Essentials of Education Poli

Essentials of Education Policy improves students' and educational leaders' understanding of the complex education policy system in the U.S.

Through an applied pedagogical approach that connects analytical concepts from public policy and education research to professional practice, the book offers academic content and applications for elementary, secondary, and postsecondary education leaders. Grounded in pillars of policy studies – educational foundations, governance structures and policy subsystems, the policy process, and specific policy issues – the book provides educational leaders with the knowledge and skills necessary to solve fundamental inequities in American education and empowers them to become change agents.

This engaging textbook will be essential reading for students and scholars in Education Policy, Leadership, and Educational Foundations, as well as for educational leaders.

William Ewell is a Teaching Professor in the Graduate School of Education at Northeastern University College of Professional Studies.

Essentials of Education Policy

Processes and Possibilities for Educational Leaders

William Ewell

Routledge
Taylor & Francis Group

NEW YORK AND LONDON

Designed cover image: SDI Productions / Getty Images

First published 2025
by Routledge
605 Third Avenue, New York, NY 10158

and by Routledge
4 Park Square, Milton Park, Abingdon, Oxon, OX14 4RN

Routledge is an imprint of the Taylor & Francis Group, an informa business

Library of Congress Cataloging-in-Publication Data
Names: Ewell, William, author.
Title: Essentials of education policy : processes and possibilities for educational leaders / William Ewell.
Description: New York, NY : Routledge, 2025. | Includes bibliographical references and index.
Identifiers: LCCN 2024031531 (print) | LCCN 2024031532 (ebook) | ISBN 9781032139364 (hardback) | ISBN 9781032139371 (paperback) | ISBN 9781003231561 (ebook)
Subjects: LCSH: Education and state—United States. | Education and state—United States—States. | Educational change—United States. | Educational equalization—United States.
Classification: LCC LC89 .E838 2025 (print) | LCC LC89 (ebook) | DDC 379—dc23/eng/20240913
LC record available at https://lccn.loc.gov/2024031531
LC ebook record available at https://lccn.loc.gov/2024031532

ISBN: 978-1-032-13936-4 (hbk)
ISBN: 978-1-032-13937-1 (pbk)
ISBN: 978-1-003-23156-1 (ebk)

DOI: 10.4324/9781003231561

Typeset in ITC Galliard Pro
by Apex CoVantage, LLC

Contents

Part I

Foundations of Education Policy

1 Introduction

Why Is Educational Policy Change So Difficult?

Gallup, one of the most well-respected public polling firms in the United States, surveyed nearly **2,000** superintendents, approximately **15%** of the nation's total, to determine the greatest needs in public education. In 2018, more than **60%** of superintendents strongly agreed that attracting and retaining highly qualified teachers was their greatest challenge (Gallup, 2018). A quick look at the national data explains why.

Each year, approximately **8%** of teachers leave the profession, and another **8%** change schools (Taie et al., 2023). This might not sound like a large number, but it means that over 5 years, a school system can experience **80%** teacher turnover. Turnover rates are even higher for Southern, urban, low-income, and high-minority school districts. The communities that most need a highly qualified, stable teaching workforce are the most likely to experience high teacher turnover and the ensuing student impacts. Teacher surveys indicate they leave the profession because of dissatisfaction with it, low pay, inadequate support, poor school leadership, and poor working conditions.

Although socioeconomic status, class size, and parental education affect student achievement, teacher effectiveness has the most significant impact on student learning (Sanders & Horn, 1998). Teacher effectiveness is cumulative: The more effective teachers a student has, the more significant their achievement growth. Studies have found that students with three effective teachers outperformed students with no effective teachers by 52 percentage points on subsequent math exams (Chingos & Peterson, 2011).

If the evidence is so clear that quality teaching has the greatest impact on student achievement, if educational leaders agree teacher recruitment and retention are the highest educational priorities, and if K–12 teacher turnover is a crisis, then why can the problem not be fixed? It's complicated – literally. Part of the problem is the system's complexity. American government and public policy are incredibly complex, and education may be the most complex issue in American politics. Consider this: In the United States, approximately **56.6** million students are enrolled in **132,853** elementary and secondary schools, **98,277** of which are public, in more than **14,000** school districts. The sector employs over 3.1 million public school teachers and **928,000** school administrators (National Center for Education Statistics, 2017). The U.S. higher education system consists of more than **4,000** institutions with a total enrollment of more than 18 million students and more than 3.6 million employees (Census Bureau, 2020).

If that scale is not enough, components of the education system fall under different levels of government, including federal, state, county, and municipal. According to the Census Bureau (2020), there are **39,044** general-purpose local governments in the United States:

DOI: 10.4324/9781003231561-2

19,492 municipal governments, 16,519 township governments, and 3,033 county governments. These government jurisdictions incorporate 13,562 public school districts.

Within this political system, collective decisions are made about the distribution of resources in society. Local, state, and federal governments can allocate scarce resources by increasing teacher pay, improving working conditions, and providing enhanced benefits and training. Scarcity means society has limited resources, which requires people to make difficult decisions about allocating resources to maximize their benefits. Consider a household's decisions to allocate the scarce resource of income or wealth. A typical household has a budget and decides how to allocate its money. For every dollar spent on housing, the household has one less dollar to spend on food, transportation, or utilities. Governments face the same constraints and difficult resource allocation decisions. *Public policy* is the study of these governmental and nongovernmental responses to public problems and allocation of scarce resources.

How Do You Make Sense of Public Policy?

This textbook aims to improve educational leaders' understanding of the education policy process, policy changes, implementation, and methods for becoming a change agent. In this section, I define government, politics, and policy. In the next section, I present 10 theoretical principles for understanding education policy changes. Throughout the text, these principles shine a flashlight into the darkest realms of education policy and politics. The 10 principles are rules that are generally accepted based on scientific evidence. Students can use these guiding principles to improve their understanding of a wide range of public policy circumstances. These principles help explain why and how an event occurred. In the final sections, I discuss the benefits educational leaders get from understanding education policy and provide a textbook overview.

What Is Government?

Government is the formal political arrangements by which a land and its people are ruled. The government comprises institutions and subordinate offices that bestow government officials with specific authority and responsibilities. *Authority* is the legal or statutory charge to make a particular decision. *Power* is a broader concept that refers to the officials' influence on government actions. A government official's authority is a critical element of their formal power. The U.S. Constitution, state constitutions, and laws grant policymakers authority. *Informal powers* are not derived from constitutional or statutory law. Informal powers include personal characteristics and skills that government officials use to influence others.

Governments vary considerably in their institutional structure. On one end of the spectrum, *autocracy* is a form of government that vests authority in a single individual. On the other end of the spectrum, *direct democracy* is a form of government in which the electorate decides directly on policy without an intermediary or representative. *Representative democracy* is a form of government in which the people vote for representatives who then vote for policy initiatives. According to the Democracy Index, an index compiled by the Economist Group that publishes the widely respected weekly magazine *The Economist*, democracies require six essential elements (Herre et al., 2023):

- a pluralistic system in which at least two legitimate but different political parties coexist;
- a free and fair electoral process that enables the people to choose between candidates of those parties;

- a government that operates openly and transparently, works for the good of all the people, respects its own rules, has proper checks and balances, and gives its citizens a free choice and control over their lives;
- politically engaged citizens who support democratic principles, fight fair, vote regularly, accept the will of the voters, and commit to a peaceful transfer of power after each election;
- an emphasis on preserving the civil liberties and personal freedoms of both the majority and minorities; and
- a free and independent media unhindered by government interference, influence, or intimidation.

Table 1.1 shows the number and percentage of countries worldwide by form of government. According to the Democracy Index, 74 of 167 countries, including the United States, were labeled full or flawed democracies in 2021. Fifty-nine countries were identified as authoritarian regimes, and another 34 demonstrated characteristics of authoritarian and democratic systems. Fewer than half of countries worldwide are considered democracies, and some 45% of the world's population lives in a democratic country.

What Is Politics?

Politics is the process through which individuals and groups reach agreement on a course of collective action. As the famous political scientist Harold Lasswell (1936) wrote, "politics is who gets what, when, and how" (p. 1). This process can be as simple as a parent and a child negotiating bedtime or as complex as international treaties on fossil fuel emissions targets. The defining characteristics of a political process are bargaining and compromise. The course of bargaining and compromise is determined by, among other factors, the complexity of the issue, the size of the group, and the trust the participants have in one another. Participants with higher levels of trust incur lower costs while determining an outcome.

Many people say they do not like politics. Politics is ultimately a process of conflict in which groups compete for control of scarce resources. Most people find conflict uncomfortable because it produces stress and they interpret it as fighting. Politics is a means of dealing with conflict to avoid more extreme measures like violence or war. The purpose of politics is also to enable members of society to achieve collective goals they could not accomplish on their own.

What Is Public Policy?

Public policy is generally defined as what government officials, and by extension the citizens they serve, choose to do or not do about public problems. *Conditions* are "concerns about

Table 1.1 Democracy Index 2021, by Regime Type

Regime type	No. of countries	% of countries	% of world population
Full democracies	21	12.6	6.4
Flawed democracies	53	31.7	39.3
Hybrid regimes	34	20.4	17.2
Authoritarian regimes	59	35.3	37.1

Note: World population refers to the total population of the 167 countries covered by the index. Because this includes only very small states, this total is nearly equal to the entire estimated world population. Source: (Herre et al., 2023)

the quality of life for large groups of people that are either held as a broad consensus among a population or voiced by social and economic elites" (Chambers & Bonk, 2012, p. 2). Conditions become defined as problems when a segment of the public decides it should do something to mitigate the condition. The problem does not necessarily need to worsen to convince the public that the condition requires a governmental solution (Kingdon, 1984). For example, high teacher turnover rates are simply a condition until they are associated with a problem that a segment of the public perceives as requiring government intervention. High teacher turnover rates drive schools to hire a disproportionate number of inexperienced and less effective teachers, increase class sizes, or reduce curricular offerings; these steps negatively impact student learning outcomes (Darling-Hammond et al., 2017). If enough of the public perceives this condition as requiring government intervention, then government representatives, officials, policy entrepreneurs, the media, and the public will call for policy action.

Why Is Government Involvement Needed?

English philosopher John Locke is considered the father of liberalism and one of the most influential thinkers of the Age of Enlightenment. In 1690, Locke wrote *Two Treatises of Government*, arguing that people are equal and vested with natural rights and that sovereignty should be placed into the hands of the people. *Natural rights* refer to rights held by all humans that are not dependent on any culture, custom, or government. They are universal. Locke (1999) held that all people are born with inalienable rights that cannot be taken away, including life, liberty, and property. People exchange some of their natural rights when they enter society, and governments enact laws that protect their property and defend their liberty. Locke's political philosophy became a cornerstone of the Declaration of Independence and the U.S. Constitution. The purposes of government can be classified into four categories: protection of life, liberty, private property, and individual rights; establishing foundations of a market economy and economic growth; mitigating the negative impacts of a market economy; and reducing inequality and promoting social justice.

The Protection of Life, Liberty, and Property

Protecting life, liberty, and private property flows directly from Locke's theories of government functions. The first purpose of government is to protect people's lives from harm. Most Americans – indeed, most citizens of Western democracies – agree that governments should maintain social order, provide security and defense, and provide for the general welfare. The oath of office for members of Congress begins: "I do solemnly swear that I will support and defend the Constitution of the United States against all enemies, foreign and domestic" (Pub. L. No. 89–554, September 6, 1966, 80 Stat. 424, n.d.) The first line of the oath focuses on defending the Constitution, and by extension, the people of the United States, from foreign or domestic enemies.

The protection of liberty refers to the government's role in protecting people from government power. *Civil liberties* refer to individual constitutional protections from government power. Civil liberties define activities the government has limited authority to interfere with, including speech, religion, privacy, assembly, and the press. In 1868, the Fourteenth Amendment to the Constitution enshrined civil rights into U.S. law at the state level by guaranteeing "equal protection of the laws." The equal protection clause of the Fourteenth Amendment reads: "No State shall make or enforce any law which shall . . . deny to any person within its jurisdiction the equal protection of the laws."

Civil rights refer to individuals' rights to receive fair treatment, with punishment a consequence for unfair treatment or discrimination. While civil liberties require the government not to infringe on individuals' rights – not an action – civil rights indicate the government must take action to ensure equal protection of the law. Individual rights also include property rights. The Fifth Amendment to the U.S. Constitution reads, in part: "Nor shall private property be taken for public use, without just compensation." The due process clause of the Fourteenth Amendment also states that the government may not "deprive any person of life, liberty, or property without due process of the law." The Fifth and Fourteenth Amendments provide legal protections against unlawful property loss.

Establishing Private Markets and Ensuring Economic Growth

The second category of government responsibilities is establishing the foundations of a market economy and economic growth. Market economies do not occur naturally. Governments must create the conditions for market economies, including establishing property rights, creating and managing money supply, and keeping order (Page & Simmons, 2000). In his seminal book *The Mystery of Capital*, economist Hernando de Soto (2000) argued one of the main differences between advanced and developing countries is not human capital, natural resources, or technological advantages but relatively strong government institutions that enable property systems and private ownership. Developing countries that lack strong government institutions and legal systems cannot ensure property rights, which erodes the economic system. For example, primary residences represent a third of U.S. household assets (Census Bureau, 2017). The accumulation of wealth and private property is made possible by complex systems of property titling, property registration, and banking finance. In developing countries with unstable government and financial systems, household assets lack the legal structure that would unlock their value. Stable government institutions are the bedrock of advanced economies.

Market Failures

Government is also necessary to overcome *market failures*, in which the free market fails to account for all the costs and benefits of providing and consuming goods. The four most common types of market failures are asymmetric information, concentrated market power, externalities, and public goods. *Private goods* refers to goods that are *rival*, meaning consumption by one consumer prevents simultaneous consumption by other consumers, and *excludable*, meaning consumers who have not paid for a good can be prevented from having access to it. For example, if a consumer purchases a pair of sneakers, that is a private good. It is rival in consumption because when the consumer wears the sneakers, no one else can simultaneously wear them. The sneakers are also excludable because it is possible to prevent consumers who have not paid for the sneakers from having access to them. Figure 1.1 identifies other examples of private goods in its upper left quadrant, including food, clothing, cars, and personal electronics.

Public goods refer to goods that are *nonrivalrous*, meaning one person's consumption of the good does not prevent another person from consuming it, and *nonexcludable*, meaning individuals cannot be effectively excluded from using them. National defense is a public good. The U.S. national defense protects everyone in the country. The military cannot exclude specific individuals from consuming its protection. Protecting one person does not prevent another person from receiving protection.

Some goods have attributes of both private and public goods. *Common goods* are nonexcludable but rival in consumption. An example is fish stocks in international waters, those beyond the reach of national law. People cannot be excluded from fishing, but consuming the fish stock reduces the available fish. Common goods can lead to a scenario called the *tragedy of the commons*, in which individuals consume resources for short-term gains while neglecting the common good by depleting the long-term viability of the resource. Without third-party protection, such as a government institution, the tragedy of the commons leads individual consumers to overutilize the resource until it is completely exhausted.

Club goods refers to goods that are excludable but nonrival in consumption. A toll road is a classic example of a club good. The road is excludable because nonpayers can be prevented from using it but nonrival in consumption because one additional car on the road does not exclude others from using it. Club goods can reach a point of saturation where the goods become congested. The toll road can have a traffic jam, or a beach can have so many visitors that no more people can enter it. Once the congestion is relieved, these goods once again become club goods.

Public education should be a public good. All children should have access to high-quality education, and one child's access to a quality education should not limit another child's access. Public education has been excluded from segments of the population for much of American history. Public education was not compulsory for all children until 1918. *Brown v. Board of Education*, the Supreme Court ruling that racial segregation in public schools violated the Fourteenth Amendment, was not issued until 1954. Even today, only half of U.S. states require school attendance until age 18, and only a handful of states require free education for students under 5. Public charter and magnet schools can exclude students based on several factors, including special needs. The United States still has work to do to ensure all students receive a high-quality education regardless of race, gender, socioeconomic status, sexual orientation and identity, disability, religion, or country of origin.

Public education is often treated as a private good because many of its benefits are conveyed to individual consumers. Public goods are particularly suitable for sustaining well-ordered societies (Kallhoff, 2014). The global increase in for-profit education in recent decades has shifted education away from its social purposes and goals and toward private interests (Locatelli, 2018). If education were solely a private good, it would be relegated to individuals in a free market and lose its public benefits and positive externalities for society. To extract the positive externalities, most developed countries make public education a de facto public good by making it compulsory and universally available (Menashy, 2009). Understanding public education as a public good has implications for ensuring equity, inclusion, and social justice within the American education system.

	Excludable	*Non-Excludable*
Rivalrous	**Private Goods**	**Common Goods**
Non-Rivalrous	**Club Goods**	**Public Goods**

Figure 1.1 Private and Public Goods

Postsecondary education is also typically considered a private good. It is excludable, through admission standards, and rivalrous, in that a student who enrolls in the university leaves one less seat for another student. Public institutions enroll nearly 80% of U.S. postsecondary students. Policymakers and the public continue to view higher education as a private good whose primary purpose is to provide consumers with increased earnings potential (Pasquarella, 2016). As a private good, wealthier Americans can afford to attend more highly ranked postsecondary institutions because access partially depends on the student's ability to pay, which is related to their parents' education and wealth. When people describe public education as a public good, they mean it is good for the public. If higher education were a public good, the capacity to pay, preparation for college admission, and enrollment would be decoupled from a student's parental education and wealth.

Externalities are another type of market failure that have positive or negative spillover effects on the broader public. Externalities occur when producing or consuming a good has a positive or negative impact on a third party not directly involved in the transaction. Vaccinations have a positive externality against disease because they have spillover benefits. Not only does the person receiving the immunization become protected, but also other community members become less likely to contract the disease. Governments often subsidize or cover the total cost of vaccinations because of the positive externalities provided to society through health and economic benefits.

Public education is another classic example of a positive externality. Education benefits those receiving it by making them better citizens, increasing their job and earnings potential, and improving their quality of life. Society also benefits because education increases an individual's economic impact; reduces social costs through lower government health, welfare, and criminal justice costs; and strengthens democracy. Positive externalities are underproduced in a free-market economy because the producers of a good do not capture the value of the societal spillover benefits. Government subsidies for positive externalities increase their production and the positive societal impacts they produce. Public funding for education increases the total production of education and allows society to capture the additional positive benefits provided by a more educated public.

Postsecondary education also produces positive externalities that justify government intervention to expand access and affordability. The private benefit of higher education is that as education grows, individual income also rises. Higher education also provides positive externalities to society through democratic citizens, an improved economy, lower unemployment rates, and higher productivity.

The government also plays a role in decreasing negative externalities. Environmental pollution is a classic example of a negative externality. For example, a company produces goods and makes production decisions based only on direct costs and profit opportunities. Suppose the company is not required to consider the costs of the pollution its factory creates on the health and well-being of a third party, the surrounding community. In that case, it benefits economically by not paying for those indirect costs. The price of the company's products will not capture all the costs related to producing the goods.

Asymmetric information is a third type of market failure. It refers to market transactions where one party has information another party lacks. In 2001, economists Joseph Stiglitz, George Akerlof, and Michael Spence received the Nobel Prize for their study of information asymmetry in the market for used cars. They explained that vehicles only a few months old sell for a much lower price than new cars. If buyers had adequate information, they would know which cars were so-called lemons and which were high quality, and this could create two separate markets. Unfortunately, buyers do not know which cars are lemons – but sellers do. This information asymmetry reduces the price of used vehicles below what buyers of high-quality used cars would be willing to pay if they had complete information; thus, market efficiency is lost. Solutions to the information asymmetry problem include car warranties and giving buyers information through a car history.

Asymmetric information problems also arise in education settings. For example, colleges and universities have an asymmetric information advantage over consumers concerning the quality of their services because they require families to provide detailed financial information. As a result of this asymmetric information advantage, higher education institutions can extract the highest price families can afford. The higher education consumer lacks information about the quality of education services. The government can reduce this asymmetric information advantage by requiring higher education institutions to be transparent about their financials, discount rates, and cost of student services and how they compare with those at other institutions.

The fourth type of market failure is *monopoly*, an imperfect market that restricts output to maximize profit. In a full monopoly, a single supplier controls a product's entire supply, so they can restrict supply to keep prices high. Google's internet search engine controls 88% of the market share, generating billions of ad revenue annually. The U.S. Department of Justice has accused Google of suppressing competition through exclusive business agreements (Department of Justice Office of Public Affairs, 2020).

Although monopolies reduce competition and represent a failure of free markets, natural monopolies occur when a product or service can be provided most efficiently if there is only one supplier. These typically involve significant upfront investments to build a physical infrastructure, like water or electrical systems. The U.S. elementary and secondary education system has some characteristics of a natural monopoly with its high fixed costs, economies of scale, and low marginal costs. Private monopolies have the incentive and opportunity to extract large profits without any democratic control over the company. A public monopoly has the advantage of creating economies of scale while ensuring all students, not just those who can afford to pay, receive a high-quality education. Public monopolies provide the advantage of offering equitable resources to all people, regardless of their ability to pay.

Minimizing the Negative Impacts of a Market Economy: Poverty, Inequality, and Equity

In an economy free of market failures, markets efficiently allocate the supply and demand of private resources, generating economic growth. This growth does not necessarily lead to declining poverty or inequality. Free markets do not care about the equitable distribution of resources. In unregulated market economies, increases in education, skills, and capital resources lead to greater inequality. Workers cannot use their labor or skills as collateral to obtain loans. In contrast, those with capital assets can use their property to make profits, borrow money, and invest (Hodgson, 2016). Capitalists can reap cumulative wealth from assets. This dichotomy allows capitalists to accumulate wealth, which drives inequality.

Governments can intervene to mitigate inequity in the distribution of resources caused by capitalism through spending, regulations, and policy. More than 70% of the global population faces increasing inequality (United Nations, 2020). This results in more significant political divisions, hampers economic and social progress, and slows overall economic growth. According to the Pew Research Center (2020), the United States ranks 35th highest in wealth gap among the 40 countries in the Organisation for Economic Cooperation and Development (OECD). The wealth gap between America's richest and poorest families doubled from 1989 to 2016. These growing economic disparities result in lower economic opportunity and mobility, lower political influence for the disadvantaged, and geographic segregation by income.

Government intervention can reduce inequities through a wide range of public policies. These include redistributing resources to families in lower income brackets, progressive taxation, minimum wages, social safety net programs such as Medicaid, earned income tax credits, and the Supplemental Nutrition Assistance Program. Government can also reduce inequality and poverty by building a ladder of opportunity through improved educational outcomes. Education programs aimed at improving economic and social outcomes for children include improving public schools; afterschool and community activities; expanded early education opportunities; and enrichment, internship, and apprenticeship programs. The government can also expand the availability of postsecondary educational opportunities through public policies that reduce their cost, including offering free and subsidized public education, grants, and loans; prohibiting discrimination in the job market and educational spheres based on gender, race, sexual orientation, age, or disability status; and providing lifelong training opportunities to acquire and retain new job skills.

This section has detailed various purposes for government intervention, including protecting life, liberty, and property; establishing a market economy; promoting growth and prosperity; overcoming market failures; and minimizing the negative impact of a market economy. People in different positions on the ideological spectrum disagree about the proper extent of government intervention in each category. Government intervention requires justification to support collective resources for the common good. *Policy* describes a course of action proposed by a governmental or nongovernmental actor to solve a public problem. The following section describes the principles students can use to understand and analyze the political and policy processes necessary to influence policy outcomes.

Case Study: Leading the World in College Completion

According to the International Institute for Management Development (2023), the United States dropped from the world's most competitive economy to the 10th most competitive between 2018 and 2020. The decline has mainly hampered American competitiveness in the global economy and its college-educated workforce. The United States ranks 19th among 28 industrialized countries in college graduation rates (National Center for Education Statistics, 2023). Economists estimate that 65% of all jobs require some postsecondary education. By 2030, postsecondary education requirements are expected to rise above 70% (Carnevale et al., 2023). According to the Bureau of Labor Statistics, four million Americans left their jobs each month in late 2021, leaving approximately 11 million open jobs (Penn & Nezamis, 2022). While the demand for highly educated workers increases, their supply stagnates and compromises American economic competitiveness. According to a Council of Foreign Relations task force chaired by Condoleezza Rice, "The education crisis is a national security crisis. . . . America's education failures pose threats to national security" (Klein et al., 2012).

To combat this problem, President Barack Obama called for the United States to "once again lead the world in college completion. This must be a national priority. We must ensure that every student graduates from high school well prepared for college and a career" (U.S. Department of Education, 2010). Making a call to solve a problem does not solve the problem. What is the size of the problem posed by low college graduation rates?

According to the Georgetown University Center on Education and the Workforce, the U.S. has been underproducing college-educated workers since the 1980s (Carnevale et al.,

2021). It identified the need for 20 million postsecondary-educated workers (Carnevale et al., 2021). More college-educated workers would improve economic efficiency and satisfy workforce demands but widen inequality. College-educated workers enhance economic efficiency by increasing productivity. The demand for college-educated workers has grown over the past several decades, while the number of college-educated workers has declined. This is a simple supply and demand problem. As the demand for college-educated workers increases and the supply of those workers declines, their wages increase. The income gap between college-educated and noncollege-educated people has widened over the last several decades, accounting for a sizable portion of economic inequality. While demand for highly skilled workers has grown, demand for low-skilled workers has declined. The result is an explosion in the wage gap based on education level. It has also resulted in a racial and gender wage gap in that the educational wage gap disproportionately impacts women and minorities (Blank, 2021).

The U.S. requires more workers with advanced degrees to remain competitive in an increasingly global economy. Who is responsible for increasing the college graduation rate? What role does the U.S. elementary and secondary school system play in increasing college graduation rates?

The U.S. public school system prepares students for career and college readiness. Its role is to ensure students leave high school prepared to enter the workforce. American public schools are largely failing this responsibility. According to an Education Trust report, only 31% of all U.S. students complete a college- and career-ready curriculum, and only 13% complete a career-ready curriculum (Bromberg & Theokas, 2016). Studies indicate that 60% of first-year college students are placed in remedial education courses, at a cost of one billion dollars annually (Jimen et al., 2016). Most students arrive at higher education institutions ill prepared to succeed. What role do higher education institutions play in increasing college completion rates?

Increasing college graduation rates requires commitment from higher education institutions. However, the U.S. higher education system comprises 4,000 colleges and universities. Each state's university, college, and community college systems operate independently and have wide-ranging governance systems. American higher education exemplifies a decentralized and disparate system in which coordinated change is, at best, incremental. The evidence suggests that, like their elementary and secondary counterparts, American higher education bears responsibility for poor college completion rates. According to the Education Data Initiative, 56% of 4-year college students drop out within 6 years, with the majority saying they dropped out for financial reasons (Hanson, 2021). The United States ranks 19th among 28 OECD countries in college graduation rates. Astonishingly, only 5% of students at 2-year colleges graduate with a degree within 2 years (OECD, 2023). Most higher education institutions lack the support services to support first-generation and underserved populations, who drop out at higher rates than their wealthier, White peers.

So, who is responsible for increasing higher education graduation rates: the university system or the public schools? The answer is that all these institutions and actors need to work together. However, coordination across the federal and 50 state governments, thousands of higher education and elementary and secondary schools, and the private sector poses a complicated problem. Public policy is the method by which a group collectively determines a course of action. Increasing college graduation rates is a policy problem that can be solved through collective action. The next section lays out a series of principles that can be used to improve understanding of public policy.

Ten Principles of Public Policy

The study of public policy is complex, but like any discipline, it is unified by a series of central theories and ideas that explain, predict, and understand political and policy phenomena. These principles build on the work of Lowi et al. (2022). This section explores 10 principles that can be used to transition from simply describing a phenomenon to generalizing about it and then to guide research, professional actions, and policy change efforts.

How People Make Decisions

Principle 1: History Matters

Choices made in the past limit the options available today. For example, someone may wish to pursue a different career path. However, previous decisions to pursue education, employment, and experiences in one field are *sunk costs*, a cost that has been incurred and cannot be recovered. Those previous decisions make switching careers more costly. Economists argue people should not consider sunk costs when making decisions because they cannot recover them. The career change may require additional education, training, and experience. The career change may also require the person to start at a lower salary and career position and may involve the risk of failing in the new career path. Previous career decisions may deter a person from considering a career change.

Policy and political choices made in the past can also limit policy choices and thus constrain decisions made today. For example, some experts argue the national achievement gap is a byproduct of an education system primarily financed by local property taxes. One solution would be to finance a higher percentage of education at the national or state level. Legal precedents and previous political and constitutional decisions make such policy changes difficult. First, there is no guarantee of education in the U.S. Constitution. Because education is not explicitly mentioned in the Constitution, it is officially the purview of state governments, according to the Tenth Amendment. Second, the Fourteenth Amendment provides equal protection for students based on race, gender, sexual orientation, and ethnicity. However, the Fourteenth Amendment does not speak to the issue of equality of economic status; therefore, a decision to fund education at the national level may violate constitutional law. Third, property values are tied to the quality of local school systems, so efforts to decouple school finance from property taxes would have significant economic consequences for most Americans. If one were to design the American education system today, one would most likely choose a different financing mechanism. These previous political and policy decisions constrict current political and policy options. Decisions made in the past restrict the decisions one can make in the future.

Principle 2: The Status Quo Matters

Status quo refers to the current state of political or policy issues. The status quo has significant built-in advantages. American political institutions are designed with high transaction costs to mitigate the possibility of tyranny, where one political actor or group can oppress the larger public. *Separation of powers* refers to the division of government responsibilities – legislative, executive, and judicial – into different branches to limit the power of each branch. The system of *checks and balances* ensures no one branch becomes too powerful by providing each with a check on the others. The president can veto congressional acts and nominate Supreme Court justices, Congress has the authority to impeach the president or Supreme Court justices, and the Supreme Court has the power to find laws unconstitutional. Enacting a law requires, at a minimum, the support of a majority of the members of the committee of jurisdiction, a majority of House members, a supermajority of Senate members, and presidential support. Scholars refer to each of these as a *veto point*, meaning the bill fails if any of these actors decline support. The American political system has numerous veto points that make change difficult. If one supports the status quo policy position, the political system is designed to take advantage of that position. Change is exceedingly difficult in this system.

Extending the example from Principle 1, the status quo is that public education is financed primarily through local property taxes. Could people change the U.S. Constitution and include an educational right? Of course! Article V allows for changes to the U.S. Constitution. The probability of a successful amendment to the U.S. Constitution is exceedingly low, however, given that two thirds of the House and Senate would need to propose it and three fourths of the states would need to ratify it. Shifting away from the status quo would require enormous support among public and elected officials and among property owners, particularly higher income owners who would need to be willing to take a financial hit, as well as the cooperation and coordination of millions of Americans. The U.S. Constitution has been changed, but given the high transaction costs, only 17 of more than 11,000 proposed amendments (a 0.1% passage rate) have been ratified since the Bill of Rights in 1789. The status quo has an enormous advantage over change.

Principle 3: Preferences Matter

Approximately 330 million people live in the United States. Each American has preferences for the rules of society and the distribution of resources. *Preferences* are rankings of attitudes derived from one's family, religion, media, peers, education, geography, and demographic characteristics (Druckman & Lupia, 2000). Individual preferences aggregate into political values that articulate what they value in society. People want public policy to reflect their political preferences by emphasizing specific values and deemphasizing others. Political values lead individuals to choose a *political ideology*, a set of ideas, beliefs, values, and opinions exhibiting a recurring pattern that justifies or explains which social and political arrangements they prefer.

In liberal democracies, *pluralism* is the political philosophy that many groups of opposing interests govern. Schattschneider (1975) quipped in his seminal *The Semisovereign People*: "The flaw in the pluralist heaven is that the heavenly choir sings with a strong upper-class accent." In other words, political power rests in the hands of those who have economic power. Scholarship indicates economic elites and business interest groups impact U.S. public policy – the average citizen's preferences have minimal influence (Achens & Bartels, 2017; Gilens & Page, 2014; Giles, 2012; Rigby & Wright, 2013). Policymakers' indifference to low-income citizens' preferences extends to state politics and policy processes (Rigby & Wright, 2013).

Principle 4: Opportunity Costs Matter

Societies have limited resources. This fact has far-reaching implications for individuals, families, governments, and societies. When individuals decide how to allocate their limited resources to purchase food, housing, education, or other options, they implicitly make a tradeoff. Spending limited resources on food means those same resources are not available to purchase other needs or wants. *Opportunity cost* refers to the value of the next best alternative. Individuals face tradeoffs in their decision making. The opportunity cost of going to the movies is what else one could purchase with the $20 and the time spent attending the cinema.

The equity–efficiency tradeoff is a prime example of the tradeoffs individuals, governments, and societies face. An *equity–efficiency tradeoff* occurs when there is a conflict between economic efficiency and the fairness of the distribution of resources in society. Maximum *economic efficiency* is a condition in which all production in an economy is allocated to the most valuable uses. Minimizing waste often leads to a reduction in *equity*, which is how fairly wealth and income are distributed. Pure utility maximization through economic efficiency conflicts with society's basic ethics and morality. Capitalism is a system that prioritizes economic efficiency. Governments often mitigate the inequities caused by that economic system with social welfare systems that ensure a broader distribution of economic gains.

How Governments Make Decisions

Principle 5: Institutions Matter

Political institutions are where the government makes decisions. In a country with 330 million people who have different preferences, disagreement is predictable and unavoidable. Aggregating preferences is the fundamental problem of democratic governments; it requires bargaining and compromise. *Collective action*, the effort of a group to reach and implement agreements, requires coordination between actors who sacrifice individual goals and rewards for the common good. In a classic example, two suspects are arrested by police and placed in different cells so they cannot communicate. Both suspects are allowed to remain silent or blame the other. Figure 1.2 illustrates the payoff for each option available to the two suspects. The top left box shows the payoff is 1 year of prison each if both suspects remain silent. The bottom right box shows the payoff is 3 years of prison each if both suspects blame one another. The top right and bottom left boxes show the payoff if one suspect remains silent and the other blames their fellow suspect. In these cases, the suspect who remains silent receives 5 years of prison time, while the person who blames their fellow suspect gets no jail time.

This prisoner's dilemma illustrates the paradox of collective action. Both suspects are better off if they remain silent. But neither suspect can trust the other to remain silent, so the most rational, self-interested decision is to blame the other suspect. If Suspect A remains silent, his possible payoffs are 1 and 5 years in prison. If Suspect A blames Suspect B, the possible payoffs are 0 and 3. Both suspects, if they are rational and self-interested, are incentivized to blame their colleagues even though both would be better off by staying silent. Mutual silence produces better results than mutual blame, but both suspects are incentivized to blame. The prisoner's dilemma extends to societies trying to overcome collective problems. A third-party intervention requires participants to adhere to the collective action and solve the trust issue.

Societies overcome collective action problems through government serving as the third-party mechanism. When designing government institutions, transaction and conformity costs influence the suitability of the government institution to the desired collective action. *Transaction costs* are the time, effort, and resources required to make collective decisions. Transaction costs rise as the number of participants increases. They pose considerable barriers to a political agreement. For example, the U.S. Constitution vests the presidency with supreme operational command and control over all military personnel, and the power

Suspect A \ Suspect B	Remain Silent	Blame
Remain Silent	1 / 1	0 / 5
Blame	5 / 0	3 / 3

Figure 1.2 Prisoner's Dilemma

to launch military operations. The Constitution provides the president with low transaction costs so that the official can use military force to defend the country from foreign or domestic attacks. Imagine if the 435 members of the House of Representatives had to debate whether to use military force during an attack on the nation. The transaction costs would be too high to allow for an immediate response. Government institutions can also be designed with high transaction costs to make collective action more difficult. To create government stability and reduce the ability of a single political faction to rewrite the Constitution, its framers created high transaction costs. Amendments to the Constitution require a two-thirds supermajority of the House and Senate and then ratification by three fourths of the states. The transaction costs are so high that the Constitution has been changed only 17 times, not counting the original 10 amendments passed as a condition for some states' initial support.

Conformity cost refers to the difference between what an individual prefers and what the collective body requires. Conformity costs in an autocracy or dictatorship, for example, are high. The dictator makes all decisions, and members of society are forced to deal with the consequences even if they differ from their preferences. Conformity costs and transaction costs are typically inversely related. As transaction costs increase, government institutions reduce conformity costs. Government institutions are designed to achieve certain ends and include structures to achieve those ends. Suppose the electorate is concerned that the government will infringe on freedoms such as privacy through surveillance. They may create institutions with high transaction costs that require a substantial burden of proof before the government can spy on the population.

Principle 6: Partisanship Matters

Partisanship is the defining characteristic of American politics in the 21st century. *Political partisanship* means strong and sometimes blind adherence to a particular party, faction, cause, or person. In the American context, partisanship focuses on adherence to one of the two major political parties. The U.S. electoral system primarily utilizes a plurality voting system in which the candidate who receives more votes than any other candidate is elected. Plurality voting differs from majority voting systems, in which the winning candidate must receive more votes than all other candidates combined. Plurality voting systems disincentivize third parties because they have difficulty winning elections or legislative representation. For example, a third party could win **30%** of the vote in every congressional or state legislative district and win no representation if it does not win a plurality of the vote in any contest.

The public's confidence in American government has decreased as partisanship has increased. According to the Pew Research Center (2020), trust in government has declined from a high of nearly **80%** in the early 1960s to a low of **17%** in 2020. The decline precisely tracks with a simultaneous rise in American political partisanship. Through the 1960s, the United States effectively had four political parties: liberal Republicans (mainly in the Northeast), conservative Republicans, conservative Democrats (mainly in the South), and liberal Democrats. Since the 1970s, *congressional member replacement*, members replaced by more ideologically polarized members, and *adaptation*, the change of member voting behavior over time, has resulted in the most polarized Congress since the Civil War (Theriault, 2006).

Principle 7: Incentive Structures Matter

Representative democracy represents a classic instance of delegation. Citizens delegate authority to representatives to make public policy decisions on their behalf rather than directly exercising authority. In other words, the principals, the voters, delegate some of their authority to their agents, the elected representatives. Why would principals be willing to delegate their authority to agents? The principal–agent relationship has numerous advantages. One is *division of labor*, the separation of tasks in an organization, economy, or governmental system so participants may specialize and improve efficiency. For example, the voter (the principal) who delegates authority to an elected representative (the agent) can focus their efforts on earning wages rather than researching policy or government processes. This labor specialization also occurs in government agencies and legislative bodies, where individuals specialize in public policy and governance to improve expertise and efficiency. The benefits of the principal–agent relationship are substantial.

What costs are associated with the principal–agent relationship? *The principal–agent problem* is that the principal and the agent may have conflicting priorities. Delegation poses a risk to the principal because the agent may act in a way that is contrary to the principal's interests. Both parties are motivated by self-interest. The agent's self-interest and the principal's self-interest may conflict. The principal must properly motivate or coerce the agent to act in the principal's interest or align the agent's self-interest with the principal's self-interest.

How does the principal align their goals with the agent's self-interest? The principal–agent problem is solved through incentive structures, rewards, or punishments that impact human behavior. The principal can align the agent's self-interest by giving the agent value for advancing the principal's interest and monitoring the agent to ensure they are advancing the principal's interest. For example, a school principal wants teachers to use a pedagogy they believe will improve student achievement outcomes. In this case, the principal is the principal, and the agent is the teacher. To ensure the teacher utilizes that method, the principal could use rewards or pay bonuses – or dole out punishments, suspensions, or termination if the teacher does not use it. They could observe and monitor teachers to ensure the agent's adherence to the principal's directive. Education stakeholders are motivated by incentive structures.

How the Policy Process Works

Principle 8: The Policy Stages Matter

A public policy goes through a series of stages from inception to completion. The stages in this model include problem definition, agenda setting, formulation, adoption, implementation, and evaluation. Figure 1.3 illustrates the stages and cyclical nature of the policy process. The problem definition stage identifies the causes and consequences of undesirable circumstances. This framing highlights particular aspects of the problem, making some solutions more or less feasible. Agenda setting refers to policy formulation, the stage at which policies are developed and considered. Implementation is the stage at which policies are put into practice. The process and outputs are reviewed during the evaluation stage to determine the policy impact. Change agents require different approaches to influence policy at each stage of the policy process.

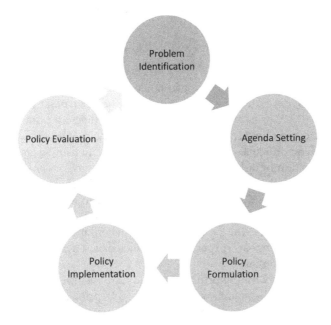

Figure 1.3 The Public Policy Process

Principle 9: The Policy Instruments Matter

Policy instruments are types of interventions and techniques that governments or public authorities use to achieve policy goals. Policy instruments are the various tools within a policymaker's toolbox. Each policy instrument has strengths and drawbacks and different applicability to a specific policy environment and public problem. *Policy typologies* divide policy instruments into categories based on their characteristics.

Why does the type of policy matter? Different policy types achieve distinctive policy outcomes and influence which policy actor has more influence over decision making and implementation. For example, regulatory policy instruments are the jurisdiction of executive branch agencies. They give executive actors, including mayors, governors, and the president, more policy influence. The type of policy matters because it determines which governmental and nongovernmental actors have the most power over a given policy.

Principle 10: Policy Choices Matter

Public policies are not just products of the political process. They also shape the political environment, electoral politics, and future policymaking (Campbell, 2012). This process is known as *policy feedback*, the potential that public policies will transform politics and, as a result, influence future courses of policy development (Pierson & Skocpol, 2002). The structure of public policies influences patterns of political change. Public policies generate resources and incentives for political actors that encourage them to interpret the political world in specific ways. Policy change invariably allocates benefits to some individuals or groups and imposes costs on others (McDonnell, 2013). For example, elementary and secondary accountability policies hold school-level administrators and teachers accountable for student achievement. Scholars have suggested that this accountability agenda has divided the Democratic Party from civil rights groups that typically support Democratic policy initiatives because accountability policies designed to lift underserved students punish underperforming schools (Rhodes, 2011). As this example suggests, policy choices have political consequences.

Five Reasons Why Educational Leaders Need to Understand Education Policy

Some may ask, "Why can't I just focus on my school, district, or university? Why do I need to understand education and policy and politics?" Many people find politics and policy divisive, uncomfortable, and downright nasty. I get it. To some degree, everyone wants to avoid conflict, yet education policy and politics are inherently adversarial. Educational leaders need to understand policy systems because that is how decisions are made in a democracy. There is political conflict to avoid physical conflict. Here are five additional reasons why it is incumbent on educational leaders to understand education policy and politics.

Understand the Educational Environment

American education is inherently political. Educational leaders must understand the impact of policymaker decisions. In 2015, the National Network of State Teachers of the Year called on educators to understand and engage in policymaking (Colvin et al., 2015). Knowledge and understanding are prerequisites for advocating, influencing, or shaping policy change. This book aims to teach educators how to understand the education policy and political environment so they can be better informed.

Understand Policy Decisions

Policy decisions are constantly influencing educators at all levels of government. District curriculum changes, state budget decisions, federal testing requirements, and university system priorities alter the environment in which educational leaders operate. To address these policy changes proactively, educational leaders need to understand the policymaking process and anticipate how policy changes will alter their budgets, options, and operating procedures.

Shape Implementation

Implementation is the stage of the policy process when a policy is put into action, monitored, adjusted, and evaluated. Educational leaders, from administrators to faculty to staff, are the actors who implement federal, state, local, university, district, and school-level policy actions. Proper implementation requires educational leaders to interpret, organize, and apply the policy to the pertinent organization. The implementing actors translate the policy into rules, guidelines, and resources, and employees organize to achieve the policy goals. As the implementers of public policy, educational leaders can assert substantial influence over policy outcomes. Understanding the policy process stages, power structures, and principal–agent incentive structures can increase educational leaders' influence over the policy implementation process.

Be a Change Agent

Hersh (2020) explained that most highly educated citizens partake in *political hobbyism*: They consume politics and policy through media without altering political or policy systems. While being educated about politics and policy is a necessary precursor to civic action, Hersh explained that this is insufficient. Changing power structures and the education system require political power. Political power requires political action in the form of canvassing to influence elections, political organizing, community action, fundraising, and lobbying. Being a change agent requires taking actions that influence political power structures. District, university, local, state, and federal policymakers need to hear educational leaders' voices. This book illustrates how educational leaders can influence political and policy systems.

Educational Leadership

An educational leader has a vision for improving a system and rallies people to move toward that better vision. Educational leaders often limit their influence on their school or organization. This book aims to provide leaders with the knowledge and skills to influence more extensive policy systems and organize change by leading others toward a better vision.

Book Overview

This book's 11 chapters are divided into four sections: the educational environment, education governance, the policy process, and education issues and solutions. Each section is critical for understanding the complex nature of public policy in general and education policy in particular.

Part I focuses on the educational environment. Chapter 2 provides an overview of the purpose and history of education policy. The chapter reviews the development of U.S. education systems to understand their historical purpose and grapple with their current implications. Understanding the collective purpose of education is a necessary precursor to considering improvements to that system. Chapter 3 explores power and public policy theories. Theories help explain, predict, or understand phenomena and extend existing knowledge. The chapter explains several prominent public policy theories that help people understand how education policy works and predict the conditions under which the existing system might produce change.

Part II examines education governance and structure. In a democracy, change occurs through the actions of government institutions in response to what the public seeks.

Educational leaders must understand how the education governance system is structured and what institutions and levels of government influence specific policies to promote change. Chapter 4 explores federal-level governance structures, politics, actors, and power. Historically, the federal government played a limited role in U.S. education, but its role has expanded dramatically in recent decades. Chapter 5 explores state-level governance, structures, politics, actors, and power. Since the 1970s, state government has played the dominant role in American education systems through policymaking and administrative oversight. This chapter explains the state governance structure and the instrumental role state government plays in administrative oversight, education policy changes, and the financing of American education. Chapter 6 examines local government institutions, educational administrative offices, and district and local-level school systems to understand their purpose, relationship, and relative power. Educational leaders have the most direct contact with local governments, yet their complexity, diversity, and numerous components make them difficult to understand.

Part III explains the policy process. As discussed in Part II, the U.S. education system operates within a complex environment that spans three levels of government, three branches, and diverse school systems. Educational leaders must understand how legislation and various instruments impact policy change within this complex environment. Chapter 7 provides an overview of the stages model, a policy analysis framework used to clarify the components of the process that develops and changes policy. The chapter elaborates on the first three stages in the policy process: issue definition, defining the policy issue; agenda setting, the process by which a policy moves from an idea to being on the agenda of government institutions; and policy formulation, developing the policy instrument details and adoption, and passing the policy through the appropriate government institution. Chapter 8 explains the last two stages in the stages model: implementation and evaluation. Educational leaders typically play a crucial role in implementation, so it is necessary to understand the complex nature of the implementation process across numerous actors and agencies throughout government and school systems. Chapter 8 also describes the range of policy instruments, from legislative action to regulations to informal authority. The chapter places policy instruments into typologies to provide a mechanism for understanding categories of policy tools used to fix the education system. Chapter 9 investigates the financing of American education and the resulting system inequities.

Part IV grapples with specific education policy issues and controversies. Chapter 10 explores elementary and secondary education, including the achievement gap, desegregation, accountability and standards systems, school choice, dropouts, teacher quality and training, teacher recruitment and turnover, school leadership, and school safety and wellness. Chapter 11 examines postsecondary education issues, including affordability, access, affirmative action, remediation, graduation rates, student debt, and disparities in higher education outcomes.

Key Terms

Discussion Questions

1. Why is it so difficult to make policy change?
2. What is the purpose of government intervention? When should the government intervene?
3. Is education a public good? Is it a common good?
4. Is education a positive externality? If so, what implications does this have for government intervention?

5. How does education ameliorate economic, political, and social inequities?
6. Which policy principle best helps you understand public policy decisions?
7. Why do educational leaders need to understand education policy?

Application

1. Choose one of these policy issues and identify why it is a public problem.

   achievement gap
   disability education
   English-language learner education
   school funding inequities
   school desegregation
   school choice
   teaching equity
   teaching diversity
   school climate
   social-emotional learning

2. Choose one of the following federal policies and identify what problem or conditions promoted its development.

   Elementary and Secondary Education Act
   Individuals with Disabilities Act
   Perkins Career and Technical Education Act
   Education Sciences Reform Act
   Family Educational Rights and Privacy Act

3. Choose one of your institution's or organization's policies and identify the problem or condition that prompted its development.

References

Achens, C. H., & Bartels, L. (2017). *Democracy for realists: Why elections do not produce responsive government*. Princeton University Press.

Blank, R. (2021, October 1). *For a competitive economy, we need a skilled workforce*. Issues in Science and Technology. https://issues.org/competitive-economy-skilled-workforce-blank/

Bromberg, M., & Theokas, C. (2016). *Meandering towards graduation: Transcript outcomes of high school graduates*. The Education Trust. https://edtrust.org/wp-content/uploads/2014/09/MeanderingTowardGraduation_EdTrust_April2016.pdf

Campbell, A. L. (2012). Policy makes mass politics. *Annual Review of Political Science, 15*(1), 333–351. https://doi.org/10.1146/annurev-polisci-012610-135202

Carnevale, A. P., Cheah, B., & Wenzinger, E. (2021). *The college payoff: More education doesn't always mean more earnings*. Georgetown University Center on Education and the Workforce. https://cew.georgetown.edu/cew-reports/collegepayoff2021/

Carnevale, A. P., Smith, N., Werf, M. V. D., & Quinn, M. C. (2023). *After everything: Projections of jobs, education and training requirements through 2031*. Georgetown University Center on Education and the Workforce. https://cew.georgetown.edu/Projections2031

Census Bureau. (2017). *The wealth of households 2017*. www.census.gov/content/dam/Census/library/publications/2020/demo/p70br-170.pdf

Census Bureau. (2020). *SAIPE school district estimates for 2020*. www.census.gov/data/datasets/2020/demo/saipe/2020-school-districts.html

Chambers, D., & Bonk, J. (2012). *Social policy and social programs: A method for the practical public policy analyst*. Pearson.

Chingos, M. M., & Peterson, P. E. (2011). It's easier to pick a good teacher than to train one: Familiar and new results on the correlates of teacher effectiveness. *Economics of Education Review, 30*(3), 449–465. https://doi.org/10.1016/j.econedurev.2010.12.010

Colvin, R. L., Bassett, K., Boffy, J., Boffy, H. F., DelColle, J., Fennell, M., Izzo, M., Lechleiter-Luke, L., Mielwocki, R., Minkel, J., Pearson, M., Poulos, C., & Woods-Murphy, M. (2015). *Engaged: Educators and the policy process*. National Network of State Teachers of the Year.

Darling-Hammond, L., Sutcher, L., & Carver-Thomas, D. (2017, November 13). *Why addressing teacher turnover matters*. Learning Policy Institute. https://learningpolicyinstitute.org/blog/why-addressing-teacher-turnover-matters

de Soto, H. (2000). *The mystery of capital: Why capitalism triumphs in the West and fails everywhere else*. Basic Books.

Department of Justice Office of Public Affairs. (2020, October 20). *Justice department sues monopolist Google for violating antitrust laws: Department files complaint against Google to restore competition in search and search advertising markets* [Press release]. www.justice.gov/opa/pr/justice-department-sues-monopolist-google-violating-antitrust-laws

Druckman, J. N., & Lupia, A. (2000). Preference formation. *Annual Review of Political Science, 3*(1), 1–24. https://doi.org/10.1146/annurev.polisci.3.1.1

Gallup. (2018). *Leadership perspectives on public education: The Gallup 2018 survey of K–12 school district superintendents*. Gallup.

Gilens, M., & Page, B. I. (2014). Testing theories of American politics: Elites, interest groups, and average citizens. *Perspectives on Politics, 12*(3), 564–581. https://doi.org/10.1017/s1537592714001595

Giles, M. (2012). *Affluence and influence: Economic inequality and political power in America*. Princeton University Press.

Hanson, M. (2021). *College dropout rates*. Education Data Initiative. Retrieved Month ##, 202x, from https://educationdata.org/college-dropout-rates

Herre, B., Rodes-Guirao, L., Ortiz-Ospina, E., & Roser, M. (2023). *Economist intelligence unit, democracy index 2021: The China challenge*. Economist Intelligence Unit. https://ourworldindata.org/grapher/democracy-index-eiu

Hersh, E. (2020). *Politics is for power: How to move beyond political hobbyism, take action, and make real change*. Scribner.

Hodgson, G. M. (2016). *Conceptualizing capitalism*. University of Chicago Press.

International Institute for Management Development. (2023). *IMD world competitiveness booklet 2023*. IMD World Competitiveness Center. https://imd.cld.bz/IMD-World-Competitiveness-Booklet-2023

Jimen, L., Moralez, J., Sargrad, S., & Thompson, M. (2016). *Remedial education: The cost of catching up*. Center for American Progress. www.americanprogress.org/article/remedial-education/

Kallhoff, A. (2014). Why societies need public goods. *Critical Review of International Social and Political Philosophy, 17*(6), 635–651. https://doi.org/10.1080/13698230.2014.904539

Kingdon, J. (1984). *Agendas, alternatives, and public policies*. Little Brown.

Klein, J. I., Rice, C., & Levy, J. (2012). *U.S. education reform and national security: Independent task force report no. 68*. Council on Foreign Relations Press.

Lasswell, H. D. (1936). *Politics: Who gets what, when, how?* McGraw-Hill Book Company.

Locatelli, R. (2018). *Education as a public and common good: Reframing the governance of education in a changing context*. United Nations Educational, Scientific and Cultural Organization.

Locke, J. (1999). *Two treatises of government* (M. Goldie, Ed.). Everyman.

Lowi, T. J., Ginsberg, B., Shepsle, K. A., Ansolabehere, S., & Han, H. (2022). *American government: Power and purpose*. W.W. Norton & Company.

McDonnell, L. M. (2013). Educational accountability and policy feedback. *Educational Policy, 27*(2), 170–189. https://doi.org/10.1177/0895904812465119

Menashy, F. (2009). Education as a global public good: The applicability and implications of a framework. *Globalisation, Societies and Education, 7*(3), 307–320.

National Center for Education Statistics. (2017). *Digest of education statistics*. https://nces.ed.gov/programs/digest/d17/tables/dt17_105.50.asp?current=yes

National Center for Education Statistics. (2023). *International education attainment: Condition of education*. https://nces.ed.gov/programs/coe/indicator/cac

Organisation for Economic Cooperation and Development. (2023). *Education at a glance 2023.* OECD Publishing. www.oecd-ilibrary.org/education/education-at-a-glance-2023_e13bef63-en

Page, B., & Simmons, J. R. (2000). *What governments can do: Dealing with poverty and inequality.* The University of Chicago Press.

Pasquarella, L. (2016, October 20). What can the next president do to keep colleges and universities from raising tuition and fees? [Opinion]. *Washington Post.* www.washingtonpost.com/news/in-theory/wp/2016/10/20/higher-education-should-be-a-public-good-not-a-private-commodity/

Penn, R., & Nezamis, E. (2022). *Job openings and quits reach record high in 2021, layoffs and discharges fall to record lows.* Monthly Labor Review, U.S. Bureau of Labor Statistics. https://doi.org/10.21916/mlr.2022.17

Pew Research Center. (2020). *Americans' views of government: Low trust, but some positive performance ratings.* www.pewresearch.org/politics/2020/09/14/americans-views-of-government-low-trust-but-some-positive-performance-ratings/

Pierson, P., & Skocpol, T. (2002). Historical institutionalism in contemporary political science. In I. Katznelson & H. Milner (Eds.), *Political science: The state of the discipline* (pp. 693–721). W.W. Norton.

Pub. L. No. 89–554, September 6, 1966, 80 Stat. 424.

Rhodes, J. H. (2011). Progressive policy making in a conservative age? Civil rights and the politics of federal education standards, testing, and accountability. *Perspectives on Politics, 9*(3), 519–544. https://doi.org/10.1017/s1537592711002738

Rigby, E., & Wright, G. C. (2013). Political parties and representation of the poor in the American states. *American Journal of Political Science, 57*(3), 552–565. https://doi.org/10.1111/ajps.12007

Sanders, W. L., & Horn, S. P. (1998). Research findings from the Tennessee value-added assessment system (TVAAS) database: Implications for educational evaluation and research. *Journal of Personnel Evaluation in Education, 12*(3), 247–256. https://doi.org/10.1023/a:1008067210518

Schattschneider, E. E. (1975). *The semisovereign people: A realist's view of democracy in America.* Cengage Learning.

Taie, S., Lewis, L., & Merlin, J. (2023). *Teacher attrition and mobility: Results from the 2021–22 teacher follow-up survey to the national teacher and principal survey, first look summary report.* National Center for Education Statistics. https://nces.ed.gov/pubs2024/2024039SummaryM.pdf

Theriault, S. M. (2006). Party polarization in the U.S. Congress. *Party Politics, 12*(4), 483–503. https://doi.org/10.1177/1354068806064730

United Nations. (2020). *World social report 2020: Inequality in a rapidly changing world.* United Nations Publication.

U.S. Department of Education (2010). *A blueprint for reform: The reauthorization of the elementary and secondary education act.* www2.ed.gov/policy/elsec/leg/blueprint

2   The History of American Education

Is Education the Great Equalizer or the Source of Inequality?

Throughout the history of the United States, education has represented the promise of the American dream, the ideal that every citizen should have an equal opportunity to achieve success and prosperity through hard work, determination, and initiative. Paradoxically, it has also been the source of economic, social, and political inequities. Horace Mann, the father of American education, stated, "Education, then, beyond all other divides of human origin, is a great equalizer of conditions of men – the balance wheel of the social machinery" (Mann, 1957). Although research indicates educational attainment is correlated with economic and social improvement, educational opportunities are disproportionately distributed based on family socioeconomic standing (Morris et al., 2018). The distribution of educational opportunities promotes intergenerational immobility: Individuals are more likely to remain in the same economic quartile as their parents in the United States than in any other advanced economy (Hertz, 2006). Education remains the great equalizer, but the distribution and lack of educational opportunity can also consign socioeconomic, racial, and other groups to their existing economic condition.

The political development of American education can best be understood as a slow and arduous expansion of educational opportunities and rights to historically oppressed groups. This progression is not linear but includes setbacks and regressions. Recall Principle 1: history matters, and current policies result from previous decisions that create positive feedback loops. Like the U.S. stock market, there are short-term fluctuations, recessions, and even wholesale depressions, but the long-term trend is one of expanding educational rights and opportunities. This chapter describes the social, economic, and political movements that have generated these trends in American education, particularly emphasizing the various racial, gender, and socioeconomic groups that have consistently been denied equal educational rights and opportunities.

Before the development of American public school systems, children received schooling only through private tutoring, home schools, tuition-charging schools for the wealthy, apprenticeships, and a patchwork of local church-supported schools organized by groups of parents. Without public funding, educational opportunities largely depended on family wealth. Except in a few New England towns, no public education systems existed before the American Revolution. From the perspective of colonial America's predominantly agricultural economy, schooling was viewed as largely unnecessary.

Religious education was the original motivation for American schooling, both public and private. In the colonial period, public schools were established primarily for political goals rather than individual benefits (Spring, 2016). Literacy was as a means of protecting settlers'

DOI: 10.4324/9781003231561-3

religious traditions. By the end of the American Revolution, New England adult male literacy was nearly universal due to the highly educated groups that migrated between 1630 and 1660 and their commitment to literacy as a cultural norm required for full religious participation. Puritans, the original settlers of New England, created communities centered on the meeting house that served as civil democratic governments and religious congregations (Cubberley, 1919). Education represented a central building block of Puritan communities as training to prepare leaders for the seminary and develop a literate congregation.

On April 14, 1642, the Massachusetts Bay Colony passed the first compulsory education law in the New World. In 1647, the Massachusetts Bay legislature, called the General Court, passed a law requiring every town composed of at least 50 families to have an elementary school and every town with at least 100 families to have a Latin school. The high population density of Massachusetts Bay, compared to other colonies, encouraged the development of government institutions, including public schools. Other New England colonies, including Hartford and New Haven, also passed laws establishing public schools (Cremin, 1970). All New England colonies except Rhode Island created a public schooling system before the American Revolution.

The Middle Atlantic colonies in the New Amsterdam and Chesapeake regions considered education a private matter. As mid-Atlantic cities, including New York and Philadelphia, developed into major economic centers, private schools opened as financial businesses (Cremin, 1970). These private educational ventures highlighted the growing disparity between religious education and more career-oriented education. The religious diversity of Middle Atlantic education far surpassed that of predominantly Puritan New England. The Middle Atlantic colonies' religious diversity – Anglicans, Baptists, Catholics, Dutch Calvinists, Jews, Lutherans, Presbyterians, and Quakers – led to higher levels of educational diversity as each denomination established its own schools.

The low population density of the Southern colonies discouraged community organizations, including schools (Urban et al., 2019). Churches of various denominations largely determined whether children received schooling. The Southern colonies incorporated an English approach to education, in which churches provided not only religious training but also literacy training so parishioners could read the Bible. Educational training in Southern colonies depended on religious affiliation, socioeconomic standing, population density, geographic location, and community support (Urban et al., 2019). As private school options expanded, socioeconomic standing became the primary driver of educational opportunities.

1636–1785: The Colonial Period and Foundations of American Higher Education

During the 17th and early 18th centuries, English settlers dominated colonial settlements in New England and Virginia. Most mid-Atlantic colonists were Dutch, Swedish, Irish, or German. Each European country of origin had a long history of higher education, establishing universities long before settlement in the New World: England (1096), Germany (1385), Sweden (1477), Ireland (1592), and Denmark (1575). By 1646, more than 100 men trained at Cambridge or Oxford University immigrated to New England (Rudolph, 1962). Early settlers arrived with an appreciation for higher education institutions and the role they played in an educated society. During the colonial period, the primary purpose of higher education was to educate and distinguish an elite class (Bailyn, 1960). Most Founders had a college education, which contributed significantly to the political and legal debates and writings about the American Revolution (Thelin, 2019). However, a college or university degree was not a

Table 2.1 Colonial Colleges and Universities

Colonial college (Original name)	Founded	Colony
Harvard University (New College)	1636	Massachusetts Bay Colony
College of William and Mary	1693	Colony of Virginia
Yale University (Collegiate School)	1701	Connecticut Colony
University of Pennsylvania (College of Philadelphia)	1740	Province of Pennsylvania
Princeton University (College of New Jersey)	1746	Province of New Jersey
Columbia University (King's College)	1754	Province of New York
Brown University (College of Rhode Island)	1764	Colony of Rhode Island
Rutgers University (Queen's College)	1766	Province of New Jersey
Dartmouth College	1769	Province of New Hampshire

prerequisite to practicing a profession, which limited the purpose and scope of higher education. Apprenticeship remained the dominant method of educating professionals. Analogous
to colonial elementary and secondary schooling, early higher education institutions' primary
purposes were religious education and training ministers and school masters.

Prior to the American Revolution, nine colleges and universities were established in the
American colonies. Commonly known as the colonial colleges, they represented an early commitment of American settlers to higher education. Table 2.1 lists the nine colonial colleges by
their location and founding date. In 1636, the Massachusetts General Court established New
College, later renamed after early benefactor John Harvard. In 1693, the College of William
and Mary received a charter as the second institution of higher learning in the English colonies (Urban et al., 2019). During the colonial period, no other college or university was established south of Chesapeake Bay. In 1701, Yale University (Collegiate School) was founded by
Congregationalists who believed Harvard had become too liberal in religious matters (Urban
et al., 2019). In 1746, Princeton University was founded as a direct reaction to the religious
inflexibility of Yale University doctrine. In the 1760s, the schism of the Protestant denominations into various sects resulted in the founding of several additional colleges, including Dartmouth College (1769), Brown University (1765), and Rutgers University (1766).

Women

The American colonies' laws derived from English common law, which held that a husband
and wife are one person in the law and that legal existence of women is "suspended during
the marriage" (Blackstone, 1765). Despite these colonial era legal restrictions on women, the
birth of the nation offered some fleeting glimpses of hope for women's rights. The American
Revolution's philosophical foundations rested on the expansion of individual rights, democracy, and equality. Women of the era, such as Abigail Adams, Mercy Otis Warren, and many
others, argued the promises of the American Revolution should extend to women. While
colonial and postcolonial restrictions on women's rights persisted, women continued to fight
for educational equality.

Women were often taught to read for religious purposes. In upper-class families, women
were often also taught math and writing. The early expansion of public schools was primarily
designed for free White boys. Some women, mostly in the New England states, were allowed
to teach in public schools. Women's educational opportunities began to gradually increase
following the American Revolution. The expanding economy placed more responsibility on
women to educate their children and purchase provisions for home and the family farm or

business (Kerber, 1980). Estimates of literacy among White women in the English colonies prior to the revolution exceed **50%** (Davidson, 1986).

African Americans and Native Americans

Indigenous peoples in North America for centuries educated through an elaborate method of transmitting knowledge called the oral tradition (Friesen, 1999). Indigenous education systems transferred values, beliefs, customs, language, knowledge, and skills to succeeding generations. The education system was based on family and community, with parents, elders, and extended relatives all contributing to knowledge and skill transition (Matthew, 2001). Experiential education was the primary pedagogical tradition, with younger generations observing, modeling, and mimicking older generations in language, knowledge, and skills. European settlers in North America failed to appreciate this unwritten, primarily oral education system. Settlers believed Western institution-based education systems were superior and sought to impose those systems on Native Americans.

In 1619, the first enslaved African people arrived in Jamestown, Virginia, commencing the institution of slavery in America. The so-called peculiar institution directly contradicted the ideals of freedom, liberty, and equality that formed the basis of the American Revolution. The American Revolution resulted in some African American educational gains, including thousands of enslaved people who were freed during and after the war. Antislavery societies established several schools for African American children in Philadelphia, Trenton, Boston, and New York (Rury & Darby, 2016). The schools educated thousands of African American children and political and intellectual leaders (Polgar, 2011; Swan, 1992). Widespread resistance to the establishment of Black schools, including the use of violence, also occurred throughout this era (Litwack, 1961; Moss, 2013). By the 1820s, the revolutionary spirit that had supported the rise of Black schools faced increased White resistance and restrictions on African American educational opportunities (Rury & Darby, 2016).

During the colonial period and beyond, the American education system not only excluded most non-Whites but was also at times complicit in supporting slavery and the removal of Native Americans (Wilder, 2013). Higher education institutions were not only beneficiaries of the exploitation of African Americans and Native Americans, but they also furthered these systems of inequality. The elite merchants and planter class provided higher education institutions the resources they required, and in return universities provided "the intellectual cover for the social and political subjugation of non-white peoples" (Wilder, 2013). Colleges and universities received funding to train missionaries to Native Americans and received Indigenous prisoners from state governments. Slave traders became major donors to colleges and universities, which invited them to prominent positions as trustees. College and university presidents, trustees, and faculty regularly owned enslaved people on campuses in both the North and the South (Bell, 2015). Scholars have broadly demonstrated the historic role of postsecondary institutions in supporting systems of oppression that exploited non-White people to further their own interests and the interests of those in power (Angulo, 2005; Brown University Steering Committee on Slavery and Justice, 2006; Meyers, 2008; Sugrue, 1994; Tomlinson & Windham, 2006; Wright, 1996).

1774–1840: Foundations of a Nation and a National Education System

The British government afforded American colonists' considerable autonomy for over 150 years between 1607 and 1764. The British Empire's 1754–1763 war with France, known in the American colonies as the French and Indian War, produced a sizeable British government debt, which it sought to alleviate by creating a series of taxes on the American colonies. The 1764 Sugar Act taxed the import of sugar and molasses; the 1765 Stamp Act taxed all printed materials; and the 1767 Townshend Acts taxed such goods as glass, lead, paper, and tea. These taxes led to widespread American colonist disapproval and protest, the most famous of which was the 1773 Boston Tea Party, when the Sons of Liberty dumped 300 chests of British tea into Boston Harbor. On April 19, 1775, the American Revolutionary War commenced with shots fired between Massachusetts militia and British soldiers at Lexington and Concord. The American Revolutionary War lasted from 1775 to 1783. On January 14, 1784, the United States Congress ratified the Treaty of Paris, officially ending the American Revolution and establishing the United States as a sovereign nation.

On June 21, 1788, the U.S. Constitution was ratified when New Hampshire became the ninth of 13 states to approve the document. Many state legislators were concerned with the limited rights guaranteed in the U.S. Constitution and called for a separate Bill of Rights, a derivative of the 1689 English Bill of Rights, as a prerequisite for constitutional approval. On December 15, 1791, the Bill of Rights, the first 10 amendments to the U.S. Constitution, were ratified. They provide specific guarantees of civil rights and civil liberties: freedom of speech, press, religion, assembly, the right to petition the government, and many others. The Tenth Amendment to the U.S. Constitution reads: "The powers not delegated to the United States by the Constitution, nor prohibited by it to the States, are reserved to the States respectively, or to the people." Given that the U.S. Constitution does not mention education, the Tenth Amendment assigns educational authority to the states rather than the federal government. According to the Constitute Project, 185 of 192 national constitutions guarantee the right to education, including all nations ranked ahead of the United States in primary and secondary education (Lawler, 2018).

Despite the absence of education from the U.S. Constitution, the Founders believed American democracy depended on the participation of educated citizens in civic life who could understand political, social, and economic issues. American leaders began developing political institutions, including an education system that could provide citizens with the civic knowledge necessary to participate in self-governance. For example, in 1779, Thomas Jefferson submitted to the Virginia legislature an education bill for the "More General Diffusion of Knowledge" (Wagoner, 2004). The bill proposed elementary schools in each ward that would provide an education for all free children without charge. The purpose of the elementary schools would be to improve citizens' moral and civic virtues and literacy and arithmetic skills so they could pursue self-sufficiency and happiness. Jefferson's educational plan envisioned education as a public good that would provide not only individual happiness but also the social benefits of self-governance, knowledgeable citizens, and equal opportunity.

On May 20, 1785, the Continental Congress passed the Land Ordinance Act, requiring each town in newly settled areas to reserve a section of land for public school use. The purpose of the provision was to promote public education by providing a financial source for schooling and centrally locate the school in each community. The Land Ordinance stated: "There shall be reserved the lot No. 16 of every township, for the maintenance of public schools with the said township (An Ordinance for Ascertaining the Mode of Disposing of Lands in the Western Territory: Be It Ordained by the United States in Congress Assembled, That the Territory Ceded by Individual States to the United States, Which Has Been Purchased of the Indian Inhabitants, Shall Be Disposed of in the Following Manner, 1785). The Land Ordinance of 1785 demonstrated growing consensus among the political elite and the public that public schooling was needed to promote democracy in the emerging republic. By 1800, seven of the 14 states that had joined the Union included requirements for public education in their state constitutions (Urban et al., 2019).

Between 1790 and 1840, state education systems expanded to provide education to a broader spectrum of the population. In 1790, the Pennsylvania Constitution required free public education for low-income children, becoming the first state to establish a statewide public school system. In 1805, the New York Free School Society established free schools open to all. In 1827, Massachusetts passed a law establishing free, public school for all children. The expansion of education in the first half of the 19th century was driven primarily by the need for a competent workforce given industrialization and urbanization. Despite these developments, public education remained inconsistent across and within states and across various demographic groups until the 1840s.

1840–1860: The Common School Movement

In the 1840s, advances in transportation began connecting communities and expanding economic opportunity. Industrialization and the creation of the factory system led to labor unrest and the need for an expanded skilled workforce. Industrialization and conditions in Europe resulted in increased immigration, particularly among Roman Catholics. The rise of the middle class coincided with the Age of Jackson, named after U.S. President Andrew Jackson, who championed greater rights for the common person and a rejection of the elite and aristocratic political leaders that had led the nation since its founding. In 1834, the Whig Party was formed among National Republicans, abolitionists, anti-Masons, and disgruntled Democrats who opposed Jacksonian Democrats. The Whigs' political platform supported the protective tariff, the national bank, and federal subsidies for expanded infrastructure. According to the Whigs' so-called American system, the federal government should take an active role in financing internal improvements in transportation infrastructure, including railroads, canals, bridges, ports, tunnels, and educational institutions.

Broad-based support for the expansion of education services became known as the common school movement. *Common schools* referred to a school with a common curriculum that supported education for all – the common person – rather than just for the economic and political elite. Common schooling advocates argued for free, universal education for all children, so long as they were White and Protestant. Common school curriculum focused on the three Rs of reading, writing, and arithmetic and were funded by public dollars, typically by the local property taxes that would become the foundation of modern-day public schools. Advocates argued public schools would strengthen the nation's economy through workforce preparation for middle- and lower-class students and improve the political and social standing of the nation by creating more participatory citizens. The common school movement was also a response to the perceived threats of social fragmentation produced by immigration and urbanization. Advocates argued that common schooling experiences would improve cohesion across social classes and improve social outcomes. Other common school supporters were driven by the nationalistic motivation of indoctrinating immigrants to American ideals.

Common school supporters were led by Massachusetts lawyer and legislator Horace Mann. In 1837, Mann was appointed to lead the first state board of education in the United States. As secretary of education, Mann constructed an education system based on the Prussian model, in which all students received a common curriculum regardless of their ability to pay tuition. Mann promoted education for all, not just the wealthy elite, believing common schools would provide citizens with commonly held political beliefs.

1785–1860: The Diffusion of Higher Education Throughout the New Nation

The period from the American Revolution to the Civil War was one of massive U.S. territorial expansion and population growth. In 1803, the Louisiana Purchase nearly doubled the size of the United States to include territory composing the modern-day states of Arkansas, Iowa, Kansas, Missouri, Nebraska, and Oklahoma as well as parts of Colorado, Louisiana, Minnesota, Montana, New Mexico, North Dakota, South Dakota, and Wyoming. In 1821, Spain ceded Florida to the United States in the Transcontinental Treaty. In 1846, the Oregon Treaty established American control over the territory including the current states of Oregon, Washington, and Idaho and parts of Montana and Wyoming. In 1848, the Treaty of Guadalupe Hidalgo ended the Mexican American War and ceded territory including the present-day states of California, Nevada, and Utah as well as parts of Arizona, Colorado, New Mexico, Texas, and Wyoming. The U.S. population expanded from less than four million at the signing of the U.S. Constitution to more than 30 million by the start of the Civil War.

This massive territorial expansion and population growth led to an explosion of postsecondary institutions. Between 1790 and 1810, more than double the number of postsecondary institutions were established as during the entire colonial period. By 1860, more than 500 postsecondary institutions had been established across the United States (Cohen, 1998). Westward expansion, religious pluralism, and low population density all contributed to the unprecedented expansion of higher education institutions. Westward migration established small communities spread over a massive area that sought to establish postsecondary institutions to mimic communities back east and promote religious teachings. Immigration further expanded religious pluralism, leading religious denominations to establish their own higher education institutions. Between 1810 and 1860, postsecondary enrollment in colleges established by Congregational, Presbyterian, and Episcopal denominations decreased from 85% to less than 50%, illustrating the diversification of American higher education institutions (Burke, 1982; Cohen, 1998). Public institutions were accompanied by a broader range of religious higher education institutions, including Baptist, Catholic, and Methodist.

The lack of government regulations and oversight allowed any group to establish postsecondary institutions if it had the financial resources and could attract students and faculty. In 1790, President George Washington in his first address to Congress proposed a national university to train political leaders and promote national unity, but skeptics argued the university system would draw political leaders from the wealthy class (Spring, 2016). In 1816, Democratic Republicans in the New Hampshire state legislature converted Dartmouth College from a private college to a public university by transferring trustee appointment power to the governor. The state court sided with the state of New Hampshire. Daniel Webster, on behalf of Dartmouth College, argued the case before the Supreme Court. The Supreme Court ruled in favor of Dartmouth College, with Chief Justice John Marshall finding that Dartmouth's charter constituted a contract that the state of New Hampshire had violated. Marshall held that in establishing a charter New Hampshire could reserve certain state powers, but the state had not created such powers in this case and therefore violated Article 1, Section 10, of the United States Constitution, also known as the Contract Clause. The Dartmouth Supreme Court ruling strengthened the independence of private and public universities. The absence of a national university or federal regulations and the Supreme Court's Dartmouth decision led to unrestrained growth among higher education institutions (Trow, 1989).

The purpose of higher education also began to shift from an exclusively religious and public good toward a means of improving individual economic standing and personal investment. American colleges moved toward preparing students for professions and away from primarily religious instruction. The changing role of higher education is also illustrated by state governments establishing public postsecondary institutions. In 1785, Georgia charted the first state university in Athens. The University of North Carolina at Chapel Hill was the first public university to graduate a class in 1798. By the Civil War, 17 states had established public universities. States supported the establishment of public colleges primarily through land grants for the purposes of religious freedom and professional preparation.

Women

During this period, women lacked access to and participation in many economic, social, and political institutions including voting, property ownership, and many professions. Common schools stood out as the exception. Women were welcomed not only as students but also as teachers in elementary schools. The biased belief that women were more nurturing than men provided the conditions for women's acceptance in the school system.

African Americans

African Americans faced more difficult obstacles to participation in common schools. Racist worries about Black advancement and the negative consequences for White political power and social standing denied African Americans access to common schools. In the South, elites and the general populace worried that literacy would lead to rebellion and the disintegration of the social order. By 1846, all states north of the Mason-Dixon line had abolished slavery, but this did not dissuade Northerners from excluding African Americans from common schools. Northerners feared race equality and wanted to use education to maintain the existing social hierarchy.

Despite the early educational successes of African American schools in some Northern cities, White opposition to African American education became more widespread as public schooling for Whites expanded (Moss, 2013). Between 1740 and 1834, Southern states enacted antiliteracy laws prohibiting teaching enslaved people how to read or write (Beaubrun, 2020). Antiliteracy laws criminalized the education of African Americans to maintain a racialized social order. In 1740, South Carolina, in response to the 1739 Stono Slave Rebellion, became the first state to forbid and criminalize educating enslaved persons. Most Southern slave states – including Alabama, Georgia, Louisiana, Mississippi, Missouri, North Carolina, South Carolina, and Virginia – had all passed antiliteracy laws. Despite these laws, churches served as pivotal institutions by promoting Black liberation through education, literacy, and African spiritual heritage.

As African Americans and their antislavery allies rallied opposition to the institution of slavery, resistance to African American education increased throughout the first half of the 19th century. The rise of antiliteracy laws in the early 1830s was a direct response Nat Turner's 1831 slave revolt. On August 21, 1831, Nate Turner led a slave revolt that led to the deaths of 55 White people. White people executed 55 Black rebels without trials, and another 19 enslaved persons were executed following a trial. While the revolt lasted only 24 hours, its political and social ramifications cannot be underestimated. Fear of slave revolts and the rise of abolitionism led to the expansion of antiliteracy laws to restrict the education of African Americans. Southern states sought to tighten control over African Americans by controlling literacy. By providing barriers to literacy, Southern slaveholders believed they could reduce the influence of abolitionists and the threat of slave revolts.

Native Americans

In 1819, Congress passed the Indian Civilization Act (ICA), which authorized funds for religious groups to live among and teach American Indians. The ICA adopted the Indian boarding school policy for the purpose of assimilating Native American children. Protestant and Catholic organizations developed religious schools to educate and assimilate Native American children. The development of boarding schools divided Native American communities and removed most American Indian children from their family and tribe. Indian boarding schools banned cultural practices and the speaking of native languages in an attempt to strip Native American children of their cultural identity.

In 1828, Jackson was elected president based partially on his military exploits against Native Americans. From 1815 to 1820, Jackson served as a federal treaty commissioner working to remove Native Americans from their lands so Southern slave plantations could expand (Howe, 2007). In 1830, Congress passed the Indian Removal Act, providing Jackson with the authority to remove Native Americans from their land, one of his top priorities. The Cherokee Nation appealed to the federal courts to avoid removal. In 1832, Marshall ruled in *Worcester v. Georgia* that the Cherokee were entitled to federal protection and that states lacked the constitutional authority to impose regulations on Native American lands. Jackson ignored the ruling and continued to remove Cherokee, Creek, Chickasaw, Choctaw, and Seminoles, also known as the five tribes, across the Mississippi River to reservation lands in Oklahoma Territory. Experts estimate that the Cherokee removal along the Trail of Tears from Georgia to Oklahoma Territory alone caused 2,000 deaths, with a similar number dying from disease once they arrived in the territory. In 1851, Congress passed the Indian Appropriations Act establishing the Indian reservation system and expanded support of Indian boarding schools.

1860–1890: The Civil War and the Rise of a National Education System

In 1860, Republican Abraham Lincoln won the presidency in a landslide. Southern state leaders believed Lincoln's election would lead to the abolition of slavery and decided to secede from the Union. The Southern state secessions resulted in huge congressional majorities for liberal Republicans, leading to a progressive era in federal policymaking. In 1862, Congress passed and Lincoln signed into law the Morrill Land Grant College Act, which set aside federal lands to create colleges for agriculture and mechanical arts. The Morrill Act granted each state 30,000 acres of land to fund the construction of public colleges and universities. The states could use the land to build higher education institutions or sell it to pay for the construction. The resulting schools are listed in Table 2.2.

The Civil War resulted in more than **600,000** casualties and the destruction of the Southern economy but also led to the rebirth of the nation and the end of slavery. The Civil War changed the economic, political, and social character of American society. The war effort had required a strong national government with expanded authority to tax and control currency, the extension of federal citizenship, and the enactment of a military draft system (White, 2017). The manufacturing effort required to sustain the Northern, and to a lesser extent the Southern, armies further advanced American industrialization. Industrialization brought increases in wealth and standard of living, but it also resulted in increased urbanization and economic inequality.

No decision more clearly exemplified the increasing role of the federal government in elementary and secondary education in the post–Civil War period than the establishment of the Department of Education. In 1867, Congress passed and President Andrew Johnson signed into law legislation establishing the Department of Education to collect information to assist states in establishing effective school systems. The Department of Education became a proxy for the toxic racial politics of the post–Civil War era. Former Confederate states that had been forced to rewrite their state constitutions and provide schooling for children regardless of race came to see any educational initiative as further overreach of the federal government into state matters for the improvement of freed slaves. In 1868, Congress demoted the Department of Education to an office in the Department of the Interior.

Between 1865 and 1870, Congress passed and the states ratified the Thirteenth, Fourteenth, and Fifteenth Amendments to the U.S. Constitution, popularly known as the Reconstruction Amendments. The Thirteenth Amendment abolished slavery, the Fourteenth Amendment provided citizenship to all persons born in the United States and equal protection of the laws, and the Fifteenth Amendment established that the right to vote could not be denied on the basis of race. The Reconstruction Amendments had a profound impact on the American legal system, social and political life, and education. While Congress clearly designed the Equal Protection Clause to strengthen the legal rights of newly freed slaves, it extended equal protection of the law to all U.S. citizens. The Equal Protection Clause requires that public institutions, including public schools, treat all equally regardless of race, religion, or national origin.

Table 2.2 1862 Morrill Land Grant College and Universities

State	University
Alabama	Auburn University, Auburn
Alaska	University of Alaska, Fairbanks
Arizona	University of Arizona, Tucson
Arkansas	University of Arkansas, Fayetteville
California	University of California, Berkeley
Colorado	Colorado State University, Fort Collins
Connecticut	University of Connecticut, Storrs
Delaware	Delaware State University, Dover
Florida	University of Florida, Gainesville
Georgia	University of Georgia, Athens
Hawaii	University of Hawaii, Honolulu
Idaho	University of Idaho, Moscow
Illinois	University of Illinois, Urbana
Indiana	Purdue University, West Lafayette
Iowa	Iowa State University, Ames
Kansas	Kansas State University, Manhattan
Kentucky	University of Kentucky, Lexington
Louisiana	Louisiana State University, Baton Rouge
Maine	University of Main, Orono
Maryland	University of Maryland, College Park
Massachusetts	University of Massachusetts, Amherst
Michigan	Michigan State University, East Lansing
Minnesota	University of Minnesota, St. Paul
Mississippi	Mississippi State University, Starkville
Missouri	University of Missouri, Columbia
Montana	Montana State University, Bozeman
Nebraska	University of Nebraska, Lincoln
Nevada	University of Nevada, Reno
New Hampshire	University of New Hampshire, Durham
New Jersey	Rutgers University, New Brunswick
New Mexico	New Mexico State University, Las Cruces
New York	Cornell University, Ithaca

(Continued)

Table 2.2 (Continued)

State	University
North Carolina	North Carolina State University, Raleigh
North Dakota	North Dakota State University, Fargo
Ohio	Ohio State University, Columbus
Oklahoma	Oklahoma State University, Stillwater
Oregon	Oregon State University, Corvallis
Pennsylvania	Pennsylvania State University, State College
Rhode Island	University of Rhode Island, Kingston
South Carolina	Clemson University, Clemson
South Dakota	South Dakota State University, Brookings
Tennessee	University of Tennessee, Knoxville
Texas	Texas A&M University, College Station
Utah	Utah State University, Logan
Vermont	University of Vermont, Burlington
Virginia	Virginia Tech, Blacksburg
Washington	Washington State University, Pullman
West Virginia	West Virginia University, Morgantown
Wisconsin	University of Wisconsin, Madison
Wyoming	University of Wyoming, Laramie

Compulsory Education

The common school movement brought forth compulsory education laws that required children, within certain age limits, to attend school. In 1852, Massachusetts passed the first compulsory attendance law. Following the Civil War, numerous states followed suit: Vermont (1867), New Hampshire (1871), Washington (1871), Connecticut (1872), California (1874), and New York (1874), Callahan (1964). Table 2.3 shows the year compulsory laws were enacted for each state. Southern states were the last to enact state education compulsory laws, between 1907 (North Carolina) and 1918 (Mississippi). By 1918, all 48 U.S. states had enacted compulsory education laws.

State compulsory education laws were motivated by industrialization and urbanization (Baker, 1999), demand for workers, and immigrant assimilation (Trow, 1961). The compulsory school movement was motivated more by social, cultural, and economic factors than by a desire to increase school attendance. Middle- and upper-income factions, particularly Protestant groups, supported compulsory education to improve the integration of immigrant children into American society and out of concern over child labor in American manufacturing. During this period, child labor laws prohibited youths from working and impacted school attendance even more than compulsory school laws that were rarely enforced (Goldin & Katz, 2008).

Teachers Unions

In 1857, 10 state education associations established the National Teachers Association. In 1870, the National Teachers Association merged with the National Association of School Superintendents and the American Normal School Association to establish the National Education Association (NEA). The NEA quickly became a leading voice in American education, particularly in promoting a more equitable education system. At its summer 1865 convention, the National Teachers Association denounced slavery and recommended that free public school systems for all children be a condition of readmitting seceded states to the

Table 2.3 State Education Compulsory Laws Enacted and Provisions

State	Year compulsory law enacted	Ages of required school attendance	Minimum age at which free education must be offered	Maximum age to which free education must be offered
Alabama	1915	6–17	5	17
Alaska	1929	7–16	5	20
Arizona	1899	6–16	6	21
Arkansas	1909	5–18	5	21
California	1874	6–18	5	21
Colorado	1889	6–17	5	21
Connecticut	1872	5–18	5	21
Delaware	1907	5–16	5	21
District of Columbia	1864	5–18	5	21
Florida	1915	6–16	4	
Georgia	1916	6–16	5	19
Hawaii	1896	5–18	5	20
Idaho	1887	7–16	5	21
Illinois	1883	6–17	4	21
Indiana	1897	7–18	5	22
Iowa	1902	6–16	5	21
Kansas	1874	7–18	5	
Kentucky	1896	6–18	5	21
Louisiana	1910	7–18	5	20
Maine	1875	7–17	5	20
Maryland	1902	5–18	5	21
Massachusetts	1852	6–16	3	22
Michigan	1871	6–18	5	20
Minnesota	1885	7–17	5	21
Mississippi	1918	6–17	5	21
Missouri	1905	7–17	5	21
Montana	1883	7–16	5	19
Nebraska	1887	6–18	5	21
Nevada	1873	7–18	5	21
New Hampshire	1871	6–18		21
New Jersey	1875	6–16	5	20
New Mexico	1891	5–18	5	
New York	1874	6–16	5	21
North Carolina	1907	7–16	5	21
North Dakota	1883	7–16	5	21
Ohio	1877	6–18	5	22
Oklahoma	1907	5–18	5	21
Oregon	1889	6–18	5	19
Pennsylvania	1895	8–17	6	21
Rhode Island	1883	5–18	5	21
South Carolina	1915	5–17	5	22
South Dakota	1883	6–18	5	21
Tennessee	1905	6–18	5	
Texas	1915	6–19	5	26
Utah	1890	6–18	5	
Vermont	1867	6–16	5	
Virginia	1908	5–18	5	20
Washington	1871	8–18	5	21
West Virginia	1897	6–17	5	22
Wisconsin	1879	6–18	4	20
Wyoming	1876	7–16	5	21

Union. In 1894, the NEA's Committee of Ten report recommended 12 years of elementary and secondary education, including 4 years of high school; equality in instruction; curriculum standards; and enhanced university training for teachers, principals, and superintendents. Teachers unions would continue to have a disproportionate impact on federal, state, and local education policy and practice from the 19th century to the modern day.

The University System

In 1865, New York Governor Reuben Eaton Fenton signed the Cornell University charter, commencing the rise of American universities focused on research and graduate training in addition to undergraduate education. Harvard, Yale, and Johns Hopkins were also early adopters of the American university model, which is dedicated to graduate education and focused on specialization of knowledge, research, and division of labor between faculty and administrators. In 1876, Johns Hopkins became the first research university in the United States (Veysey, 1965). American universities prioritized research for the advancement of knowledge and industries and to educate students to be scientific leaders and innovators who would expand economic growth and prosperity, develop industry, be civic and academic leaders, and improve American economic competitiveness and standard of living. Between 1870 and 1930, the number of American graduate students increased from 200 to nearly 50,000 and the number of doctorates awarded increased from 44 to more than 2,000 (Hofstadter, 1952). During the end of the 19th century, the rise of the American university was one of the most significant moments in the evolution of American higher education.

In 1900, the Association of American Universities (AAU) was founded at the University of Chicago to consider "matters of common interest relating to graduate study" (Selingo, 2017). The founding member institutions were Clark University, Catholic University of America, Columbia University, Cornell University, Harvard University, Johns Hopkins University, Princeton University, Stanford University, University of California, University of Chicago, University of Michigan, University of Pennsylvania, University of Wisconsin, and Yale University. At the turn of the 20th century, the American higher education system was viewed as inferior to the European system due to its decentralized nature and lack of uniform graduation and curriculum standards. The original goals of the AAU included improving uniformity of graduate degree requirements, improving American universities' reputation, and raising the standards of all university institutions (Selingo, 2017). Professional associations also were established during this time to identify standards for academic subjects. Table 2.4 lists AAU members and their founding date and date of membership. The table illustrates that most American research universities were established by 1900, the California University System being the primary exception. AAU membership is by invitation only and based on the quality of the university program of research and graduate and undergraduate education. The development of the university system placed American higher education on the path to being the preeminent postsecondary education system in the world.

Women

In 1790, men were twice as likely as women to be literate (Tyack & Hansot, 1992). By 1870, White women's literacy rate surpassed men's (Rury, 2020). The common school movement had opened the elementary grades to women, and the literacy rates illustrate the impact (Strober & Lanford, 1986). The educational progress of women in American education spurred a debate about coeducation in the latter half of the 19th century. A public debate

Table 2.4 Association of American University Members

Research University	Member date	Founding date
Harvard University	1900	1636
Yale University	1900	1701
University of Pennsylvania	1900	1740
Princeton University	1900	1746
Columbia University	1900	1754
Brown University	1933	1764
Rutgers University	1989	1766
Dartmouth College	2019	1769
University of Pittsburgh	1974	1787
University of North Carolina at Chapel Hill	1922	1789
University of Michigan	1900	1817
University of Virginia	1904	1819
Indiana University Bloomington	1909	1820
George Washington University	2023	1821
McGill University	1926	1821
Case Western Reserve University	1969	1826
University of Toronto	1926	1827
New York University	1950	1831
Tulane University	1958	1834
Emory University	1995	1836
Duke University	1938	1838
Boston University	2012	1839
University of Missouri	1908	1839
University of Notre Dame	2023	1842
University at Buffalo	1989	1846
University of Iowa	1909	1847
University of Wisconsin at Madison	1900	1848
University of Rochester	1941	1850
University of Utah	2019	1850
Northwestern University	1917	1851
University of Minnesota, Twin Cities	1908	1851
Tufts University	2021	1852
University of Florida	1985	1853
Washington University at St. Louis	1923	1853
Michigan State University	1964	1855
Pennsylvania State University	1958	1855
University of Maryland at College Park	1969	1856
Massachusetts Institute of Technology	1934	1861
University of Washington	1950	1861
Cornell University	1900	1865
University of Kansas	1909	1865
University of Illinois Urbana-Champaign	1908	1867
University of California, Berkeley	1900	1868
Purdue University	1958	1869
Ohio State University	1916	1870
Vanderbilt University	1950	1873
Johns Hopkins University	1900	1876
Texas A&M University	2001	1876
University of Colorado Boulder	1966	1876
University of Oregon	1969	1876
University of Southern California	1969	1880
University of Texas at Austin	1929	1883

(Continued)

Table 2.4 (Continued)

Research University	Member date	Founding date
Arizona State University	2023	1885
Georgia Institute of Technology	2010	1885
University of Arizona	1985	1885
University of Chicago	1900	1890
California Institute of Technology	1934	1891
Stanford University	1900	1891
Carnegie Mellon University	1982	1900
University of California, Davis	1996	1905
University of California, Riverside	2023	1907
Rice University	1985	1912
University of California, Los Angeles	1974	1919
University of Miami	2023	1925
University of California, Santa Barbara	1995	1944
Brandeis University	1985	1948
University of South Florida	2023	1956
Stony Brook University	2001	1957
University of California, San Diego	1982	1960
University of California, Irvine	1996	1965
University of California, Santa Cruz	2019	1965

about gender segregation commenced, with more conservative areas advocating for single-sex education, particularly in secondary schools (Tyack & Hansot, 1992). Coeducational schools became the norm because the cost of gender segregation made such plans impractical. The education system did not challenge traditional gender roles but rather reinforced them, making it less of a threat to the status quo. The 1848 Seneca Falls Women's Rights Convention was a seminal moment in the women's rights movement. The convention called for women's equality and suffrage. Among the resolutions passed by the convention were a call for equal educational rights for women.

Domestic societal norms of the time limited which professions were open to women. Teaching was one of the few socially acceptable jobs outside the home, so it became a popular female professional choice. Women were welcomed to the teaching profession for elementary grades, but men dominated higher grades. Scholars have called this political development the feminization of the teaching industry (Rury, 2020; Rury & Hurst, 2022). The feminization of the teaching industry drove away men, who increasingly viewed the profession as solely for women. By the 1880s, 63% of all public school teachers were women and the percentage was much higher in elementary schools. The increasing cost of public schools as enrollments increased made hiring female teachers, who were paid far less than their male counterparts, more economical for local school districts. Historians argue that men moving out of the teaching profession was a central cause of the feminization of the teaching profession (Strober & Lanford, 1986). Teaching did not provide a career ladder for women, who typically left the profession after a short time for marriage.

Prior to 1835, no U.S. colleges admitted women. Advocates for higher educational opportunities for women supported both the expansion of coeducational opportunities at existing colleges and the development of women's colleges. In the mid-19th century, women's colleges were established to provide educational opportunities for women, who were still excluded from most American colleges and universities. By 1870, women's colleges comprised 60% of total female undergraduate enrollment (Newcomer, 1959). The Seven Sisters were a group of women's colleges that became the equivalent of the Ivy League schools for women: Mount Holyoke (1837), Vassar (1861), Wellesley (1870), Smith (1871), Radcliffe (1879), Bryn Mawr (1885), and Barnard (1889). More than 50 women's colleges were founded between 1835 and 1900.

After the Civil War, enrollment of women in American higher education increased significantly. Between 1870 and 1900, the percentage of coeducational colleges increased from 30% to 70%. By 1900, women comprised 30% of American higher education enrollments. Most women entered higher education to prepare for secondary teaching positions.

African Americans

On March 3, 1865, a month before General Robert E. Lee's surrender at Appomattox Court House, Congress established the Freedman's Bureau to provide food, shelter, clothing, medical services, and land to displaced Southerners and newly freed African Americans. The Freedman's Bureau also established schools to address African American educational needs. Rather than run schools itself, the Bureau helped private aid societies establish schools and offered military protection. The organization assisted in the establishment of more than 4,000 schools. Southern Whites fought against African American educational opportunities by burning many of the schools established by the Freedman's Bureau (Sitton & Conrad, 2005). A primary goal of the Freedman's Bureau was improving literacy rates and providing the educational foundation to incorporate African Americans into the wage labor economy. African American demand for education was so high that school enrollment matched or exceeded that of Whites across the South (Rury & Darby, 2016). Thanks also to an inflow of missionaries into the South to educate freed persons, literacy rates rose rapidly. Literacy rates among African Americans in the South prior to the Civil War have been estimated at 5%–10% (Schweiger, 2013). By the end of Reconstruction, 30% of African Americans had achieved literacy.

The Freedman's Bureau was also responsible for most of the African American colleges founded after the Civil War, including Atlanta University, Fisk University, Howard University, and Hampton University. In 1872, Congress abolished the Freedman's Bureau due largely to pressure from Southern Whites. The Compromise of 1877 awarded Republican Rutherford B. Hayes the presidency in exchange for concessions including the removal of U.S. military forces from the former Confederate states. The Compromise ended Reconstruction and the federal government turned its back on African Americans. Southern White leaders quickly filled the vacuum and installed a system of racial segregation in all areas including public schools. The loss of political power and civil rights ended the expansion of Black schools and ushered in an era of poorly funded, segregated schooling designed to oppress African Americans.

Native Americans

During 1870–1900, federal policy toward Native Americans shifted from removal to reservations to breaking up reservations by allotting tribal and federal land to individual Native Americans. In 1887, Congress passed the General Allotment Act, also known as the Dawes Act, authorizing the president to allot lands to individual tribal members to civilize them and bring them into the mainstream of American society. While some supporters of the policy had positive intentions, the impact was to further devastate Native American culture.

In 1878, the federal Indian Office established day and boarding schools to assimilate Native American children. Although treaties between the United States and many native tribes required the federal government to provide educational services, the federal government delegated authority to religious groups to run the schools. In 1879, the first off-reservation school was established in Carlisle, Pennsylvania. The school's founder, Army Captain Richard Henry Pratt, said his goal for the school was to civilize Indians through cultural assimilation. In an 1892 speech, Pratt bluntly stated his educational goal: "Kill the Indian in him, and save the man."

Chinese Americans

On January 24, 1848, gold was discovered at Sutter's Mill, 50 miles outside Sacramento, California. The impact of the Gold Rush on California cannot be overstated. Between 1850 and 1860, California's population increased from approximately 92,000 to 380,000, a 310% expansion. In 1849, the first major wave of Chinese Americans arrived in California due to the discovery of gold. In 1848, only a handful of people of Chinese descent were living in the U.S., but by 1851 that number had increased to 25,000. In 1858, the California Legislature passed the Chinese Exclusion Law, banning Chinese laborers from entering the United States. In 1859, the Chinese School was opened in the Chinatown neighborhood of San Francisco, California. Students of Chinese descent were excluded from public schools. In 1870, the California School Law repealed prior legislation that limited public education to White children, but the law mentioned only African Americans, Indians, and Mongolians. For the next 15 years, children of Chinese descent were the only racial group denied access to public education. In 1885, the California Supreme Court ruled in *Tape v. Hurley* that it was unlawful to exclude children of Chinese descent from public schools.

Americans With Disabilities

Prior to the 18th century, people with disabilities typically received contemptuous or even brutal treatment by societies that believed they were not capable of learning or participating in social or economic activity (Winzer, 2009). In the 18th century, the European Enlightenment, a period of scientific, political, and philosophical discovery and reason, increased literacy rates, scientific understanding, individual liberty, and religious tolerance. The Enlightenment improved societal understanding of the causes of disabilities and toward the education of people with disabilities. In the 19th century, the first institutions to educate persons with disabilities were established in Europe. From the colonial era through the early 19th century, people with disabilities in the United States were primarily supported in the home by the family unit (Osgood, 2008).

In the 19th century, the first efforts to formally educate students with disabilities in the United States came in the form of institutions. In 1817, Thomas Hopkins Gallaudet opened the Connecticut Asylum for the Education and Instruction of Deaf and Dumb persons in Hartford, Connecticut. The term *dumb* meant the inability to speak. In 1832, the Asylum for the Blind opened in Boston, Massachusetts, with support from its first director, Samuel Gridley Howe. In 1848, Howe, with support from the Massachusetts state government, established the Massachusetts School for Idiotic and Feeble-Minded Youth in Boston to educate youth with intellectual disabilities. While the academics and philanthropists who founded these institutions sought to improve the condition and treatment of students with disabilities, the larger society often supported them as a way to separate these children from the general population (Winzer, 2009). The early institutions primarily served students who were deaf, blind, or intellectually disabled.

Despite early successes in promoting the education of persons with disabilities, public and private institutions shifted away from education and toward isolating them. This custodial shift coincided with the expansion of public and private institutions throughout the United States. By the 1890s, most states supported institutions for persons with disabilities through public funding (Osgood, 2008). Educational opportunities for persons with disabilities from colonial America through the 20th century were mixed. On the one hand, educators, philanthropists, advocates, and state governments utilized scientific innovations to improve their understanding of the causes and educational needs of those with disabilities to develop educational services. On the other, the movement to educate persons with disabilities quickly became a means of isolating individuals from the broader society rather than providing them equal opportunity.

1890–1920: Assimilating Immigrants and Building an Industrial Economy

The United States more than doubled in population between 1880 and 1920, increasing from 50 million to 106 million. During that 40-year span, U.S. immigration exploded, with more than 20 million people coming to the United States. This period attracted primarily Eastern and Southern European immigrants seeking economic opportunity and freedom from religious persecution. They settled primarily in industrial centers. By 1920, first- and second-generation immigrants comprised two thirds of U.S. manufacturing labor (Hirschman & Mogford, 2009). While the proliferation in immigration labor proved central to the U.S. industrial revolution and economic growth, it posed a challenge to the American social, cultural, and political system. In 1892, Francis Bellamy wrote the Pledge of Allegiance as part of the 400th anniversary of Christopher Columbus's arrival in the New World. His purpose was to instill a sense of patriotism and nationalism in school children, particularly the millions of immigrant children.

The American industrial revolution developed mass production methods through new technology and manufacturing methods. Robber barons like John D. Rockefeller, J.P. Morgan, and Andrew Carnegie formed huge corporations. Lack of competition allowed trusts to dictate prices and wages. The richest 1% of the U.S. population amassed more than 50% of all wealth.

The progressive era saw a social and political response to the negative externalities of industrialization, urbanization, immigration, and political corruption that characterized the Industrial Revolution. Progressive reformers pursued more economic, political, and social equality. To reduce the political power of economic elites and political machines, state legislatures instituted initiatives and referendums, direct primaries, and municipal reforms. Progressive reformers were also responsible for a series of constitutional amendments, including the Sixteenth Amendment, legalizing a national income tax; the Seventeenth Amendment, transferring the selection of U.S. Senators from state legislatures to popular elections; and the Nineteenth Amendment, granting women the right to vote.

The progressive era also witnessed significant administrative and pedagogical education reforms. Population growth combined with state compulsory education laws significantly increased school enrollments. The unprecedented growth in school enrollments motivated school systems to centralize school governance by decreasing the authority of individual schools and transferring that authority to local governments and school boards, particularly in urban districts. Professionally trained administrators became the leaders of public schools predicated on corporate organizational structures. School superintendents became the administrative heads of these new centralized school systems. Research universities developed schools of education to provide school leaders with the specialized knowledge to manage school systems.

Progressive era education administrative reforms also extended to the specialization of the education system. By 1900, the principal U.S. public education school structure was 8 years of primary school and, for a minority of students, 4 years of secondary school (Juvonnen et al., 2004). According to the National Center for Education Statistics (2001), of the 17.1 million students in 1900, only 600,000 (4%) attended high school and 200,000 (1%) enrolled in postsecondary institutions. The increasingly complex economy of the Industrial Revolution and the advanced training of school leaders led to specialization of the common school system. The newly developing educational organizational structure incorporated kindergarten, middle and junior high schools, high schools, and the research university.

Common schools typically began teaching students at 6 years old, which created a problem for the increasingly industrialized workforce, particularly among urban and lower income populations that needed to ensure their young children were prepared for public school. Urban schools borrowed the idea of early education from Germany, specifically the educational theorist Friedrich Froebel. He believed children should learn from an early age through creative and imaginative play. In 1856, the first U.S. kindergarten opened in Watertown, Wisconsin. By 1914, all major American urban school systems had developed kindergartens. Their purpose was less about teaching 3- to 6-year-old students to read and write and more about ensuring children were healthy and developing cognitive and social–emotional skills. While kindergartens initially developed outside the public school system, states slowly incorporated them into the publicly financed school system.

The turn of the century also brought calls from educational leaders to reorganize secondary schooling to meet the needs of the 20th century economy and societal structure. Educational leaders sought to align the secondary curriculum and structure to better prepare students for college; serve the growing, increasingly nonnative, urban student population; and train a better educated workforce for industrial labor (Juvonnen et al., 2004). In 1911, the NEA published a report that argued for starting college preparation in seventh rather than ninth grade. In 1918, the Commission on the Reorganization of Secondary Education recommended dividing secondary education into junior and senior levels (Cuban, 1992). The commission also recommended a highly differentiated secondary school curriculum with tracks based on a student's post–high school plans. The political and public pressure placed on the education system to reorganize also drew from an anti-immigrant fear that America was losing traditional values and that a middle school could provide cultural assimilation and social services to improve urban conditions (Spring, 2016).

Progressive pedagogical reforms were promoted by academics, the most influential and notable being John Dewey. He served as a professor at the University of Chicago from 1894 to 1904 and then at Columbia University from 1904 to 1930. Dewey promoted the democratization of the American school system so schools would serve not only as places of learning but also of social change. Dewey described his educational philosophy as one in which student growth, not some predetermined end, should represent educational purpose. Dewey argued for active learning and student participation to engage students in the learning process and relate education to real-world applications. The purpose of education, he argued, was not the communication of knowledge but the sharing of social experience so children become integrated into a democratic community. Dewey's philosophy had widespread impact on American educational practices. His approach influenced teaching practices to increase student participation and engagement through active learning strategies. His vision was juxtaposed against an authoritarian education system in which a teacher provided students with knowledge through lectures and discipline. Dewey believed schools were at the center of a democratic republic and should reflect democratic norms that educate all children to be thoughtful, critically reflective, socially engaged citizens. Critics have argued that Dewey's philosophy undermines classroom order and teacher authority, resulting in the failure of children to acquire necessary academic skills and knowledge (Urban et al., 2019).

Efforts to segregate and disenfranchise African Americans immediately followed the end of the Civil War and the passage of the Thirteenth Amendment. State and local laws legalizing limits to formerly enslaved people's freedom, referred to as the Black Codes, became common. Black Codes restricted voting rights, employment opportunities, and housing options. The legal and policing systems were used as a means of reenslaving African Americans.

In 1896, the Supreme Court held in *Plessy v. Ferguson* that there was nothing inherently unequal about separate accommodations for different races if they were equal. The "separate but equal" doctrine, affirming that racial segregation did not violate the Fourteenth Amendment's Equal Protection Clause, established the constitutional basis for legalized segregation. By 1910, nearly all the former Confederate states passed new state constitutions that practically disenfranchised African Americans. The public school system segregated African American children into separate schools that were in no way equal to their White counterparts' schools. Segregated schools lacked basic building safety and sanitation, contained overcrowded and underresourced classrooms, and were staffed by underpaid teachers and administrators.

In 1890, Congress passed a second Morrill Act, providing additional funding for land grant universities with an additional critical requirement. To receive the funding, land grant colleges were required to provide equal access to existing land grant colleges or establish additional higher education institutions for "people of color." The second Morrill Act is controversial because it simultaneously expanded and segregated higher education opportunities for African Americans. Table 2.5 lists the 17 historically Black colleges and universities established or reorganized by the second Morrill Act.

In 1887, Congress passed the Hatch Act, funding state land grant colleges to establish agriculture experiment stations. The legislation fostered scientific research for improving

Table 2.5 1890 Second Morrill Act Land Grant Universities

State	Institution	Founded
Alabama	Alabama A&M University	1875
Mississippi	Alcorn State University	1871
Ohio	Central State University	1887
Delaware	Delaware State University	1891
Florida	Florida A&M University	1887
Georgia	Fort Valley State University	1895
Kentucky	Kentucky State University	1886
Oklahoma	Langston University	1897
Missouri	Lincoln University	1854
North Carolina	North Carolina A&T State University	1891
Texas	Prairie View A&M University	1876
South Carolina	South Carolina State University	1896
Louisiana	Southern University	1880
Tennessee	Tennessee State University	1912
Alabama	Tuskegee University	1881
Arkansas	University of Arkansas Pine Bluff	1873
Maryland	University of Maryland Eastern Shore	1886
Virginia	Virginia State University	1882
West Virginia	West Virginia State University	1891

farming, conservation, and rural life. These research investments were a significant federal investment in both higher education and American agriculture that led to increased efficiency in agricultural practices and crop production. State experiment stations funded by the Hatch Act and housed at land grant universities also trained researchers to expand agricultural education. In 1914, Congress passed the Smith Lever Act, which expanded land grant universities by establishing cooperative extension services to extend new agricultural techniques to a broader distribution of farmers. The Smith Lever Act created partnerships between agricultural colleges and the United States Department of Agriculture, requiring states to match federal funds. The Hatch and Smith Lever Acts illustrate the commitment of the federal government to support postsecondary education into the early 20th century.

1920–1945: The Great Depression and the High School Movement

The Great Depression challenged the nation to reassess all aspects of American life, including education. The Great Depression financially impacted education through short-term decreases in funding and resources that disproportionately affected lower income communities. The Depression's long-term impact on school finances was lagged, as the stock market crash of 1929 did not reverberate to local governments until the 1932–1933 school year. However, the depression would have a long-term impact on public school finances just as secondary schools witnessed the greatest expansion and enrollment increase in history. The political response was longer lasting, with progressive teachers' unions supporting educational reforms.

The High School Movement

In the first half of the 20th century, the United States became the world leader in publicly financed secondary school education. By 1910, most youth outside the South attended primary school until the age of 14 (Goldin & Katz, 2008). Between 1910 and World War II, high school graduation rates expanded from 10% to 53% and the percent of high school enrollment increased from 18% to 73%. This educational transformation became known as the high school movement. According to Goldin and Katz (2008), in 1955 the United States achieved a secondary enrollment rate of 80% while no country in Europe had achieved a 25% rate. The expansion of secondary school enrollment was one of America's greatest accomplishments of the 20th century.

The foundations of the high school movement were laid in the 19th century. In 1821, Boston established the first public English high school as an alternative to grammar school to prepare boys between 12 and 15 (Tyack & Hansot, 1992). Its original purpose was not to prepare students for college but to prepare them for white-collar jobs. In 1827, the Massachusetts General Assembly passed a law requiring all communities of more than 500 families to establish public high schools. By 1865, Massachusetts established more high schools than any other state. Early adoptees of public high schools included Eastern and Midwestern urban areas like Cleveland and Cincinnati, Ohio; Detroit, Michigan; New York, New York; Portland, Maine; Providence, Rhode Island; and New Orleans, Louisiana.

The Rise of Public Higher Education and the Research University

The high school movement also empowered the expansion of American postsecondary education throughout the 20th century. During the first half of the 20th century, the two dominant trends in American higher education were the development of the comprehensive research university and the disproportionate development of public sector postsecondary institutions. According to the American Council of Education, universities provide advanced degrees in a variety of fields in addition to undergraduate education. Between 1900 and 1940, student enrollment at public colleges and universities increased from 22% to nearly 50% (Goldin & Katz, 1998).

What caused the rise of the American higher education public sector? American higher education's increasing division of labor and specialization provided research universities an advantage in meeting the need for advanced training in an increasingly technologically driven labor force. Public universities that developed to meet state economic needs gave them a first mover advantage in the changing higher education landscape. Public universities also had the advantage of developing and expanding professional programs in emerging professions at a lower cost than their private sector counterparts. According to Goldin and Katz (2008), the size, reputation, and research resources required to compete with public universities increased the barriers to entry for private sector research universities. The 1910–1940 high school movement also increased the higher education enrollment pool, with a disproportionate percentage selecting professional-oriented programs at public universities. Another factor influencing the rise of the public research university was the level of state support. Between 1900 and 1940, the level of state support for public higher education doubled, with increased funding particularly strong in regions outside the Northeast where private postsecondary institutions presented less competition.

1945–1960: National Involvement in American Education

World War II, like previous wars, impacted American education in profound ways. World War II centered American education on the need to fight Nazi racism because of the atrocities that had been witnessed (Berman, 1970; Berstein, 1970; Gardner, 2002). Americans returned from war and came face to face with the difficult realization that the nation had developed systems of oppression to disenfranchise African Americans. The Civil War had abolished slavery, but it had not abolished American racism or systems of oppression. In the United States, racial segregation laws and restrictions on Black suffrage sought to reduce African Americans to second-class status. Scientific advances in genetics, evolutionary biology, and intelligence testing had been distorted to wrongly justify racist behavior in Germany, Japan, and in the United States. The atrocities of World War II forced Americans to look in the mirror and come to terms with systems of racial oppression. More than one million African American men and women served in World War II and returned to face terrible mistreatment, violence, and lynching.

President Harry Truman led several federal government efforts to face these difficult realities. In 1946, Truman established the Committee on Civil Rights to make recommendations to strengthen civil rights in the United States. In 1948, Truman signed Executive Order 9981, which established the President's Committee on Equality of Treatment and Opportunity in the Armed Services and mandated the desegregation of the U.S. military.

Brown v. Board of Education (1954)

In 1954, the United States Supreme Court unanimously ruled that racial segregation in schools was unconstitutional in *Brown v. Board of Education*. The Topeka, Kansas, public school system had forced Linda Brown to attend an all-Black elementary school even though another public elementary school was located closer to her home. Brown and 12 other families filed a class-action lawsuit in U.S. federal court arguing the segregationist policy was unconstitutional. The Supreme Court overturned its 1896 decision in *Plessy v. Ferguson* that legalized separate but equal public facilities. Chief Justice Earl Warren declared in his majority opinion: "In the field of public education, the doctrine of 'separate, but equal' has no place. Separate educational facilities are inherently unequal" (Ferguson, 1896).

Brown v. Board of Education did not immediately lead to the desegregation of America's schools. Many school districts and local governments ignored the Supreme Court ruling. Protests and violence were common responses to integration efforts, particularly in the Southern states. In 1957, nine African American students enrolled in Little Rock Central High School. Arkansas Governor Orval Faubus prevented the students from entering the racially segregated school and protests blocked the school entrance for weeks. President Dwight Eisenhower sent National Guard troops to restrict the protesters and force Faubus to allow the students to attend the school. The bravery of the Little Rock Nine, as they became popularly known, inspired further school desegregation and the broader civil rights movement (Perry, 2015). Southern states also resorted to removing constitutional educational requirements and passing laws claiming they could ignore the federal government's school integration requirements.

The postwar economic boom also had profound impacts on American elementary and secondary education. Since 1900, the United States had maintained the largest economy in the world and the highest standard of living (O'Hara & O'Hara, 2000). The postwar economic boom allowed the United States to invest significant public and private resources into primary, secondary, and postsecondary education. These investments paid off, making the United States the most educated country in the world through much of the 20th century.

Women

The high school movement, although originally intended for men, quickly became coeducational. In 1826, the first high schools for women opened in Boston and New York. By 1900, girls constituted 59% of the national high school population (Tyack & Hansot, 1992). The expansion of secondary schools benefited women by providing previously unavailable educational opportunities. Teacher shortages, improved teacher conditions, and modest increases in teacher salaries increased the percentage of male teachers to 25% by 1940 (Sedlak & Schlossman, 1986). Teacher shortages also forced school districts to end the long-standing practice of excluding married women from teaching. Women continued to have limited job prospects outside public education, which drew a disproportionate number of highly qualified women to the profession (Rury, 2020). During a period of misogyny, teaching was a socially acceptable profession because women could continue to fill a domestic role. Many teachers would teach until they had children and then return to the profession once their children attended school (Sedlak & Schlossman, 1986). While women had occupied most of the elementary school principalships since 1905, men occupied most higher level school leadership positions, including high school principalships and district superintendents (Rury, 2020).

World War I was a watershed moment for women's suffrage. The U.S. war effort catalyzed American capital, technological, and labor resources. The U.S. war effort mobilized nearly five million men into all military branches, which was more than 20% of the male population aged 21 to 45. More than 20,000 women also served in the military as field nurses, clerical administrators, and in other noncombat roles. Women also filled the millions of civilian jobs left vacant by the precipitous decline in the supply of human labor wrought by military mobilization. Industries historically unavailable to women, particularly in manufacturing and agriculture, became dependent on their labor. World War I catalyzed women's economic responsibilities, strengthening the women's movement for political suffrage and social empowerment. In 1920, the Nineteenth Amendment to the U.S. Constitution expanded voting rights to women. This key moment in American gender equality was wrought by the women's suffrage movement and intensified by the expanded role women played during World War I. Women's suffrage had far-reaching impacts for American society and for education. Studies indicate the Nineteenth Amendment corresponded with increases in government spending, decreases in child mortality, and improved student education retention (Kose et al., 2021). Despite advances in U.S. gender equality, during and after the war the percentage of female elementary and secondary teachers continued to increase through World War II, as postwar employment opportunities began to return to their prewar patterns.

African Americans

Prior to World War I, the African American population continued to reside predominantly in the South. Progressive political and education reforms of the early 20th century strategically excluded Black participation to gain political favor with Southern constituencies (Woodward, 1971). Conservative and progressive reformers supported racial segregation of the developing American education system. In 1941, following the Japanese bombing of Pearl Harbor, the United States declared war on the Axis Powers of Japan, Germany, and Italy and joined the Allied Powers, including Great Britain and the Soviet Union. More than 1.2 million African Americans served in World War II in support and combat roles. African American contributions to the war effort and American denunciation of Nazi theories of Aryan supremacy led to a reassessment of U.S. racial segregation and discrimination (Rury & Darby, 2016). The Nazi ideology of racist superiority highlighted the contradiction between America's ideals of American liberty and equality and U.S. treatment of racial minorities.

Black soldiers who had risked their lives to fight against a racist regime and defend American democracy returned home to a society of bigotry, segregation, and injustice. The contradiction motivated the rise of the civil rights movement, which included political protests, lobbying for civil rights legislation, and legal action to combat segregation in public services including education. The civil rights movement and *Brown v. Board of Education* shifted the focus of American education toward greater equity. During the Cold War, a period of geopolitical tension between the United States and the Soviet Union for global influence that followed World War II, the United States sought the support of nations around the globe, including African and Asian nations. The Cold War helped foreground the contradiction between American ideals of equality and the oppression of African Americans, prompting continued policy change. African Americans witnessed their largest gains in educational achievement in U.S. history. Between 1940 and 1960, African American school enrollment increased from **68.4%** to **86.1%**, nearly matching the enrollment of their White counterparts.

Native Americans

By 1926, nearly **83%** of Indian school-age children attended 367 boarding schools operating in 29 states (National Native American Boarding School Healing Coalition, 2023). In 1928, the Brookings Institution conducted an independent investigation of federally run schools for Native Americans and produced the Meriam Report. The report called for reform of the schools to be more consistent with progressive education reforms in the broader public education system. In 1934, President Franklin D. Roosevelt passed the Indian Reorganization Act (IRA), referred to as the Indian New Deal, granting additional educational rights to Native Americans. The IRA for the first time provided Native Americans the right to determine where their children went to school. In 1934, Congress also passed the Johnson O'Malley Act, authorizing the U.S. Interior Department to contract with states and territories to educate Native American children.

1960–1980: The Federal Role in Education – Protecting Educational Rights

The *Brown v. Board of Education* Supreme Court decision and school desegregation efforts inspired a broader civil rights movement. In 1955, the arrest of Rosa Parks for refusing to give up her seat on a bus in Montgomery, Alabama, led to a citywide boycott against racial segregation in public transportation. In 1960, African American college students protested segregated lunch counters by refusing to leave their seats at a Woolworth's in Greensboro, North Carolina. Sit-ins spread to other college campuses, with more than 50,000 students participating in the protests. In 1961, the Nonviolent Coordinating Committee, the National Association of Colored People, and Martin Luther King Jr.'s Christian Leadership Conference worked with local activists to protest racial segregation in transportation and other public facilities throughout Albany, Georgia. In 1963, civil rights groups protested discriminatory economic policies in Birmingham, Alabama, through boycotts, sit-ins, and marches. Police turned dogs and high-pressure water hoses against protesters; this was caught on television and demonstrated the violence perpetrated against nonviolent protesters. Also in 1963, King led the largest political rally for human rights in the United States, in Washington, DC, to protest for jobs and freedoms for African Americans. These pivotal civil rights moments and many others had a profound social and political impact on the nation. The protests would soon lead to several pieces of federal legislation that had broad impacts on American education.

On July 2, 1964, President Lyndon Johnson translated American unity following President John F. Kennedy's assassination into the passage of the Civil Rights Act of 1964, which prohibited discrimination based on race, color, religion, sex, or national origin. Table 2.6 outlines the 11 titles of the 1964 Civil Rights Act. Titles IV and VI relate directly to education. Title IV prohibits segregation and authorizes the U.S. attorney general to address equal protection violations in public schools and institutions of higher education. Although Title IV receives most of the attention, Title VI allows federal funds to be withheld from segregated public school systems, providing a powerful incentive for school desegregation. Title VI states:

> No person in the United States shall, on the ground of race, color or national origin, be excluded from participation in, be denied the benefits of, or be subjected to discrimination under any program or activity receiving federal financial assistance.
>
> (Civil Rights Act, 1964)

The law protects students against harassment or discrimination based on a student's race, color, or national origin.

Table 2.6 The Civil Rights Act of 1964 Titles

Title	Title name	Title purpose
I	Discriminatory Voting Tactics	Prohibits disqualification of voters based on race, including literacy tests and qualifying standards
II	Discrimination Against Patrons of Commercial Business	Prohibits segregation and discrimination against patrons in private businesses
III	Desegregation of Public Libraries, Parks, and Other Facilities	Prohibits segregation and discrimination in public facilities, including parks, recreational facilities, libraries, and prisons
IV	Desegregation of Public Schools and Colleges	Prohibits segregation and discrimination in public schools and university systems and directs the Department of Education to provide assistance to facilitate school desegregation
V	The U.S. Commission on Civil Rights	Expands the authority and responsibilities of the Commission on Civil Rights
VI	Discrimination in Federally Funded Programs	Prohibits discrimination by recipients of federal funding or participants in federally funded programs
VII	Discrimination in Employment	Prohibits discrimination by private sector and federal government employees. Title VII was later interpreted by the Supreme Court to also prohibit discrimination based on sexual orientation or gender identity
VIII	Voting Statistics	Directs the secretary of commerce to conduct a survey of registration and voting statistics capturing data related to race, color, and national origin
IX	Appellate Review and Attorney General	Permits individuals subjected to state prosecutions of violations of civil rights to remove the case to federal court
X	Community Relations Service	Established the Community Relations Service to resolve civil rights disputes
XI	Preemption and Other Matters	Addresses interactions between the Civil Rights Act of 1964 and state and local antidiscrimination laws

Elementary and Secondary Education Act

Johnson made civil rights and education the centerpieces of his War on Poverty, a legislative agenda to reduce American poverty that included Medicare; Medicaid; job and income support; urban renewal programs; and elementary, secondary, and postsecondary federal aid. In 1965, Congress approved the Elementary and Secondary Education Act (ESEA), which was designed to provide financial support to school districts serving low-income students and combat racial segregation in schools. Johnson believed that educational inequality disadvantaged low-income and minority students in public school systems and that reform was critical to breaking the cycle of poverty. ESEA includes a broad range of education programs and funding to combat educational inequities in poor urban and rural areas. ESEA's Title I provides financial assistance to local education agencies and schools with high percentages of students from low-income families to improve their educational opportunities and close achievement gaps. Public schools with at least 40% of students classified as low income qualify for Title I funds. The Civil Rights Act's ban on federal funding to segregated schools combined with ESEA Title I funding provide a powerful incentive for school systems to desegregate.

Federal education funding has never risen above 12% of total U.S. education spending; it currently represents 8% of total education spending (Skinner, 2019). The national government's relatively small contribution leverages state and local government cooperation to enact national education reforms. State and local governments consistently face education funding shortfalls and typically cannot afford to turn down federal funds, particularly those aimed toward lower-income school systems. ESEA provided federal funding, but the original legislation left curriculum, standards, and personal matters delegated to state and local governments.

Teachers Unions

In 1916, teachers established the American Federation of Teachers (AFT) as an alternative to the NEA, which excluded school administrators. Until the 1950s, the NEA and AFT focused on broadly improving the education profession. In the 1950s, the AFT became more politically active, filing amicus briefs in *Brown v. Board of Education* and others. Teacher strikes in the early 1960s have been credited with convincing Kennedy to issue Executive Order 10968, giving federal employees collective bargaining rights. This led 22 states to adopt laws granting collective bargaining rights to state and local employees. Following Kennedy's executive order, the NEA adopted union activities and the right to strike and denied school administrators organizational membership.

Teachers unions developed into a powerful political actor that bargained for improvements in teacher pay and benefits, teacher working conditions, and protections against discrimination. Between 1960 and 1974, teachers unions sponsored more than 1,000 strikes involving more than 800,000 teachers (Shelton, 2017). Teachers union collective bargaining led to increased teacher salaries and benefits, professionalized the work environment, ended discriminatory employment practices, and ended noneducational tasks.

During the 1976 presidential election campaign, Democratic presidential candidate Jimmy Carter promised NEA leadership that, if elected, he would support the establishment of a cabinet-level Department of Education. As a result, the NEA conferred its first presidential endorsement to Carter. On October 17, 1979, Carter signed the Department of Education Organization Act, establishing the Department of Education as a cabinet-level organization. The act divided the Department of Health, Education, and Welfare into the Department of Education and the Department of Health and Human Services. According to the Department of Education's mission statement, the organization has four key functions: (a) establishing policies on federal financial aid for education and distributing and monitoring those funds, (b) collecting data on America's schools and disseminating research, (c) focusing national attention on key educational issues, and (d) prohibiting discrimination and ensuring equal access to education (U.S. Department of Education, 2024).

In 1973, the 12 countries of the Organization of the Petroleum Exporting Countries (OPEC) commenced an oil embargo that led to a U.S. recession and *stagflation* – persistent inflation combined with high unemployment and stagnant demand – that resulted in widespread economic pessimism through the late 1970s and early 1980s. Many Americans believed America's economic failures were caused by deteriorating educational competitiveness relative to developing nations. An inadequate education system had failed to develop the workforce necessary to compete in an increasingly competitive global economy, leading to declining American economic standing and standard of living.

1945–1975: The Golden Age of American Higher Education

Historians have characterized the post–World War II era as the golden age of American education due to the unprecedented expansion of institutions and student enrollment. The postwar baby boom increased the population from 140 to 215 million between 1945 and 1975,

a 60% growth. The population surge, an extraordinary economic expansion, and diversification of the U.S. economy increased demand for postsecondary education. Between 1945 and
1975, higher education enrollment increased from two to 11 million, a 450% increase. What
caused this historic expansion of American higher education?

In 1944, Roosevelt signed the Servicemen's Readjustment Act of 1944, better known as
the GI bill, providing World War II veterans with federal assistance for college education,
unemployment insurance, and housing. With more than 15 million soldiers, the U.S. government sought to avoid a postwar depression, massive unemployment, or civil unrest. The
GI Bill was designed to help veterans adjust to civilian life primarily through education and
other forms of government assistance. The GI Bill is considered one of the most successful
pieces of federal legislation ever produced. It invested more than $14.5 billion in education
and training for more than eight million veterans. This resulted in the largest surge in higher
education enrollments and public college expansion in U.S. history.

The GI Bill proved so successful that more than 6,000 for-profit schools were established
to take advantage of the historic investment in higher education by the federal government.
The GI Bill allowed veterans to use funds for any qualified postsecondary institution but
delegated authority to the states for determining accreditation standards. The goal of postsecondary accreditation is to ensure institutions meet minimum quality standards. When
federal oversight of these for-profit institutions exposed widespread fraud, Congress had to
decide between the development of a federal accreditation system or a private sector accrediting system (Kelchen, 2017). The Veteran's Readjustment Act of 1952 required accreditation
of postsecondary institutions as a means of ensuring a minimum standard of quality control
(Harcleroad, 1980). Accreditation began as a voluntary process at the turn of the 20th century, but the 1944 and 1952 GI Bills transformed accreditation into a required practice of
higher education institutions by connecting the process to federal funding (Conway, 1979).

Sputnik and the National Defense Act

In 1957, the Soviet Union successfully launched the first satellite, commencing the space
race. Sputnik's launch symbolized Soviet technological dominance in the Cold War, and
the United States perceived the event as a national security threat (Logsdon & Launius,
2003). The space race became a microcosm of the Cold War conflict between Russia and the
United States – communism versus democracy, freedom versus authoritarianism – and raised
the stakes of the conflict to new heights. The U.S. education system received most of the
blame for America's failure to keep pace with Russian technological advances (Clowse, 1981;
Finding & Thackery, 1996; Rudolph, 2002). Conservative leaders said declining standards
stemming from the 1918 Principles of Secondary Education, which recommended differentiated college and noncollege curriculum tracks, had diluted educational achievement (Clowse,
1981; Divine, 1993; Jeynes, 2007; Logsdon & Launius, 2003). Liberals blamed the lack of
education funding for the crisis.

In 1958, Congress approved the National Defense Education Act (NDEA) to improve
American education and train the next generation of students in science, technology, engineering, and mathematics (STEM) fields. The legislation provided more than $1 billion
(nearly $11 billion in 2023 dollars), including over 40,000 loans, 40,000 scholarships, and
1,500 fellowships, for the expansion of undergraduate and graduate STEM training (Fleming, 1960). The NDEA also provided matching funds for states to improve secondary science, mathematics, and foreign languages. This incentivized states, particularly in the South,
to provide a minimum education funding foundation to improve education for all students

while centralizing funding at the state level. The long-term impact of the NDEA would far exceed its financial support of secondary and postsecondary education. The bipartisan legislation, under the pretense of national defense, had set a precedent of federal aid for education. This set the stage for the expansion of federal support of education in the decades to follow.

The Higher Education Act

In 1965, Johnson also passed, as part of his War on Poverty, the Higher Education Act, an omnibus bill that included federal funding for student financial aid, facility construction, and aid to institutions. In 1972 Congress reauthorized and President Richard Nixon signed amendments to the Higher Education Act, including need-based federal student aid and civil rights protections. Basic Education Opportunity Grants, later called Pell Grants after bill sponsor Rhode Island Senator Claiborne Pell, provided federal financial aid to eligible, low-income undergraduate students. During the past 50 years, Pell Grants have become a cornerstone of U.S. postsecondary financial aid. In the 2020–2021 academic year, 6.4 million students received Pell Grants averaging $4,568 per undergraduate student recipient. Pell Grants were awarded to nearly 40% of undergraduate students – a total federal expenditure of $26.5 billion.

The 1972 Education Amendments also included Title IX, which stated: "No person in the United States shall, on the basis of sex, be excluded from participation in, denied the benefits of, or be subjected to discrimination under any education program or activity receiving federal financial assistance." Title VII of the 1964 Civil Rights Act had banned sex discrimination in hiring practices, but those protections did not apply to education institutions. Title IX increased female participation from 15% to 45% of NCAA student athletes between 1971 and 2021. Although collegiate athletics receives a disproportionate amount of popular and scholarly attention, Title IX had a much broader impact on women's access to higher education. Title IX banned sex discrimination in college admissions, forever altering the gender dynamics of higher education.

Community Colleges

The golden age of higher education continued the prewar growth of public institutions and student enrollment. In 1945, student enrollments split evenly between public and private institutions. By 1975, more than three quarters of college students were enrolled in public institutions. The development of public community colleges produced a significant portion of the growth in public sector enrollment. In the 20th century, community colleges were developed to offer technical and vocational training in response to industrialization, produce professionals in specific fields to meet local economic demands, and to extend high school education (Ricketts, 2009). In 1892, University of Chicago President William Rainey Harper divided instruction into two sets of 2 years, calling the lower set of courses junior college (Brint & Karabel, 1989). Students who completed the first 2 years of study were awarded associate degrees. During the Great Depression, many Americans sought educational opportunities to improve their economic standing. This led to significant enrollment expansion at community colleges. Between 1929 and 1939, community college enrollment increased from 56,000 to 150,000 (Brint & Karabel, 1989). After World War II, federal and state governments invested in community colleges, particularly in Florida, Maryland, New York, North Carolina, and Washington. Community colleges filled a niche in American higher education. They served students who could not attend 4-year institutions due to acceptance standards or finances and those whose educational needs did not require a 4-year degree. By 1975, community college enrollment increased to nearly four million students, which was nearly half of public sector enrollments and a fourth of all higher education enrollments.

Post-WWII America witnessed the greatest expansion of higher education enrollment in history. Postsecondary enrollment remained highly unequal along socioeconomic and racial demographics. By the mid-1970s, the federal and state governments had developed a higher education system focused on expanding educational opportunities for all students. All states had developed subsidized public universities and community college systems to expand educational opportunity. The federal government had expanded financial aid programs and placed safeguards for equal treatment based on gender, race, or ethnicity. During this period, a paradigm shift occurred in American society: College enrollment became the cultural expectation for most high school graduates.

Women

The increase in women's higher education attainment in the second half of the 20th century is one of the most important advancements in American history (Rose, 2015, 2016). Between 1950 and 1975, female higher education enrollment increased from 30% to more than 50%. In 1950, women received approximately 20% of all bachelor's and master's degrees and less than 10% of doctoral degrees conferred by U.S. postsecondary institutions. By 1980, women received more than 50% of all bachelor's and master's degrees and approximately 40% of doctoral degrees.

For more than 3 centuries, gender inequality characterized postsecondary education. This limited women's economic, social, and political inclusion in American society (Marshall, 1950; Shklar, 1991). Private financial support was disproportionately directed toward men due to social stereotypes of men as the breadwinners. Men were seen as better recipients of limited family financial resources than women, who were typecast as exiting the labor force to marry and raise a family (Davis, 1991; Hanson et al., 2009; Rose, 2015). Higher education practices like gender quotas, exclusion of women, and other discriminatory admissions policies were institutional barriers to female participation. Title IX of the 1972 Education Amendments ensured equal college access for women. Between 1971 and 1983, the gender gap in college enrollment shifted from men outnumbering women by 1.4 million to women outnumbering men by 400,000. Between 1970 and 2021, the percent of women obtaining a high school diploma increased from 59% to nearly 92%. During that same period, the percent of women receiving a college degree increased from 8% to nearly 40%. In 1971, women also received only 9% of medical degrees, 7% of law degrees, and 1% of dental degrees. Today, a majority of U.S. medical, law, and dental students are women (Rights, 1997).

African Americans

The 1954 *Brown v. Board of Education* Supreme Court ruling required all U.S. colleges and universities to admit Black students. Few colleges and universities complied with the federal mandate without pressure from legislative and executive branch actors. The Civil Rights Act of 1964 provided the impetus for the desegregation of American colleges and universities. The desegregation of U.S. colleges and universities initiated declining enrollment at predominately Black institutions. Historically Black colleges and universities enrolled over 90% of African American undergraduate students prior to integration but only 18% by 1976. The Civil Rights Act of 1964 had a profound impact on the desegregation of U.S. colleges and universities.

Native Americans

In 1946, Congress enacted the Indian Claims Commission Act, granting Native Americans the right to file claims against the United States for illegally seized lands. In 1953, Congress passed House Resolution 108, announcing the federal government resolved to terminate the trustee relationship between Native tribes and the United States. The policy encouraged Native Americans to leave reservations and pursue economic opportunities elsewhere. Paradoxically, even as the federal government was terminating its responsibilities for Native American tribes, it was increasing federal involvement in their education. In 1950, Congress included reservations in the school construction and impact aid programs (Deloria & Lytle, 1983). In 1952, of the 127,957 Native children between the ages of 6 and 18, approximately 37,000 attended the 233 schools operated by the Bureau of Indian Affairs in 14 states and another 52,000 attended public schools (Reyhner & Eder, 2017).

The civil rights movement's achievements in increasing public awareness and changing federal policy inspired Native American activists to change their tactics in the 1960s and 1970s. According to the Census Bureau, those who identify at least partially as American Indian or Alaska Native make up approximately 2.5% of the population, concentrated in a handful of states. Historically, the relatively small size of the Native American population and racism toward them made influencing U.S. policy deeply challenging. By incorporating the tactics of the civil rights movement – building coalitions, staging public demonstrations, and performing acts of civil disobedience – Native Americans achieved a series of policy gains in the 1960s and 1970s.

The ESEA did not originally provide Title I funding to schools administered by the Bureau of Indian Affairs, but a year later, in 1966, funding was made available for these schools. In 1969, a U.S. Senate subcommittee released *Indian Education: A National Tragedy, a National Challenge.* The report highlighted the alarming status of Native American education. The report led to the passage of the 1972 Indian Education Act, which established the Office of Indian Education and the National Advisory Council on Indian Education. The legislation also provided a formal program and several competitive grant programs for Native American children and adults. In 1974, Congress amended the act to include teacher training and fellowship programs.

In 1975, Congress passed the Indian Self Determination and Education Assistance Act, allowing tribes to have greater autonomy and to administer federal programs through contractual agreements. The legislative goal was to increase tribal self-government by allowing more control over the administration of federal programs. The act gave tribal governments control over their own schools for the first time. Tribal governments now control 70 schools that incorporate Native languages and cultural traditions into their curriculum.

This era also witnessed increased interest in Native American higher education. In 1972, the American Indian Higher Education Consortium was established to represent all such postsecondary institutions and create a Native American accreditation agency to improve tribal sovereignty and self-determination. In 1977, the Navajo tribal council founded Navajo Community College as the first tribal college. The following year, Congress passed the Tribally Controlled Community College Assistance Act, providing federal funds to support higher education institutions controlled by Native American tribes. Today, there are 35 tribal colleges in 13 states. In 1959, Arizona State University established the Center for Indian Education. Several journals have also been established to provide research on American Indian education, including *Journal of American Indian Education* in 1961, *Canadian Journal of Native Education* in 1980, and *Journal of Navajo Education* in 1981 (Reyhner & Eder, 2017). In 1969, the National Indian Education Association was established to advance comprehensive, culture-based educational opportunities for American Indians, Alaska Natives, and Native Hawaiians. Several prominent higher education studies of Native American education have influenced U.S. policymaking, including the University of Chicago's *National Study of American Indian Education (1967–1971)*.

Americans With Disabilities

The civil rights movement inspired other interest groups to seek equal protection under the law, including Americans with disabilities (An et al., 2011). The disability rights movement advocated for broader civil rights for all Americans with disabilities, including children. The movement was successful in achieving numerous federal disability protections in the 1960s and early 1970s, but no federal laws addressed mainstreaming school children with disabilities or compulsory school attendance (Winzer, 2009). As late as 1970, only one in five children with disabilities were educated in public schools.

In the 1970s, the disability movement coopted civil rights movement tactics and used the courts to expand disability protections after failing to achieve educational institutional reforms at the state or local level. In 1972, disability advocates argued in *Pennsylvania Association for Retarded Citizens (PARC) v. Commonwealth of Pennsylvania* that separate education for children with disabilities violated *Brown v. Board of Education*: It was inherently unequal and a violation of the Equal Protection Clause of the Fourteenth Amendment. The case was the first right-to-education suit in the country for children with disabilities and resulted in a consent decree in which states agreed to provide free public education for children with mental health problem (*Mills v. Board of Education of the District of Columbia expanded PARC*) to include students with behavioral, cognitive, physical, and emotional disabilities. State and local government officials concerned that the court decisions placed a massive financial obligation on school systems lobbied the federal government for financial support (Winzer, 2009).

In 1973, Congress passed the Rehabilitation Act, which prohibited discrimination based on disability in federal agencies and programs receiving federal financial assistance. The Rehabilitation Act was one of the first civil rights laws to protect individuals with disabilities. Section 504 of the Rehabilitation Act provides legal protections for students with disabilities (Murphy, 2020). The Fourteenth Amendment's Equal Protection Clause provides the framework for Congress to establish additional legal protections for students with disabilities in American school systems (Decker et al., 2021).

In 1975, Congress passed and President Gerald Ford signed the Education for All Handicapped Children Act (EAHCA), guaranteeing a free, appropriate public education to all children with a disability. The legislation included four significant provisions: (a) guaranteed the right to a free, appropriate education for all children with a disability; (b) protected the rights of children with disabilities by providing a fair and appropriate education in the least restrictive environment; (c) required clear procedures for identifying and delivering special education services at all levels; and (4) provided federal funding to help states and local governments and school systems provide an education for all children with a disability.

What did Congress mean by a free, appropriate public education? EAHCA required that all students with disabilities be placed in the least restrictive environment, meaning in a classroom with their peers, to the greatest extent appropriate. Students are only separated from the mainstream classroom when the severity of their disability requires it. Special education services must delivered utilizing an individual education plan (IEP) for each child receiving disability education services. The IEP includes annual goals, progress monitoring, accommodations, and modifications. EAHCA committed to providing 40% of the average per-pupil expenditure in the U.S. multiplied by the number of special education students in each state. Because these federal funds are discretionary rather than mandatory, the federal government has historically covered less than 15% of the costs of special education. State and local governments must cover the difference.

1980–2000: The Rise of Standards and Accountability Systems

The 1965 ESEA mandated that every school district receiving Title I federal funds be evaluated (Ryan & Shepard, 2010). In 1969, the National Assessment of Educational Progress began collecting sample education performance data across the 50 states to identify educational problems and develop sound public policy. In 1980, Ronald Reagan won the presidency on a conservative Republican ideology of tax cuts, increased defense spending, family values, conservative Judeo-Christian morality, and deregulation. Tax cuts combined with significant increases in defense spending led to cuts in most domestic programs, including education. Between 1980 and 1988, federal defense spending increased from $267 billion (4.9% of GDP) to $393 billion (5.8%), a 32% increase, while education spending increased from $39.3 to $62.8 billion, equivalent to a 2% inflation-adjusted spending increase (National Center for Education Statistics, 2001). Reagan shifted the federal education agenda toward free market approaches and academic excellence including school choice, rigorous academic standards, parental responsibility, character education, and religious freedom.

In 1981, Secretary of Education T.H. Bell established the National Commission on Excellence in Education to study the quality of U.S. education and its impact on U.S. economic competitiveness. In 1983, the commission produced a report called *A Nation at Risk: The Imperative for Educational Reform* that described the failure of American education (United States National Commission on Excellence in Education, 1983). According to the report, the U.S. was falling behind other developed countries economically because of its failing education system (Vinovskis, 1999). The risk in the report's title referred to the inability of the United States to compete internationally due to the gap between high-achieving countries like Japan and Germany and the low educational performance of American students. The report recommended raising high school graduation rates, raising academic performance expectations, improving teacher preparation and effectiveness, and holding education leaders responsible for educational achievement.

A Nation at Risk would provide the impetus for the development of state standard and accountability models (Mehta, 2012). The report elevated the economic role of education as the primary goal of schooling in a globally competitive economy. Student achievement became the responsibility of schools rather a broader social responsibility (McGuinn, 2009). *A Nation at Risk* also shifted accountability for student performance and educational results from local school boards toward state leadership. This shift, combined with increasing state spending as a percentage of total education spending, placed greater accountability and responsibility with state leadership, including the governors, state legislators, and chief state school officers.

In the 1988 presidential election, Vice President George H.W. Bush announced, "I want to be the education president. I want to lead a renaissance of quality in our schools." Tennessee Governor Lamar Alexander, Bush's future secretary of education, served as chair of the National Governors Association (NGA) in 1985–1986 when it produced a report called *A Time for Results*. The governors proposed tracking state progress, clearly defining education standards, and providing local school districts autonomy to achieve results. In 1989, Bush convened a bipartisan Governors Education Summit in Charlottesville, Virginia, to produce the nation's first education goals based on the NGA report. At the summit, Bush and the nation's governors developed the America 2000 goals:

1. All children in America will start school ready to learn.
2. The high school graduation rate will increase to at least 90%.
3. American students will leave Grades 4, 8, and 12 having demonstrated competency over challenging subject matter including English, mathematics, science, foreign languages, civics and government, economics, art, history, and geography.
4. U.S. students will be first in the world in science and mathematics achievement.
5. Every adult American will be literate and will possess the knowledge and skills necessary to compete in a global economy and exercise rights and responsibilities of citizenship.
6. Every school in the United States will be free of drugs, violence, and the unauthorized presence of firearms and alcohol and will offer a disciplined environment conducive to learning (Public Law 103–227).

As cochair of the NGA taskforce, Arkansas Governor Bill Clinton played a central role in the 1989 education summit. Clinton also served as chair of the Democratic Governors Association and aided in the development of the America 2000 goals. Clinton later defeated Bush in the 1992 presidential election. Despite their political and policy differences on most issues, their collaborative effort to develop the America 2000 goals resulted in relative continuity in the federal education policy agenda. Clinton's Goals 2000 program made only minor changes to the America 2000 goals. Clinton's education agenda resulted in continuity in federal education policy through the final 2 decades of the century.

The 1989 education summit's calls for national standards, national tests, and school choice were translated into the America 2000 legislation. The Charlottesville summit is broadly regarded as the first step toward the federal government playing a more central role in the standards-based movement (McGuinn, 2009; Mehta, 2012). The plan proposed voluntary curriculum standards and national tests, strategies for improving teaching including private sector-based strategies such as merit pay, and school choice models. The legislation did not make it out of committee due to Democratic failure to support the private sector strategies, but the standards and accountability model approach would serve as the educational foundation for both Clinton's and future President George W. Bush's educational approach. While George H.W. Bush was ultimately unsuccessful in achieving his educational goals, he laid the groundwork for the federal and state educational approach that continues today.

In 1994, Clinton signed a reauthorization of the ESEA entitled the Improving America's Schools Act. It required states to adopt curriculum standards and accountability measures to ensure schools were making adequate yearly progress (AYP). AYP would develop into a central and controversial measure of academic proficiency in the 2002 No Child Left Behind reauthorization. The legislation also granted states and local education agencies increased autonomy to utilize Title I federal funding. Clinton pushed back against a Democratic-controlled Congress focused on providing increasing federal funding for high-poverty districts, arguing that high standards and accountability models would be more effective at improving student achievement. Clinton's education agenda converged with those of Republicans and state leaders and signaled bipartisan support for standards and accountability rather than equity over the next several decades. The legislation signified a national commitment to standards-based reforms and set the stage for George W. Bush's standards-based reform proposals in the 2000 presidential election.

Higher Education

By the 1980s, despite the relative lack of federal or state government oversight, the American higher education system had evolved into a complex yet standardized system. Each tier of the system contained institutions that provided standardized curriculum, policies, students, and faculty. While institutions remained diverse in their institutional resources, the accreditation process and degrees conferred required all institutions to conform to the system's requirements. A national system of higher education had been achieved.

American higher education continued to expand rapidly, but at a slower pace than in the post-WWII era. Between 1945 and 1975, the number of higher education institutions grew from 1,763 to 3,026, a 70% increase. By 2000, the number of higher education institutions increased to 4,084, a 34% increase. Most of this growth occurred in the community college and private for-profit sectors. Between 1975 and 2000, the growth of public and private 4-year nonprofit institutions increased from 1,866 to 2,363, a 26% increase. More than 57 million Americans, 32% of the more than 180 million adults, participated in some form of postsecondary education. Between 1980 and 2000, the percent of recent high school completers enrolled in college increased from 49.3% to 63.3%.

In 1984, Congress passed the Perkins Vocational Education Act to support career and technical education at secondary and postsecondary institutions that would prepare students for the workforce. Vocational education provides occupational preparation primarily for high school students and community college students who do not pursue a bachelor's degree. Federal funding for vocational education dates to the 1917 Smith-Hughes Act. Perkins was reauthorized in 1990, 1998, 2006, and 2018. Perkins V funds career and technical education for approximately seven million secondary and four million postsecondary students. Federal funding is distributed to state governments to fund professional and technical programs and schools. Perkins was enacted to improve the academic knowledge and technical employability skills of secondary and postsecondary students.

Native Americans

In 1978, Congress passed the Indian Child Welfare Act (ICWA), which recognizes tribal sovereignty, prioritizes the preservation of Native families, and gives preferences for a child's placement to their extended family and tribe. Despite the law's passage, a disproportionate number of Native children continued to be removed from their families and tribes and placed in non-Native homes. In 1988, the Bureau of Indian Affairs (BIA) released *Report on BIA Education*, detailing the decline of Indian boarding schools (Reyhner & Eder, 2017). The report found that between 1965 and 1988, BIA boarding school student enrollment declined from 24,051 to 11,264 and total BIA school enrollment declined from 51,448 to 38,475. The student enrollment reductions resulted from a massive transition of Indian students to non-BIA schools.

In 1990, Congress passed the Native American Languages Act (NALA) to preserve, protect, and promote the right of Native Americans to develop their languages. This led to the development of language-immersion schools that teach Native children their tribal languages. NALA represented a continuation of self-determination policies and a reversal of long-standing federal government English-only policies prohibiting the speaking of Native languages (Reyhner & Eder, 2017). The same year, the Indian Nations at Risk Task Force investigated the condition of American Indian education and found the education system had failed to educate large numbers of Indian students and adults. The task force found that approximately 40,000 Native American students attended BIA-funded schools and

Table 2.7 1994 Land Grant Institutions

College	State
Aaniih Nakoda College	Montana
Bay Mills Community College	Michigan
Blackfeet Community College	Montana
Cankdeska Cikana Community College	North Dakota
Chief Dull Knife College	Montana
College of the Muscogee Nation	Oklahoma
College of Menominee Nation	Wisconsin
Diné College	New Mexico
Fond du Lac Tribal and Community College	Minnesota
Fort Berthold Community College	North Dakota
Fort Peck Community College	Montana
Haskell Indian Nations University	Kansas
Ilisagvik College	Arkansas
Institute of American Indian Arts	New Mexico
Keweenaw Bay Ojibwa Community College	Michigan
Lac Courte Oreilles Ojibwa Community College	Wisconsin
Leech Lake Tribal College	Minnesota
Little Big Horn College	Montana
Little Priest Tribal College	Nebraska
Navajo Technical University	New Mexico
Nebraska Indian Community College	Nebraska
Northwest Indian College	Washington
Oglala Lakota College	South Dakota
Saginaw Chippewa Tribal College	Michigan
Salish Kootenai College	Montana
Sinte Gleska University	South Dakota
Sisseton Wahpeton College	South Dakota
Sitting Bull College	North Dakota
Southwestern Indian Polytechnic Institute	New Mexico
Stone Child College	Montana
Tohono O'odham Community College	Arizona
Turtle Mountain Community College	North Dakota
United Tribes Technical College	North Dakota
White Earth Tribal and Community College	Minnesota

more than **333,000** attended public schools – 87% of all Native students. The task force highlighted the need for Native community involvement in Native American education to revitalize their communities and improve social and academic outcomes. Bush and Alexander held a White House conference in 1992 to demonstrate support for the task force's recommendations.

In 1994, Congress passed the Equity in Educational Land-Grant Status Act, authorizing a $23 million endowment, $1.7 million grant program, and $5 million cooperative extension service to facilitate collaboration (Association of Public and Land-Grant Universities, 2012). Table 2.7 lists the tribal colleges and universities that received land grant designation. These higher education institutions provide a comprehensive set of educational and community services that extend beyond higher education, including high school equivalency, developmental education, college credentials, and job training (U.S. Department of Agriculture, 2024).

2000-Present: Standards, Accountability, and Testing Proliferate

In the 2000 presidential election, Republican Texas Governor George W. Bush defeated Democratic Vice President Al Gore. Bush had campaigned on one of his central accomplishments as Texas governor, the state's improvements in student achievement based on Texas Assessment of Academic Skills exams. He campaigned on the academic success of his education standards and accountability program, particularly academic improvements for Black and Latino students. Republicans continued to prioritize school choice, parental choice, and local control in their education platform. Democrats prioritized funding increases specifically for teacher pay and for high-poverty districts. In the ESEA reauthorization, Democrats pursued higher federal funding and assessments that measured subgroups by race and disability status, and Republicans sought a standards and accountability system combined with school choice options. Bush and congressional Republicans were also motivated to coopt a policy issue that traditionally favored Democrats.

On January 8, 2002, the No Child Left Behind Act reauthorized the ESEA. It included the following elements:

- Required states to implement standards-based assessments in reading and mathematics for students in Grades 3–8 by the 2005–2006 school year and in three grade levels in science by the 2007–2008 school year.
- Required states to annually apply adequate yearly progress standards, incorporating a goal of all students reaching proficient by the end of the 2013–2014 school year.
- Required states to participate in the National Assessment of Educational Progress tests in fourth and eighth grade reading and mathematics.
- If states fail to meet AYP for any subgroup for 2 or more consecutive years, they would be subject to consequences, including public school choice and supplemental services.
- Increased Title I funding for high-poverty districts.
- States and local education agencies receiving Title I funding required to ensure teachers meet the definition of "highly qualified teacher" by the end of the 2005–2006 school year.
- Student assessment results for individual schools, districts, and states must be reported to parents and the public by the 2002–2003 school year (United States Congress (107th, 1st session, 2001)).

While Goals 2000 and the 1994 Improving America's Schools Act encouraged the development of standards and accountability models, the 2002 No Child Left Behind (NCLB) Act required them. NCLB should be viewed as the culmination of a 2-decade-long movement that began with 1983's *A Nation at Risk*, which characterized American education as the key determinant of economic success and global competitiveness and said underperforming American schools were responsible for this failure (Mehta, 2012). NCLB shifted public responsibility for student achievement from local school boards to the federal and state governments (McDonnell, 2013).

While NCLB goals were broadly supported at the outset, stakeholder resistance quickly mobilized. Standards and accountability policies empowered a top-down approach unprecedented in American education. Federal and state officials imposed prescriptive requirements on administrators and teachers. For example, teachers unions objected to the loss of teacher agency and increased public scrutiny created by NCLB. Civil rights groups objected that raising standards and punitive accountability measures without increased resources to lift underserved populations only exacerbated existing educational inequities. Conservatives argued NCLB empowered the federal government to control education and reduced the power of local communities. In 2015, President Barack Obama and the Republican-controlled Congress reauthorized the ESEA. They increased flexibility for NCLB requirements in exchange for developing high standards designed to close achievement gaps and improve outcomes for all students.

Common Core

During the George H.W. Bush and Clinton administrations, policymakers and policy entrepreneurs pursued the creation of national education standards to ensure a high-quality education that would prepare all students for success in college and work. Conservatives opposed increasing the federal government's role in education and liberals opposed raising standards without providing the necessary resources for underserved students. Policy entrepreneurs led by former North Carolina Governor James B. Hunt Jr., and West Virginia Governor Bob Wise worked with the NGA, the Council of Chief State School Officers, and Achieve Inc. to lobby state-level policymakers and educational organizations to develop common standards. By making Common Core a state-led effort, the proponents avoided the political obstacles faced by previous common curriculums.

Elementary and Secondary Education in the 21st Century

Historically, the U.S. elementary and secondary education system has been a world leader in educational achievement. As an early adopter of common schools and compulsory education., the U.S. led the world in primary education enrollment in the mid-19th century (Goldin & Katz, 1999). The common school movement made schooling universally available to women, leading to gender equality in literacy rates. From 1910 to 1940, the high school movement made the U.S. the world leader in secondary education (Goldin & Katz, 1999). By 1940, the United States achieved near universal literacy (90%) and ranked among the most literate nations. The expansion of secondary education provided the human capital that allowed the United States to become the world's most productive economy by the start of the 20th century.

Despite the historical achievements of the U.S. elementary education system, it was exceedingly inequitable. This led to opportunity and achievement gaps that persist today. Through the Civil War, students of color were largely excluded from public education. Forced segregation endured until *Brown v. Board of Education* in 1954, and de facto segregation persisted throughout American history. These historical trends and an education finance system that disproportionately allocates school resources to the wealthiest communities have resulted in educational achievement and opportunity gaps. For example, 22% of children living in high-poverty districts drop out of school, compared to only 6% of children who have never lived in poverty (Hernandez, 2012). The American Dream is the ideal that every citizen should have an equal opportunity to achieve success and prosperity through hard work. The American education system is the primary mechanism for providing all citizens equality of opportunity. Historical trends in the inequitable distribution of educational opportunities persist today. They increase U.S. inequality and reduce social mobility.

Higher Education in the 21st Century

Today, the U.S. higher education system remains a product of the trends that marked its development. The historical trend of increasing access and inclusivity has continued: More than two thirds of high school graduates enroll in higher education. The U.S. boasts one of the highest shares of population with postsecondary education in the world. Federal and state investments increased the percentage of U.S. college graduates from 7.7% to 37.7% between 1960 and 2022 (Bureau, 2022). In 1980, 20.9% of men received bachelor's degrees compared to 13.6% of women, a 53% difference. In 2019, women surpassed men in the percentage of the college educated labor force in the United States. In 2023, 39% of women completed a bachelor's degree compared to 36.2% of men, and women are expected to significantly widen the postsecondary educational attainment gender gap in the next decade. Women have overcome a long history of discrimination in higher education practices. The private benefits of postsecondary education are substantial: improved income, employment, health, social, and civic outcomes (Gonzalez et al., 2023; Ma et al., 2019; Tamborini et al., 2015). The private benefits also have positive public externalities by improving the economy, tax revenue, and social and civic engagement.

Historically, the benefits of U.S. higher education have not been distributed equitably (Gonzalez et al., 2023). The U.S. higher education system remains highly stratified by socioeconomic status, perpetuating inequality in economic and social opportunities. According to the U.S. Census, the percentage of adults 25 and older with bachelor's degrees increased to 41.8% for the non-Hispanic White population, but only 27.6% for the Black population and 20.9% for the Hispanic population (Census Bureau, 2023).

The U.S. higher education system disproportionately provides access to elite 4-year institutions and research universities to higher socioeconomic families, while underserved populations attend 2-year community colleges and for-profit institutions. Highly selective institutions have significantly higher graduation rates than less selective 4-year, 2-year, and for-profit institutions (Pike & Robbins, 2020). For example, Ivy League colleges graduate approximately 96% of enrolled students, compared to 20% of community college students. More than a million students drop out of college each year. Postsecondary student debt has exceeded $1.7 trillion and disproportionately impacts underserved students. College dropouts face higher consumer debt without the benefit of improved employment or earnings potential. The stratification of U.S. higher education in the 21st century along socioeconomic and racial characteristics perpetuates historical trends.

Key Terms

American Indian Higher Education Consortium
antislavery societies
Association of American Universities
Bill of Rights
Brown v. Board of Education of Topeka, Kansas
civil liberties
civil rights
Civil Rights Act of 1964
colonial colleges
Common Core
common school movement
community colleges
compulsory education
Controlled Community College Assistance Act of 1978
Dartmouth College v. Woodward
Education Amendments of 1972
Education for All Handicapped Children Act of 1975

Elementary and Secondary Education Act of 1965
elementary schooling
English common law
Equal Protection Clause
Equity in Educational Land-Grant Status Act of 1994
Executive Order 9981
feedback loops
Fifteenth Amendment
Fourteenth Amendment
Freedman's Bureau
General Allotment Act of 1887
Hatch Act of 1887
high school movement
Higher Education Act of 1965
home schooling
Indian Civilization Act of 1819
Indian Child Welfare Act of 1978
Indian Claims Commission Act of 1946
Indian Reorganization Act of 1934
Indian Self Determination and Education Assistance Act of 1975
Land Ordinance Act of 1785
literacy
Mills v. Board of Education of the District of Columbia
Morrill Act of 1862
National Defense Act of 1958
oral traditions
Pennsylvania Association for Retarded Citizens (PARC) v. Commonwealth of Pennsylvania
Perkins Vocational Education Act of 1984
Plessy v. Ferguson
political development
progressive era
research university
Second Continental Congress
Second Morrill Act of 1890
secondary schooling
Servicemen's Readjustment Act of 1944
Smith-Lever Act of 1914
Tape v. Hurley
teachers unions
Tenth Amendment
Thirteenth Amendment
United States Department of Education
university system
women's suffrage

Discussion Questions

1. How were children and adults educated in the colonial period? During this period which groups were excluded or denied educational opportunities?

2. What early signs demonstrated a commitment to elementary, secondary, and postsecondary Americans education?

3. How did the early development of American public education sow the seeds for an inequitable system?

4. What economic, political, and social factors led to the common school movement?

5. What economic, political, and social factors led to the Morrill Act of 1862 and the Second Morrill Act of 1890? How did the political development of postsecondary education exclude or deny certain groups educational opportunities?

6. What economic, political, and social factors led to the high school movement?

7. What led to the development of the university system and how did it change American postsecondary education?

8. How did the Great Depression and World War II influence the development of elementary, secondary, and postsecondary American education?

9. How did the Supreme Court decision *Brown v. Board of Education of Topeka, Kansas* change the landscape of American education?

10. How did President Johnson's War on Poverty influence efforts to make American education more equitable?

11. How did the standards and accountability system change American education?

12. What disparities remain in American elementary and secondary education? What disparities remain in American postsecondary education?

Application

1. Explain the political development of your policy issue.
2. Explain how your policy issue fits within the political development of American education.
3. Explain what economic educational, political, and social factors led to the need for your policy.
4. Explain how your policy addresses inequities in the American education system.

References

An, S., Roessler, R. T., & McMahon, B. T. (2011). Workplace discrimination and Americans with psychiatric disabilities: A comparative study. *Rehabilitation Counseling Bulletin, 55*(1), 7–19.

Angulo, A. J. (2005). William Barton Rogers and the southern sieve: Revisiting science, slavery, and higher learning in the old South. *History of Education Quarterly, 45*(1), 18–37.

Association of Public and Land-Grant Universities. (2012). *The land-grant tradition.* https://aplu.org/library/the-land-grant-tradition

Bailyn, B. (1960). *Education in the forming of American society.* University of North Carolina Press.

Baker, D. P. (1999). Schooling all the masses: Reconsidering the origins of American schooling in the Postbellum Era. *Sociology of Education, 72*(4), 197. https://doi.org/10.2307/2673153

Beaubrun, G. G. (2020). Talking Black: Destigmatizing Black English and funding bi-dialectal education programs. *Columbia Journal of Race and Law, 10*(2), 196.

Bell, J. (2015). Race, power, and education in early America. *Education's Histories, 2*(1).

Berman, W. C. (1970). *The politics of civil rights in the Truman administration.* Ohio State University Press.

Berstein, B. (1970). *Politics and policies of the Truman administration.* Quadrangle Books.

Blackstone, S. W. (1765–1769). *Commentaries on the laws of England, book the first: Chapter the fifteenth: Of husband and wife* (4 Vols.). Printed at the Clarendon Press.

Brint, S. G., & Karabel, J. (1989). *The diverted dream: Community colleges and the promise of educational opportunity in America, 1900–1985.* Oxford.

Brown University Steering Committee on Slavery and Justice. (2006). *Slavery and justice.* Brown University.

Brown v. Board of Education, 347 U.S. 483 (1954).

Burke, C. B. (1982). *American collegiate populations: A test of the traditional view.* University Press.

Callahan, R. E. (1964). *Education and the cult of efficiency.* University of Chicago Press.

Census Bureau. (2023). *Census bureau releases new educational data.* www.census.gov/newsroom/press-releases/2023/educational-attainment-data.html

Civil Rights Act of 1964, Pub. L. No. 88–352, 78 Stat. 241 (1964). www.govinfo.gov/content/pkg/STATUTE-78/pdf/STATUTE-78-Pg241.pdf

Clowse, B. B. (1981). *Brainpower for the cold war: The Sputnik crisis and national defense education act of 1958.* Greenwood.

Cohen, A. M. (1998). *The shaping of American higher education: Emergence and growth of the contemporary system.* Jossey-Bass.

Conway, M. M. (1979). The commissioner's authority to list accrediting agencies and associations: Necessity for an eligibility issue. *The Journal of Higher Education, 50*(2), 158–170.

Cremin, L. (1970). *American education: The colonial experience, 1607–1783.* Harper & Row.

Cuban, L. (1992). What happens to reforms that last: The case of the junior high school. *American Educational Research Journal, 29*(2), 227–251.

Cubberley, E. P. (1919). *Public education in the United States: A study and interpretation of American educational history.* Houghton Mifflin.

Davidson, C. N. (1986). Female education, literacy and the politics of sentimental fiction. *Women's Studies International Forum, 9*(4), 309–312. https://doi.org/10.1016/0277-5395(86)90003-8

Davis, F. (1991). *Moving the mountain: The women's movement in America since 1960.* University of Illinois Press.

Decker, J. R., Fetter-Harrott, A., & Rippner, J. (2021). Beyond speech: Students' civil rights in schools. *Laws, 10*(80). https://doi.org/10.3390/laws10040080

Deloria, V., Jr., & Lytle, C. M. (1983). *American Indians, American justice.* University of Texas Press.

Divine, R. A. (1993). *The Sputnik challenge.* Oxford University Press.

Ferguson, 163 U.S. 537 (1896).

Finding, J. E., & Thackery, F. W. (1996). *Events that changed America in the twentieth century.* Greenwood.

Fleming, A. S. (1960). The philosophy and objectives of the national defense education act. *Annals of the American Academy of Political and Social Science, 327,* 132–138.

Friesen, J. W. (1999). The function of legends as a teaching tool in pre-colonial first nations' societies. *Interchange, 30*(3), 305–322. https://doi.org/10.1023/a:1007601310865

Gardner, M. R. (2002). *Harry Truman and civil rights: Moral courage and political risks.* Southern Illinois University Press.

Goldin, C., & Katz, L. F. (1998). The origins of state-level differences in the public provision of higher education: 1890–1940. *American Economic Review, 88*(2), 303–308.

Goldin, C., & Katz, L. F. (1999). Human capital and social capital: The rise of secondary schooling in America, 1910–1940. *The Journal of Interdisciplinary History, 29*(4), 683–723. https://doi.org/10.1162/002219599551868

Goldin, C., & Katz, L. F. (2008). *The race between education and technology.* Harvard University Press.

Gonzalez, D., Law, J., Oladiran, F., Rounsaville, T., Sanghbi, S., & Scott, D. (2023). *Fulfilling the potential of U.S. higher education.* McKinsey & Company. www.mckinsey.com/industries/education/our-insights/fulfilling-the-potential-of-us-higher-education#/

Hanson, K., Guilfoy, V., & Pillai, S. (2009). *More than title IX: How equity in education has shaped the nation.* Rowan & Littlefield.

Harcleroad, F. F. (1980). *Accreditation: History, process, and problems.* American Association of Higher Education.

Hernandez, D. J. (2012). *Double jeopardy: How third-grade reading skills and poverty influence high school graduation.* The Annie E. Casey Foundation.

Hertz, T. (2006). *Understanding mobility in America.* Center for American Progress. chrome-extension://efaidnbmnnnibpcajpcg/https://cdn.americanprogress.org/wp-content/uploads/issues/2006/04/Hertz_MobilityAnalysis.pdf

Hirschman, C., & Mogford, E. (2009). Immigration and the American industrial revolution from 1880 to 1920. *Social Science Research, 38*(4), 897–920. https://doi.org/10.1016/j.ssresearch.2009.04.001

Hofstadter, R. (1952). *The development and scope of higher education in the United States.* Columbia University Press.

Howe, D. W. (2007). *What hath God wrought: The transformation of America, 1815–1848.* Oxford University Press.

Jeynes, W. H. (2007). *American educational history: Schools, society, and the common good.* Sage.

Juvonnen, J., Vi-Nhuan, L., Kaganoff, T., Augustine, C., & Constant, L. (2004). *Focus on the wonder years: Challenges facing the American middle school.* RAND.

Kelchen, R. (2017). *Higher education accreditation and the federal government.* Urban Institute. www.urban.org/sites/default/files/publication/93306/higher-education-accreditation-and-the-federal-government.pdf

Kerber, L. (1980). *Women of the republic: Intellect and ideology in revolutionary America.* Norton.

Kose, E., Kuka, E., & Shenhav, N. (2021). Women's suffrage and children's education. *American Economic Journal: Economic Policy, 13*(3), 374–405.

Lawler, N. (2018). The right to education in the United States and abroad: A comparative analysis of constitutional language and academic achievement. *The Federal Lawyer.*

Litwack, L. F. (1961). *North of slavery: The negro in the free states, 1790–1860.* The University of Chicago Press.

Logsdon, J. M., & Launius, R. D. (2003). *Reconsidering Sputnik: Forty years since the soviet satellite.* Harwood Academic.

Ma, J., Pender, M., & Welch, M. (2019). *Education pays 2019: The benefits of higher education for individuals and society.* College Board. https://research.collegeboard.org/media/pdf/education-pays-2019-full-report.pdf

Mann, H. (1957). *The republic and the school: Horace Mann on the education of free men* (L. A. Cremin, Ed.). Teachers College Press.

Marshall, T. H. (1950). *Citizenship and social class and other essays.* Cambridge University Press.

Matthew, N. (2001). *First nations education financing.* First Nations Education Steering Committee.

McDonnell, L. M. (2013). Educational accountability and policy feedback. *Educational Policy, 27*(2), 170–189. https://doi.org/10.1177/0895904812465119

McGuinn, P. (2009). Education policy from the great society to 1980: The expansion and institutionalization of the federal role in schools. In B. Glen & S. Teles (Eds.), *Conservatism and American political development* (pp. 188–222). Oxford University Press.

Mehta, J. (2012). How paradigms create politics. *American Educational Research Journal, 50*(2), 285–324. https://doi.org/10.3102/0002831212471417

Meyers, T. L. (2008). A first look at the worst: Slavery and race relations at the college of William and Mary. *The William and Mary Bill of Rights Journal, 16*, 1141–1168.

Morris, T., Dorling, D., & Smith, G. D. (2018). How well can we predict educational outcomes? Examining the roles of cognitive ability and social position in educational attainment. In J. Jarman & P. Lambert (Eds.), *Exploring social inequality in the 21st century* (pp. 52–66). Routledge Press.

Moss, H. (2013). *Schooling citizens: The struggle for African American education in antebellum America.* University of Chicago Press.

Murphy, K. L. (2020). Civil rights laws: Americans with disabilities act of 1990 and section 504 of the rehabilitation act of 1973. *Journal of Physical Education, Recreation & Dance, 92*(1), 57–59. https://doi.org/10.1080/07303084.2021.1844555

National Center for Education Statistics. (2001). *Federal support for education, fiscal years 1980 to 2001.* https://nces.ed.gov/pubs2002/2002129

National Native American Boarding School Healing Coalition. (2023). *List of Indian boarding schools in the United States.* https://boardingschoolhealing.org/list/

Newcomer, M. (1959). *A century of higher education for American women.* Harper & Brothers.

O'Hara, F., & O'Hara, F. M. (2000). *Handbook of United States economic and financial indicators.* Greenwood.

An Ordinance for Ascertaining the Mode of Disposing of Lands in the Western Territory: Be It Ordained by the United States in Congress Assembled, That the Territory Ceded by Individual States to the United States, Which Has Been Purchased of the Indian Inhabitants, Shall Be Disposed of in the Following Manner (1785).

Osgood, R. L. (2008). *The history of special education: A struggle for equality in American public schools.* Praeger.

Perry, R. K. (2015). *The Little Rock Crisis: What Desegregation Politics Says About Us.* Springer.

Pike, G. R., & Robbins, K. R. (2020). Using panel data to identify the effects of institutional characteristics, cohort characteristics, and institutional actions on graduation rates. *Research in Higher Education, 61*(4), 485–509. https://doi.org/10.1007/s11162-019-09567-7

Polgar, P. J. (2011). "To raise them to an equal participation": Early national abolitionism, gradual emancipation, and the promise of African American citizenship. *Journal of the Early Republic, 31*(2), 229–258. https://doi.org/10.1353/jer.2011.0023

Pub. L. No. 103–227.

Reyhner, J., & Eder, J. (2017). *American Indian education, a history* (2nd ed.). University of Oklahoma Press.

Reynolds v. Sims, 377 U.S. 533 (1964).

Ricketts, G. (2009). *Community colleges: A brief history*. National Association of Scholars.

Rose, D. (2015). Regulating opportunity: Title IX and the birth of gender-conscious higher education policy. *Journal of Policy History, 27*(1), 157–183. https://doi.org/10.1017/s0898030614000396

Rose, D. (2016). The public policy roots of women's increasing college degree attainment: The national defense education act of 1958 and the higher education act of 1965. *Studies in American Political Development, 30*(1), 62–93. https://doi.org/10.1017/s0898588x1600002x

Rudolph, F. (1962). *The American college and university: A history*. University of Georgia Press.

Rudolph, J. L. (2002). *Scientists in the classroom: The cold war reconstruction of American science education*. Palgrave Macmillan.

Rury, J. L. (Ed.). (2020). *Education and social change: Contours in the history of American schooling* (6th ed.). Routledge.

Rury, J. L., & Darby, D. (2016). War and education in the United States: Racial ideology and inequality in three historical episodes. *Paedagogica Historica, 52*(1–2), 8–24. https://doi.org/10.1080/0030 9230.2015.1133675

Rury, J. L., & Hurst, J. (2022). The segmentation of teacher professionalization. In X. Dumay & K. Burn (Eds.), *The status of the teaching profession: Interactions between historical and new forms of segmentation* (pp. 38–61). Routledge.

Ryan, K., & Shepard, L. (2010). *The future of test-based educational accountability*. Routledge.

Schweiger, B. B. (2013). The literate South: Reading before emancipation. *The Journal of the Civil War Era, 3*(3), 331–359. https://doi.org/10.1353/cwe.2013.0049

Sedlak, M., & Schlossman, S. (1986). *Who will teach? Historical perspectives on the changing appeal of teaching as a profession*. Rand Corporation.

Selingo, J. J. (2017). *The networked university: Building alliances for innovation in higher education*. Pearson.

Shelton, J. (2017). *Teacher strike! Public education and the making of a new American political order*. University of Illinois Press.

Shklar, J. N. (1991). *American citizenship: The quest for inclusion*. Harvard University Press.

Sitton, T., & Conrad, J. H. (2005). *Freedman colonies: Independent Black Texans in the time of Jim Crow*. University of Texas Press.

Skinner, R. R. (2019). *State and local financing of public schools*. Congressional Research Service.

Spring, J. (2016). *American education*. Routledge.

Strober, M. H., & Lanford, A. G. (1986). The feminization of public school teaching: Cross-sectional analysis, 1850–1880. *Signs: Journal of Women in Culture and Society, 11*(2), 212–235. https://doi.org/10.1086/494217

Sugrue, M. (1994). We desired our future rulers to be educated men: South Carolina College, the defense of slavery, and the development of secessionist politics. *Higher Education Annual, 14*, 39–71.

Swan, R. J. (1992). John Teasman: African-American educator and the emergence of community in early Black New York City, 1787–1815. *Journal of the Early Republic, 12*(3), 331. https://doi.org/10.2307/3123834

Tamborini, C. R., Kim, C., & Sakamoto, A. (2015). Education and lifetime earnings in the United States. *Demography, 52*(4), 1383–1407. https://doi.org/10.1007/s13524-015-0407-0

Thelin, J. R. (2019). *A history of American higher education*. Johns Hopkins University Press.

Tomlinson, S., & Windham, K. (2006). Northern piety and Southern honor: Alva Woods and the problem of discipline at the University of Alabama. *Perspectives in the History of Education, 25*, 1–42.

Trow, M. A. (1961). The second transformation of American secondary education. *International Journal of Comparative Sociology, 2*(2), 144–166. https://doi.org/10.1163/156854261x00156

Trow, M. A. (1989). American higher education: Past, present, future. *Studies in Higher Education, 14*(1), 5–22.

Tyack, D., & Hansot, E. (1992). *Learning together: A history of coeducation in American public schools*. Russell Sage Foundation.

United States Census Bureau. (2022). *2022 current population survey*. www.census.gov/programs-surveys/cps.html

United States Congress (107th, 1st session: 2001). No child left behind act of 2001.

United States Department of Education. (2024). *About ED overview and mission statement.* https://www2.ed.gov/about/landing.jhtml

United States Department of Education, Office of Civil Rights. (1997). *Title IX: 25 years of progress.* https://purl.fdlp.gov/GPO/LPS12198

United States National Commission on Excellence in Education. (1983). *A nation at risk: The imperative for educational reform.* The National Commission on Excellence in Education.

U.S. Department of Agriculture. (2024). *1994 land-grant college and universities map.* www.nifa.usda.gov/1994-land-grant-colleges-universities-map

Urban, W., Wagoner, J. L., & Gathier, M. (2019). *American education: A history.* Routledge.

Veysey, L. R. (1965). *The emergence of the American university.* The University of Chicago Press.

Vinovskis, M. A. (1999). *The road to Charlottesville: The 1989 education summit.* National Education Goals Panel.

Wagoner, J. L. (2004). *Jefferson and education.* University of North Carolina Press.

White, R. (2017). *The republic for which it stands: The United States during reconstruction and the Gilded age, 1865–1896.* Oxford University Press.

Wilder, C. S. (2013). *Ebony and ivy: Race, slavery, and the troubled history of America's universities.* Bloomsbury Press.

Winzer, M. A. (2009). *From integration to inclusion: A history of special education in the 20th century.* Gallaudet University Press.

Woodward, C. V. (1971). *Origins of the new south, 1877–1913: A history of the south.* LSU Press.

Wright, R. N. (1996). Ambivalent bastions of slavery: The "peculiar institution" on college campuses in antebellum Georgia. *The Georgia Historical Quarterly, 80*(3), 467–485.

3   Theories of Power and Education Policy

The 2022 congressional midterm elections did not go as expected. Most political pundits predicted a red wave, meaning Republicans would gain majority control of the House and Senate and achieve significant gains in state legislatures and governorships. Instead, Democrats held control of the United States Senate. Republicans won control of the House of Representatives but gained only 10 seats rather than the predicted 42 (Campbell, 2022). Democrats flipped four statehouse chambers – the Michigan House and Senate, Minnesota Senate, and Pennsylvania House – and none flipped to Republican control. Democrats also gained three governorships, in Arizona, Massachusetts, and Maryland. After the election, Republicans had majority party control of the U.S. House of Representatives, 55 state legislative chambers, and 26 governor's offices, and Democrats had majority control of the White House, U.S. Senate, 40 state legislative chambers, and 24 governor's offices.

The 2022 midterm results illustrate the dispersed, complex nature of power in American politics. Historically, political power has shifted from the president's party to the opposition in their first midterm election as voters blame the newly elected president for political and economic failures. What changed that dynamic in the 2022 midterm elections? Did President Joe Biden's legislative successes win over swing voters? Did the Supreme Court decision to overturn *Roe v. Wade* create a backlash against Republicans? Did former President Donald Trump endorse candidates who did not appeal to moderates or did his low approval ratings drag down Republican candidates? What impact will these political elections have on education policy at the federal, state, and local levels? To answer these questions, it is necessary to analyze theories of power. This chapter explores the concept of power and introduces political and policy theories that explain who has power and the impact of distribution of power on public policy outcomes.

Definitions of Power

What is power? Power is central to understanding politics and public policy, but the concept is abstract and belies clear and concise definitions. Political scientist Harold Lasswell (1936) famously wrote that politics is the study of "who gets what, when, and how." Political actors who can produce intended effects, such as enacting certain public policies, have power (Russell, 1938). To study who has power and how they utilize that power to determine who gets what, when, and how, one must have a clear understanding of the concept. Fundamental understandings of education policy begin with questions about power. Who has power and how do they acquire it? How do institutions and systems structure power relationships? How do belief systems and ideological perspectives shape political power? Defining the abstract term of power is a prerequisite to answering these questions.

DOI: 10.4324/9781003231561-4

Political power is commonly defined as the ability to control outcomes or shape the behavior of others. Political scientist Robert Dahl (1956) defined it this way: "A has power over B to the extent that he can get B to do something that B would not do otherwise" (p. 202). Dahl defined power as a coercive control mechanism. According to political theorist Max Weber, "Power is the probability that one actor within a social relationship will be in a position to carry out his own will despite resistance, regardless of the basis on which this probability rests" (Weber et al., 1978, p. 171). Power can be explicit and coercive or unseen and noncoercive. If a school board restricts the options of a superintendent and other school leaders, then it is exercising second-dimension power or agenda-setting power rather than direct or overt power. If political elites are trying to shape ideological preferences toward an LGBTQ-inclusive curriculum, they are exercising third-dimension power.

Historically, autocratic systems have dominated most societies. Half of all countries are still autocracies today. Only 14 countries have been electoral democracies for more than a century, including Australia, Belgium, Canada, Denmark, Finland, Iceland, Ireland, Luxemburg, the Netherlands, New Zealand, Sweden, Switzerland, the United Kingdom, and the United States (Herre, 2022). During most of human history, autocratic rule meant political power was concentrated in the hands of a small group or single person. The Industrial Revolution distributed wealth to a broader spectrum of the public, leading the masses to pursue greater political power through democratic government. One school of scholars argues power shifted from autocratic rule toward democratic rule as the wealth, education, and social standing of the middle class improved through industrialization (Dahl, 1961). While this school agrees inequalities still exist, it argues concentration of wealth, status, and education no longer translate into dominance by the minority over the majority. An opposing theoretical perspective holds that the concentration of power in the economic, social, and political elite still dominates modern politics. The concentration or diffusion of power within government and society is central to understanding democracy.

Dimensions of Political Power

Political theorist Steven Lukes classified power into three types or dimensions based on the work of political theorists including Robert Dahl, Peter Bachrach, and Morton Baratz (Lukes, 2004). The first dimension is direct power: coercive or noncoercive action to get B to do what A wants. First-dimension power is direct and observable. The second dimension of power concerns structural aspects of power relations. Second-dimension power is exercised as A influences the agenda or options available to B. An individual or group exercises second-dimension power by limiting the scope of debate and controlling the agenda. The third dimension of power considers the ability to avoid conflict by shaping perceptions of a situation. Third-dimension power involves those who hold power using people's belief in the system to manipulate their preferences into alignment with the preferences of the leader.

Decision-Making Power

The first dimension of power refers to the ability of an actor to influence the behavior of others or secure the compliance of another when interests conflict. The first dimension of power requires three conditions (Dahl, 1957). First, the actions of actor A must precede the response from actor B. Second, B's actions must be a direct result of A's actions and not the product of outside or exterior forces. Third, A's capacity to enforce their actions and subsequent outcomes against B is due to the ability of A to alter B's losses if they do not comply.

If a teacher asks students to read a book and complete an assignment, the student can decide whether they want to comply with the teacher's request. The teacher can alter the student's potential losses by saying, "If you do not read the book and complete the assignment, you will fail the assignment." The student is coerced to complete the assignment by the potential losses they face if they do not comply with the teacher's request.

In 1961, Dahl argued elites compete for decision-making power (Dahl, 1961). This first dimension of power refers to explicit exercises of power, and Dahl (1961) described power in the following terms:

> Suppose a policeman is standing in the middle of an intersection at which most traffic ordinarily moves ahead; he orders all traffic to turn right or left; the traffic moves as he orders it to do. Then it accords with what I conceive to be the bedrock idea of power.

In Dahl's scenario, the driver is forced to turn one direction regardless of their preference. The driver is forced to comply with the officer or face potential consequences or losses. A state legislature utilizes first-dimension power when it establishes a standards and accountability system to ensure academic rigor, evaluates schools on student achievement, and incentivizes compliance. The state legislative action is observable and coercive.

Both individuals and groups can exert power. Power is the capacity of actor or group A to influence actor or group B (Muth, 1984). In educational systems, individuals exercising power include the president, governor, postsecondary governing board executive officer, state superintendent, state public university system presidents, district superintendents, principals, and teachers. Most of these individuals operate in an executive branch capacity, bestowed by legislative branch institutions with the power to implement public policy directives. Education legislative institutions with power include Congress, state legislatures, postsecondary governing and coordinating boards, state school boards, and local school boards. Federal and state constitutions confer legislative powers to these organizations to create education policy and allocate resources. Interest groups also wield informal power, including teachers unions, administrator organizations, business coalitions, and PTAs. These groups combine their membership, resources, and lobbying tactics to wield informal power. The power of each of these groups and individuals is context specific. A local school board has broad authority to influence district curriculum standards and hire administrators, but the group has little influence over state legislative decisions.

According to Bachrach and Baratz (1970), the four types of first-dimension power are force, authority, influence, and manipulation. Education systems include each type of power.

Force

Force indicates A achieves their preferred outcome in the face of B's noncompliance by restricting B's choices. This ordinarily occurs through physical force. Physical force can be either violent or nonviolent (Wrong, 1988). Physical punishment, called corporal punishment in schools, refers to the use of physical force to cause deliberate pain or discomfort to change student behavior. Corporal punishment remains legal in 17 states. The National Center for Education Statistics (NCES, 2022) estimates that more than 70,000 public school students receive physical punishment at least once during the school year. Physical discipline is associated with depression, low self-esteem, self-harm, suicide attempts, substance abuse, higher dropout rates, and poor school performance (Ferguson, 2013).

Physical discipline is disproportionately levied against minoritized and disabled students (MacSuga-Gage et al., 2021).

Teacher strikes and student protests are examples of nonviolent physical force. Striking teachers refuse to appear in the workplace during labor negotiations to achieve concessions, including salaries, working conditions, and state and local financial resources. In 37 states and the District of Columbia, teacher strikes are illegal. According to the Bureau of Labor Statistics (2023), teacher strikes of at least 1,000 employees have occurred 75 times in the past 30 years. In recent years, higher education worker strikes have surged, with 20 occurring since January 2022 including faculty, staff, postdoctoral, and student worker strikes (Milkman & Naald, 2023).

Authority

Authority refers to B complying with A's request when they respect A's position and find their commands reasonable. Authority gives an actor the ability to inflict reward or penalty. According to Bachrach and Baratz (1963), this authority is a necessary but not sufficient condition to maintain control only if several conditions are met: (a) the person threatened is aware of the threat, (b) the threat has real consequences, (c) the perceived harm of the sanctions outweigh the agent's perceived benefits of noncompliance, and (d) the entity threatened believes the authority would actually impose the penalty. If these conditions are not met, then authority is insufficient to achieve compliance. In such cases, influence is required.

Influence

To maintain influence means A achieves B's compliance without using overt or tacit threats. Influence can derive from formal institutional authority or from informal powers. Formal powers provide influence through the ability to keep issues off the agenda and achieve policy or political goals without force. Informal powers allow an actor to convince others to submit voluntarily to the desired action. Influence is different from authority because it does not depend upon sanctions. Influence requires that B comply with A's demands not due to fear of sanctions but because of relationships, persuasion, and respect.

Manipulation

Manipulation occurs when the power holder conceals intent from the power subject (Wrong, 1988). Manipulation denotes A achieving B's compliance by restricting B's choices without B being aware of A's intentions. Manipulation also occurs when A alters B's environment to achieve a desired response without interacting directly with B at all (Wrong, 1988). There are countless power asymmetries in educational settings, the most fundamental of which are between a teacher and a student and supervisors and supervisees. Teachers understand the content and pedagogical approach, and students do not. Teachers have a moral obligation not to abuse their power through student manipulation. University, college, and school leaders can manipulate their faculty and staff by concealing the intent of their actions and robbing their supervisees of the ability to make informed decisions.

First-dimension power receives disproportionate attention from researchers because it is easier to observe and measure. Second- and third-dimension power are more subtle forms of power. Despite the difficulty in measuring second- and third-dimension power, they can be just as dominant in A's effort to get B to achieve their desired outcome.

Non-Decision-Making Power

The second dimension of power focuses on the structural aspects of restricting groups' participation or their ability to exercise power (Bachrach & Botwinick, 1992). This dimension represents the "mobilization of bias" in a system to influence power implicitly rather than explicitly (Gaventa, 1980, p. 3). By controlling the agenda, political actors can control debate and limit discussion of policy issues that challenge the status quo. By limiting debate or preventing a decision, A can prevent B from obtaining what B wants without using coercive force. Those who wield second-dimension power suppress conflict, rather than create it, by limiting the scope of debate.

Second-dimension power is inherently more difficult to identify than first-dimension power when lack of action is the dominant strategy of those in power. Those in a position of power may seek to direct the attention of others away from a particular issue by focusing on alternative issues that are comparatively harmless (Bachrach & Baratz, 1970). This type of power is difficult to identify because those in power successfully restrict attention to innocuous issues. Power is exercised when a political actor or group establishes or reinforces social and political values or institutional practices that limit consideration of political issues to those that are inoffensive to those in power. Elites utilize second-dimension power to avoid the potential negative political consequences of utilizing first-dimension power.

Former Republican Speaker of the House Dennis Hastert developed what is known today as the Hastert Rule. The Hastert Rule is an informal agreement that the speaker will not schedule a floor vote on any bill that does not have majority support among the speaker's political party. According to the Hastert Rule, legislative proposals that have majority support in the House of Representatives, but not among a majority of the majority party, would not be scheduled for a vote. A majority of the majority party, a minority of all House members, maintains power over scheduling votes in the House of Representatives. Why would House speakers maintain such an informal rule? Party leaders' priorities include reelection of their party members, winning chamber majority control, and good public policy. All three goals are achieved by allowing a majority of the majority party to control agenda setting. The Hastert Rule represents a second dimension of power because it restricts the ability of the minority party to pass legislation that appeals to a minority of the majority party. The majority party improves their political position by avoiding policy issues that divide their party and putting forth policy issues that divide the opposition party.

Ideological Power

The third dimension of power refers to belief systems that can be manipulated through the control of information. Lukes proposed a third dimension of power based not on coercive or noncoercive power but on shaping preferences (Lukes, 2004). Lukes argued the first dimension of power, the pluralist view of power, involved A's preferences winning out over B's in a formal institution; in the second dimension, A manipulates the rules of the game so B's preferences are never heard. In the third dimension of power, A and B share the same preferences. What is the power dynamic? This scenario may still indicate a power dynamic where B has internalized A's preferences because A controls the information B consumes.

The third dimension of power is ideological and therefore difficult to observe or measure. The third dimension of power aligns with elite theory, in which a small group of economic, political, and social elites influence and dominate politics. These elites shape mass preferences. For example, ideological media is designed to manipulate individual preferences to align with those of the political elites. The power of elites is then furthered by the political ideology espoused by political groups and media sources. The third dimension of power seeks to manipulate individual and group preferences, so they comply.

Theories of Politics and Policy

The world is infinitely complex. To identify causal relationships and correlations between dependent and independent variables, it is necessary to utilize theories. Theories are systems of ideas intended to explain or predict behavior, facts, or events. Valid theories are verified by research and guide action and discovery. Researchers test theories to contradict false theories, understand accurate theories, and revise developing theories. Social scientists have developed theories for analyzing and predicting policymaking, including elite, institutional, political systems, incremental, rational choice, punctuated equilibrium, and advocacy coalition theory.

Elite Theory

Elite theory posits that a small economic, social, and political elite holds most power and that this power is largely independent of democratic elections. According to elite theory, power is concentrated in the hands of a small number of people or organizations that control policy processes. According to elite theory, a wealthy and influential minority has disproportionate power, which displaces any real participation by the majority of citizens in the American democratic process. The primary assumption of elite theory is that the public is less influential in shaping public policy than a small group of wealthy elites (Dye, 2001). Elites are disproportionately drawn from the upper socioeconomic strata of society.

Elite theory views public policy as reflecting the values and preferences of the wealthy, politically connected elite rather than those of the broader public. According to elite theory, public policy is a top-down process determined by the elite and applied to the masses. The elites believe they are better equipped to determine public policies to promote the welfare of the masses. Elites prefer the status quo to radical changes because the status quo generally benefits the elite. Elite preference for the status quo leads to incremental policy change and stability in the political and policy environment.

Institutional Theory

Policymaking does not occur in a vacuum; rather, policy actors operate within political institutions. Institutions are more than the collection of political actors in legislative, executive, and judicial government organizations. Institutions include the rules, norms, practices, and relationships that influence the behavior of institutional actors. Institutional rules and norms can be formal or informal. Formal rules include the U.S. Constitution detailing the relationships between the legislative, executive, and judicial branches and between the federal government and state and local governments. Formal rules also include state constitutions, federal and state laws, judicial rulings, executive orders, and those governing how government institutions operate internally. Informal rules refer to norms and nonstatutory rules that govern patterns of behavior and the relationships between various formal and informal political actors.

Institutional structures and rules constrain and shape policy processes and the options and opportunities available to political actors. These rules and structures exert enormous influence to empower or obstruct the policy interests of political actors. Rules are not neutral. For example, the Higher Education Act (HEA) authorizes federal aid programs for postsecondary education within the Department of Education, including programs that increase higher education access for low-income and first-generation students, regulations for higher education institutions to be eligible for Title IV federal student aid programs, and rules governing the accreditation process. HEA is supposed to be reauthorized every 5 years, but it has not been reauthorized since 2008. Although the House of Representatives Education and Labor Committee passed the College Affordability Act reauthorizing HEA, the Senate was unable to make any progress on HEA reauthorization legislation. Institutional differences between the House and the Senate make passing major legislation more difficult in the Senate. The Senate rules provide individual senators with significant autonomy. The filibuster is a Senate rule allowing senators to delay or block a Senate floor vote on a piece of legislation or confirmation. Like the House of Representatives, the Senate requires a simple majority to pass legislation. However, before Senate legislation can come to a vote, the chamber rules require 60 votes to end debate. The HEA has not been reauthorized for 14 years because the Senate filibuster rule requiring 60 senators to agree to end debate has been too high a hurdle for the legislation to clear. Institutional rules have enormous impact on policy outputs because they dictate the rules of the game.

Historical Institutionalism

Historical institutionalism is a social science approach that focuses on the ways in which institutions structure and shape behavior and outcomes. Historical contingency refers to how decisions made in the past contribute to the formation of institutions that influence current practices. Path dependence is a concept referring to past events or decisions that constrain later events or decisions. Path dependence holds that once an institution has been established and resources committed, deviations from that path become increasingly costly (Ackrill & Kay, 2006; Peters et al., 2005; Pierson, 1993; Pierson & Skocpol, 2002).

The historical institutionalism literature refers to critical junctures, key events or decisions made in the past that led to the development of an institution. A famous example of a critical juncture is the global use of the QWERTY keyboard. The QWERTY keyboard is the standard English-language keyboard layout. The title originates from the first six letter keys at the top left of the keyboard. Originally, typewriters were constructed with keys in alphabetical order, but they tended to jam when keys in physical proximity were utilized consistently. In the 1880s, the critical juncture arrived when typewriter manufacturers rearranged the letter layout so the letters used most often in the English language were distributed across the keyboard. This solved the jamming problem, but it also created a less efficient keyboard. More efficient keyboards exist, including the Dvorak keyboard, that improve the efficiency and speed of typing. Why then does most of the English-speaking world still use the QWERTY keyboard? The answer is path dependence. The initial decision to adopt the QWERTY keyboard was a critical juncture that led to millions of people learning the system. Deviations from the QWERTY keyboard now would require changing computers, smart phones, and other hardware devices and retraining millions of people on a new keyboard system. The sunk costs associated with the existing system are too high to make widespread changes.

Path dependence can be applied to numerous education policy systems. For example, the U.S. elementary and secondary education finance system primarily funds public education with state (47%) and local (46%) money. Federal funding accounts for only 7% of total public education funding. As discussed in Chapter 2, a strong culture of local control and low public school enrollment rates through most of American history led to public education being financed primarily through local taxing sources, especially local property taxes. Property values vary significantly from district to district, with wealthier areas collecting more in revenue than less wealthy areas. Most scholars would argue that if one were to develop a public education system today, financing through a property tax would not be a good idea. The inequities that such a system creates are inconsistent with the American ideal of equal opportunity for all. Applying a path dependence lens to the problem suggests that transitioning to a new education finance system would involve dealing with massive sunk costs, making a change in the system very costly. These examples illustrate how past events or decisions constrain later decisions by increasing the costs associated with change. The system becomes a self-reinforcing process as decisions close off other options (Capoccia & Kelemen, 2007).

Historical institutionalism also focuses on how institutions originate in order to understand their purpose and evolution and their impact on policymaking. Historical contingency addresses political developments and how those events and trends impact how institutions became established. However distinctive the original circumstances, institutions produce increasing returns once established, making it increasingly costly to divert the institutional purpose (Pierson, 2000). The order of events in institutional development is often critical to understanding the current state of the policies developed.

Political Systems Theory

Political systems theory concentrates on the impact of external factors, including the cultural, economic, physical, and social environments, on policymakers' actions and policy outputs. The theory posits that changes in these environments produce groups demanding and supporting change in the policy environment. The theory defines these external demands and supporting groups as inputs on the political system. The external demands and supporting groups apply pressure on the political system to produce a solution or output. Political groups compete to shape the solution within the political system. Once the political system produces an output, it impacts the cultural, economic, physical, or social environment. If the outputs result in a change in the environment, these changes are called outcomes. The policy outputs can then engender new demands and opposition groups against the policy, which is called feedback. Policy feedback refers to the policies shaping politics and policymaking. Policy feedback produces demands on the political system that change the system inputs and restart the cycle of systems changes.

In 1953, political scientist David Easton developed political systems theory to establish the connection between the political system and the broader cultural, economic, physical, and social environment (Easton, 1953). The theory depicts how government responds to societal demands rather than simply focusing on political actors and institutional structures. The political system is the primary unit of analysis and the authoritative system that determines resource allocations within any society. The political system responds to positive and negative impacts emerging from the broader societal environment. More stable political systems like governments in developed nations like the United States are better equipped to deal with societal environmental shocks than those in the Global South. According to political systems theory, responses of the political system to changes in the societal environment occur within a critical range, meaning the system can handle a certain amount of stress caused by the broader cultural, economic, physical, or social environment. All political systems have a stress limit. Once shocks to the system move beyond the critical range, they cannot cope with the stress, and, in some cases, the political system collapses.

Rationality, Incrementalism, and Punctuated Equilibrium

Representative democracy is composed of elected leaders representing a group of people called constituents. In theory, a representative democracy is designed to have elected leaders serve as delegates who only consider the preferences of their electorate when making decisions. In practice, constituents rarely agree on a course of action or policy position. Elected representatives must consider the opinion of their constituents and weigh that against their understanding of the consequences of policy action.

Rational choice theory posits that individuals use rational calculations to make rational choices and achieve outcomes aligned with their own self-interest. This theory is employed in economics to understand the behavior of consumers and sellers in market economies. When used in public policy and political science, the theory holds that history and culture are not central to understanding political or policy action. Instead, the theory states that individuals make decisions based on their self-interest and that social behavior can be understood by aggregating individuals' rational decisions. Rational choice theory is based on a series of assumptions:

- All actions are rational and made after considering costs and rewards.
- The benefits of a relationship or action must outweigh the costs. Costs and benefits are not only monetary but can include emotional considerations.
- When the value of the benefit diminishes below the value of the costs incurred, the person will discontinue the action.
- Individuals will use the resources at their disposal to optimize rewards.
  Rational choice theory begins with the concept of comprehensive rationality, an ideal type of decision making in which policymakers translate their values and goals into policy following a comprehensive study of all choices and their outcomes. This is an unrealistic simplification in comparison to more realistic models. Herbert Simon developed the concept of bounded rationality based on limited human and organizational capacity (Simon, 1947, 1955, 1977, 1983, 1985). Political systems cannot consider all policy issues simultaneously. Bounded rationality, a more realistic theory of reality, is based on three primary assumptions:
- Humans are cognitively constrained and make decisions based on limited information. Political systems also have limited capacity to consider.
- These constraints impact decision making.
- Difficult problems reveal constraints and highlight their significance.

Human beings have mental constraints such as limited attention, time, and working memory and therefore they use heuristics to compensate for their limitations (Simon, 1955). Elected leaders have three primary goals: reelection, good public policy, and institutional power. Rational choice theory explains public policy by aggregating the preferences of individual actors including voters, legislators, and executive agency officials. The classic study of rational choice theory in understanding legislator decisions is political scientist David Mayhew's *Congress: The Electoral Connection* (Mayhew, 1974).

Incrementalism

Political scientist Charles Lindblom developed incrementalism theory to emphasize the collaborative process of policymaking and the incentives for political actors to build on past policies rather than make wholesale changes (Lindblom, 1959). Incrementalism theory is a practical alternative and a theoretical advance to comprehensive rationality, bounded rationality, and rational choice theory. According to incrementalism, policymaking involves significant transaction costs, which are the time, effort, and resources required to make collective decisions. Policymaking typically requires determining winners and losers. Entrenched interest groups, the public, and political parties on the losing side seek to increase the political costs of policy change. The opportunity costs, the perceived benefit of not choosing the next best option when resources are limited, associated with developing major new policy outputs disincentivize bold policy changes and incentivize incremental changes. Incremental change refers to nonradical policy change involving small adjustments to the status quo.

Why are policymakers incentivized to pursue incremental versus nonincremental policy change? Government efficiency increases as policymakers make slight adjustments to previous policies rather than expend the resources necessary for bold policy changes. Nonincremental policy changes require high transaction costs and opportunity costs without any guarantee of success. Nonincremental policy change also increases the likelihood of unintended consequences. Chapter 9 further details the problem of unintended consequences in policy implementation. Unintended consequences refer to policy impacts that differ from the expected policy outcomes. Policymakers can minimize the risk of unintended consequences by making incremental changes to the policy status quo. The U.S. political system places high transaction costs on policy change through the separation of power between the legislative, executive, and judicial branches and through federalism, in which the same territory is controlled by multiple levels of government. While the purpose of this high transaction cost system is to reduce the likelihood of tyranny, the structure also decreases the probability of nonincremental policy change. Policymakers have professional and structural incentives to make incremental changes to the policy status quo.

Public budgeting is an area of policy research where incrementalism has been applied and found to impact decision making. State governments pass annual or biannual budgets to fund programs and activities, including elementary, secondary, and postsecondary education. Unlike the federal government, state governments are constrained by balanced budget amendments prohibiting deficit spending. States are required to adjust budgets based on economic conditions and tax collection totals. Despite this natural fluctuation in government revenues and spending, state education spending remains exceedingly consistent. State-level education spending follows the state's previous year's budget allocation with incremental shifts based on tax revenues and political priorities. The best predictor of one year's state elementary, secondary, and postsecondary education spending is the previous year's education spending. Studies indicate incremental budgeting occurs not only in total education spending but also in the various spending subcategories.

Punctuated Equilibrium

Punctuated equilibrium theory uses a theoretical concept appropriated from evolutionary biology to explain the stability of dynamic systems. Social scientists applying the theory find that policymaking processes demonstrate long periods of stability interspersed with brief and dramatic instability (Cairney, 2012). Baumgartner and Jones (2002) argued most policy models explain either stability (incrementalism, path dependency) or change (policy process model, political systems theory, and advocacy coalition framework), but few can explain patterns of stability and change (True et al., 2006).

Punctuated equilibrium builds upon previous models of incrementalism and bounded rationality to explain periods of stability. Bounded rationality and incrementalism theories are predicated on the cognitive limitations of decision makers and apply that logic to governments. Government institutions are a collection of policymakers and are influenced by the public, interest groups, and other political actors. Governments and the public have limited capacity to focus on a particular policy issue.

Theories of conflict expansion and agenda setting emphasize the difficulty of getting policymaking institutions to consider policy ideas (Cobb & Elder, 1983; Schattschneider, 1960). Political systems are designed to favor the status quo. As with other theories, the complexity of the political system, including separation of powers, separate levels of government sharing power, and jurisdictional boundaries of policy subsystems, combine to create high transaction costs that incentivize policy incrementalism. Baumgartner and Jones (1991, 1993) argued those complex systems occasionally engender nonincremental change. Once a policy issue rises on the political agenda, the policy subsystem is expanded, and formal and informal subsystem actors become advocates of status quo change. The U.S. constitutional system established high transaction costs to force broad coalition building to achieve policy change. However, when political coalitions mobilize to overcome these barriers, nonincremental policy change results.

Punctuated equilibrium theory posits that equilibrium occurs when policy subsystems capture the policymaking process. Disequilibrium, resulting in short periods of nonincremental change, occur when an issue makes it onto the macropolitical agenda, an expanded agenda that incorporates policymakers, interest group actors, media, and the public outside the typical policy subsystem. Policy systems in equilibrium experience negative feedback, maintaining the restricted policy subsystem. Positive feedback occurs when a change in the system amplifies the likelihood of further change (Baumgartner & Jones, 2002). A policy subsystem can become a policy monopoly when institutional arrangements limit participation and policy imagination to reinforce the dominance of the existing policy subsystem (Baumgartner & Jones, 1993). When policy monopolies move into disequilibrium, dramatic policy change can occur.

Punctuated equilibrium theory has most commonly been used to explain budgetary changes, including among educational institutions. Educational institutions' dependence on limited funding sources can lead to sudden punctuations (Ecton & Dziensinski, 2022). Higher education institutions that rely heavily on tuition or state appropriations experience more budget punctuations (Lacy et al., 2017). Higher education state appropriations demonstrate incremental change over time disrupted by nonincremental changes based on a state's changing economic or political standing (Li, 2017). Punctuated equilibrium studies of institutional-level budgeting reveal that public institutions had fewer budgetary punctuations than nonprofit ones. For-profit institutions experienced the most budgetary volatility and least financial stability (Epp, 2015).

Multiple Streams Theory

Comprehensive rationality represents an idealized form of decision making in which policy is developed by a comprehensive study of all policy choices and environmental variables (Cairney, 2012). In contrast, multiple streams theory (MST) posits that organizational decision making is "organized anarchy" with contradictory preferences difficult to define or rank (Cohen et al., 1972). Analysis of the policy environment and policy options are not comprehensive. Instead, preferences are based on policy experimentation, and policymakers revise policy outputs based on learning from previous successes and failures.

MST explains why, when, and how some policy issues gain prominence among policymakers. MST, also known as the garbage can model, perceives policy change as organized chaos in which problems, solutions, and decision-making venues are arbitrary and episodic. Like a garbage can, problems, solutions, and politics represent independent streams with mixed-up, volatile relationships (Cairney, 2012). As shown in Figure 3.1, the three streams combine in unpredictable ways due to the cognitive limitations of policy actors and organizational fragmentation, which leads to disjointed policymaking.

The problem stream is comprised of conditions policymakers and the public deem as requiring government intervention. It includes indicators, focusing events, and policy feedback. Figure 3.1 illustrates the Multiple Streams Framework developed by Kingdon (1984). Policymakers and the public elevate conditions to problems. Constant agenda-setting conflicts determine which public problems deserve government attention. Focusing events can increase public attention on a policy issue. Focusing events are critical moments that bring widespread public attention and group mobilization and place a policy issue on the public agenda (Birkland, 1997). Issue framing is a political phenomenon in which interest groups present an issue in a way that will receive the most agreement from others. Issue framing is a process of selecting certain aspects of a policy issue, increasing its prominence to elicit certain interpretations and evaluations of the issue (Weaver, 2007).

The policy stream consists of policy solutions that have been developed by specialists including academics, think tanks, interest groups, and policy entrepreneurs. While some theories and models view the problem and policy solutions as a linear process, MST sees problems and solutions as independent streams. Problems and solutions typically operate on separate timelines. Problems rapidly rise and fall on the public agenda, but solutions can take a long period of time to develop and refine (Kingdon, 1984). Solutions are often developed by policymakers, academics, think tanks, and interest groups without a specific problem. Interest groups wait for a problem to develop and then offer the policy solution (Kingdon, 1984).

Politics is the third stream, referring to the acceptability of a solution to policymakers and the broader public at a particular time. Endogenous factors including institutional structures, routines, and election-based turnover alter political conditions that open or close windows of

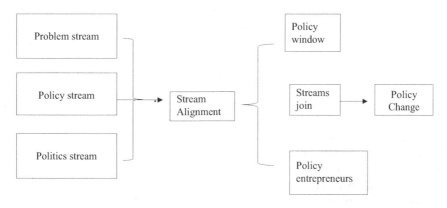

Figure 3.1 Multiple Streams Framework

opportunity. Political elections can dramatically shift the political environment. As President Barack Obama's second term ended, Congress reauthorized the Elementary and Secondary Education Act (ESEA). It transitioned from the controversial No Child Left Behind version of the ESEA passed under President George W. Bush in 2001 to the new Every Student Succeeds Act. Democrats made the political calculation that their political party might lose the White House, so a policy compromise while Obama was still in office would be more conducive to their policy preferences. Republicans were able to extract concessions from Democrats with a highly contested presidential election forthcoming.

Exogenous changes in the demographic, economic, political, and social environment can increase or decrease the acceptability of policy solutions. In December 2019, a new pneumonia began infecting people in Wuhan, China. The International Committee on the Taxonomy of Viruses identified the infectious disease as severe acute respiratory syndrome coronavirus 2, later named COVID-19 by the World Health Organization (Center for Disaster Philanthropy, 2023). In spring 2020, 48 states closed schools for the remainder of the academic year, impacting nearly 51 million children. According to the National Council of State Legislatures, more than 1,300 colleges and universities in all 50 states canceled in-person classes or shifted to online instruction. According to the College Crisis Initiative, 44% of colleges and universities remained primarily online through the 2020–2021 school year. The COVID pandemic was a focusing event that directed public attention to the issue of public health in elementary, secondary, and postsecondary educational institutions.

The COVID-19 pandemic placed public health, particularly among the nation's educational institutions, on the decision agenda. On March 27, 2020, Congress passed the Coronavirus Aid, Relief and Economic Security Act, appropriating $2.2 trillion in direct economic aid with $31 billion for elementary and secondary public schools and $14 billion for higher education institutions. Nearly every state government also passed legislation providing guidelines and funding for educational institutions to protect student health and plan for the transition back to in-person learning. The COVID-19 pandemic and its severe health consequences rapidly raised public attention and led to immediate and widespread federal, state, and local policy outputs to deal with the crisis.

The Policy Process Models

The stages model, also known as the policy process model, characterizes the policy process as a series of stages: problem identification, agenda setting, policy formulation, policy adoption, implementation, and evaluation. The policy process model portrays the stages of the policy process as connected but not linear. The model is typically described as a cyclical process to illustrate that public policy continues to cycle back to policy issues. While the policy process model depicts the stages as distinct, in practice the stages often overlap, entire stages are omitted, and the stages can occur in a different order. For example, a policy solution may be formulated but the public and elected policymakers may not recognize the problem requiring the solution.

Table 3.1 describes the policy process stages. The purpose of the policy process model is to understand that each stage includes distinct challenges and opportunities, involves different government and nongovernmental institutions and policy actors, and requires different empirical approaches to measure policy process. The problem definition stage identifies the root cause of the problem and the scope of the impact. Agenda setting is the process of directing broader attention to a policy issue. Formulation is the process of translating policy goals into substantive policy instruments. Implementation describes governmental or

Table 3.1 The Policy Process Model Stages

Stage	Definition
Problem definition	Clearly ascertaining the root cause of the problem and its impact on the target population.
Agenda setting	The process of directing public, media, and policymaker attention to a policy issue.
Policy formulation	The process of designing policy that transforms goals into government programs.
Policy adoption	The process of approving policy by government institutions.
Policy implementation	The activities undertaken by government and others to achieve goals and objectives articulated in policy statements.
Policy evaluation	The process of identifying the content, impact, or implementation of a public policy.

organizational action to achieve the articulated policy goals. Evaluation is the process of identifying the impact of the policy on the target population. Policy evaluation can lead to a change in the problem definition and eventually to broader attention to the problem, making the stages model a cyclical process. Chapters 7–9 provide an in-depth overview of the policy stages.

Policy Diffusion

Policy diffusion theory is the study of how and why policy ideas spread (Walker, 1969). Policy diffusion occurs when an innovation spreads from one governmental jurisdiction to another by policy, political, and normative information and competitive pressure (Volden et al., 2008). Policy diffusion studies have explored endogenous spread of policy innovations within subunits of a nation's government and exogenous spread of policy innovations among countries (Sabatier, 1987). The American federal system is an ideal laboratory for testing the interdependence of federal, state, and local government influence on policy diffusion. Diffusion can occur horizontally across governments at the same level or vertically across governments at different levels (Mallinson, 2021).

Policy diffusion seeks to understand how government policy innovations spread intergovernmental competition, policy learning, political learning, federal coercion, and social contagion (Pacheco, 2012; Shipan & Volden, 2012). Diffusion processes identified by scholars include regional, vertical, leader-laggard, and national interaction models (Gándara & Woolley, 2023). Policymaking innovations originating from geographically proximal governments is termed regional diffusion (Shipan & Volden, 2012). Vertical diffusion results when state governments are influenced by national or local government policies. (Karch, 2007). Leader-laggard models identify states that are considered leaders in a policy area. State leaders spread policy innovations to others (Grupp & Richards, 1975; Volden, 2006). Policy innovation can also occur through policy actors' communication networks, including membership organizations, in a diffusion mechanism called national interaction (Orphan et al., 2021). Policy diffusion studies also measure the impact of internal determinants on innovation, including economic, political, and social issues (Gray, 1994).

Why are governments influenced by the policy decisions of other governments? First, research indicates economic competition drives state policy decisions (Ingle et al., 2007). State leaders see themselves in competition with other states for industries, companies, and jobs. If other states, particularly geographically proximate ones, make investments in education that improve their education system or ability to attract job producers, other states feel pressure to make similar policy changes. Second, policy diffusion is facilitated by national organizations designed to inform policymakers about best practices in education policy. This information sharing among political networks is called policy learning (Mooney & Lee, 1995). Organizations including the Education Commission of the States, National Governors Association Center for Best Practices, and the Hunt Institute convene conferences and disseminate policy information to influence policy change (Karch, 2007; Mintrom, 1997).

Group Theory

Group theory is the study of how individual actors assemble to form political groups including voters, interest groups, political campaigns, political parties, and governmental organizations. Group theory includes a category of theories and models that seek to explain how these groups compete for political power and its impact on political behavior and policy outcomes. Pluralism is a fundamental concept of group theory. *Pluralism* is the philosophy that the diffusion of power among a broad range of political actors prevents any single group from gaining dominance (Polsby, 1980). According to Dahl, increases in political, economic, and social heterogeneity, the quality or state of being diverse in content, disperses political power to the benefit of democratic government. The concentration of power in individuals or groups, such as wealthy business interests, has long been considered a threat to democratic rule. Pluralists argue the fragmentation of the system both horizontally, the separation of powers and diffusion of interests within one level of government, and vertically, a federal system that divides power among multiple levels of government institutions and actors, ensures that no one faction will control political power or policy outcomes.

In contrast to elite theory, pluralism holds that power is dispersed among interest groups throughout the political system. Multiple interests or factions disperse power or at least mitigate the ability of any one interest group to seize total power. Interest groups counter the power of opposing interest groups to balance political power and not allow any one group to dominate the political system. For example, teachers unions have significant political power in each state and nationally due to their membership size and their substantial resources. The Business Roundtable, composed of chief executives of 200 leading corporations, has enormous resources, access to vast amounts of campaign contributions and lobbying resources, and access to influential policymakers. Even pluralists acknowledge that some groups might dominate areas of public policy where their interests are paramount. While this domination in certain policy areas is inevitable, overlapping membership among interest groups and underrepresented interests establishing new interest groups mitigate the threat of minority interest group control.

Critics of pluralism argue that dispersed interest groups require opportunities to use political resources. The inequality of interest group resources, membership size, money, and political skills ensures control by wealthy interest groups. The working class and poor, particularly following the decline of unions during the past 40 years, lack the financial and political resources to counteract business interests, leading to increasing business dominance over labor interests. Business, trade, and professional associations comprise nearly 85% of all interest group representation in Washington, DC (Baumgartner & Leech, 2001).

Advocacy Coalition Framework

The advocacy coalition framework (ACF) is a group theory that concentrates on competing advocacy coalitions or interest groups within a policy subsystem (Sabatier, 1988; Sabatier & Jenkins-Smith, 1999). Advocacy coalitions are groups of political actors with shared policy goals who coordinate their political activity (Sabatier & Jenkins-Smith, 1999). The policy process is complicated, involving multiple policy actors, institutions, and levels of government. ACF holds that to understand the complex policy process one must focus on how coalitions are tied together through shared belief systems and compete with other coalitions to achieve policy outputs (Weible & Sabatier, 2005).

ACF distinguishes salient and technical policy issues. Technical policy issues that lack widespread public interest minimize conflict and produce compromises between coalitions (Ingold & Gschwend, 2014). Salient policy issues that mobilize widespread public attention lead to policymaking stability because coalitions stand on principle and are unwilling to compromise on core beliefs. The framework identifies dominant and nondominant policy subsystems but holds that significant coalitions and policy actors differ across policy issue areas. The framework also highlights policy learning, in which policy actors incorporate new information into their deliberations and strategic actions, resulting in minor changes to the policy subsystem over time. Alternatively, external and internal shocks can create major changes in the coalitions and subsystems. For example, an election can change the elected representatives and the coalitions involved in the policy subsystem. Policymaking institutional structures incentivize specialization of policy knowledge, resulting in subsystems or groups of coalitions grouped by policy jurisdiction (Weible & Sabatier, 2005).

ACF expands beyond policy subsystems, comprised of legislative committees, executive agencies, and interest groups, to incorporate a broader range of political and policy elites including the media, researchers, and policy experts. Its relatively stable political, economic, and social variables include the constitutional structure, values, and resources available to coalition groups (Cairney, 2012). External subsystem events impact the stable parameters through changes including economic fluctuations, elections and partisan control of government, and resource fluctuations such as government funding. For example, a downturn in the economy reduces government tax collection, which reduces public resources and impacts the money available to spend on policy initiatives. Long-term coalition opportunity structures represent consensus among the coalition groups required to enact changes to the policy status quo. The external subsystem events and long-term coalition opportunity structures result in short-term opportunities that advocacy coalitions can manipulate to promote change or defend against attempted policy changes.

Policy Subsystems

Governments and the public problems they confront are so vast that policymaking typically occurs within a specific policy area with a small number of vested and knowledgeable participants (Cairney et al., 2019). Policy subsystems include the actors and institutions found in each policy area (Sabatier & Jenkins-Smith, 1999). The policy subsystem concept has evolved from the original concept of iron triangles of legislators, bureaucrats, and interest groups (Adams, 1981). Subgovernment theory also focuses on the relationship between congressional committees, interest groups, and executive branch agencies, all of which are concerned about the formulation, adoption, and implementation of policy in a particular area (DeHaven-Smith, 1984). Organizations and actors in a policy subsystem form relatively stable relationships and exchange political and policy resources (Compston, 2009). Formal institutions require knowledge, expertise, and financial support from informal actors, and informal actors require the legislative authority and bureaucratic implementation of government organizations. Compston (2009) defined three conditions for a policy subsystem:

- resource control by a political actor;
- the resource is desire by another political actor; and
- the resource can be transferred.

Policy subsystems, also known as policy network analysis or policy domains, consist of a network or coalition of individuals and organizations working together in a policy domain.

Education is a policy subsystem consisting of the legislative and executive branch actors that formulate, adopt, administer, and implement education policy. Education policy subsystems also include nongovernmental actors like interest groups, think tanks, foundations, and nonprofit organizations. Galey-Horn and Ferrare (2020) utilized policy network analysis to explain market-based education policy change including charter school expansion. Between the 2010–2011 and 2021–2022 school years, charter school enrollment more than doubled from 1.8 to 3.7 million students (NCES, 2023). Intermediary organizations strategically utilize research to build policy coalitions in states and cities to expand charter school reforms. Intermediary organizations engage in information transmission, advocacy work, and political lobbying to build coalitions and influence policy change in local and state governments.

Key Terms

advocacy coalition framework
authority
autocracy
bounded rationality
comprehensive rationality
decision making
democracy
elite theory
endogenous change
exogenous change
first-dimension of power
force
group theory
historical institutionalism
horizontal diffusion
ideological power
incrementalism
influence
institutional power goal
institutional theory
manipulation
multiple streams theory
nonincremental policy change
path dependence

pluralism
policy diffusion
policy innovations
policy learning
policy process model
policy subsystems
political systems theory
power
public policy goal
punctuated equilibrium theory
rational choice theory
rationality
reelection goal
second dimension of power
status quo
subgovernment theory
third dimension of power
vertical diffusion

Discussion Questions

1. How do you define power? What are the different types of power?
2. What is institutional theory? What is historical institutionalism? What is path dependence?
3. What is rational choice theory? What is bounded rationality? What is comprehensive rationality and its assumptions?
4. What is incremental versus nonincremental policy change? What does punctuated equilibrium theory predict about incremental versus nonincremental policy change?
5. What is policy diffusion? How does policy diffusion occur?
6. What are policy subsystems? How do policy subsystems influence policy status quo and change?
7. What is advocacy coalition framework?

Application

1. Explain what policy theory best explains the development of your policy issue.
2. Compare and contrast how different policy theories explain your policy issue.

References

Ackrill, R., & Kay, A. (2006). Historical-institutionalist perspectives on the development of the EU budget system. *Journal of European Public Policy, 13*(1), 113–133. https://doi.org/10.1080/13501760500380775

Adams, G. (1981). *The iron triangle: The politics of defense contracting.* Council of Economic Priorities.

Bachrach, P., & Baratz, M. S. (1963). Decisions and nondecisions: An analytical framework. *The American Political Science Review, 57*(3), 632–642.

Bachrach, P., & Baratz, M. S. (1970). *Power and poverty: Theory and practice.* Oxford University Press.

Bachrach, P., & Botwinick, A. (1992). *Power and empowerment: A radical theory of participatory democracy.* Temple University Press.

Baumgartner, F. R., & Jones, B. D. (1991). Agenda dynamics and policy subsystems. *The Journal of Politics, 53*(4), 1044–1074. https://doi.org/10.2307/2131866

Baumgartner, F. R., & Jones, B. D. (1993). *Agendas and instability in American politics*. The University of Chicago Press.

Baumgartner, F. R., & Jones, B. D. (2002). *Policy dynamics*. The University of Chicago Press.

Baumgartner, F. R., & Leech, B. L. (2001). Interest niches and policy bandwagons: Patterns of interest group involvement in national politics. *Journal of Politics*, *63*(4), 1191–1213. https://doi.org/10.1111/0022-3816.00106

Birkland, T. A. (1997). *After disaster: Agenda setting, public policy, and focusing events*. Georgetown University Press.

Bureau of Labor Statistics. (2023). *Work stoppages*. www.bls.gov/wsp/

Cairney, P. (2012). *Understanding public policy: Theories and issues*. Palgrave Macmillan.

Cairney, P., Heikkila, T., & Wood, M. (2019). *Making policy in a complex world*. Cambridge University Press.

Campbell, J. E. (2022). *The seats-in-trouble forecasts of the 2022 midterm congressional elections*. University of Virginia Center for Politics. https://centerforpolitics.org/crystalball/articles/the-seats-in-trouble-forecasts-of-the-2022-midterm-congressional-elections/

Capoccia, G., & Kelemen, R. D. (2007). The study of critical junctures: Theory, narrative, and counterfactuals in historical institutionalism. *World Politics*, *59*(3), 341–369. https://doi.org/10.1017/s0043887100020852

Center for Disaster Philanthropy. (2023). *COVID-19 coronavirus*. https://disasterphilanthropy.org/disasters/covid-19-coronavirus

Cobb, R. W., & Elder, C. D. (1983). *Participation in American politics: The dynamics of agenda-building*. Johns Hopkins University Press.

Cohen, M. D., March, J. G., & Olsen, J. P. (1972). A garbage can model of organizational choice. *Administrative Science Quarterly*, *17*(1), 1–25.

Compston, H. (2009). *Policy networks and policy change: Putting policy network theory to the test*. Palgrave Macmillan.

Dahl, R. A. (1956). *A preface to democratic theory*. University of Chicago Press.

Dahl, R. A. (1957). The concept of power. *Behavior Science*, *2*(3), 201–215.

Dahl, R. A. (1961). *Who governs? Democracy and power in an American city*. Yale University Press.

DeHaven-Smith, L., & Horn, C. E. V. (1984). Subgovernment conflict in public policy. *Policy Studies Journal*, *12*(4), 627.

Dye, T. R. (2001). *Top down policymaking*. Sage.

Easton, D. (1953). *The political system: An inquiry into the state of political science*. Alfred A. Knopf.

Ecton, W. G., & Diziensinski, A. B. (2022). Using punctuated equilibrium to understand patterns of institutional budget change in higher education. *The Journal of Higher Education*, *93*(3), 424–451.

Epp, D. A. (2015). Punctuated equilibria in the private sector and the stability of market-systems. *Policy Studies Journal*, *43*(4), 417–436.

Ferguson, C. J. (2013). Spanking, corporal punishment and negative long-term outcomes: A meta-analytic review of longitudinal studies. *Clinical Psychology Review*, *33*(1), 196–208. https://doi.org/10.1016/j.cpr.2012.11.002

Galey-Horn, S., & Ferrare, J. J. (2020). Using policy network analysis to understand ideological convergence and change in educational subsystems. *Education Policy Analysis Archives*, *28*(118). https://doi.org/10.14507/epaa.28.4508

Gándara, D., & Woolley, C. (2023). Comparative higher education politics, policymaking in North America and Western Europe. *Higher Education Dynamics*, 455–475. https://doi.org/10.1007/978-3-031-25867-1_19

Gaventa, J. (1980). *Power and powerlessness: Quiescence and rebellion in an Appalachian valley*. University of Illinois Press.

Gray, V. (1994). Competition, emulation, and policy innovation. In L. Dodd & C. Jillson (Eds.), *New perspectives on American politics* (pp. 650–666). CQ Press.

Grupp, F. W., & Richards, A. R. (1975). Variations in elite perceptions of American states as referents for public policy making. *American Political Science Review*, *69*(3), 850–858. https://doi.org/10.2307/1958394

Herre, B. (2022). *In most countries, democracy is a recent achievement: Dictatorship is far from a distant memory*. Our World in Data. https://ourworldindata.org/democracies-age

Ingle, W. K., Cohen-Vogel, L., & Hughes, R. (2007). The public policy process among Southeastern states: Elaborating theories of regional adoption and hold-out behavior. *Policy Studies Journal*, *35*(4), 607–628. https://doi.org/10.1111/j.1541-0072.2007.00239.x

Ingold, K., & Gschwend, M. (2014). Science in policy-making: Neutral experts or strategic policy-makers? *West European Politics, 37*(5), 993–1018.

Karch, A. (2007). Emerging issues and future directions in state policy diffusion research. *State Politics & Policy Quarterly, 7*(1), 54–80. https://doi.org/10.1177/153244000700700104

Kingdon, J. (1984). *Agendas, alternatives, and public policies*. Little Brown.

Lacy, T. A., Fowles, J., Tandberg, D. A., & Hu, S. (2017). U.S. state higher education appropriations: Assessing the relationships between agency politicization, centralization, and volatility. *Policy and Society, 36*(1), 16–33.

Lasswell, H. D. (1936). *Politics: Who gets what, when, how?* McGraw-Hill Book Company.

Li, A. Y. (2017). Dramatic declines in higher education appropriations: State conditions for budget punctuations. *Research in Higher Education, 58*(4), 1045–1066.

Lindblom, C. (1959). The science of "muddling through." *Public Administrative Review, 19,* 79–88.

Lukes, S. (2004). *Power: A radical view*. Palgrave Macmillan.

MacSuga-Gage, A. S., Gage, N. A., Katsiyannis, A., Hirsch, S. E., & Kisner, H. (2021). Disproportionate corporal punishment of students with disabilities and Black and Hispanic students. *Journal of Disability Policy Studies, 32*(3), 212–223. https://doi.org/10.1177/1044207320949960

Mallinson, D. J. (2021). Growth and gaps: A meta-review of policy diffusion studies in the American states. *Policy & Politics, 49*(3), 369–389.

Mayhew. (1974). *Congress: The electoral connection*. Yale University Press.

Milkman, R., & Naald, J. V. D. (2023). *The state of the unions 2023: A profile of organized labor in New York City, New York state, and the United States*. CUNY School of Labor and Urban Studies. https://slu.cuny.edu/wp-content/uploads/2023/08/Union-Density-2023.pdf

Mintrom, M. (1997). Policy entrepreneurs and the diffusion of innovation. *American Journal of Political Science, 41*(3), 738. https://doi.org/10.2307/2111674

Mooney, C., & Lee, M. H. (1995). Legislating morality in the American states: The case of pre-Roe regulation reform. *American Journal of Political Science, 39*(3), 599–627.

Muth, R. (1984). Toward an integrative theory of power and educational organizations. *Educational Administration Quarterly, 20*(2), 25–42. https://doi.org/10.1177/0013161x84020002003

National Center for Education Statistics. (2022). *2017–18 discipline estimations by discipline type*. https://nces.ed.gov/programs/digest/d21/tables/dt21_233.27.asp?current=yes

National Center for Education Statistics. (2023). *Public charter school enrollment: Condition of education*. U.S. Department of Education, Institute of Education Sciences. https://nces.ed.gov/fastfacts/display.asp?id=30

Orphan, C. M., Laderman, S., & Gildersleeve, R. E. (2021). Advocates or honest information brokers? Examining the higher education public policy agenda-setting processes of intermediary organizations. *The Review of Higher Education, 44*(3), 325–355. https://doi.org/10.1353/rhe.2021.0002

Pacheco, J. (2012). The social contagion model: Exploring the role of public opinion on the diffusion of antismoking legislation across the American states. *Journal of Politics, 74*(1), 187–202.

Peters, B. G., Pierre, J., & King, D. S. (2005). The politics of path dependency: Political conflict in historical institutionalism. *The Journal of Politics, 67*(4), 1275–1300.

Pierson, P. (1993). When effect becomes cause: Policy feedback and political change. *World Politics, 45*(4), 595–628. https://doi.org/10.2307/2950710

Pierson, P. (2000). Increasing returns, path dependence, and the study of politics. *American Political Science Review, 94*(2), 251–267.

Pierson, P., & Skocpol, T. (2002). Historical institutionalism in contemporary political science. In I. Katznelson & H. Milner (Eds.), *Political science: The state of the discipline* (pp. 693–721). W.W. Norton.

Polsby, N. W. (1980). *Community power and political theory*. Yale University Press.

Russell, B. (1938). *Power: A new social analysis*. Allen & Unwin.

Sabatier, P. A. (1987). Knowledge, policy-oriented learning, and policy change: An advocacy coalition framework. *Knowledge: Creation, Diffusion, Utilization, 8*(4), 649–692.

Sabatier, P. A. (1988, Fall). An advocacy coalition model of policy change and the role of policy-oriented learning therein. *Policy Science, 21,* 129–168.

Sabatier, P. A., & Jenkins-Smith, H. C. (1999). The advocacy coalition framework: An assessment. In P. A. Sabatier (Ed.), *Theories of the policy process* (pp. 117–166). Westview Press.

Schattschneider, E. (1960). *The semi sovereign people*. Holt, Rinehart, and Winston.

Shipan, C. R., & Volden, C. (2012). Policy diffusion: Seven lessons for scholars and practitioners. *Public Administration Review, 72*(6), 788–796. https://doi.org/10.1111/j.1540-6210.2012.02610.x

Simon, H. A. (1947). *Administrative behavior: A study of decision-making processes in administrative organization.* Macmillan.

Simon, H. A. (1955). A behavioral model of rational choice. *Quarterly Journal of Economics, 69*(1), 99–118.

Simon, H. A. (1977). The logic of heuristic decision-making. In R. S. Cohen & M. W. Wartofsky (Eds.), *Models of discovery* (pp. 154–175). D. Reidel.

Simon, H. A. (1983). *Reason in human affairs.* Stanford University Press.

Simon, H. A. (1985). Human nature in politics: The dialogue of psychology with political science. *American Political Science Review, 79,* 293–304.

True, J. L., Jones, B. D., & Baumgartner, F. R. (2006). Punctuated-equilibrium theory: Explaining stability and change in American policymaking. In P. A. Sabatier (Ed.), *Theories of the policy process* (pp. 97–116). Westview Press.

Volden, C. (2006). States as policy laboratories: Emulating success in the children's health insurance program. *American Journal of Political Science, 50*(2), 294–312. https://doi.org/10.1111/j.1540-5907.2006.00185.x

Volden, C., Ting, M. M., & Carpenter, D. P. (2008). A formal model of learning and policy diffusion. *American Political Science Review, 102*(3), 319–332. https://doi.org/10.1017/s0003055408080271

Walker, J. L. (1969). The diffusion of innovations among the American states. *American Political Science Review, 63*(3), 880–899.

Weaver, D. H. (2007). Thoughts on agenda setting, framing and priming. *Journal of Communications, 57,* 142–147.

Weber, M., Roth, G., & Wittich, C. (1978). *Economy and society: An outline of interpretive sociology* (4th ed.). University of California Press.

Weible, C. M., & Sabatier, P. A. (2005). Comparing policy networks: Marine protected areas in California. *Policy Studies Journal, 33*(2), 181–201.

Wrong, D. H. (1988). *Power: Its forms, bases, and uses.* The University of Chicago Press.

Part II
Education Governance

4 Federal Education Governance

The U.S. Constitution delegates authority over education to state governments. Despite the lack of constitutional authority, the federal government has occupied an increasingly central role in American education. This chapter examines the federal government's role in U.S. education and the influence of that impact. It seeks to answer the following questions: What role does the federal government play in education policy? What is a policy subsystem and who are the key education policy subsystem actors at the federal level? What major federal laws influence education policy? What policy mechanisms does the federal government utilize to influence education policy at the state and local level?

The funding structure of American education highlights the predominant role of state and local actors in establishing, operating, and funding schools and colleges. In 2020–2021, the U.S. federal, state, and local governments spent $1.15 trillion on elementary, secondary, and higher education (Education, 2024). Federal contributions accounted for just 8% of the total; state and local governments provided 92%. Despite limited federal funding, the U.S. government has developed a broad range of policy mechanisms to influence American education.

Power

The United States Constitution and the Federal Role in Education

American national government support of education preceded the establishment of the U.S. Constitution. On July 13, 1787, the Confederation Congress, organized under the Articles of Confederation, adopted the Northwest Ordinance, officially titled "An Ordinance for the Government of the Territory of the United States Northwest of the River Ohio." The Northwest Ordinance is considered one of the key founding documents, together with the U.S. Constitution, Declaration of Independence, and Federalist Papers. The Northwest Ordinance provided a process for achieving statehood for Illinois, Indiana, Michigan, Minnesota, Ohio, and Wisconsin. The Northwest Ordinance articulated that schools and means of education were to be encouraged because religion, morality, and knowledge were necessary to "good government and the happiness of mankind." It required every town to reserve a center lot for public schools and to generate school resources. These rules applied to all states established west of the Mississippi River and therefore influenced the development of 31 U.S. states (Black, 2021).

Although the United States Constitution does not include the word "education," the Tenth and Fourteenth Amendments play a prominent role in American education. On December 15, 1791, three fourths of the states had ratified the 10 amendments known as the

DOI: 10.4324/9781003231561-6

Bill of Rights. The Tenth Amendment states, "The powers not delegated to the United States by the Constitution, nor prohibited by it to the States, are reserved to the States respectively, or to the people." Because public education is not mentioned in the Constitution, the Tenth Amendment delegates education responsibilities to state and local governments.

On July 9, 1868, the Fourteenth Amendment was ratified by the states. It says, in part:

> All persons born or naturalized in the United States, and subject to the jurisdiction thereof, are citizens in the United States and the state wherein they reside. No state shall make or enforce any law which shall abridge the privileges and immunities of citizens of the United States; nor shall any state deprive any person of life, liberty, or property, without due process of law; nor deny to any person within its jurisdiction the equal protection of the law.

Most of the former Confederate states refused to ratify the Fourteenth Amendment, so Congress passed the Reconstruction Act of 1867 mandating the establishment of new governments in those states. It required ratification of the Fourteenth Amendment as a condition of readmission to the Union (Epps, 2006; Foner, 2019; Hannah-Jones et al., 2021).

Federalism

During the American Revolution, the Continental Congress faced enormous problems raising and supplying the army it needed to win the war because each state had to volunteer troops, supplies, and funding. From 1777 to 1789, the United States operated under the Articles of Confederation. The Articles provided each state with one vote in Congress; established no executive branch to enforce legislative acts or judicial branch to adjudicate disputes; and failed to provide the national government with the power to tax, respond to internal rebellions, or regulate foreign and interstate commerce. The 1787 Constitutional Convention sought to address the inherent weaknesses in the Articles of Confederation by establishing a stronger national government. The Constitution's framers were unwilling to assign all authority to a national government because of well-entrenched popular identification with states and well-established state governments that did not want their power diminished.

The Constitutional Convention created a federal system as a compromise between delegates arguing for a unitary national government and those arguing for the status quo of state autonomy and supremacy. In a federal system, powers and functions are divided between the national and state governments. *Federalism* creates two sovereign governments, each with the ability to restrain the power of the other. Article I, Section 8 of the Constitution articulates national government authority, including the power to collect taxes, coin money, declare war, and regulate commerce. Article VI of the Constitution includes the *supremacy clause*, stipulating that all national laws and treaties are the "supreme law of the land." The Tenth Amendment limited national power by reserving to the states or the people all powers not expressly delegated to the national government or denied to the states.

From the ratification of the Constitution to the 1930s, the U.S. federal system was what scholars call *dual federalism*, a division of powers between national and state governments in which states exercise most of the governing authority. In the 1930s, economic and social problems facing the nation, beginning with the Great Depression, altered the relationship between the national and state governments. Scholars refer to this evolved federal system as *cooperative federalism*, in which the federal government provides funding to encourage state and local governments to pursue nationally defined goals.

In the 1960s, U.S. federalism evolved further in the direction of national power as the federal government expanded its use of *categorical grants*, federal funds provided to state and local governments that are earmarked for specific policy purposes (Palmer, 1984). Categorical grants are a mechanism the national government can use to expand beyond its constitutionally defined policy role by financially incentivizing state and local governments to address federal priorities. According to the U.S. Office of Management and Budget, federal grant outlays to state and local governments increased from $2.3 billion to $750 billion between 1950 and 2019 (OMB, 2019). *Regulatory federalism* is the term scholars use to describe the current relationship between the national and state governments.

The Federal Role in Education

From the founding of the nation through the Civil War, the federal role in education was limited primarily to land grants, including 77 million acres of public lands provided to the states for public schools, and mandates for the development of local schools. In 1867, the National Association of State and City School Superintendents petitioned Congress to establish a Bureau of Education. President Andrew Johnson signed legislation giving the federal government a role in the collection of information on schools to assist state education systems.

Through the 19th century, the federal government played a larger role in higher education than in elementary and secondary education. In 1862, President Abraham Lincoln signed the Morrill Act to donate land to states so they could endow or establish agricultural colleges. In 1890, the second Morrill Act provided an annual appropriation to each state to support land grant colleges, forbade racial discrimination in admissions policies for colleges receiving federal funds, and required states establish 19 Black land-grant institutions.

The first half of the 20th century witnessed a similarly limited role for the federal government in American education. The Smith-Hughes Act of 1917 provided funding for vocational schools to prepare students for the workforce. Through World War II, the primary federal role in education continued to be higher education funding. In 1944, the Servicemen's Readjustment Act, commonly known as the G.I. Bill, provided postsecondary education benefits to World War II veterans. More than eight million veterans used the postsecondary benefits provided by the G.I. Bill to attend a U.S. college or university.

Two monumental shifts in the status quo in 1950s led to a considerable expansion of the federal government's role in elementary, secondary, and postsecondary education during the 1960s. First, the 1954 Supreme Court decision in *Brown v. Board of Education* mandated the desegregation of public schools and provided the federal government with a legal precedent and civil rights mandate to enforce equal access to education. Second, on October 4, 1957, the Soviet Union launched the Sputnik satellite into Earth's orbit, beginning the U.S.-Soviet space race. The United States interpreted the launch as a serious threat to American national security and economic dominance, prompting it to make considerable investments in federal education and research.

These events spurred federal involvement in education to promote American national security, economic competitiveness, and equal access to education. National political leaders realized the states alone could not provide the education resources and legal protections necessary to ensure American security and prosperity. This resulted in a series of federal legislative acts. In 1958, Congress passed the National Education Act, which provided student loans for postsecondary study in science, mathematics, and foreign languages.

The civil rights movement of the 1960s also increased the role of the federal government in public education. Constitutionally, states maintain authority over education, but the federal government has authority over protecting civil rights. Congress expanded the role of the federal government in protecting civil rights through a series of legislative acts in the 1960s and 1970s. The Civil Rights Act of 1964 called for the desegregation of schools by prohibiting schools from discriminating on the basis of color, race, religion, or national origin. In 1965, Congress passed the Elementary and Secondary Education Act and the Higher Education Act as part of President Lyndon Johnson's War on Poverty initiatives.

Formal Actors

Legislative Branch

Article I of the U.S. Constitution establishes the legislative branch, making it the first branch of government and the center of American democracy. The 1787 Constitutional Convention reached a stalemate when states with larger populations demanded congressional representation based on population and smaller states demanded equal representation. The Great Compromise created a *bicameral legislature*, a legislative body with two chambers representing different constituencies. Members of the House of Representatives, the *lower chamber*, would be allocated according to state population. In the Senate, the *upper chamber*, states would have two representatives regardless of population size. House elections occur every 2 years, with all 435 seats up for election. Senate elections occur every 6 years, with approximately one third of the seats up for election every 2 years.

In 1929, Congress passed the Permanent Apportionment Act, fixing the number of House seats at 435. The Constitution required at least one representative per state based on state population. This type of electoral system is called *proportional representation*, as parties gain seats in proportion to the number of votes cast for that party. The population growth of the United States led Congress to cap the number of House seats at a manageable number so it could continue to legislate. Apportionment is the process of allocating the 435 House seats among the 50 states. Every 10 years, the United States Census Bureau conducts a *decennial census* to determine the U.S. population. The census results are used to calculate the number of House members each state is entitled to. During the past several decades, this has caused a shift of House seats away from regions with declining population like the Northeast and Midwest and toward regions with growing populations like the South and Southwest. For example, since 1980 Texas has gained 11 House seats and New York has lost 13. States have the authority to draw congressional districts. Redrawing congressional districts has become a highly political process in which the state legislative majority party often seeks to gain advantage by drawing districts to maximize their party's congressional seat numbers.

The Constitution bestows Congress with both enumerated and implied powers. *Enumerated powers* are those expressly authorized to Congress by the Constitution. Article I, Section 8 lists the enumerated powers, including collect taxes, pay debts and borrow money, regulate commerce, coin money, establish a post office, protect patents and copyrights, establish lower courts, declare war, raise and support an Army and Navy, enact legislation, confirm or reject presidential appointments, regulate interstate commerce, and investigate. The House of Representatives has the exclusive power to initiate revenue bills, impeach federal officials, and elect the president in case of an Electoral College tie. The Senate has sole power to confirm presidential appointments, ratify treaties, and try impeachment cases referred by the House. The authority to enact legislation is Congress's preeminent power.

Implied powers are powers exercised by Congress that are not expressly granted in the Constitution. Implied powers are deemed necessary to perform constitutionally granted powers. Implied powers derive from the *elastic clause*, also known as the *necessary and proper clause*, contained in Article I, Section 9 of the Constitution. In 1816, Congress established the Second National Bank to regulate state currency. Maryland imposed a tax on the Second National Bank under its practice of taxing all banks not chartered by the state. James W. McCulloch, a federal cashier at the Baltimore branch of the U.S. bank, refused to pay the tax, and the state of Maryland filed suit against him. The state appeals court held that the Second National Bank was unconstitutional because the Constitution did not enumerate a power to charter a bank. In 1819, the Supreme Court ruled that chartering a bank was an implied power of the Constitution under Article I, Section 8: Congress has the authority to make laws that are "necessary and proper" to carry out their enumerated powers.

Congressional Organization

The 535 members of the United States Congress represent nearly 330 million people, each with different political and policy priorities. To represent their constituents and govern, Congress must coordinate the actions of hundreds of representatives with highly polarized political beliefs, resolve conflicts, and collectively act. To overcome these organizational challenges, the Congress primarily utilizes two institutional structures: political parties and the committee system.

Political parties are a fundamental aspect of legislative organization, despite their absence from the Constitution. The party system embodies the key organizing system that constructs political coalitions to overcome obstacles to collective action. Political parties are institutions that help political actors achieve goals including reelection, policy achievements, and power and prestige within government (Aldrich & Battista, 2002; Mayhew, 1974). Political parties provide members of Congress with a shared reputation under the party label, which incentivizes party members to work together to achieve policy goals and ultimately reelection.

On January 3, 2021, the 117th Congress began its new term. According to the Twentieth Amendment to the Constitution, Congress convenes in odd-numbered years following congressional elections the previous November.[1] Members of each party start the session by electing congressional leaders. The *party caucus* (Democrats) and *conference* (Republicans) are meetings of all party members in each chamber. The majority, referring to the party controlling a majority of the House or Senate seats, and the minority, the party with the second most members, meet in each chamber to vote for party leadership. The party leadership system is a hierarchy of power in which members of each party concede authority to a subset of party leaders to further their goals of reelection, legislative achievements, and increasing power within the institution. The concentration of power in a centralized authority helps maintain party discipline and make defections costly.

The House of Representatives majority party chooses the speaker of the House, majority leader, majority whip, and assistant speaker. Table 4.1 identifies the people who serve in these roles. The *speaker of the House*, the presiding officer, administrative head, and leader of the majority party, has agenda-setting authority through legislative scheduling. The speaker alone determines which bills will be put to a vote in the chamber. The concentration of power in the House speaker means bills that have significant bipartisan support but split the votes of the majority party will not be submitted for a vote. The leader of the majority party is incentivized to only allow votes on the floor that the majority party favors.

The *majority leader*, the top leadership position in the Senate, has an agenda-setting role similar to the speaker of the House through the power of legislative scheduling. According to Senate rules, the majority leader has the privilege to decide what legislation the Senate

Table 4.1 House of Representatives Leadership Positions, April 2024

Republicans	Democrats
Speaker of the house: Mike Johnson (LA)	
Majority leader: Steve Scalise (LA)	Minority leader: Hakeem Jeffries (NY)
Majority whip: Tom Emmer (MN)	Minority whip: Katherine Clark (MA)
Assistant speaker: Elise Stefanik (NY)	Minority caucus chair: Pete Aguilar (CA)
Policy Committee chair: Gary Palmer (AL)	Assistant leader: James Clyburn (SC)

Table 4.2 Senate Leadership Positions and Current Members, April 2024

Democrats	Republicans
Vice president: Kamala Harris	
President pro tempore: Patty Murray (WA)	
Majority leader: Charles Schumer (NY)	Minority leader: Mitch McConnell (KY)
Majority whip: Dick Durbin (IL)	Minority whip: John Thune (SD)
Policy and Communications Committee chair: Debbie Stabenow (MI)	Minority conference chair: John Barrasso (WY)
Majority caucus chair: Debbie Stabenow (MI)	Minority Policy Committee chair: Joni Ernst (IA)
Vice chairs of the conference	Vice chair of the conference: Shelley Moore
Mark Warner (VA)	Capito (WV)
Elizabeth Warren (MA)	

will consider. Table 4.2 identifies the Senate majority and minority party leadership positions. The House and Senate leadership also have the authority to appoint members to congressional committees.

The congressional committee system is the second organizational structure utilized to overcome collective action problems. The congressional *committee system* divides labor and gives each member the opportunity to specialize. Members pursue committee assignments that appeal to their constituents, align with their professional expertise, and achieve their policy goals. For example, Appropriations and Ways and Means, the committees with jurisdiction over the budget, taxation, and revenue raising, are dominated by members interested in reelection. Members join the Agriculture Committees because it appeals to their constituents and helps them get reelected. Members join the Education Committees because they are interested in impacting education policy (Bullock, 1976). Party leaders want members to win reelection so they can achieve majority control; therefore, they defer to members' committee assignment preferences. Committee service allows members to develop expertise and have more influence on policy issues under their jurisdiction. Committee membership serves both individuals and the institution. Members benefit by developing policy expertise, allowing them to take a leadership role on issues significant to their constituency and improving their ability to achieve their three goals of reelection, policy influence, and prestige and power within Congress. Congress as an institution benefits from individual members who provide guidance to other members in their area of expertise. The congressional committee system is designed to achieve both institutional and member goals.

Congress divides its legislative jurisdictions into approximately 250 committees and subcommittees. There are three main types of committees: standing, select, and joint. *Standing committees* are permanent committees that exist across congressional terms unless they are explicitly terminated. Standing committees consider bills; maintain oversight of agencies, programs, and activities; and recommend funding levels for government agencies within their jurisdiction. Standing committees have jurisdiction over a specific set of legislative topics. The jurisdictions of the standing committees typically correspond with executive branch departments. For example, Department of Education authorizations and appropriations fall under the jurisdiction of the House Education and Labor Committee and the Senate Health, Education, Labor, and Pensions Committee. *Select or special committees* are established for emerging issues that do not clearly fit within the existing standing committee jurisdictions or span multiple committee jurisdictions. For example, the House of Representatives currently has a Select Committee on the Climate Crisis that spans the jurisdictions of numerous House standing committees. *Joint committees* include House and Senate members, deal with narrow jurisdictional issues, and lack the authority to report legislation. Table 4.3 identifies the House and Senate standing committees in the 118th Congress.

Legislative bills are referred to the committee of jurisdiction by the speaker of the House or the Senate majority leader. Bills are placed on the calendar of the committee to which they have been assigned. The *committee chair*, who serves as the parliamentary head of the committee, sets the committee agenda and presides over its meetings. Committees and their members are agents of the party and the institution. Committees are the step in the legislative process when most proposed bills die. Table 4.4 provides the percentage of bills introduced and enacted in each of the past four congressional terms. On average, 1%–3% of congressional bills get enacted. For example, in the 117th Congress, 16,833 bills were introduced and 212 were enacted into law. On average, fewer than 1,000 bills get acted upon by the committees of jurisdiction, which is 5%–10% of introduced bills. Committees are the gatekeepers of the legislative process and are where most policy proposals fail.

Table 4.3 The Standing Committees of the 118th Congress

House	Senate
Agriculture	Agriculture, Nutrition, and Forestry
Appropriations	Appropriations
Armed Services	Armed Services
Budget	Banking, Housing, and Urban Affairs
Education and the Workforce	Budget
Energy and Commerce	Commerce, Science, and Transportation
Ethics	Energy and Natural Resources
Financial Services	Environment and Public Works
Foreign Affairs	Finance
Homeland Security	Foreign Relations
House Administration	Health, Education, Labor, and Pensions
Judiciary	Homeland Security and Governmental Affairs
Natural Resources	Indian Affairs
Oversight and Accountability	Judiciary
Rules	Rules and Administration
Science, Space, and Technology	Small Business and Entrepreneurship
Small Business	Veterans' Affairs
Transportation and Infrastructure	
Veterans' Affairs	
Ways and Means	

Table 4.4 Number of Congressional Bills Introduced and Enacted (114th–117th Congress)

Congress	Dates	Proposed bills	Enacted legislation	Percentage of bills enacted
117th	2021–2023	16,833	212	1%
116th	2019–2021	16,601	344	2%
115th	2017–2019	13,556	443	3%
114th	2015–2017	12,063	329	3%

Note: Data from www.govtrack.us/congress/bills/statistics

House and Senate Education Committees

The House and Senate maintain standing committees with jurisdiction over education policy issues. The House Education and the Workforce Committee has jurisdiction over federal education programs and initiatives from preschool to higher education. Table 4.5 provides an overview of the committee's areas of education policy jurisdiction, including elementary and secondary education, postsecondary education, and adult education. The committee also maintains oversight of the U.S. Department of Education and educational research, among other related policy issues.

The Education and the Workforce Committee maintains four subcommittees, including the Early Childhood, Elementary, and Secondary Education Subcommittee and the Higher Education and Workforce Investment Subcommittee. The Early Childhood, Elementary, and Secondary Education Subcommittee has jurisdiction over elementary and secondary education. The Higher Education and Workforce Investment Subcommittee has jurisdiction over education and workforce development beyond the secondary level.

The Senate Health, Education, Labor, and Pensions (HELP) Committee is comprised of 21 Senators, 11 Democrats and 10 Republicans. It has jurisdiction over education, health care, labor and employment laws, workplace health and safety, and retirement policies. The committee was established in 1869 as the Committee on Education. The HELP Committee has three subcommittees, including the Subcommittee on Children and Families, which has primary jurisdiction over education issues including Head Start, individuals with disabilities, and student loans. The HELP Committee has jurisdiction over federal education legislation including the Elementary and Secondary Education Act and the Higher Education Act. The HELP Committee's educational jurisdictions mirror those of the House Education and the Workforce Committee.

Executive Branch

Article II, Section 1 of the Constitution vests executive power in the president of the United States. The executive branch is composed of the Executive Office of the President, the Cabinet, and independent federal agencies and commissions. The Executive Office of the President is managed by the White House chief of staff and is composed of offices and agencies that directly support the president, including the White House Office, National Security Council, and Office of Management and Budget.

Article II, Section 2 of the Constitution establishes the Cabinet's role to advise the president. The *Cabinet* is composed of the vice president, 15 executive department secretaries, and 10 Cabinet-level officials. Table 4.6 lists all the permanent members of the Cabinet of the United States. The president has the authority to designate additional positions as Cabinet-level officials. The Cabinet currently includes 10 cabinet-level officials: the

Table 4.5 House Committee on Education and the Workforce Policy Jurisdiction

Subcommittee	Jurisdiction
Elementary and Secondary Education	Career and technical education
	Elementary and Secondary Education Act (ESEA)
	School choice
	Special education including the Individuals with Disabilities Education Act (IDEA)
	Teacher quality and training
	School safety and alcohol and drug abuse prevention
	Scientifically based reading instruction
	Vocational and technical education
Postsecondary Education	Career and technical education
	Higher Education Act (HEA)
	College access for low- and middle-income students
	Agricultural colleges
	Student loans
	Title IX of the Education Amendments of 1972
	Workforce Innovation and Opportunity Act
Early Childhood Education	Head Start
	Childcare and afterschool programs
	Child Care and Development Block Grant Act
	Preschool and early care
Educational Research	National Center for Education Research
	Institute of Education Sciences
Adult Education	Citizenship education and training
	Twenty-first century learning centers
	Literacy education
Child Nutrition	School lunch
	Child nutrition programs
U.S. Department of Education	Financial and program oversight
At-Risk Youth	At-risk youth programs and services
	Child abuse prevention
	Child adoption
Antipoverty	Community services block grant
	Low Income Home Energy Assistance Program

Environmental Protection Agency administrator, Office of Management and Budget director, National Intelligence director, Central Intelligence Agency director, trade representative, ambassador to the United Nations, Council of Economic Advisors chair, Small Business Administration chair, Office of Science and Technology Policy director, and the White House chief of staff.

Department of Education

The Department of Education (DOE) is a Cabinet-level department of the United States. The DOE mission statement identifies four core roles: (a) establishing policies on federal financial aid for education and distributing and monitoring those funds, (b) collecting data on America's schools and disseminating research, (c) focusing national attention on key educational issues, and (d) prohibiting discrimination and ensuring equal access to education. These functions represent a very limited scope of authority. Most countries utilize a centralized education governance structure in which the national government administers

Table 4.6 Cabinet-Level Officials, April 2024

Department	Established	Employees	Total budget (billions)	Secretary
State	1789	30,000	58.1	Antony Blinken
Treasury	1789	100,000	16.4	Janet Yellen
Interior	1849	70,000	35	Deb Haaland
Agriculture	1862	100,000	242	Tom Vilsack
Justice	1870	115,000	37.5	Merrick Garland
Commerce	1903	41,000	16.3	Gina Raimondo
Labor	1913	15,000	97.5	Julie Su
Defense	1947	3,200,000	852	Lloyd Austin
Health and Human Services	1953	65,000	1,772	Xavier Becerra
Housing and Urban Development	1965	9,000	61.7	Marcia Fudge
Transportation	1967	55,000	145	Pete Buttigieg
Energy	1977	10,000	45.8	Jennifer Granholm
Education	1979	4,400	79.6	Miguel Cardona
Veterans Affairs	1989	235,000	308.5	Denis McDonough
Homeland Security	2002	250,000	101.6	Alejandro Mayorkas

elementary, secondary, and postsecondary education. In the United States, the DOE is limited to monitoring education funding and financial aid, data collection, research dissemination, and prohibiting discrimination in educational institutions.

In 1867, the DOE was established to collect data and provide consultation to the nation's schools. Despite the department's limited authority and funding – it had only four employees and a budget of $15,000 – it immediately faced substantial backlash. In the post–Civil War era, education became conflated with race politics. Congress required Confederate states to include education for all students, regardless of color, as a condition of readmission to the Union. From 1865 to 1877, the U.S. Army occupied the South to restore the Southern states to the Union and protect Black citizens against violence. In 1865, Congress established the Freedmen's Bureau, whose many responsibilities included establishing schools for freed Blacks. Conservatives viewed any federal role in education as further control of the national government over the Southern states. Congress, with support from President Andrew Johnson, who was hostile to Reconstruction, demoted the DOE to an office in the Department of the Interior. For more than 100 years, the federal government would play a minor role in American education.

In 1979, the Department of Education Organization Act established the U.S. Department of Education with primary responsibility for administering federal elementary, secondary, and postsecondary education programs. President Jimmy Carter claimed education represented the country's most important national investment, involved more than 60 million Americans, and would determine Americans' economic future. In the 1976 presidential campaign, the National Education Association endorsed Carter – the first such endorsement in its history – due in part to his promise to establish a Cabinet-level education department. The NEA endorsement further politicized the issue, resulting in Republican Party opposition. Despite numerous attempts to dismantle the DOE, today it employs 4,400 and has a budget of $79.6 billion.

The secretary of education oversees the DOE and is the president's primary advisor on issues related to American education. The secretary is nominated by the president and confirmed by the Senate. Cabinet secretaries are in the line of presidential succession following the vice president, speaker of the House of Representatives, and the Senate president pro tempore. The cabinet members follow the order in which the departments were established, meaning the secretary of education is 15th in line for the presidency.

The DOE encompasses six program offices that oversee and implement educational services (see Figure 4.1). The Office of Elementary and Secondary Education supports local education agencies including public and private preschools, elementary, and secondary education institutions in underserved communities. The Office of English Language Acquisition supports English language learners and immigrant students in their attainment of English proficiency, preservation of heritage languages, and bilingual education and disseminates best practices through the National Clearinghouse for English Language Acquisition. The Office of Special Education and Rehabilitation Services supports programs to improve early childhood education and employment outcomes.

The Office of Postsecondary Education helps colleges and universities expand access, increase college completion rates, and improve global competitiveness. The Office of Federal Student Aid administers federal financial aid programs including loans, grants, and work-study and disseminates financial aid information to students, parents, postsecondary institutions, and lending institutions. The Office of Career, Technical, and Adult Education administers programs in adult literacy and education, career and technical education, and community colleges and workforce development.

The Office of Civil Rights (OCR) ensures equal access to education in all educational institutions that receive federal aid, including elementary and secondary schools, state education

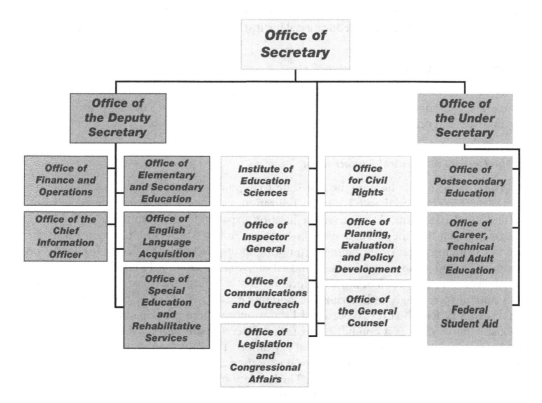

Figure 4.1 U.S. Department of Education Organizational Structure

Table 4.7 Department of Education Office of Civil Rights Regional Enforcement Offices

OCR regional office	State, district, or territory jurisdiction
Atlanta, GA	AL, FL, GA, TN
Boston, MA	CT, MA, ME, NH, RI, VT
Chicago, IL	IL, IN, IA, MN, ND, WI
Cleveland, OH	OH, MI
Dallas, TX	LA, MS, TX
Denver, CO	AZ, CO, NM, UT, WY
Kansas City, MO	AR, KS, MO, NE, OK, SD
New York, NY	NJ, NY, Puerto Rico, U.S. Virgin Islands
Philadelphia, PA	DE, KY, MD, PA, WV
San Francisco, CA	CA
Seattle, WA	AK, HI, ID, MT, NV, OR, WA, American Samoa, Guam, Northern Marianas Islands
Washington, DC	DC, NC, SC, VA

agencies, colleges and universities, vocational schools, proprietary schools, and state vocational rehabilitation agencies. The OCR enforces discrimination based on race, color, and national origin (Title VI of the Civil Rights Act), sex (Title IX of the Education Amendments of 1972), disability (Section 504 of the Rehabilitation Act of 1973), and age (Age Discrimination Act of 1975). Table 4.7 identifies the location of OCR's 12 regional offices and their jurisdiction over states, districts, and territories. The OCR district offices investigate discrimination claims against any educational institution receiving federal financial assistance.

Federal Education Laws

The DOE has primary responsibility for administering federal education programs to support elementary, secondary, and postsecondary education. Most federal education funding and programs are authorized by the education laws outlined in this section.

Perkins Career and Technical Education Act

In 1905, Massachusetts became the first state to appoint a commission, the Massachusetts Commission on Industrial and Technical Education, calling for the expansion of technical and industrial education. As vocational education expanded across many states and cities, Congress established the Commission on National Aid to Vocational Education with the goal of expanding vocational training, promoting industrial efficiency, decreasing labor and social unrest, and promoting a higher standard of living (Friedel, 2011). In 1917, Congress passed the Smith-Hughes Vocational Education Act as a response to a shortage of skilled labor and an increasingly industrialized economy (Friedel, 2011). The Smith-Hughes Act established a Federal Board of Vocational Education, required participating states to establish a state institution as a conduit between the federal board and local districts, and provided matching grant-in-aid for vocational education. The matching grant was designed to incentivize states to increase their vocational education spending on teacher salaries, teacher preparation, and Federal Board activities. The legislation proved effective at expanding vocational program education, with agriculture program enrollments increasing from 31,000 in 1920 to 853,000 in 1970 (Scott & Sarkees-Wircenski, 2004). The Smith-Hughes Act was reauthorized in 1984 as the Carl D. Perkins Act, named after Kentucky Democratic Congressman Carl D. Perkins.

Elementary and Secondary Education Act

Federal education legislation had been repeatedly defeated between the Civil War and 1965 due to concerns about federal government involvement in state and local education. On April 11, 1965, President Lyndon Johnson signed the Elementary and Secondary Education Act (ESEA), saying it "represents a major new commitment of the federal government to quality and equality in the schooling that we offer our young people" (Johnson, 1965). The bill provided approximately $10 billion (in 2022 dollars) in federal grants for state departments of education, education research, and school libraries. While the ESEA provided federal education funding to state governments, it did not fundamentally alter the relationship between the federal and state governments. Education policymaking remained decentralized, with management of public schools remaining in state and local hands. ESEA's original purpose was to improve educational opportunity for the poor through funds sent to low-income districts (Jennings, 2001).

Table 4.8 describes the ESEA titles and their purpose. Title V provided $25 million to state education agencies to improve their capacity to apply for and administer federal education grants. State agencies had to evolve from simple administrative agencies to more professionalized institutions capable of collecting educational data, applying for federal grants, and administering the increasingly complex programs.

ESEA appropriations and other federal education funding has never accounted for more than 10% of total elementary and secondary education spending, but the strings attached to

Table 4.8 Elementary and Secondary Education Act Titles and Purpose

Title	*Purpose*
Title I: Improving the academic achievement of disadvantaged students	Authorizes funding to school districts with a high percentage of low-income students based on the number of students who qualify for free or reduced-price lunch.
Title II: Preparing, training, and recruiting high-quality teachers, principals, and other school leaders	Authorizes programs that prepare, train, and recruit high-quality teachers, principals, and other school leaders.
Title III: Language instruction for English language learners and immigrant students	Authorizes programs that promote English language acquisition, language enhancement, and academic achievement.
Title IV: 21st century schools	Authorizes block grants for student support and academic enrichment, 21st century community learning centers, charter and magnet schools, and family enhancement in education programs.
Title V: State innovation and local flexibility	Authorizes programs for state and local education agencies and rural education initiatives.
Title VI: Indian, Native Hawaiian, and Alaska Native education	Authorizes Indian, Native Hawaiian, and Alaska Native education programs.
Title VII: Impact aid	Authorizes funding designed to assist local school districts that have lost property tax revenue due to the presence of tax-exempt federal property.
Title VIII: General provisions	

it have leveraged significant changes in state and local education policy. Federal policymakers have used the grant-in-aid system to incentivize states to pursue federal education goals.

Prior to the 1994 ESEA reauthorization, the federal–state relationship on education policy was characterized by cooperation. A considerable portion of state education agency budgets came from federal appropriations (McGuinn, 2015). The federal government's primary role from 1965 to 1994 was to pursue the civil rights of minoritized students, English language learners, and special education students based on the Fourteenth Amendment to the Constitution and several Supreme Court rulings between 1950 and 1975 (McGuinn, 2015).

Higher Education Act

In 1965, Congress passed the Higher Education Act (HEA) to expand postsecondary opportunity and affordability, particularly for underserved populations. HEA authorizes federal financial support for student aid programs; institutional aid; and services and supports to underserved, international, graduate, and professional students. Congressional reauthorizations are typically every 5 years. Since its last reauthorization in 2013, the HEA has been authorized through a series of temporary extensions. Table 4.9 describes the purpose of the HEA titles.

The HEA is credited with making U.S. higher education accessible to millions of students via grants, loans, and work-study. In 2023, the DOE expanded Pell grant access to more than 5.2 million recipients, more than a third of all undergraduate students. More than 44 million students have paid for higher education using federal Stafford loans. The HEA designates Title I schools as postsecondary institutions that have been authorized to receive

Table 4.9 Higher Education Act Titles

Titles	Purpose
Title I: General provisions	Defines higher education institutions; establishes general provisions including antidiscrimination, student speech, and accrediting agencies; and requires the collection of data on college costs and prices.
Title II: Teacher quality enhancement	Authorizes grants for improving teacher education programs, strengthening teacher recruitment and training, and state and IHE reporting requirements.
Title III: Institutional aid	Provides support for less-advantaged institutions serving low-income and underserved populations including historically Black college and universities.
Title IV: Student assistance	Authorizes student federal assistance including Pell grants, Perkins loans, supplemental educational opportunity grants, family education loans, Stafford loans, direct loans, PLUS loans, consolidated loans, and federal work-study programs. Also authorizes programs including the TRIO programs, High School Equivalency Program, and the College Assistance Migrant Program.
Title V: Developing institutions	Authorizes grants to Hispanic-serving institutions with a minimum population of 25% full-time, Hispanic undergraduate student enrollment.
Title VI: International education programs	Authorizes international and foreign language studies programs and business and international education programs including programs, centers, and fellowships.
Title VII: Graduate and postsecondary improvement programs	Authorizes graduate education programs and funds for improving postsecondary education.

direct federal financial assistance including student aid programs. The HEA has made college accessible to millions of underserved students per year who would not otherwise have afforded higher education.

Individuals With Disabilities Education Act

In 1975, Congress passed the Individuals with Disabilities Act (IDEA), originally the Education for all Handicapped Children Act (EHA). IDEA authorizes federal funds for special education and related services and extends rights to children with disabilities. IDEA establishes how more than eight million public school children receive early intervention, special education, and related services. Table 4.10 provides an overview of IDEA's four parts (Dragoo, 2019). Prior to 1975, 1.8 million disabled children were excluded from public schools. More than two thirds of children with disabilities spend at least 80% of their school day in a general education classroom.

IDEA guarantees that all children with disabilities are entitled to special education services as part of a free appropriate public education. To meet the needs of children with disabilities, public schools are required to work with students and their guardians to create an individualized education plan (IEP), a legal document tailored to meet the individual needs of a student with disabilities. Children are identified as possibly requiring special education services by a teacher, parent, or student. The student is evaluated in areas related to the child's suspected disability. A team of qualified professionals and the parents review the test results and determine whether the student is eligible for disability services. If the parents disagree with the evaluation, they can obtain an independent educational evaluation. If the student is found eligible for services as defined by IDEA, the school team must meet within 30 days to create the student's IEP. The school is responsible for ensuring the IEP is implemented as written and progress is measured toward annual goals. The student's IEP is reviewed annually to determine whether it requires revision. IDEA regulations require each student to be reevaluated every 3 years to determine eligibility. The IEP includes current academic performance, annual goals, special education and related services, participation with nondisabled children, participation in state or districtwide tests, dates and places where services will be administered, transition service needs, and how progress will be measured. The IEP team is typically composed of the student (as appropriate), special education teacher or provider, regular education teacher, school system representative, a person qualified to interpret the evaluation results or with special knowledge about the child, and parents. IDEA does not apply to higher education institutions, so a student's IEP does not transition with the student to a postsecondary education environment.

IDEA prioritizes keeping children with disabilities in a general education setting. It requires a least restrictive environment (LRE) standard, meaning children with disabilities are

Table 4.10 IDEA Structure

IDEA part	Description
Part A	Describes general provisions, purposes, and definitions.
Part B	Authorizes provisions to school-aged children, including state grants.
Part C	Authorizes provisions to infants and toddlers, including state grants.
Part D	Authorizes provisions and requirements for national activities to improve education for children with disabilities.

educated with nondisabled children to the maximum extent possible. This guiding principle means that removal of children with disabilities from the general educational environment occurs only "if the nature or severity of the disability is such that education in regular classes with the use of supplementary aids and services cannot be achieved satisfactorily" (§ 1412 (a)(5) of U.S. Code Title 20). The LRE standard promotes socialization and integration of disabled students with their nondisabled peers to learn critical social skills, friendships, and belonging. Figure 4.2 illustrates placement options from the least restrictive environment on the left, the general education classroom, to the most restrictive environment on the right. In determining the education environment, the IEP team considers benefit to the student, effect on peers, appropriateness and inclusion, and use of supplementary aids and services. The LRE standard places additional burdens on teachers to provide the necessary accommodations to support students with disabilities in a general classroom setting.

Education Sciences Reform Act

In 2002, Congress passed the Education Sciences Reform Act (ESRA), updating the federal government's data collection and research on U.S. education. Part A of ESRA established the Institute of Education Sciences, an independent research institute that provides scientific evidence to improve education practice and policy. Part B established the National Center for Education Research to support rigorous education research through national research centers. Part C established the National Center for Education Statistics, which collects and analyzes public school district finance data and conducts international education comparisons. Part D established the National Center for Education Evaluation and Regional Assistance to evaluate federal education programs and provide technical assistance to educational agencies, state boards of education, local school boards, and school administrations. Part E established the National Center for Special Education Research to sponsor research for students with disabilities and support the implementation of IDEA. ESRA also authorized the National Assessment of Education Progress (NAEP) to measure student academic achievement in reading, mathematics, and other subjects. The NAEP assessment is conducted every 2 years in Grades 4 and 8 in mathematics and reading and at regular intervals for Grade 12. NAEP measures student achievement over time to track changes in relation to established content frameworks.

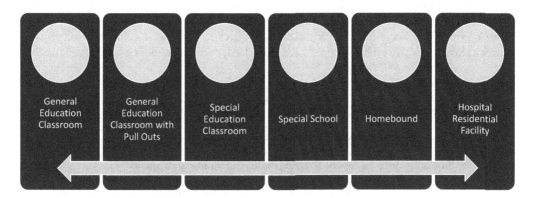

Figure 4.2 Continuum of IDEA Least Restrictive Environment Educational Placements

Protection of Student and Parental Rights

The Civil Rights Act of 1964

The Civil Rights Act (CRA) of 1964 prohibits discrimination based on race, color, religion, or sex. The CRA prohibits racial segregation from public services including public schools and colleges, libraries, parks, recreation systems, restaurants, hotels, businesses, performance halls, hospitals, and medical facilities. Title VI addresses discrimination in federally funded programs. Title IV prohibits discrimination based on race, color, national origin, sex, and religion in public schools and institutions of higher education. The CRA represents a federal effort to end discrimination in education.

Title IX of the Education Amendments of 1972

In 1972, Congress reauthorized the HEA and the ESEA with amendments including Title IX, which prohibited discrimination on the basis of sex in federally assisted education programs or activities. While much of the public discourse and academic research has focused on Title IX's application to athletics, it also applies to academic programs, admissions, counseling, employment, financial aid, grading, housing, student services, and vocational education. The purpose of Title IX is to reduce systemic barriers limiting females' employment and educational opportunities. Title IX defines discrimination on the basis of sex to include sexual harassment, sexual violence, sexual assault, sexual battery, and sexual coercion. Schools are required to develop and distribute a policy prohibiting sex discrimination, designate a Title IX coordinator, and publish a procedure for filing sex discrimination complaints.

Rehabilitation Act of 1973

The Rehabilitation Act of 1973 provided the first civil rights protections for individuals with disabilities (Brougher, 2010). Section 504 of the Rehabilitation Act prohibits discrimination against individuals with disabilities in any program receiving federal financial assistance, including private elementary and secondary schools and colleges and universities. Section 504 requires school districts to provide access to programs and activities for anyone with a physical or mental impairment that substantially limits one or more major life activities, including learning. School districts are required to provide eligible students with special education services to ensure they receive a free appropriate public education. A Section 504 plan lists the accommodations an eligible student would receive to access academic and extracurricular activities. Unlike an IEP, a 504 plan does not identify measurable learning goals, educational modifications, or how progress will be measured. The plan pertains to assurance of equal access to education rather than specialized instruction.

Family Educational Rights and Privacy Act of 1974

In 1974, Congress passed the Family Educational Rights and Privacy Act (FERPA), which regulates access to educational information and disclosure of student education records. Elementary, secondary, and postsecondary schools manage student records including contact information, disciplinary actions, grades, and health. Educational institutions receiving DOE funds, including private and independent schools, are prohibited from releasing children's education records without the written consent of their parents. Consent transfers to the student once they turn 18 years old or enroll in a postsecondary education institution.

FERPA defines educational records as materials that are directly related to a student and are maintained by an education agency or institution. FERPA exempts certain materials from the release prohibition, including employment, instructional, and law enforcement records.

FERPA requires schools to establish procedures to allow access to records within 45 days of a request and a process to challenge records' contents to confirm their accuracy. Schools are allowed to disclose student records without consent to certain parties under particular circumstances, including to accrediting agencies, school officials for legitimate educational interest, judicial orders, health and safety officials in an emergency, and state and local authorities to comply with specific laws. FERPA is intended to give parents and eligible students more control over their educational records and protect their privacy. Violation of FERPA can result in loss of DOE institutional funding.

Protection of Pupil Rights Amendment of 1978

In 1978, Congress passed the Protection of Pupil Rights Amendment (PPRA), which requires parental consent before student participation in the collection and use of information for marketing, surveys, or physical exams. Parental consent is required for students before participating in a survey funded by the DOE if the following information is collected: political affiliation, mental or psychological health information, income, sex behavior, appraisals of family relationships, privileged communication, religious practices, affiliations, or beliefs. PPRA rights transfer to the student when they turn 18 years old.

Title II of the Americans With Disabilities Act of 1990

In 1990, Congress passed the Americans with Disabilities Act (ADA), prohibiting discrimination against individuals with disabilities in employment, public services, public accommodations, transportation, and telecommunication. Title II prohibits discrimination based on disability by state and local governments including public school districts, public colleges and universities, and public libraries. Title III prohibits discrimination based on disability by privately funded elementary, secondary, and postsecondary education institutions. If a private school does not receive any federal assistance, including student or family federal financial assistance, then Title II does not apply.

Unlike IDEA, the ADA and Section 504 of the Rehabilitation Act of 1973 are federal civil rights laws that apply to postsecondary institutions. Colleges and universities are required to provide students with disabilities services that allow an equal opportunity to learn. Students and their families are required to register with the college or university disability services office to receive accommodations. The change in legal protections shifts the burden from the school to the student. Higher education administrators have broad discretion over student eligibility for accommodations.

Judicial Branch

Article III, Section I of the Constitution established the U.S. Supreme Court but left the development of lower court systems to Congress and the states. It reads:

> The judicial Power of the United States, shall be vested in one supreme Court, and in such inferior Courts as the Congress may from time to time ordain and establish. The Judges, both of the supreme and inferior Courts, shall hold their Offices during good Behavior,

and shall, at stated Times, receive for their Services, a Compensation, which shall not be diminished during their Continuance in Office.

In 1789, Congress, in one of its first official actions, established the federal court system by passing the Judiciary Act. In 1891, due largely to the expansion of the United States, Congress created a tier of appellate circuit courts.

The United States court system consists of both federal and state courts. More than 99% of all court cases are heard in state courts. Chapter 5 provides a thorough overview of the state court system and its impact on education litigation (see Table 4.11 for a summary). The federal courts have jurisdiction over cases involving federal laws, treaties, or the U.S. Constitution and violations of federal statutes. The federal court system consists of three main levels: district courts, circuit courts, and the Supreme Court of the United States.

The district courts, the first tier of federal courts, are divided into 94 judicial districts mainly based on geography. The district courts are the general trial courts of the federal system and the starting point for any case deriving from civil and criminal federal statutes. Each court has both a United States district judge, appointed by the president and confirmed by the Senate, and a U.S. attorney who serves as the district prosecutor for the federal government.

District court cases can be appealed to the federal circuit courts. The circuit courts divide the country into 13 federal jurisdictions. Circuit court judges are also appointed by the president and confirmed by the Senate. The First Circuit Court represents Maine, Massachusetts, New Hampshire, Rhode Island, and Vermont and consists of six judges. The Ninth Circuit

Table 4.11 Federal Versus State Court Structures

Federal court system	*State court systems*
Article III of the Constitution invests the judicial power of the United States in the federal court system. Article III, Section 1 specifically creates the U.S. Supreme Court and gives Congress the authority to create the lower federal courts.	The constitution and laws of each state establish the state courts. A court of last resort, often known as a supreme court, is usually the highest court. Some states also have an intermediate court of appeals. Below these appeals courts are state trial courts. Some are referred to as circuit or district courts.
Congress has used this power to establish the 13 U.S. courts of appeals, the 94 U.S. district courts, the U.S. Court of Claims, and the U.S. Court of International Trade. U.S. bankruptcy courts handle bankruptcy cases. Magistrate judges handle some district court matters.	States also usually have courts that handle specific legal matters, e.g., probate court (wills and estates), juvenile court, and family court.
Parties dissatisfied with a decision of a U.S. district court, the U.S. Court of Claims, or the U.S. Court of International Trade may appeal to a U.S. court of appeals.	Parties dissatisfied with the decision of the trial court may take their case to the intermediate court of appeals.
A party may ask the U.S. Supreme Court to review a decision of a U.S. court of appeals, but the Supreme Court usually is under no obligation to do so. The U.S. Supreme Court is the final arbiter of federal constitutional questions.	Parties have the option to ask the highest state court to hear the case.
	Only certain cases are eligible for review by the U.S. Supreme Court.

Court represents Alaska, Arizona, California, Hawaii, Idaho, Montana, Nevada, Oregon, and Washington, as well as U.S. territories Guam and Northern Mariana Islands, and consists of 29 judges. Approximately 20% of district court decisions are reviewed by a circuit court of appeals. Except for the 100–150 cases the Supreme Court agrees to hear each year, appeals court decisions are final.

The United States Supreme Court is referred to as the umpire of the federal system, meaning it has the power to decide appeals on all cases brought in federal court or those brought in state courts dealing with federal law. Once a federal circuit court or a state supreme court rules on a case, either party can appeal the case to the Supreme Court. The Supreme Court, unlike any other court in the federal system, has the power to decide which cases it considers. The Supreme Court hears less than 1% of the more than 7,000 cases it is asked to review each year. Supreme Court justices typically choose cases that have national significance. According to the internal rules of the Supreme Court, four of the nine justices must vote to accept a case. The chief justice, currently John Roberts, presides over the Court's proceedings. While the chief justice is the last to vote and decides who writes the majority opinion if he votes with the majority, he has no more authority than the other eight justices. Each of the nine justices has one vote in deciding cases.

History of Supreme Court Decisions Impacting American Education

Numerous landmark Supreme Court decisions have impacted elementary, secondary, and postsecondary American education. While state courts have focused on issues related to the right to a quality education deriving from state constitutions, the federal courts focus on issues of equal protection and prohibiting discrimination derived from the equal protection clause of the Fourteenth Amendment of the U.S. Constitution. Supreme Court decisions have focused on issues of discrimination, from desegregation to special education services. Supreme Court decisions influencing American education also focus on First Amendment rights, from freedom of expression to censorship. This section discusses many of the landmark Supreme Court decisions that have changed American education.

Desegregation and Educational Equity

While most of the landmark Supreme Court cases discussed in this section focus on decisions that expanded rights, particularly civil rights, *Plessy v. Ferguson*, one of the most notorious Supreme Court decisions, rescinded civil rights. In 1896, the U.S. Supreme Court upheld the constitutionality of racial segregation in *Plessy v. Ferguson*. In 1892, Homer Plessy sat in a Whites-only train car and was arrested for violating Louisiana's 1890 law segregating railroad cars. Plessy filed a petition claiming the law violated the equal protection clause. The Supreme Court rejected Plessy's argument that his constitutional rights were violated, reasoning that laws that merely imply a legal distinction between races were not unconstitutional. The case established the doctrine of "separate but equal" as a legal justification for segregation. Three years later, in 1899, three Georgia citizens filed suit against the Richmond County Board of Education following its closing of the only school for non-Whites. The plaintiffs argued that county funding of Whites-only schools violated not only the equal protection clause but also the separate but equal doctrine established in *Plessy* because there was no public school option for non-White students. The decision against the plaintiffs in *Cummings v. Board of Education* implied that public education for Black high school students was not a right protected by the U.S. Constitution. These two Supreme Court cases provided the legal basis for segregated public schools and Jim Crow laws for the next half century. Both cases are considered by scholars to be among the worst decisions in U.S. history.

On September 8, 1953, Supreme Court Chief Justice Fred Vinson died in his home of a heart attack. Few Americans could appreciate at that moment the transformation his death would have on American jurisprudence and education equality. President Dwight Eisenhower nominated California Governor Earl Warren to chief justice. The Warren Court, as it would come to be known, is considered by historians to be the most liberal Supreme Court in U.S. history and would have a profound impact on civil rights, civil liberties, and segregation in American education.

In 1954, the Supreme Court ruled unanimously in *Brown v. Board of Education of Topeka* that racial segregation of children in public schools was unconstitutional. In 1951, Oliver Brown filed a class-action suit against the Topeka, Kansas, Board of Education after his daughter was denied entrance to Topeka's all-White elementary schools. The suit claimed that schools for Black children were not equal to schools for White children and that segregation violated the equal protection clause. The district court conceded that segregated public schools had a "detrimental effect upon the Black children" and contributed to a sense of inferiority, but it still upheld the separate but equal doctrine (Brown, 1954). The Supreme Court ruled that "in the field of public education the doctrine of 'separate but equal' has no place as segregated schools are inherently unequal." The ruling held that Brown and other plaintiffs were being deprived of the equal protection of the Fourteenth Amendment. The decision is considered one of the most consequential in the history of the Supreme Court. Chief Justice Earl Warren, convinced segregation was morally and legally indefensible, lobbied fellow justices to reach a unanimous decision, recognizing that unanimous decisions in landmark cases provide greater legal weight. The decision became a cornerstone of the civil rights movement by establishing that "separate but equal" education and other public services were not equal at all. More than 30 subsequent Supreme Court decisions have dealt with the implications of *Brown* enshrining in law the unconstitutionality of segregation in American society.

Brown v. Board of Education ruled de jure segregation, segregation by government-enacted laws, illegal, but did not address de facto segregation, segregation or racial imbalance derived from unintentional actions by state or private actors. In *Green v. County School Board of New Kent County*, the Supreme Court ruled that a "freedom of choice" plan was not sufficient to desegregate a school system. Virginia's New Kent County School System had two schools, one that taught all White students and another that taught all Black students. After *Brown*, the school system allowed all students to choose to attend either school, but only a few Black students chose to attend the White school and no White students chose to attend the Black school. Parents sued, arguing the school system's plan did not adequately integrate the schools. The Supreme Court held that the freedom of choice plan was not sufficient to desegregate the schools. The ruling provided a higher bar for school systems to dismantle desegregation.

Most of the nation's school systems defied *Brown v. Board of Education* and maintained racial segregation in public school systems. In 1971, the Supreme Court ruled in *Swann v. Charlotte-Mecklenburg Board of Education* that federal courts had the authority to require the desegregation of public schools. The Charlotte-Mecklenburg School District had failed to develop a plan for the desegregation of schools following *Brown*. Under this Supreme Court decision, Charlotte mandated a student reassignment plan that bused children across the metropolitan region. Between 1976 and 1986, the reassignment plan maintained desegregated city schools and led to academic improvements for Black students (Smith, 2004). Cities across the country implemented mandatory busing plans, but the plans consistently faced political backlash and resulted in White flight from urban to suburban areas (Yumi, 2013).

Following the retirement of Chief Justice Warren in 1969, the Supreme Court began to moderate and limit government requirements to desegregate education. In 1974, the Supreme Court ruled in *Milliken v. Bradley* that busing students between Detroit and 53 suburban school districts was unconstitutional. The decision held that integration plans could only be legally enforced in districts that displayed de jure segregation.

In 1991's *Board of Education of Oklahoma City Public Schools v. Dowell*, the Supreme Court ruled that once a school system has demonstrated earnest compliance with a desegregation injunction, the federal court can remove the injunction. In 1992's *Freeman v. Pitts*, the Supreme Court ruled that federal district courts can relinquish control of public school desegregation plans incrementally. In 1995's *Missouri v. Jenkins*, the Supreme Court overruled a lower court order for across-the-board state-funded salary increases to improve education equity. The three rulings lowered the bar for removing school desegregation plans and paved the way for resegregation of public schools (Yumi, 2013).

Special Education

Throughout most of U.S. history, disabled students were excluded from public schools. This began to change in 1954. *Brown v. Board of Education* determined that separate educational facilities are inherently unequal, reversing the 1896 *Plessy v. Ferguson* ruling. The majority brief held "education is perhaps the most important function of state and local governments . . . such an opportunity where the state has undertaken to provide it, is a right that must be made available to all on equal terms." *Brown* empowered special education advocates to seek equal accommodation for disabled students. Special education advocates succeeded in incorporating programs and funding for "children with handicaps" into the 1965 ESEA. From the 1970s through the 1990s, federal and state court rulings would expand educational rights of disabled children and transform U.S. special education.

In 1971, the Pennsylvania Association for Retarded Children (PARC) sued the Commonwealth of Pennsylvania claiming that state law denied public education to 8-year-old students who had not reached the mental capacity of a 5-year-old. PARC argued on behalf of the children and their families that *Brown v. Board of Education* meant the students' rights were violated under the equal protection clause. The district court entered into a consent agreement, an agreement or settlement that resolves a dispute without admission of liability, that laid the foundation for student disability rights in the 1975 EHA, now known as IDEA.

In 1972, the National Legal Aid and Defender Association sued the District of Columbia Board of Education on behalf of seven disabled children who had been denied proper public education accommodations. The District of Columbia agreed the school system had the legal obligation to educate all children but said it lacked the financial resources to educate high-needs children. The U.S. district court ruled disabled students cannot be denied an education based on school costs. This *Mills* decision extended *PARC* by expanding education rights to all children with disabilities. *PARC* and *Mills* formed the basis of the landmark congressional legislation, the EHA of 1975, now known as IDEA.

In 1982's *Board of Education of Hendrick Hudson Central School District v. Rowley*, the Supreme Court held disabled students are entitled to access free appropriate public education, but schools do not need to maximize their potential. Amy Rowley was a deaf student in a mainstream classroom who was meeting all grade-level expectations. During her IEP meeting, her parents requested a sign-language interpreter they deemed an appropriate measure under EHA, now known as IDEA. The Supreme Court ruled the school was providing personalized instruction and accommodations that allowed Rowley to participate equally with her peers. The ruling defined the term "free appropriate public education" as schools permitting students to benefit educationally, not maximize their potential.

In 1988, the Supreme Court in *Honig v. Doe* prohibited unilateral exclusionary discipline resulting from a student's disability. John Doe was a 17-year-old with an impulse control disability who attacked other students and kicked out a classroom window. Doe sued the school district after he was suspended pending expulsion proceedings, arguing suspension for a disability-related misconduct violated the EHA. The decision established the 10-day rule, restricting school districts to only suspend a child for up to 10 days without parental consent or court intervention. A school district seeking a suspension or expulsion beyond 10 days must schedule a hearing, known as a manifestation determination review, to determine whether the behavior was a manifestation of a disability.

In 1989, the U.S. First Circuit Court of Appeals ruled in *Timothy v. Rochester, New Hampshire, School District* that the EHA required school districts to provide special education services to any disabled student regardless of the severity of the disability. The school district argued Timothy was ineligible for special education services because his disability was so severe that he could not benefit from them. The First Circuit held that the EHA had a zero-rejection policy and that the eligibility criteria did not include a capacity to benefit.

Freedom of Speech and Expression

In 1969, the Supreme Court ruled in *Tinker v. Des Moines Independent Community School District* that the public school district violated students' right of expression when it suspended students for a silent protest (*Tinker v. Des Moines Independent Community School District*, 1969). A group of students decided to wear black armbands to protest the Vietnam War. The principal learned of the plan and established a policy stating that any student wearing armbands would be suspended. A student's parents sued, and the lower and district court agreed with the public schools that their actions were reasonable to maintain school discipline. The Supreme Court ruled that students do not lose their First Amendment rights to freedom of speech in public schools. To justify the suppression of free speech, public schools must prove student conduct would materially and substantially interfere with school operations and student learning.

In 1973's *Lemon v. Kurtzman*, the Supreme Court ruled that Pennsylvania and Rhode Island laws allocating state funds to supplement private school teacher salaries and educational materials were constitutional under certain conditions. Opponents argued that because the laws funded religious schools, they violated the establishment clause of the First Amendment, prohibiting the government from establishing a religion.

Affirmative Action

In 1973 and 1974, a University of California Davis Medical School applicant sued, alleging less qualified minority candidates had been accepted due to program quotas, violating his rights under the equal protection clause. Allan Bakke argued he had been excluded based on race because his qualifications exceeded those of many admitted minority candidates. In 1978's *Regents of the University of California v. Bakke*, the Supreme Court sided with Bakke, required the law school to admit him, and ruled the rigid use of race in admissions decisions violated the equal protection clause. The Supreme Court held race could be used as a plus in a particular application file but not as a strike against students in narrowly defined criteria.

In 2003, the Supreme Court in *Gutter v. Bollinger* held the equal protection clause does not prohibit the use of race in narrowly tailored admissions decisions. Barbara Gutter sued the University of Michigan Law School for denying her admission despite having qualifications that exceeded admissions standards. The Supreme Court cited *Bakke* as precedent establishing diversity as a compelling government interest that met the strict scrutiny standard. The Court held the law school conducted individualized review of applications, admissions decisions were based on a complicated set of criteria where race was only one limited factor, and did not unduly harm nonminority applicants.

In 2023, the Supreme Court in *Students for Fair Admissions, Inc. v. President & Fellows of Harvard College* and *Students for Fair Admissions, Inc. v. University of North Carolina* held that higher education admissions programs that consider race violate the equal protection clause. Harvard and North Carolina argued they used race in narrowly tailored admissions decisions consistent with *Gutter v. Bollinger* and previous Supreme Court precedent. Students for Fair Admissions argued precedent was wrong and that the use of race in admissions decisions violated Title VI of the CRA and the equal protection clause. The Supreme Court held that race-based admissions decisions must pass a strict scrutiny standard, meaning the government must have a compelling interest and the law must be narrowly tailored to achieve that interest. Justices Sonia Sotomayor and Ketanji Brown Jackson filed a dissenting opinion, noting the Court "rolls back decades of precedent and momentous progress . . . and cements a superficial rule of colorblindness as a constitutional principal in an endemically segregated society where race has always mattered and continues to matter."

Key Terms

Americans with Disabilities Act
Articles of Confederation
bicameral legislature
Board of Education of Hendrick Hudson Central School District v. Rowley
Board of Education of Oklahoma City Public Schools v. Dowell
Brown v. Board of Education
categorical grants
circuit courts
Civil Rights Act of 1964
committee chair
committee system
decennial census
Department of Education
Department of Education Organization Act
district courts
dual federalism
Education Amendments of 1972
Education Science and Reform Act
Education and the Workforce Committee
elastic clause
Elementary and Secondary Education Act
enumerated powers

equal protection clause
Executive Office of the President
Family Educational Rights and Privacy Act of 1974
federalism
Fourteenth Amendment
Freeman v. Pitts
Gutter v. Bollinger
Health, Education, Labor, and Pensions Committee
Higher Education Act
Honig v. Doe
implied powers
Individuals with Disabilities Education Act
joint committees
Judiciary Act
Lemon v. Kurtzman
lower chamber
majority leader
Milliken v. Bradley the Detroit Public School System
Mills v. Board of Education the District of Columbia
Missouri v. Jenkins
Morrill Act
Northwest Ordinance
PARC v. Commonwealth of Pennsylvania
party caucus
party conference
Perkins Career and Technical Education Act
Plessy v. Ferguson
president's cabinet
proportional representation
Protection of Pupil Rights Amendment of 1978
Regents of the University of California v. Bakke
Rehabilitation Act of 1973
Secretary of Education
select committees
Serrano v. Priest
Smith-Hughes Act
speaker of the House
standing committees
Students for Fair Admissions, Inc. v. President & Fellows of Harvard College and Students for Fair Admissions, Inc. v. University of North Carolina
supremacy clause
Supreme Court
Swann v. Charlotte-Mecklenburg Board of Education
Tenth Amendment
Timothy v. Rochester, New Hampshire School District
Tinker v. Des Moines Independent Community School District
upper chamber

Discussion Questions

1. Does the federal government have authority over education?
2. Historically, what has been the federal government's role in education?
3. What is the role of the legislative branch in education policy?
4. What is the role of the executive branch in education policy?
5. What is the role of the judicial branch in education policy?
6. If state and local governments have authority over education, how does the federal government influence education?
7. Has your state supreme court decided any education finance or higher education cases?

Activities and Assignments

1. Identify a federal policy issue closely related to your research. Provide an overview of the policy issue. Utilize website resources and newspaper articles to discuss who was involved with the creation of the policy issue.
2. Discuss the power relationships between federal actors. Who has the power in your policy issue area?
3. Identify which educational jurisdictions the federal government has direct influence over. Discuss whether federal government influence in those areas should be expanded or constrained.

Note

1 Prior to the passage of the Twentieth Amendment in 1933, the opening date of the new Congress was March 4. Transportation advances reduced the time required to travel to Washington, enabling the new Congress to start at an earlier date.

References

Aldrich, J. H., & Battista, J. S. C. (2002). Conditional party government in the states. *American Journal of Political Science, 46*(1), 164. https://doi.org/10.2307/3088420

Black, D. W. (2021). The American right to education: The Northwest ordinance, reconstruction, and the current challenge. *Poverty & Race Research Action Council, 30*(1).

Brougher, C. (2010). *Section 504 of the rehabilitation act of 1973: Prohibiting discrimination against individuals with disabilities in programs or activities receiving federal assistance.* Congressional Research Service.

Brown v. Board of Education, 347 U.S. 483 (1954).

Bullock, C. S. (1976). Motivations for U. S. congressional committee preferences: Freshmen of the 92nd congress. *Legislative Studies Quarterly, 1*(2), 201. https://doi.org/10.2307/439513

Dragoo, H. E. (2019). *The individuals with disabilities education act (IDEA) funding: A primer.* Congressional Research Service. www.everycrsreport.com/files/20190829_R44624_c85f49a0d2b1c25913346932a5bf6b9c30831c8d.pdf

Epps, G. (2006). *Democracy reborn: The 14th amendment and the fight for civil rights in post-civil war America.* Holt.

Foner, E. (2019). *The second founding: How the civil war and reconstruction remade the constitution.* Norton Press.

Friedel, J. N. (2011). Where has vocational education gone? The impact of federal legislation on the expectations, design, and function of vocational education as reflected in the reauthorization of the Carl D. Perkins career and technical education act of 2006. *American Educational History Journal, 38*(1), 37–53.

Hannah-Jones, N., Roper, C., Silverman, I., & Silverstein, J. (Eds.). (2021). *The 1619 project.* One World Press.

Jennings, J. F. (2001). Title I: Its legislative history and its promise. In G. D. Borman, S. C. Stringfield, & R. E. Slavin (Eds.), *Title I: Compensatory education at the crossroads* (pp. 1–23). Erlbaum.

Lyndon, B. Johnson (1965). *Remarks in Johnson City, Tex., Upon signing the elementary and secondary education bill online by Gerhard Peters and John T. Woolley.* The American Presidency Project. https://www.presidency.ucsb.edu/node/241886

Mayhew, D. (1974). *Congress: The electoral connection.* Yale University Press.

McGuinn, P. (2015). Schooling the state: ESEA and the evolution of the U.S. department of education. *RSF: The Russell Sage Foundation Journal of the Social Sciences, 1*(3), 77. https://doi.org/10.7758/rsf.2015.1.3.04

OMB. (2019). *Budget of the United States Government, Fiscal Year 2019, analytical perspectives: Special topics, aid to state and local governments.* https://www.govinfo.gov/content/pkg/BUDGET-2019-PER/pdf/BUDGET-2019-PER.pdf.

Palmer, K. T. (1984). The evolution of grant policies. In L. D. Brown, J. W. Fossett, & K. T. Palmer (Eds.), *The changing politics of federal grants.* Brookings Institution.

Scott, J., & Sarkees-Wircenski, M. (2004). *Overview of career and technical education* (3rd ed.). American Technical Publishers.

Smith, S. S. (2004). *Boon for whom?* State University of New York Press.

Tinker v. Des Moines Independent Community School District, 393 U.S. 503 (1969).

United States Department of Education. (2024). *About ED overview and mission statement.* https://www2.ed.gov/about/landing.jhtml

Yumi, S. (2013). Resegregation of American public schools: A case study of Charlotte-Mecklenburg schools, North Carolina. *Nanzan Review of American Studies, 35,* 47–68.

5 State Education Governance

On July 1, 2010, the Pennsylvania State Board of Education adopted Common Core standards in English and mathematics. They were to be phased in during the 2010–2011 academic year, with full implementation occurring by the 2013–2014 academic year (Carmichael et al., 2010). The Common Core State Standards Initiative was established through a joint venture of the Council of Chief State School Officers, an organization representing the 50 chief state school officers; the National Governors Association, an association representing the 50 state governors; and Achieve, a nonprofit education reform organization funded by education philanthropies to develop consistent and internationally benchmarked curriculum standards across all states. The Pennsylvania State Board of Education scheduled roundtable sessions across the state throughout the implementation phase to solicit public feedback; authorized a study to compare Common Core with existing state curriculum standards; and invited written feedback from educators, policymakers, and the public (Carmichael et al., 2010).

In May 2013, Republican Governor Tom Corbett delayed the implementation of the Common Core standards less than 2 months before they were to be fully implemented (Murphy, 2013). Corbett consulted with members of the House and Senate Education Committees. Many conservative Republicans and Democrats objected to the similarities between Common Core and Pennsylvania standards, the testing graduation requirement, and the cost of standards implementation. State Board of Education Chair Larry Wittig said Corbett had mandated that Common Core be replaced, not just revised (Kraft, 2019).

Corbett's delay marked an abrupt shift in Pennsylvania education policy and placed local school districts in a precarious position. Pennsylvania school leaders had been working on implementation of the standards for nearly 3 years, and the call for delay sowed confusion among school administrators. Pennsylvania Association of School Administrators Executive Director Jim Buckheit said more than 80% of school administrators had communicated in a survey that they were more than halfway done aligning their programs with the standards. Despite the confusion caused by the delay, Secretary of Education Ellar said the governor asked the State Board of Education to hold additional public hearings and work to revise the curriculum standards so they could be submitted to the legislative education committees for final approval (Murphy, 2013). In the end, the General Assembly did not pass legislation mandating changes to the Common Core standards.

Interest groups from both sides of the political spectrum played a central role in shaping public opinion and mobilizing support and opposition to the Common Core standards. Business, military, and higher education interest groups had long supported the standards and graduation testing requirements as necessary to ensure students graduated with the skills to succeed in college and the workplace. However, the American Federation of Teachers, a

DOI: 10.4324/9781003231561-7

teachers union, joined numerous conservative interest groups in support of the delay, stating teachers required additional professional development and resources to implement the new standards.

The Pennsylvania state curriculum standards example raises more questions than it answers. What changed in Pennsylvania to motivate the state to switch the curriculum standards so quickly and who was responsible for the change? Who was ultimately in charge of state education policymaking in Pennsylvania and where did that authority derive from? Why did the state legislature not pass legislation to rewrite the standards? Why did the State Board of Education and the chief state school officer follow the governor's directions to revise the state standards? Why did the state court system not step in to determine the curriculum standards? Harold Lasswell famously quipped that politics is a competition about who gets what and when (Lasswell, 1936). This chapter answers this for state education policy systems: Who gets what, when, and especially why?

Historically, education policy has been the province of local governments. Since the 1980s, the power and authority of state governments have grown relative to local and federal governments because of a series of political and financial pressures (Bowman & Kearney, 2008). Academic achievement stagnation, American student performance scores and graduation rates dropping relative to other developed countries, and growing achievement gaps have increased the pressure on governmental actors to improve state-level educational performance. State education governance centralization is also a product of increased pressure for local school districts to equalize funding. Historically, property taxes have funded a high percentage of K–12 public education, resulting in significant funding disparities between high- and low-wealth areas. Because of political and economic pressures, interest groups from teachers unions to businesses to parent groups have called for state governments to centralize authority to confront these challenges.

Educational leaders who seek to change education policy must understand the power and authority of state government policy actors. Education change agents require knowledge of the policy environment beyond the school district. For educational leaders to influence education policy outcomes, they must understand the power dynamics of state-level policy subsystems consisting of governmental and nongovernmental actors. Policy change also requires the knowledge to access policy leaders and the skills to influence them. This chapter provides insights for how educational leaders can access state education policy leaders and influence power dynamics.

Sources of State Government Power

State government power derives from two main sources: the state constitution and statutory law. *State constitutions* enumerate the basis of legal authority, articulate the rights of state residents, and are superior to statutory law. *Statutory law* is the law established by acts of a state legislature. Like the federal government, all 50 state constitutions establish and allocate power among three branches of government, establish the scope of state and local government authority, and protect individual rights. While state constitutions are similar in the basic structure of state government, the terms, qualifications for holding office, and voting requirements, there are significant variations in their constitutional makeup and how they are amended.

There are four methods for amending state constitutions: legislative proposal, initiative, constitutional convention, and constitutional commission. Historically, the legislative proposal is the most common, comprising **90%** of all state constitutional changes. It is an established practice in all 50 states. Constitutional legislative amendments in 18 states require only a majority vote of both legislative chambers for ratification, while another 18 require a two-thirds supermajority and eight others require a three-fifths supermajority. Constitutional amendments by ballot initiative are authorized in 18 states, making them the second most common method for amending state constitutions. *Ballot initiatives* are a form of direct democracy in which proposed laws or constitutional amendments are placed on the ballot for popular vote. If propositions are placed directly on the ballot by citizens, the procedure is called a *direct initiative*; if the legislature participates by voting on the proposition, the procedure is called an *indirect initiative. Constitutional conventions* are an assembly of delegates chosen by popular election or appointed by the state legislature or governor to revise or establish a new state constitution. While constitutional conventions are rarely used to amend state constitutions, they are appropriate for considering substantial constitutional revisions or wholesale changes. In 1986, Rhode Island held the most recent state constitutional convention. A *constitutional commission* is a meeting of delegates appointed by the state legislature or the governor to study constitutional problems and propose solutions. All state constitutional amendment procedures require ratification by voters, save Delaware where a supermajority in both legislative chambers can ratify a constitutional change (Dinan, 2016).

The relative ease of changing state constitutions has led to a series of problems that directly impact education policy, including excessive length, contradictions, and outdated text. These problems make it difficult for state courts to rule on constitutionality, which has far-reaching policy implications for elementary, secondary, and postsecondary education institutions. Unlike the U.S. Constitution, to which Congress has approved 33 amendments and 27 have been ratified, each state has considered more than 200 amendments. State constitutions that were developed early in the nation's history reflected distrust of the English king and colonial governors and afforded governing supremacy to the legislative branch. Twenty states still operate under their original state constitution, including Massachusetts, whose state constitution was written by future President John Adams in 1780 and is the oldest functioning written constitution in effect in the world (Levy, 1995). States functioning under a historically dated constitution still provide disproportionate power to the legislative branch, while more modern state constitutions provide more authority to the executive branch. State constitutions reflect a wide range of amendment behavior, from Alabama's 926 amendments to Illinois's 15 (Erickson, 2019). State constitutions vary in length from 388,882 words (Alabama) to 8,565 (Utah) words, with an average length of 39,000 words. (Erickson, 2019). What implications do state constitutional shortcomings have on education policy litigation and policy disputes?

Elementary and Secondary Education Constitutional Obligations

All 50 state constitutions mandate the creation of a public elementary and secondary education system (Parker, 2016). However, the strength of the constitutional language varies widely, which has significant consequences. Some state constitutions require only the establishment of a free and public education system (Dallman & Nath, 2020). Table 5.1 identifies state constitutional language that requires education provisions beyond that minimum standard. The stronger the constitutional language, the more leverage advocates possess to pursue adequate or equitable funding for all students, regardless of the socioeconomic or demographic composition of the school district.

Since 1970, 49 states have faced school finance litigation cases involving legal challenges to the state education finance system. Typically, these lawsuits seek either an adequate level or

Table 5.1 State Constitutions' Education Clause Language

Provision	States
Uniform	Arizona, Colorado, Florida, Idaho, Indiana, Minnesota, Nevada, New Mexico, North Carolina, North Dakota, Oregon, South Dakota, Washington, Wisconsin, Wyoming
Thorough/efficient	Arkansas, Colorado, Delaware, Florida, Idaho, Illinois, Kentucky, Maryland, Minnesota, New Jersey, Ohio, Pennsylvania, South Dakota, Texas, West Virginia, Wyoming
Equal rights	Florida, Indiana, Illinois, Louisiana, Michigan, Montana, Washington
Paramount/primary duty	Florida, Washington
High-quality education	Florida, Illinois, Virginia
Provisions defined for "all children"	Alaska, Florida, New Mexico, New York, North Carolina, North Dakota, Oklahoma, South Carolina, Utah, Virginia, Washington

more equitable distribution of funding across school districts. State constitutions define the type and level of education that students should receive, and these legal definitions influence the outcomes of funding lawsuits.

Postsecondary Constitutional Obligations

American higher education needs to have the independence to manage their internal affairs and academic freedom while also being responsive to the public interest (Hutchens, 2008). Thirty states establish a postsecondary education system in their constitutions, while the remaining 20 establish a state higher education system through statutory language. Fourteen states have constitutional provisions to limit excessive state government intrusion: Alabama, California, Florida, Georgia, Hawaii, Idaho, Louisiana, Michigan, Minnesota, Montana, Nebraska, Nevada, North Dakota, and Oklahoma. Constitutional autonomy is a legal principle establishing that a state postsecondary institution is a separate department or government rather than an agency of the executive or legislative branches. The purpose of these legal provisions is to preserve the institutional autonomy of postsecondary institutions.

Most states establish the authority and responsibilities of higher education governing or coordinating boards through statutory authority. Even among the 30 states that establish their postsecondary system through constitutional provisions, postsecondary authority and powers are subject to legislative control in 16. In most states, postsecondary stakeholders consistently seek more substantive autonomy through statutory language. Like elementary and secondary public education, the specific constitutional and statutory language has significant implications for policy differences litigated in the state courts and for administrative implementation.

Neither constitutional autonomy nor substantive autonomy completely shield postsecondary institutions from state government influence. The state legislature and the governor retain control over appropriations, a shrinking yet significant source of funding for public postsecondary institutions. Postsecondary institutions, no matter their level of autonomy, have incentives to adhere to executive and legislative branch priorities.

The dominant trend since the 1980s has been greater centralization of governance structures in response to increasing higher education costs and decreasing state resources

(Mills, 2016). For example, in 1997, Florida's Constitutional Revision Commission proposed an education clause for voter approval that read:

> The education of children is a fundamental value to the people of the State of Florida. It is, therefore, a paramount duty of the state to make adequate provision of the education of all children residing within its borders. Adequate provision shall be made by law for a uniform, efficient, safe, secure, and high-quality system of free public schools that allows students to obtain a high-quality education and for the establishment, maintenance, and operation of institutions of higher learning and other public education programs that the needs of the people may require.

In the 1998 election, the amendment passed with 71% support (Dallman & Nath, 2020). The Florida Constitution was also revised to allow a reorganization of the Florida education system to centralize its governance structure and establish better accountability for academic performance throughout the education system. The reorganization created the Florida State Board of Education, appointed by the governor, with authority for education from prekindergarten through graduate school (K–20). Prior to the reorganization, Florida postsecondary governance consisted of two major bodies: the Board of Regents overseeing the 10 public state universities and the State Board of Community Colleges overseeing the 28 community colleges. The new Florida Board of Education is also referred to as the superboard. Florida's constitutional and statutory revisions made it the financial responsibility of the state to adequately educate all citizens and centralized the governance structures, shifting the relationship between governmental actors. To understand the complex power relationships between governmental actors, the next sections explore the legislative, executive, and judicial branches' authority, organizational structures, and core functions.

Legislative Branch

State governments largely mirror the institutional structure of the federal government by having separation of powers among three branches of government: legislative, executive, and judicial. State legislatures, like the U.S. Congress, are the most direct, democratic link between the people and their state government. State legislatures are institutions of popularly elected representatives. All state legislatures have an institutional structure called *bicameralism*, a lower and upper chamber, except Nebraska, which has only one chamber. The lower chamber, often called the house of representatives, is composed of elected members who serve shorter terms in office and represent fewer constituents. The house typically has the constitutional authority to initiate taxing and spending legislation and articles of impeachment. The upper chamber, usually called the senate, has fewer representatives who typically serve longer terms and represent a larger number of constituents. The senate typically has the exclusive power to confirm gubernatorial appointments and try articles of impeachment. The 50 state legislatures have 7,383 individual legislators. Houses of representatives range in size from 40 (Alaska) to 400 (New Hampshire) members. Senates range in size from 20 (Alaska) to 67 (Minnesota) members. Forty-six state lower chambers maintain 2-year terms; Alabama, Maryland, Mississippi, and North Dakota stipulate 4-year terms. Forty state upper chambers maintain 4-year terms and the other 10 stipulate 2-year terms.

State legislatures elect their representatives primarily, although not exclusively, using single-member districts and plurality rule. An *electoral district* is a subdivision of a state created to provide the population within that geographical area with representation in state government. The number of constituents per legislative district varies significantly across states based on population size, population density, and the size of the legislative chamber. California's state senators represent nearly a million residents each, more than the average member of Congress, while members of the New Hampshire House represent on average only 3,300 residents. A *single-member district*, also referred to as winner take all, refers to an electoral district where the voters choose a single person to fill an office. The *plurality* method of voting means the person who receives more votes than any other candidate in a particular district wins. The plurality method differs from a *majority* method of voting, in which a candidate must win a majority of votes $(50\% + 1)$; if no candidate wins a majority of votes, then the two candidates with the most votes enter a run-off election. Single-member districts with plurality voting systems are rarely used outside the United States. Most other countries utilize some form of *proportional representation*, in which multiple members are elected per district and the number of seats a party receives is proportional to the number of votes it receives.

State house and senate districts must be redrawn every 10 years when the U.S. census updates nationwide population estimates. The U.S. Supreme Court ruled in *Baker v. Carr* (1962) and *Reynolds v. Sims* (1964) that the Fourteenth Amendment of the U.S. Constitution requires the principle of "one person, one vote." This principle that individuals should have equal representation in voting applies to both chambers of state legislatures. The purpose of the redistricting process is to ensure equal representation in government. In 34 states, the legislature has primary control over drawing district lines. In seven states – Arkansas, Hawaii, Missouri, New Jersey, Ohio, Pennsylvania, and Virginia – political commissions composed of both legislators and nonlegislators draw legislative districts. Nine states – Alaska, Arizona, Colorado, Hawaii, Idaho, Michigan, Montana, New Jersey, and Washington – pursue an apolitical redistricting process by prohibiting public officials from serving on independent commissions. State legislators frequently redraw district lines to strengthen the majority party and weaken the minority party, a process known as *gerrymandering*. Gerrymandering entails concentrating or spreading out the minority party's voters among districts to maximize the number of legislative districts where the majority party gains an electoral advantage.

Legislative Professionalism

While their institutional structures and constitutional duties and authority are similar, state legislatures vary significantly in their professionalism, member composition, and party competition. *Legislative professionalism* refers to the capacity of the legislature to act as an effective and independent institution. Some state legislatures are like the U.S. Congress in that they are composed of full-time legislators, the chambers meet full time, there is a robust and permanent legislative professional staff, and legislators get paid professional wages. These are considered more professionalized. Other state legislatures are composed of part-time, low-paid legislators who meet for only part of the year and lack a robust permanent professional staff. These are considered less professionalized.

Beginning in the 1960s and 1970s, state legislatures increased professionalization by increasing salaries, the length of sessions, and resources including staff capacity. Legislative professionalism scholarship breaks state legislatures into three categories: professional, hybrid, and citizen. *Professional state legislatures* consider state legislators to have full-time jobs, meaning they are paid a living wage that does not require additional income. Scholars have found that state population and income are strong predictors of increases in state legislative professionalism, with larger and wealthier states choosing a more professionalized legislative structure (Squire & Hamm, 2005). Table 5.2 illustrates measures of state legislative professionalism. Squire's professionalism ranking is based on a composite score of measures of state legislative professionalization. States with a large population and high per capita income, including New York, California, Pennsylvania, and Michigan, top the list of the most professionalized state legislatures.

What implications does state legislative professionalism have for state education systems? Professional legislatures have more power than hybrid or citizen legislatures relative to other government actors. Professional legislatures have longer sessions, annual sessions, annual budgets, and substantial resources that give them more power to push their legislative agenda and budgetary priorities. In states with hybrid or citizen legislatures, the governor, the executive bureaucracy, and interest group actors develop greater political and policy power relative to the state legislature.

State Legislative Demographic Composition

Many observers argue state legislatures should emulate the demographic composition of the public they represent. Research indicates race and gender matter in political representation and that female and Black legislators sponsor a higher number of bills that support those demographic groups than White men do (Clark, 2019; Orey et al., 2006). The racial and gender diversity of state legislatures has increased dramatically in recent decades, particularly among Democratic Party members. However, women and people of color are underrepresented in nearly all state legislative chambers.

Gender

State legislatures, like the U.S. Congress, have historically underrepresented women and minorities. Women comprise more than half of the U.S. population but only **29.4%** of state representatives. However, the share of state legislative seats held by women has risen precipitously over the past 50 years. Since 1970, women have increased from only **4.5%** to the current **29.4%** of all state legislators. Female representation in state legislatures is not equal across political parties. Two thirds of all female state legislators are Democrats. Republican women comprise only **9%** of all state legislators and only **17.5%** of Republican legislators, while Democratic women comprise nearly **20%** of all state legislators and **42%** of Democratic state legislators. Table 5.3 illustrates that women are underrepresented in every state compared to their percentage of the state population.

Despite significant gains in female representation over the past 50 years, why do women continue to be underrepresented in state legislatures? Research finds that women win electoral contests at roughly the same rate as their male counterparts, so women are just as electable as men. Women self-select to run for office at lower rates and get recruited at lower rates. There is also a structural issue related to the incumbency effect: Those already holding political office are more likely to win reelection. Because men control a supermajority of state legislative seats, they have an advantage in dissuading female candidates from challenging them (Darcy & Choike, 1986). Women also tend to face environmental roadblocks, including fewer financial resources, lower education levels, and occupations that make it more challenging to run for political office (Arceneaux, 2001).

While women are less likely to run for state legislative office, once they run, they win at the same rate as men; when they arrive in state legislatures, they are just as effective as men and better representatives for women. Researchers have consistently found that female legislators

Table 5.2 Measures of State Legislative Professionalism

State	Squire's 2015 professionalism rank	2020 annual salary	Session length (months)	Permanent staff	Annual/biannual session/budget
California	1	114,877	9	2,098	AA
Massachusetts	2	66,256	12	759	AA
New York	3	110,000	12	2,776	AA
Pennsylvania	4	90,335	12	2,358	AA
Michigan	5	71,685	12	817	AA
Ohio	6	65,528	12	476	AB
Hawaii	7	62,604	3	307	AB
Alaska	8	50,400	3	341	AA
Illinois	9	69,464	12	784	AA
Maryland	10	50,330	3	656	AA
Washington	11	52,766	3	536	AB
Colorado	12	40,242	4	228	AA
Connecticut	13	28,000	4	465	AB
Arizona	14	24,000	3.5	521	AA
Florida	15	29,697	2	1,446	AA
Missouri	16	35,915	4.5	403	AA
Iowa	17	25,000	3.5	167	AA
North Carolina	18	13,951	4	370	AB
Texas	19	7,200	5/0	2,057	BB
New Jersey	20	49,000	12	727	AA
Nebraska	21	12,000	4	229	AB
Oklahoma	22	35,021	4	224	AA
Oregon	23	31,200	5/1	303	AB
Arkansas	24	42,428	2/1	435	AA
Minnesota	25	46,500	3.5	568	AB
Wisconsin	26	52,999	12	649	AB
Delaware	27	47,291	5.5	79	AA
Rhode Island	28	15,959	5.5	259	AA
Louisiana	29	16,800	2.5	743	AA
Nevada	30	4,389	4/0	284	BB
Kansas	31	8,432	4.5	148	AA
Virginia	32	18,000	2	533	AB
Vermont	33	11,221	4.5	55	AA
Alabama	34	49,861	3.5	349	AA
Idaho	35	18,415	3	76	AA
Kentucky	36	21,462	3.5	375	AB
Mississippi	37	23,500	3.5	140	AA
West Virginia	38	20,000	2	201	AA
South Carolina	39	10,400	5	280	AA
Indiana	40	27,204	3	252	AB
Maine	41	14,862	4	171	AB
Georgia	42	17,342	3.5	525	AA
New Mexico	43	0	1.5	168	AA
Tennessee	44	24,316	4.5	264	AA
Montana	45	3,719	3.5/0	136	BB
Utah	46	12,285	1.5	133	AA
North Dakota	47	9,315	3.5/0	37	BB
South Dakota	48	11,892	2	58	AA
Wyoming	49	4,500	2	36	AB
New Hampshire	50	100	5	129	AB

Table 5.3 Women and People of Color in State Legislatures, April 2024

State	Total female legislators/total legislators	Percentage of women in legislature	Percentage of people of color: legislators	Percentage of people of color: state population
Alabama	22/140	15.7	25	34.5
Alaska	22/60	36.7	15	39.4
Arizona	35/90	38.9	29	45.3
Arkansas	34/135	25.2	12	17.7
California	38/120	31.7	39	63.0
Colorado	44/100	44.0	17	31.8
Connecticut	60/187	32.1	26	33.3
Delaware	15/62	24.2	10	37.8
Florida	47/160	29.4	30	46.2
Georgia	72/236	30.5	28	47.4
Hawaii	25/76	32.9	78	78.2
Idaho	33/105	31.4	3	18.0
Illinois	66/177	37.3	25	38.8
Indiana	38/150	25.3	12	20.8
Iowa	44/150	29.3	7	14.1
Kansas	47/165	28.5	11	24.1
Kentucky	34/138	24.6	9	15.4
Louisiana	26/144	18.1	24	41.5
Maine	70/186	37.6	11	6.6
Maryland	76/188	40.4	33	49.3
Massachusetts	58/200	29.0	8	28.5
Michigan	54/148	36.5	16	25.0
Minnesota	64/201	31.8	5	20.1
Mississippi	28/174	16.1	29	43.4
Missouri	48/197	24.4	13	20.6
Montana	46/150	30.7	14	13.7
Nebraska	14/49	28.6	8	21.0
Nevada	34/63	54.0	30	51.2
New Hampshire	144/424	34.0	6	9.7
New Jersey	37/120	30.8	26	45.2
New Mexico	41/112	36.6	49	62.6
New York	67/213	31.5	27	44.9
North Carolina	43/170	25.3	1	37.0
North Dakota	31/141	22.0	1	15.6
Ohio	36/132	27.3	14	21.1
Oklahoma	32/149	21.5	18	34.4
Oregon	39/90	43.3	6	24.4
Pennsylvania	68/253	26.9	9	23.6
Rhode Island	42/113	37.2	12	17.9
South Carolina	29/170	17.1	24	36.4
South Dakota	26/105	24.8	6	17.7
Tennessee	20/132	15.2	15	26.1
Texas	45/181	24.9	35	58.1
Utah	27/104	26	10	21.7
Vermont	73/180	40.6	4	7.2
Virginia	41/140	29.3	17	38.3
Washington	60/147	40.8	9	31.4
West Virginia	19/134	14.2	3	8.0
Wisconsin	34/132	25.8	6	18.8
Wyoming	14/90	15.6	3	16.0
Nation	2,162	29.3	18.1	39.9

sponsor bills that benefit women more often than men do (Bratton, 2002; Bratton & Haynie, 1999). Even after controlling for political party, female legislators are more liberal than their male counterparts (Barrett, 1995). They are also just as likely as male legislators to achieve passage of legislative bills (Barrett, 1995).

Race

People of color face even higher levels of underrepresentation in state legislatures than women. African Americans, who comprise 13% of the U.S. population, account for only 9% of state legislators. Latinos comprise 17% of the U.S. population but only 5% of state legislators. Asian Americans comprise 5% of the U.S. population but only 1% of state legislators. Women of color comprise nearly 40% of all women and 20% of the U.S. population but comprise only 7.5% of state legislators. Table 5.3 illustrates that only two state legislatures, Maine and Montana, have a higher percentage of legislators of color than the states' respective minority populations (6% and 13%). Numerous state legislatures have less than half the percentage of representatives of color than their percentage of the state population.

Thirty-two state legislatures have established a Black caucus, a group of legislative members who meet to pursue common legislative objectives (Clark, 2019). Not surprisingly, researchers find that state legislative seat share percentage is directly correlated with the state population's racial breakdown. African American voter turnout is positively correlated with the Black share of state legislative seats (Frymer, 1999). Research does not find much evidence of biracial coalitions. African American majority districts elect African Americans and Latino majority districts elect Latinos, but in most state legislative districts biracial coalitions do not support one another (Casellas, 2009).

Research also finds that Black state legislative seat share is not associated with either higher levels of per pupil education spending or less rigid welfare-to-work requirements (Frymer, 1999). Electoral capture theory or White backlash holds that centrist Democratic Party leaders seek to court White moderates and therefore push for more conservative policies when a higher percentage of state legislative seats are held by Blacks. African Americans are less likely to achieve legislative passage than their White counterparts (Barrett, 1995).

Profession

Ten state legislatures are full-time, professional organizations with salaries that allow their members to be full-time legislators. Figure 5.1 illustrates this: Only 1% of state legislators identify their profession as "state legislator." Thirty percent of state legislators identify their profession as business, followed by attorney (15%), other (12%), consultant/nonprofit (8%), retired (8%), and agriculture (5%). Only 6% of state legislators nationwide identify as an educator in either K–12 or higher education. The 50 state legislatures average 148 legislators in their two chambers but have fewer than nine educators on average. This professional breakdown illustrates a dearth of educator experience and knowledge in state legislatures.

Collective Action Problems

State legislatures are extraordinarily complex institutions with hundreds of members, thousands of staff members, external interest groups seeking to influence the legislative process, a complex array of formal legislative rules, and in most cases millions of constituents with wide-ranging policy preferences. This complexity presents significant problems with

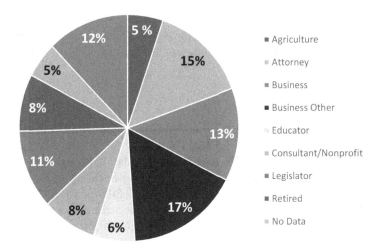

Figure 5.1 State Legislator Requirements and Characteristics

coordination, the ability of a group of actors to work together toward a common goal. These coordination problems are generally referred to as *collective action problems*, situations in which individuals would be better off if they cooperated but have incentives not to cooperate if others are cooperating. Legislative members are incentivized to act in their own self-interest to build their reputation with constituents and win reelection. Sometimes this behavior can come at the cost of collective legislative or societal goals. State legislatures, like Congress, use two primary methods to overcome collective action problems: party leaders and committees.

Leadership

Each state legislative chamber has at least four leadership positions. The *speaker* is a partisan leadership position in state house chambers elected by members of the house. The speaker's official duties and authority typically include presiding over the daily session of the house; preserving order in the chamber; making parliamentary motions; appointing committee chairs and members; referring bills to committee; signing legislation, writs, and warrants; and acting as the official spokesperson for the house. The *speaker pro tempore* presides in the absence of the house speaker (National Conference of State Legislatures, 2020). The speaker's unofficial duties have expanded over time to include building legislative coalitions, providing services and information to individual members, acting as a liaison with the executive branch and senate leadership, serving as a public liaison, and supporting candidates' political campaigns. The speaker pro tempore typically presides over the house in the speaker's absence but has few other duties or responsibilities.

Senate leadership positions are more varied than those in houses of representatives. Senate chambers are led by an elected president in 23 state senates, the lieutenant governor in 26 states, and a speaker in one state. Where the lieutenant governor serves as the senate president, states limit their legislative power and authority resides with the *president pro tempore*. The leader of the senate's duties and authorities typically include presiding over the daily sessions of the senate; preserving order in the chamber; making parliamentary motions; ruling on parliamentary questions; appointing committee chairs and members; referring bills to committee; signing legislation, writs, and warrants; and acting as the official spokesman for the senate (National Conference of State Legislatures, 2020).

House and senate chambers also each have two political party leadership positions, a majority leader and minority leader. The *majority leader* serves as the leader of the majority party in the chamber, represents the majority party during floor debates, develops the chamber's legislative calendar, and works with the chamber leader on policy development. The *minority leader* serves a similar role for the minority party in each chamber. Research indicates that legislative leaders' power is greater when the legislative chamber has more members, a higher level of legislative professionalism, more turnover, more homogeneity among members, and more competitive elections (Mooney, 2013).

Legislative leaders are empowered with agenda-setting powers to overcome coordination problems. The majority leader generally decides which committee bills receive consideration by the full chamber. This agenda-setting authority allows the majority party to avoid legislative bills that split its caucus and to consider bills that split the minority caucus. As discussed in Chapter 4, legislative members voluntarily delegate more authority to legislative leaders when they think it will help overcome collective action problems. In other words: To improve their chance of reelection and ability to advance policy priorities, members delegate greater authority to legislative leaders who improve their chance of achieving shared legislative goals.

Committee Systems

While legislative leaders wield agenda-setting authority and orchestrate legislative business, most legislative work occurs in committees. Legislative leaders assign all members to small working groups called committees that consider, review, revise, and vote on legislative bills. Each committee has jurisdiction over a specific policy area. Most education bills are sent to the chamber's committee with jurisdiction over education issues.

Types of Committees. State legislatures utilize several types of committees to conduct business. Most state legislatures have standing committees specifically for education policy issues in both houses. *Standing committees* are permanent unless the legislature formally abolishes them. Most standing committees also have subcommittees, a subdivision of the full committee that considers bills within a more concise policy jurisdiction. For example, the South Carolina House of Representatives' Education and Public Works Standing Committee includes five subcommittees: K–12, Higher Education, Motor Vehicles, Public Safety, and Transportation. Table 5.4 identifies the state legislative committees with jurisdiction over education issues in each of the 99 state legislative chambers. Although some states, such as Hawaii and North Carolina, have separate standing committees for K–12 education and higher education policy issues, most states' education committees have jurisdiction over all education issues. State legislators are drawn to education committees if their constituents care deeply about those issues – for instance if they represent districts with public colleges and universities or public school districts with highly engaged teachers unions and parents.

Committee membership is typically restricted to members of a chamber, but 29 states have *joint committees* composed of members of both legislative chambers. Table 5.5 identifies nine states that utilize joint education committees: Arkansas, Connecticut, Massachusetts, Maine, Montana, New Jersey, Oregon, Utah, and Washington. The objective of joint committees is to develop better communication and cooperation across legislative chambers.

Special or select committees are established for specific purposes and theoretically are disbanded after accomplishing their goals. For example, the California General Assembly has a Select Committee on Early Childhood Development whose purpose is to develop policy

Table 5.4 State Legislative Committees With Jurisdiction Over Education Issues

State	House	Senate	Joint
Alabama	Education Policy Ways and Means Education	Education and Youth Affairs	
Alaska	Education	Education	
Arizona	Education Appropriations Subcommittee on Education	Education	
Arkansas	Education Early Childhood Subcommittee K–12, Vocational–Technical Institutions Subcommittee	Education AR Comprehensive School Improvement Plans Subcommittee Education/Joint Ad Hoc Subcommittee Public School Employee Health Insurance Subcommittee	Joint Committee on Education Facilities ALC-JBC Education K–12
California	Education Subcommittee on Education Finance	Education	
Colorado	Education	Education	
Connecticut			Joint Committee on Education
Delaware	Education	Education	
Florida	Subcommittee on Pre-K–12 Appropriations Education	Subcommittee on Pre-K–12 Appropriations Education	
Georgia	Education	Education and Youth	
Hawaii	Education Higher Education	Education Higher Education	
Idaho	Education	Education	
Illinois	Elementary and Secondary Education Licensing Administration and Charter Policy Elementary and Secondary Education School Curriculum Policies	Education	
Indiana	Education	Education and Career Development	
Iowa	Education	Education	
Kansas	Education	Education	
Kentucky	Education Budget Review Subcommittee on Postsecondary Education Budget Review Subcommittee on Primary and Secondary and Workforce Development	Education Budget Review Subcommittee on Education	
Louisiana	Education	Education	
Maine			Joint Committee on Education and Cultural Affairs

(Continued)

Table 5.4 (Continued)

State	House	Senate	Joint
Maryland	Ways and Means	Education, Health, and Environmental Affairs	
Massachusetts			Joint Committee on Education Joint Committee on Higher Education
Michigan	Education Reform	Education	
Minnesota	Education Finance Education Innovation Policy	Education-12 Finance Education-12 Policy	
Mississippi	Education	Education	
Missouri	Elementary and Secondary Education	Education	
Montana	Education	Education and Cultural Resources	Joint Education Committee
Nebraska	Education		
Nevada	Education	Education	
New Hampshire	Education	Education	
New Jersey	Education	Education	Joint Committee on Public Education
New Mexico	Education	Education	
New York	Education	Education	
North Carolina	Education Community Colleges Education K–12 Education Universities	Education/Higher Education	
North Dakota	Education	Education	
Ohio	Education and Career Readiness	Education	
Oklahoma	Education	Education	
Oregon	Education	Education	Public Education Appropriations Ways and Means Subcommittee on Education
Pennsylvania	Education	Education	
Rhode Island	Health, Education, and Welfare	Education	
South Carolina	Education and Public Works	Education	
South Dakota	Education	Education	
Tennessee	Education Administration and Planning Education Instruction and Programs	Education	
Texas	Public Education	Education	
Utah	Education	Education	Public Education Appropriations Subcommittee
Vermont	Education	Education	
Virginia	Education	Education and Health	
Washington	Education	Early Learning & K–12 Education	Education Accountability System Oversight Education Funding
West Virginia	Education	Education	
Wisconsin	Education	Education	
Wyoming	Education	Education	

solutions for supporting the health, growth, and development of every California child. While these committees in theory only last for a limited number of state legislative sessions, in practice they can last for decades and become part of the standard legislative committee structure.

Conference committees include representatives from both the house and senate chambers. As previously discussed, bicameralism requires both legislative chambers to pass independent bills and then reconcile the differences between the bills before they can receive executive branch approval.

Committee Membership. Each committee has a chair who serves as the parliamentary head of the committee. The chair sets the committee agenda by determining when and whether legislation is considered. Committee chairs wield significant agenda-setting authority: They can determine the fate of bills by bringing them up for consideration, ignoring them, or amending them to substantially alter their original purpose. Legislative committees are an organizational system designed to serve the individual members, the legislative institution, and constituents. The committee system serves the members' interests by fragmenting legislative power, allowing members to play a role in crafting the legislation and earn credit from constituents for legislative victories. Members seek committee assignments with oversight over issues of concern to their constituents so they can credibly claim that they are powerful, can deliver appropriations and services to their communities, and deserve reelection. The committee system also serves institutional and state goals as members develop expertise in specific policy areas, share that expertise with their legislative colleagues, and improve the quality of lawmaking. Members can build expertise on specific policy issues, such as education, that benefit their constituents, the legislature, and the entire state.

State legislatures face coordination problems like those of any group working to take collective action. As the group size and complexity of the work increases, so too does the coordination problem. State legislatures solve these coordination problems by delegating authority to party leaders to make collective decisions to serve the party caucus's goals. Political party leaders and committee chairs cannot compel compliance from members, but they can incentivize their behavior by offering prized committee assignments. The committee system also allows the state legislature to overcome coordination problems more easily by delegating much of the work to smaller groups of legislators.

Why should educational leaders care about state legislative leadership and committee systems? To act, state legislatures abdicate significant authority to party and committee leaders. Therefore, as educational leaders seek to change policy, party and committee leaders are the most meaningful actors in the policy process. Without the support of party and education committee leaders, legislative and state funding changes are nearly impossible.

State Legislative Functions

State legislatures perform four central functions: representing constituents, policymaking, developing and approving state budgets, and conducting oversight of executive branch agencies. The state legislature represents constituents in terms of policy, services, and allocation of public goods. Members of state legislatures are considered single-minded seekers of reelection, meaning they are motivated to represent their constituents to keep their seat in the legislature (Mayhew, 1974). State legislators contend for committee assignments, sponsor, and work to pass legislative bills, steer resources toward their districts, and provide services in order to serve their constituents and improve their electoral prospects.

The legislature is considered the most influential political institution in a state because of its policymaking and budgetary authority. State legislatures have the sole authority to pass state laws, change the state constitution, and restructure education institutions. While state legislatures delegate many policy issues to other political and administrative institutions, they retain the authority to override those decisions by passing statutory or constitutional changes. For example, states typically delegate the definition of state curriculum standards to a state board of education. Nevertheless, if the state legislature disagrees with a decision by the state board of education, the chief state school officer, or even the governor, it can pass statutory or constitutional changes to override the decision of other policymaking institutions.

The state legislative process is like the congressional policymaking process described in Chapter 4, but there are slight variations across the 50 states. For example, some states have bills expire at the end of the session, while others allow bills to stay active through a 2-year session. The percentage of state legislative bills that become law is substantially higher than the congressional rate of 3%–4%. On average, state legislatures pass 18% of all bills introduced, but this varies from a low of 3% in New York to a high of 63% in Utah (Squire & Moncrief, 2019). Research suggests several reasons for higher rates of policymaking success, including fewer interest groups, higher rates of bill introductions, more state bills that only apply to specific localities, unified control of the legislature, a greater number of budget bills, and carryover provisions for bill introductions (Squire & Moncrief, 2019).

The *power of the purse*, the authority to pass regular state budgets, is another powerful legislative function. As discussed in Chapter 4, state legislatures maintain two separate but related processes: authorization and appropriations. *Authorization* is legislation that can establish, continue, or modify an agency, program, or activity for a fixed or indefinite period (Heniff, 2012). *Appropriations* allow agencies to spend money that had been previously authorized. In other words, authorization creates policy changes and appropriations provide the money for those policy changes. Thirty-one state legislatures pass a budget on an annual basis, like Congress, while 19 states pass *biannual budgets*, a state budget that includes funding for a 2-year period. In 1940, 44 states enacted biannual budgets. Over the past 80 years, states have shifted toward annual budgeting as state budgets grew and became more complex and state legislatures tried to increase their power relative to the governor. The power of the purse endows the state legislature with additional influence over the education bureaucracy. For example, the state board of education or department of education technically reports to the governor in many states, but their budget relies on legislative appropriations. Therefore, educational actors have incentives to serve the interests of both executive and legislative branch actors.

The state legislature also performs administrative oversight functions. *Administrative oversight* authorizes the legislature to ensure that laws it passed are administered by executive branch agencies in a manner consistent with legislative intent. The oversight functions typically occur as part of reviews of state agencies and programs and through budget and legislative hearings. Most states perform regular reviews of administrative rules and regulations to ensure compliance. The ability of states to perform administrative oversight is closely tied to their level of legislative professionalism. Administrative oversight is perceived as a lower priority for state legislators because those functions rarely give an electoral advantage to individual members. More professionalized legislatures have more time and staff resources to carry out the functions.

Why do educational leaders need to understand state legislatures? The state legislature is the most constitutionally powerful actor in state government. State legislative leaders wield considerable power to build legislative coalitions, and their support of a policy issue is critical to its success. Education committee members are the most influential education policy subsystem actors for the development of education legislation. If educational leaders seek to influence education legislation, education committee members are the key representatives to address. If, however, educational leaders want to influence education funding levels, then they should go to the appropriations and budget committee members who retain authority over state budgets. Given the size, diversity, and complexity of state legislatures, they face significant coordination problems as they build coalitions to pass education legislation and state budgets under the best of circumstances. In political and policy environments where a state legislature cannot overcome collective action problems or the problem deals with policy implementation, executive branch actors accept a more powerful role in state education policy subsystems. The next section focuses on the various executive branch institutions, their roles and responsibilities, and their relative power within the education policy subsystem.

Executive Branch

State executive branches implement and enforce laws passed by the legislative branch. All 50 states have an executive branch headed by a governor, attorney general, secretary of state, auditors, and commissioners. Forty-five states also have a lieutenant governor who is first in the line of succession and serves a role like the vice president at the federal level. In addition to overseeing the executive branch bureaucracy, the governor is also regarded as the head of the state education system. Other executive branch institutions charged with K–12 education implementation and oversight include the state board of education, the chief state school officer, and the department of education. There is considerably more variation in higher education governance structures among the 50 states, but they typically include a statewide coordinating or governing board that performs administrative oversight of public universities in addition to the governor. This section provides an overview of the various executive branch actors involved in state education system oversight and explains their power and governing dynamics.

Governor

While all 50 states constitutionally establish the office of the governor, they vary significantly in qualifications and powers. Governors serve 4-year terms in all states except New Hampshire and Vermont, which use 2-year terms. Virginia is the only state that limits the governor to a single term in office. The constitutional minimum age for a governor varies from no minimum (Kansas and Massachusetts) to age 31 (Oklahoma). All but five states require gubernatorial candidates to be U.S. citizens, and all but two (Kansas and Tennessee) require state residency for a period ranging from 30 days (Rhode Island) to 10 years (Oklahoma and Missouri). If the governor cannot complete their term of office, 45 states designate the lieutenant governor to succeed the governor; in the other five, the line of succession identifies the secretary of state or leader of the state senate. All state constitutions except Oregon's provide a mechanism to impeach the governor. Like the federal government, the impeachment process starts in the house and ends with a trial in the senate. Removal requires a two-thirds majority except in Alaska and Nebraska.

The governor is the most visible leader of the state government. As the chief executive officer, the governor is responsible for overseeing the operation of the state executive branch, implementing state laws, and pursuing policy objectives. Governors also serve as head of their state political party, legislative leader, chief state liaison, intergovernmental actor, and chief crisis manager. All governors have the authority to issue executive orders and emergency actions. Like the president, governors typically see their primary role as keeping their citizens safe and ensuring a strong economy with job opportunities for all citizens. While many governors view education as preparing citizens to participate in a representative democracy, all see it as an economic development program that prepares citizens for the workforce. Gubernatorial influence over education policy issues depends on their formal and informal powers.

Formal Powers

Gubernatorial powers are typically divided into institutional (formal) and personal (informal) powers. Institutional or formal powers refer to authority provided to the governor in the state constitution and statutes and by the voters through ballot initiatives. Institutional powers typically include appointments, budget, party control, and veto authority.

Appointment Power. Gubernatorial appointment power refers to the authority to select people to fill key positions in state administration. Governors typically enjoy broad authority to nominate officials to serve in state executive branch positions. Gubernatorial powers of appointment related to education differ considerably across the states, which influences the governor's ability to impact policy decisions and policy implementation. For example, the Colorado governor and its state board of education (SBE) are separately elected, and the SBE chooses the chief state school officer (CSSO), the commissioner of education. In Virginia, the governor appoints both the SBE members and the CSSO. Education leaders appointed directly by the governor have more incentives to make decisions aligned with the governor's priorities and are more likely to have policy preferences aligned with the governor. This section, details the variation in gubernatorial appointment powers and the implications of that variation.

The governor's appointment powers related to elementary and secondary education and higher education are typically limited. The education department head is appointed by a board or agency in 20 states and elected in another 14 states. In most states, the higher education head is appointed by a board independent of gubernatorial approval.

Budget Authority. Executive budget authority is another institutional power the governor enjoys in all 50 states. Executive budgets refer to the authority to collect agency and department budget requests and develop policy priorities in a proposed budget for legislative consideration and approval. The level of budgetary authority varies with the governor's institutional powers and the political makeup of the state legislature. State legislatures controlled by the opposing party can ignore the governor's budget request and craft their own budget, subject to the governor's veto authority.

Veto Authority. In 44 states, the governor has a *line-item veto*, the power to nullify or cancel specific provisions of a bill without vetoing the entire bill. Thirty-four states provide line-item veto authority on appropriations bills, which gives governors in those states more influence over executive branch agencies. Ten states provide the governor with the authority to line-item veto or change language in any legislative bill, which significantly increases their power relative to the state legislature (Moe, 1988). Only five states (Indiana, Nevada, North Carolina, Rhode Island, and Vermont) limit the governor's veto authority to whole legislative bills, like the president's veto authority. All state legislatures have constitutional authority to override a gubernatorial veto. Thirty-six states require a two-thirds vote from both chambers of the legislature, seven states require a three-fifths vote from both chambers, and seven states require a simple majority vote from both legislative chambers. Only 5% of gubernatorial vetoes are overridden by state legislatures (Squire & Moncrief, 2019).

Informal Powers

Gubernatorial informal or personal powers refer to the personal attributes and environmental circumstances that strengthen or weaken a governor's power to achieve their political goals. Informal powers include the governor's electoral margin and public approval, party control, and political future.

Performance Rating. In a democracy, elected leaders remain in power based on receiving a plurality of the vote. Popularity is directly tied to votes and translates to political power. The more popular governors are among the public, the more influence they have among state legislators and other political actors. The governor's margin of victory serves as their initial performance rating. The larger the margin of victory, the greater the governor's perceived political mandate to pursue their policy agenda. State legislative members seek reelection, so if a governor's policy agenda is very popular, they are more likely to support it. Approval ratings, measured through public polling, provide regular snapshots of gubernatorial popularity that influence informal powers.

Party Control. As at the federal level, a governor's ability to pursue a legislative and budgetary agenda depends on the partisan makeup of the state legislature. Elected leaders of the same party generally adopt closer policy positions. Members of a political party seek to improve the reputation of their shared political party with the public – and diminish the reputation of the opposing political party – to win elections and increase their political power. Therefore, even if members of a party disagree on policy goals, they maintain electoral incentives to achieve legislative victories so their party can improve its reputation and to deny the opposing party legislative victories and decrease its reputation. Governors who share a party affiliation with the state legislative chambers have more ability to achieve their policy goals and increase their personal power.

Personal Future. Governors who are at the beginning of their term or have the constitutional capacity to run for reelection have more power than those who are leaving office (Ferguson, 2018). While governors who are near the end of their term or are term limited are less able to assist supporters and campaign against detractors, governors with substantial time or potential time in office have a longer period during which they can use their power. The longer the potential tenure of the governor, the greater the level of personal power.

Governor as Education Leader

Historically, governors have viewed education as a local issue and delegated implementation and oversight to school boards and state superintendents. States provided a comparatively small percentage of K–12 and higher education spending. Beginning in the 1980s, governors' power increased as they started to take more direct leadership over education policy issues and the state became the dominant level of government (Shober, 2012). Gubernatorial leadership was pushed to the forefront after state courts forced many states to expand state spending to equalize spending across districts, the federal government required accountability, and education increased as a percentage of state budgets (Henig, 2009). According to education scholars, governors have become the pivot of education policymaking in the American states (Wirt & Grove, 1990).

Executive Bureaucracy

The governor is the elected chief administrator of the executive branch and oversees a broad range of elected, appointed, and career state employees. The governor appoints a small number of the top positions of the executive branch. Most members of the executive branch are unelected bureaucrats. *State government bureaucracy* refers to a body of unelected government officials working within administrative agencies and offices characterized by specialization of functions and adherence to fixed rules who are within a hierarchy of authority that carries out the tasks of government (Weber, 1948). State and local government comprises 19 million bureaucrats. In the education bureaucracy, these public servants extend from appointed SBE members to state education department employees to principals, teachers, and school staff. The purpose of the government bureaucracy is to maximize the effectiveness and efficiency of policy implementation.

Bureaucrats face a common collective action problem called the principal–agent problem. The *principal–agent problem* refers to a dilemma in which a principal contracts with an agent authorized to work on the principal's behalf. The principal has no assurances that the agent shares their preferences and lacks the means to observe all the agent's behavior. Government bureaucracies delegate responsibilities from principals to agents. The elected governor promises to improve student achievement and graduation outcomes but must delegate responsibility for achieving those goals to the education bureaucracy with limited ability to observe the behavior of the bureaucrats. Bureaucrats often have multiple principals with differing priorities. For instance, the state education department directly works for the governor who leads the executive branch; however, the department's annual budget is determined by the state legislature. How do the bureaucratic actors determine which principal to appease if the two are in conflict? How does the principal ensure the bureaucrat does their job and follows their direction? This section provides an overview of the various institutions and actors that make up the state education bureaucracy and their relationships within the governance structure.

State Board of Education

SBEs provide general supervision of the public schools, including articulating the short- and long-term vision and needs of the education system and making policy decisions to achieve those goals. While SBEs' authority varies widely across states, the National Association of State Boards of Education has identified four common roles: (a) policymakers who are responsible for policies that promote educational quality, (b) advocates who are responsible for quality education for all students, (c) liaisons who seek to foster relationships and communication between education and others, and (d) consensus builders who work to find common ground between disparate interests (www.nasbe.org/about-state-boards-of-education/). Most SBEs have authority to determine qualifications for education personnel, including teacher licensure standards; establish high school graduation requirements; establish accountability and assessment programs, including state standards; and establish standards for accreditation of local school districts and preparation programs for teachers and administrators.

Since their inception in the 1800s, SBEs have evolved in both policy authority and selection methods (Henig, 2013; Shober, 2012). Twenty-five SBEs are established by constitutional authority, 22 by statute, and three states do not have SBEs. Elected SBEs grew in popularity until the 1990s, when a shift toward gubernatorial-appointed selection methods occurred ((Henig, 2013); Shober, 2012). Table 5.5 provides an overview of SBE selection methods. Governors now make appointments in all but 12 states; seven use partisan ballot elections (Alabama, Colorado, Kansas, Michigan, Nebraska, Texas, and Utah), four do not have an SBE (Minnesota, New Mexico, North Dakota, and Wisconsin), and the legislature appoints the SBE in New York. Governors appoint all members of the SBE, typically with senate approval, in 28 states. Eight states utilize a mixed approach in which the governor

Table 5.5 State Board of Education Governance Structures

State	Member selection	Selection of state board chair	Number of voting SBE members	Length of term	Authority for teacher licensure	Authority for standards adoption
Alabama	Partisan ballot	Governor serves as president	8 and governor	4	SBE	SBE
Alaska	Governor appoints, legislature confirms	SBE elects	7	5	SBE	SBE
Arizona	Governor appoints, Senate confirms	SBE elects	11	4	SBE	SBE
Arkansas	Governor appoints, Senate confirms	SBE elects	9	7	SBE	SBE
California	Governor appoints, Senate confirms	SBE elects	11	4	Professional Standards Commission (PSC)	SBE
Colorado	Partisan ballot	SBE elects	7	6	SBE	SBE
Connecticut	Governor appoints, legislature confirms	Governor appoints	11	4	SBE	SBE
Delaware	Governor appoints, Senate confirms	Governor appoints	7	6	SBE	SBE
District of Columbia	Nonpartisan ballot	SBE elects	9	4	SBE	SBE
Florida	Governor appoints, Senate confirms	SBE elects	7	4	SBE	SBE
Georgia	Governor appoints, Senate confirms	SBE elects	14	7	PSC	SBE
Hawaii	Governor appoints, Senate confirms	Governor appoints	9	3	Standards board	SBE
Idaho	Governor appoints, Senate confirms	SBE elects	8	5	SBE	SBE
Illinois	Governor appoints, Senate confirms	Governor appoints	9	4	SBE	SBE

(Continued)

Table 5.5 (Continued)

State	Member selection	Selection of state board chair	Number of voting SBE members	Length of term	Authority for teacher licensure	Authority for standards adoption
Indiana	Governor appoints 8, speaker of house 1, president pro tempore 1	CSSO serves as chair	11	4	State Education Agency (SEA)	SBE
Iowa	Governor appoints, Senate confirms	SBE elects	9	6	Independent board	SBE
Kansas	Partisan ballot	SBE elects	10	4	SBE	SBE
Kentucky	Governor appoints, Senate confirms	SBE elects	11	4	PSC	SBE
Louisiana	8 nonpartisan ballot; 3 governor appoints, Senate confirms	SBE elects	11	4	SBE	SBE
Maine	Governor appoints	SBE elects	9	5	SBE	SEA
Maryland	Governor appoints, Senate confirms; teachers elect 1	SBE elects	14 including 1 teacher, parent, and student	4	SBE	SBE
Massachusetts	Governor appoints, Senate confirms	Governor appoints	11 including voting student	5	SBE	SBE
Michigan	Partisan ballot	SBE elects	8	8	CSSO	SBE
Minnesota	None	NA	NA	NA	Standards board	CSSO
Mississippi	Governor appoints 2, lt. governor appts. 2, speaker appts. 2	SBE elects	9	9	SBE	SBE
Missouri	Governor appoints, Senate confirms	SBE elects	8	8	SBE	SBE
Montana	Governor appoints, Senate confirms	SBE elects	7	7	SBE	SBE

(Continued)

Table 5.5 (Continued)

State	Member selection	Selection of state board chair	Number of voting SBE members	Length of term	Authority for teacher licensure	Authority for standards adoption
Nebraska	Nonpartisan ballot	SBE elects	8	4	SBE	SBE
Nevada	4 nonpartisan ballot, 3 governor appoints	SBE elects	7	4	Standards board	SBE
New Hampshire	Governor appoints	Governor appoints	7	5	SBE	SBE
New Jersey	Governor appoints, Senate confirms	SBE elects	13	6	SBE	SBE
New Mexico	None	NA	NA	NA	SEA	SEA
New York	Legislature appoints	SBE elects	17	5	SBE	SBE
North Carolina	Governor appoints, legislature confirms; lt. gov. and state treasurer ex officio members	SBE elects	13	8	SBE	SBE
North Dakota	None	NA	NA	NA	Standards board	CSSO
Ohio	11 nonpartisan ballot; governor appoints 8, Senate confirms	SBE elects	19	4	SBE	SBE
Oklahoma	Governor appoints, Senate confirms	CSSO serves as chair	7	4	SBE	SBE
Oregon	Governor appoints, Senate confirms	SBE elects	7	4	Standards board	SBE
Pennsylvania	Governor appoints, Senate confirms 17; legislature appts. 4	Governor appoints	21	6	SBE	SBE
Rhode Island	Governor appoints, Senate confirms	Governor appoints	17	3	SBE	SBE

(Continued)

Table 5.5 (Continued)

State	Member selection	Selection of state board chair	Number of voting SBE members	Length of term	Authority for teacher licensure	Authority for standards adoption
South Carolina	Legislature appts. 16, governor appts. 1	SBE elects	17	4	SBE	SBE
South Dakota	Governor appoints, Senate confirms	SBE elects	7	4	SBE	SBE
Tennessee	Governor appoints, legislature confirms	SBE elects	10 including 1 voting student	5	SBE	SBE
Texas	Partisan ballot	Governor appoints	15	4	Independent board	SEA
Utah	Partisan ballot	SBE elects	15	4	SBE	SBE
Vermont	Governor appoints, Senate confirms	SBE elects	9 including 1 voting student	6	Standards board	SBE
Virginia	Governor appoints, legislature confirms	SBE elects	9	4	SBE	SBE
Washington	Governor appoints, Senate confirms 7; local school boards elect 5; private schools elect 1	SBE elects	14	4	Standards board	CSSO
West Virginia	Governor appoints, Senate confirms	SBE elects	9	9	SBE	SBE
Wisconsin	None	NA	NA	NA	SBE	SBE
Wyoming	Governor appoints, Senate confirms	SBE elects	12	6	SBE	SBE

appoints some members and other members are elected or appointed by legislative or other political institutions.

Why does the SBE selection method matter? Appointed SBE members are incentivized to align with the governor's education priorities, both because the governor chose them partially based on their education priorities and because they owe their position to the governor. This alignment decreases transaction costs and increases the likelihood that these executive branch institutions successfully implement policies.

State Department of Education

Historically, state education departments were established to oversee elementary and secondary education and administer federal and state education grants, laws, and regulations (Brown et al., 2011). When Congress passed the Elementary and Secondary Education Act (ESEA) in 1965, it fundamentally shifted the relationship between the federal government and local school districts by increasing federal aid, specifically to high-poverty districts through Title I funding. State education agencies had been organizations with low resources, meager staffs, and limited authority. Gubernatorial efforts in the 1980s and 1990s to develop standards and accountability systems increased the authority and purpose of state education agencies. In 1994, the ESEA reauthorization, the Improving America's Schools Act, tied state actions on standards, assessments, and accountability to federal funding. In 2001, the No Child Left Behind (NCLB) Act resulted in a dramatic shift in the role of state education agencies, which became responsible for helping develop state standards, assessments, and accountability systems; develop data systems to track student academic growth; and identify and turn around low-performing schools in some states. While the responsibilities of state education departments have continued to grow since 1965, these organizations' resources and capacity remain inadequate to successfully administer their expanded roles (Brown et al., 2011).

State education departments vary significantly in size, scope, and approach toward supporting local school districts because of each state's unique history, culture, and decentralization or commitment to local control (Weiss & McGuinn, 2017). State education departments are limited by state cultures that value decentralization, local control, and trust between local and state officials. What are state departments of education best suited to accomplish? According to the Consortium for Policy Research in Education, state education departments perform five essential roles: articulating the state's educational vision and goals; selecting and implementing the state's standards and assessments; designing and implementing the state's accountability system; administering, implementing, and overseeing state and federal funding and other programs; and communicating about critical educational issues with stakeholders across the states. Additional roles vary significantly from state to state (Weiss & McGuinn, 2017). Some state education departments also focus on turning around low-performing schools and districts, as in Louisiana, New Jersey, Michigan, and Massachusetts, while others take a hands-off approach. While NCLB defined highly qualified teachers, the Every Student Succeeds Act (ESSA) deferred to states on how to define and achieve a quality teaching workforce. Some states also design and offer leadership for teacher and administrator professional development, particularly on state-level issues including new standards and assessments (Loeb et al., 2009).

As discussed in Chapter 4, the 2015 ESSA reauthorized the ESEA, shifting considerable authority from the federal government back to state governments. This reauthorization also transferred education accountability system authority from the U.S. Department of Education to the state departments of education. The state departments needed to develop accountability performance measures, identify low-performing schools, and establish evidence-based strategies to improve low-performing schools. States significantly vary in the percentage of schools identified as low performing. For example, Rhode Island has identified 99% of all schools as falling into one of these three categories, while Alabama, Georgia, and Virginia have only identified 5% of schools as falling into these categories (Renter et al., 2019).

State education agencies face a litany of challenges as they try to reform their departments and meet their growing organizational responsibilities, including state restrictions on their authority, shrinking budgets, and dwindling staff levels (Brown et al., 2011). Researchers have found that state education agencies were largely successful in implementing NCLB's data collection and testing requirements, but they lacked the funding, staff, expertise, and organizational structure to support large-scale educational changes at low-performing schools (Sunderman & Orfield, 2007). State education agencies also lack the financial capacity to hire and retain highly qualified staff, who can earn substantially more in the private sector or at the school district level (Timar, 1997). State education agencies were originally designed to funnel funds from federal and state entities to local school districts rather than lead education reform, which limits their capacity (Brown et al., 2011). In an effort to overcome these shortcomings, many state education agencies have reorganized around specific district needs and away from the traditional organizational structure based on funding sources such as Title I funding (Weiss & McGuinn, 2017). The question remains whether most state education agencies have the resources or capacity to fulfill this broad set of goals. Table 5.6 illustrates the variation in state education agency staffing.

Chief State School Officer

The CSSO, a generic term used to define a position whose title varies across states, heads the department of elementary and secondary education in all 50 states. This position is equivalent to the secretary of education at the federal level. In 1812, New York established the first CSSO (First & Quaglia, 1990). By 1850, all states had established a CSSO position either by constitutional provision or state statute. During the past 170 years, the position has expanded considerably along with the number of children attending elementary and secondary schools, increasing the need for a larger state education bureaucracy.

A CSSO's primary responsibilities include serving as the chief executive officer of the department of education; executive officer of the SBE; and the state administrative officer for executing education laws, rules, and regulations. The CSSO runs the day-to-day state-level education bureaucracy and communicates with the state legislature, governor, and SBE to improve education policy and ameliorate education problems. While local school districts retain autonomy over personal decisions, the CSSO can guide local school district actions through regulatory and funding changes. The CSSO is responsible for state oversight of education quality, district spending, and monitoring of student achievement and therefore can be seen as an advisor to local education leaders (Louis et al., 2010).

During the past 25 years, states have taken the lead role in education policymaking. This has placed CSSOs in the critical role of ensuring that local school districts are meeting the needs of all students. The CSSO engages stakeholders from the state legislature, governor, and SBE to local district leaders, superintendents, principals, families, and parents to create conditions in districts and schools that provide opportunities for all students.

The Council of Chief State School Officers (CCSSO) is an association composed of all the heads of departments of elementary and secondary education in the 50 states, the District of Columbia, and the five U.S. territories. The purpose of the CCSSO is to advocate for federal education policy, aid chief state school officers and their education agencies, and partner with federal agencies and private foundations to develop research studies and manage projects to support state education actions. For example, the CCSSO partnered with the National Governor's Association, Achieve, and other nonprofit groups to develop the Common Core State Standards Initiative to establish consistent educational standards across the states and ensure high school graduates are prepared for higher education or the workforce.

Table 5.6 State Education Agency Staff

State	State agency staff	State student enrollment	Number of students per education staff
Alabama	888	744,000	838
Alaska	634	131,000	207
Arizona	481	1,087,000	2,260
Arkansas	366	479,000	1,309
California	1,200	6,070,000	5,058
Colorado	369	802,000	2,173
Connecticut	325	568,000	1,748
Delaware	222	123,000	554
Florida	1,128	2,667,000	2,364
Georgia	537	1,650,000	3,073
Hawaii	215	180,000	837
Idaho	128	272,000	2,125
Illinois	487	2,113,000	4,339
Indiana	239	1,046,000	4,377
Iowa	225	482,000	2,142
Kansas	251	468,000	1,865
Kentucky	315	666,000	2,114
Louisiana	650	681,000	1,048
Maine	139	191,000	1,374
Maryland	548	846,000	1,544
Massachusetts	500	963,000	1,926
Michigan	460	1,666,000	3,622
Minnesota	400	838,000	2,095
Mississippi		494,000	
Missouri	251	917,000	3,653
Montana	166	143,000	861
Nebraska	215	291,000	1,353
Nevada	100	429,000	4,290
New Hampshire	284	201,000	708
New Jersey		1,380,000	
New Mexico	245	328,000	1,339
New York	519	2,765,000	5,328
North Carolina	779	1,458,000	1,872
North Dakota	101	95,000	941
Ohio	582	1,822,000	3,131
Oklahoma	300	642,000	2,140
Oregon	268	559,000	2,086
Pennsylvania	493	1,788,000	3,627
Rhode Island	133	146,000	1,098
South Carolina		712,000	
South Dakota	135	120,000	889
Tennessee	695	964,000	1,387
Texas		4,673,000	
Utah	328	576,000	1,756
Vermont	158	92,000	582
Virginia	265	1,231,000	4,645
Washington	400	1,030,000	2,575
West Virginia	675	283,000	419
Wisconsin	437	874,000	2,000
Wyoming	135	86,000	637

The CCSSO, in concert with the nation's CSSOs, developed a 2020 strategic plan with the following five goals:

1. Students: States set high expectations for student success by creating opportunities and removing barriers.
2. Critical student transitions: States create multiple pathways for each student to successfully transition into, through, and beyond the K–12 system.
3. Teachers: States support teachers so each student experiences high-quality instruction.
4. School and district leaders: States support school and district leaders to continuously improve schools.
5. State leaders: Chiefs maximize the effectiveness of their state education agencies both in service of and as partners with district and local leaders (Officers, 2017).

These strategic goals communicate CSSO priorities by working with stakeholders throughout the complex state education system.

State constitutional and statutory minimum qualifications for CSSOs vary widely across states. Some states require previous professional experience, including prior education experience (13), administrative experience (11), and a minimum level of education (12). Other states require the CSSO to be a U.S. citizen (12) and meet a minimum age requirement (14) and a state residency requirement (13). The variability across the states demonstrates the broad range of roles that state political leaders envision for the CSSO.

Selection methods for CSSOs include election, gubernatorial appointment, and state board of education appointment. Table 5.7 shows that the governor appoints the CSSO in 17 states, 20 states appoint the CSSO through the SBE, and 13 CSSOs are elected. The state governance structure has implications for the CSSO's priorities and relationship with other state and local education and political stakeholders. CSSOs appointed by the governor are more likely to let the governor take the lead on setting educational priorities. CSSOs appointed by the state board of education or popularly elected are more likely to act independently and set a policy agenda and priorities that may at times conflict with the priorities of the governor or state legislature and therefore lead to a more decentralized system.

Table 5.7 Chief State School Officer Selection Method

CSSO selection method	*States*
Elected	Arizona, California, Georgia, Idaho, Indiana, Montana, North Carolina, North Dakota, Oklahoma, South Carolina, Washington, Wisconsin, Wyoming
Appointed by governor	Maine, Minnesota, Nevada, New Hampshire, Tennessee
Appointed by governor with consent of Senate	Delaware, Iowa, Minnesota, Nevada, New Jersey, New Mexico, Pennsylvania, South Dakota, Texas, Vermont, Virginia
Appointed by state board of education	Alabama, Colorado, Florida, Hawaii, Illinois, Kansas, Kentucky, Louisiana, Maryland, Massachusetts, Michigan, Mississippi, Missouri, Nebraska, Ohio, Utah, West Virginia
Appointed by the state board of education, subject to approval by the governor	Alaska, Arkansas, Connecticut, Massachusetts, Rhode Island
Other	New York, Oregon

Elementary and Secondary State Education Governance Models

Education is one of the most complex areas of public policy, largely because of the far-reaching horizontal and vertical expansion of governance across federal, state, and local government; across numerous government branches and agencies; and within layers of school system bureaucracies. Governance structures matter. Different types of education governance structures produce vastly different relationships between elected leaders, government agencies, school leaders, and the voting public. A governance framework helps explain the spectrum of governance structures and their implications for education policy. Figure 5.2 illustrates a two-dimensional space in which the vertical dimension depicts the governor's relationship with the CSSO. The authority–centralization dimension spans from high to low levels of centralization. High levels of centralization mean the governor has strong direct authority over the education system through appointments of other education officials. The horizontal dimension graphs the governor's relationship with the SBE, with high levels of centralization on the left and lower levels on the right.

State education governance centralization provides a classic political system tradeoff between high transaction costs and high conformity costs. *Transaction costs* are the costs incurred from the time and effort required to compare preferences and negotiate compromises in making collective decisions. *Conformity costs* are the difference between what a person would ideally prefer and what a group decides. Conformity costs rise when collective decisions produce policy outcomes that do not best serve a particular individual's interest. For example, a dictatorship has low transaction costs and high conformity costs. The dictator can make decisions without significant transaction costs and therefore has a greater ability to deal with potential problems in the system, but the tradeoff is high conformity costs because all other citizens must accept the dictator's decisions without input. Conversely, *direct democracy*, a form of democracy in which all people in a particular political geographic area decide

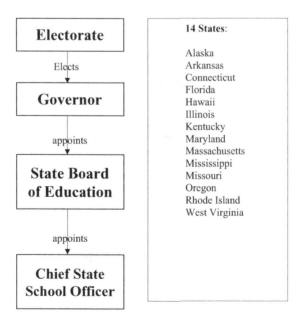

Figure 5.2 State Education Governance Model 1

on policy initiatives directly, has high transaction costs and low conformity costs. In direct democracies, such as some New England towns, conformity costs are low because everyone in the community has a voice in the decision making, but the tradeoff is that transaction costs are extremely high, making policy change difficult to achieve. Centralized state education governance models that give the governor a high level of authority decrease transaction costs but raise conformity costs. A governor with direct control over the education system actors can more closely control policy reform and change than one with weak or shared authority over educational system actors.

The 50 states have four primary education governance structures, with differing levels of centralization. Figure 5.2 illustrates Model 1, in which the governor appoints both the SBE and the CSSO. This model is the second most centralized of the education governance structures. The governor has enormous authority and accountability in this system. Through direct appointment of the SBE, the governor controls the key policymaking institution in the state education structure. By appointing the CSSO, the governor has authority over the state education agency charged with implementing policy.

Figure 5.3 depicts Model 2, which is utilized in seven states. In Model 2, the SBE members are elected, and they collectively appoint the CSSO. This is the most decentralized education governance model. Neither the SBE nor the CSSO are appointed by the governor, so they can act with political independence from the governor. This disperses power between the executive branch institutions. The governor has less direct authority over implementation and administration of the education system because they have less influence over the SBE and CSSO. Model 2 is the education governance structure that has the highest transaction costs. The independently elected SBE lacks any political incentive to follow the governor's lead on policy issues. The CSSO is appointed by the SBE and acts independently of the governor. The high transaction costs derive from the sovereignty of all three state-level policymaking institutions and increase the likelihood of maintaining the status quo in the education policy environment.

Figure 5.4 illustrates Model 3: an independently elected CSSO and a governor appointed SBE. Nine states utilize this structure. Model 3 represents a middle ground between the more centralized Model 1 and the decentralized Model 2. While the governor has education policymaking authority through the appointment of the SBE, the independently elected

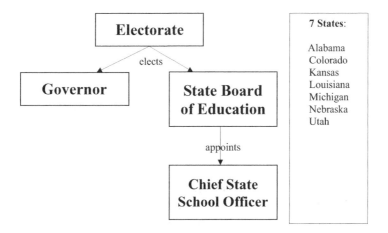

Figure 5.3 State Education Governance Model 2

CSSO reduces the governor's influence over the administration, oversight, and implementation of the education bureaucracy. Model 3 has moderate centralization. Members of the SBE, and by extension the state education agency, are beholden to the governor through their appointed positions, but the CSSO is not.

Figure 5.5 illustrates Model 4, which is utilized by 11 states. In Model 4, the governor appoints both the SBE and the CSSO. This model is the most centralized governance structure, as both the SBE and the CSSO are indebted to the governor for their positions. This model centralizes education policy power in the governor, who has significant policymaking authority. Model 4 places accountability squarely in the office of the governor. Model 4 has the lowest transaction costs but the highest conformity costs. The CSSO and the members of the SBE, and by extension the state education agency, are beholden to the governor through their appointed positions.

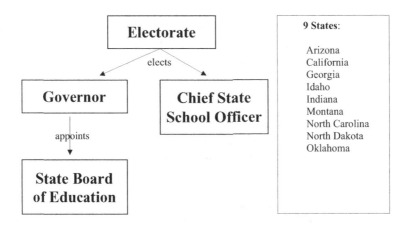

Figure 5.4 State Education Governance Model 3

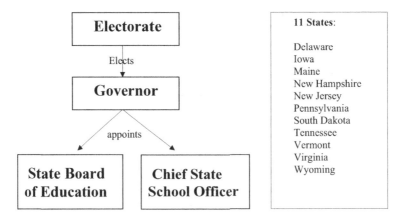

Figure 5.5 State Education Governance Model 4

Higher Education Governance Structures

All states have a higher education governance structure, but the authority, power, and complexity of these systems vary widely. Seventeen states provide legal authority to establish postsecondary governance systems in their constitutions, while 36 states do so through statute. Counterintuitively, governance systems established by statute typically give policy leaders more authority over higher education decisions than constitutionally established governance systems. Constitutional authority is typically dated, while state statutes developed in the past several decades are more likely to vest additional authority in a centralized governance system. State higher education governance structures fall into one of four categories: a single statewide coordinating board, a single statewide governing board, one or more major statewide coordinating or governing boards, and an administrative or service agency.

Coordinating boards typically have the authority to approve institutional missions; develop systemwide strategic plans; develop and maintain academic policies, programs, and initiatives; and provide recommendations to state leaders. Typically, coordinating boards have little or no role in personnel and institutional operations, with those responsibilities falling to individual higher education institutions' local boards. Table 5.8 lists the 20 states that utilize a higher education governance structure with a single state coordinating board. These states are disproportionately clustered in the South and the Midwest. For example, Oklahoma's statewide coordinating board has authority over public higher education institutions and more limited authority over independent institutions. All higher education institutions are governed by their own local boards. State community colleges are not governed by state coordinating boards. (Fulton, 2019).

Statewide governing boards are empowered with the responsibilities of coordinating boards but have additional university-level authority. The statewide governing boards typically also have direct responsibility for personnel decisions, institutional operations including hiring college presidents and determining compensation agreements, and authority for approving institutional budgets and recommending systemwide budgets to the state legislature. Statewide governing boards centralize more authority than coordinating boards. Only eight states utilize a statewide governing board. These states are typically low-population states where a statewide governing board creates economies of scale by centralizing authority and reducing the decision-making responsibilities of individual colleges. For example,

Table 5.8 State Higher Education Governance Models

Higher education board type	States
Single statewide coordinating board	Alabama, Arkansas, Colorado, Illinois, Indiana, Kentucky, Louisiana, Maryland, Massachusetts, Missouri, Nebraska, New Mexico, Ohio, Oklahoma, Oregon, South Carolina, Tennessee, Texas, Virginia, Washington
Single statewide governing board	Alaska, Hawaii, Idaho, Kansas, Montana, Nevada, North Dakota, Rhode Island
One or more major statewide governing boards	Arizona, California (3), Connecticut, Florida (2), Georgia (2), Iowa (2), Maine (2), Minnesota (2), Mississippi, New Hampshire (2), New York (2), North Carolina (2), Pennsylvania, South Dakota, Utah (2), Vermont, West Virginia, Wisconsin, Wyoming
Administrative or service agency	Alaska, Arizona, Connecticut, Delaware, Florida, Iowa, Minnesota, New Hampshire, Mississippi (2), South Dakota (2), Wisconsin (2)

the Nevada Board of Regents governs the state's 4- and 2-year institutions, rather than local governing boards (Fulton, 2019).

While more populous states typically have more than one systemwide coordinating board, some medium and lower population states do as well. For example, the California higher education system has three governing systems: the University of California system, the California State University, and the California Community Colleges. The state also has 150 private nonprofit colleges and 160 for-profit institutions that do not fall under any of the higher education governance structures. The lack of a coordinating body for higher education makes goal setting, oversight, and coordination more challenging (Johnson & Mejia, 2019). Given the recent challenges of increasing tuition and declining enrollments, the California state legislature has discussed legislation that would reestablish a higher education authority.

The 11 states that utilize administrative agencies to oversee components of their higher education systems also have system-level coordinating or governing boards. Five states have standalone postsecondary agencies – Alaska, Arizona, Connecticut, Minnesota, and New Jersey – while six states have postsecondary divisions within the K–12 education department: Delaware, Florida, Iowa, New Hampshire, New York, and Pennsylvania (Fulton, 2019). These agencies fall under the auspices of the governor and the state education bureaucracy. Postsecondary administrative agencies typically advise or provide recommendations to state policy and education leaders, conduct research, administer programs, and engage in statewide planning (Fulton, 2019).

Coordinating and Governing Board Selection Methods

State higher education coordinating and governance boards consist of appointed members who oversee the development, implementation, and evaluation of policies and practices of the university systems. Table 5.9 identifies the selection methods for postsecondary coordinating

Table 5.9 Appointing Authority for Postsecondary Coordinating and Governing Boards

Appointing authority	States
Governor appoints	Arizona (12), Arkansas (12), Illinois (8), Iowa (14), Minnesota (13), Virginia (13)
Governor appoints some board members	Alabama (12/10), Connecticut (21), New Jersey (29), Tennessee (6/14), Vermont (5/15)
Governor appoints with approval of legislature	Alaska (11), California (18), Colorado (11), Florida (14), Georgia (19), Hawaii (23), Idaho (11), Kansas (9), Kentucky (9), Louisiana (13), Maine (16), Maryland (16), Massachusetts (15), Mississippi (15), Missouri (12), Montana (10), Nebraska (9), Nevada (10), New Hampshire (10), North Carolina (17), North Dakota (18), Oklahoma (9), Oregon (14), Pennsylvania (20), Rhode Island (10), South Carolina (15), South Dakota (9), Texas (10), Utah (18), Washington (9), West Virginia (9), Wisconsin (18), Wyoming (9)
State legislature appoints	Mississippi (12), New York (17), North Carolina (25)

Note: Number in parentheses denotes the number of board members.

and governing boards. Governors have some level of appointment power in all states. The governor appoints board members with approval from the state legislature in 33 states. Six states provide the governor with appointment power without approval from the state legislature. In another five states, the governor appoints some of the members, but other entities including the state legislature have authority over appointing some of the members. Mississippi, New York, and North Carolina have multiple postsecondary boards, with one of the boards appointed by the state legislature. In all states, the governor plays a central role in determining the composition of postsecondary coordinating and governing boards.

Executive Officer Selection Methods

Postsecondary education officers lead postsecondary governance systems in goal setting, administration, and policy development. In 41 states, the postsecondary executive officers are appointed by the coordinating or governing board. In only three states, New Hampshire, Pennsylvania, and Washington, does the governor have sole authority to appoint the executive officers. Table 5.10 shows that in an additional seven states the governor appoints the executive officers with approval of the state legislature. The SBE or secretary of education appoints the executive officers in five states: Florida, Idaho, Iowa, Massachusetts, and New York.

Table 5.10 Appointing Authority of Postsecondary Executive Officers

Appointing authority	*Number*	*Number of boards or agencies*	*States*
Agency board or agency committee	2	2	Alaska, Delaware
Coordinating board	18	19	Alabama, Illinois, Indiana, Kentucky, Louisiana, Mississippi, Missouri, Nebraska, Oklahoma, Oregon, South Carolina, South Dakota, Tennessee, Texas, Virginia, Wisconsin, West Virginia (2), Wyoming
Coordinating board with approval of governor	1	1	Arkansas
Governing board	23	31	Alaska, Arizona, California (3), Connecticut, Florida, Georgia (2), Hawaii, Iowa, Kansas, Maine (2), Minnesota (2), Mississippi, Montana, Nevada, New Hampshire (2), New York (2), North Carolina (2), North Dakota, Pennsylvania, Rhode Island, South Dakota, Vermont, Wisconsin
Governing board with approval of governor or Senate	1	2	Utah (2)
Governor	3	3	New Hampshire, Pennsylvania, Washington
Governor with approval of legislature	7	7	Colorado, Connecticut, Maryland, Minnesota, New Jersey, New Mexico, Ohio
SBE or secretary of education	5	5	Florida, Idaho, Iowa, Massachusetts, New York

Judicial Branch

On April 14, 2016, a California appeals court reversed a lower court ruling that teacher tenure and other job protections violated the California Constitution's equal protection clause. The Los Angeles County Superior Court had ruled that teacher tenure was unconstitutional. In June 2014, the plaintiffs in that case argued teacher tenure protected ineffective teachers and therefore violated the equal protection rights of students who were taught by those low-performing teachers. The Los Angeles schools superintendent had testified for the plaintiffs, arguing teacher tenure was unconstitutional, while California Attorney General Kamala Harris argued for teacher protections with support from the California Teachers Association and the California Federation of Teachers, the two largest teachers unions in the state (Blume & Ceasar, 2014; Blume et al., 2016).

The superior court found that district administrators placed ineffective teachers primarily in low-income and racially diverse schools and thereby violated the equal protection clause. The appeals court agreed that low-income and racially diverse schools disproportionately placed teachers in low-income schools, but found that placement by administrators did not flow from the teacher protections. This case sparked a national debate over teacher tenure and the distribution of teachers across districts and schools.

This case, *Vergara v. California*, illustrates the central role of state courts in influencing education policy. Court systems are reactive institutions: They do not set policy agendas but can only react to cases brought before them. Despite this limitation, court decisions have influenced student civil rights, school finance, special education, bilingual education, desegregation, and teacher rights through the interpretation of federal and state constitutions (Reid, 2016). When political factions or interest groups fail to achieve policy change through the legislative or regulatory framework, they often turn to the courts to achieve their policy goals. Opponents of judicial influence argue unelected judges should not allow political actors to achieve policy goals they failed to achieve through the legislative process. Proponents argue the courts are designed to be independent of political influence and can defend minority rights against oppression by the majority. This section reviews the structure of state court systems and selection methods.

State Court Structure

Each state's constitution and laws establish a state court system. While its structure varies significantly across the 50 states, the basic judicial hierarchy is a pyramid, like the federal judicial system. *Limited jurisdictional trial courts* (LJCs), sometimes called inferior, circuit, or district courts, are at the bottom of the hierarchy. LJCs hear minor civil cases, crimes classified as misdemeanors, small claims, and other minor disputes. States have varying numbers of LJCs.

General jurisdiction courts (GJCs), also referred to as major trial courts, sit above LJCs and have primary jurisdiction on issues not delegated to LJCs, including serious criminal or civil cases. Cases are typically designated to GJCs based on the severity of punishment or the monetary value of a case, including felony prosecutions. Seven states have single-tiered trial courts without general and limited jurisdiction divisions: California, Iowa, Idaho, Illinois, Maine, Minnesota, and Vermont. Twenty-one states have three or more GLC and LJC types, nine have two GLC and LJC types, and 16 utilize one type of GLC and LJC trial courts.

The next level up the pyramid in the state court hierarchy is state courts of appeals, also known as *intermediate appellate courts*. Appellate courts hear appeals on cases decided in the lower courts and from administrative agencies. Thirty-nine states have appellate courts that typically hear the first, and often only, appeal because they exercise both mandatory and discretionary review of cases. Eleven states do not have appellate courts because their caseloads are such that all appeals go directly to the court of last resort.

State supreme courts, also called the *courts of last resort*, maintain final authority over appeals filed in state courts. Most states have a single state supreme court, but Oklahoma and Texas maintain separate state supreme courts for civil and criminal cases. State supreme courts are at the top of a judicial system that oversees more than 95% of all cases filed in the United States and decides more than 10,000 cases annually (National Center for State Courts, 2014). While the U.S. Supreme Court receives the most attention from scholars, media, and the public, state court systems resolve most of the civil and criminal court cases decided annually in the U.S.

Selection Methods

Judicial selection methods vary substantially across states but generally fall into five categories: partisan election, nonpartisan election, legislative appointment, gubernatorial appointment, and assisted appointment (National Center for State Courts, 2020). Table 5.11 shows the number of states that utilize each selection method for the three levels of state judicial systems. State supreme courts often have assisted appointment; 24 of 52 courts (recall that Texas and Oklahoma have two supreme courts) use this selection method. Assisted appointment, also known as the Missouri Plan or merit selection, is a judicial selection process in which the governor appoints judges based on the recommendation of a commission or board (Goelzhauser, 2019). The nominating commission reviews judicial candidate qualifications and submits a list to the governor, who appoints judges from among the nominees submitted. Typically, after serving for an initial period, judges participate in a retention election (American Bar Association, 2008).

Nonpartisan elections are the second most common state judicial selection method, with 15 states utilizing this method for the supreme court, 15 for appeals courts, and 34 for trial courts. Nonpartisan candidates on the ballot are listed without their party affiliation, while in partisan judicial elections they are listed with their party affiliation. Seven states use partisan elections for the supreme court, and 39 do for trial courts. Table 5.11 illustrates that elections are more commonly used for lower courts than for state supreme or appellate courts. Gubernatorial appointment of state supreme court judges occurs in only five states, and legislative appointments are used in only two states.

Supreme Court judicial terms range from 6 years to life. Table 5.12 denotes the terms of office for all state supreme court justices. States with partisan and nonpartisan elections

Table 5.11 State Courts Selection Methods

Method	Supreme court	Court of appeals	Trial courts
Partisan election	7	6	39
Nonpartisan election	15	15	34
Legislative appointment	2	2	5
Gubernatorial appointment	5	3	6
Assisted appointment	24	18	46
Combination or other	0	1	17
Total	52	45	147

Table 5.12 State Supreme Court Judicial Selection Systems and Terms of Office

Partisan election	Nonpartisan election	Assisted appointment	Gubernatorial or legislative appointment
Alabama (6)	Arkansas (8)	Alaska (10)	California (12)
Illinois (10)	Georgia (8)	Arizona (6)	Maine (7)
Louisiana (10)	Idaho (8)	Colorado (10)	Massachusetts (Life)
North Carolina (8)	Kentucky (8)	Connecticut (8)	New Jersey (7)
Pennsylvania (10)	Michigan (8)	Delaware (12)	Tennessee (8)
Texas (6)	Minnesota (6)	Florida (6)	South Carolina (10)
	Mississippi (8)	Hawaii (10)	Virginia (12)
	Montana (8)	Indiana (10)	
	Nevada (6)	Iowa (8)	
	North Dakota (10)	Kansas (6)	
	Ohio (6)	Maryland (10)	
	Oregon (6)	Missouri (12)	
	Washington (6)	Nebraska (6)	
	West Virginia (12)	New Hampshire (Life)	
	Wisconsin (10)	New York (14)	
		Oklahoma (6)	
		Rhode Island (Life)	
		South Dakota (8)	
		Utah (10)	
		Vermont (6)	
		Wyoming (8)	

average 8-year terms, while states with assisted, gubernatorial, or legislative appointments average over 10 years. Only three states, New Hampshire, Massachusetts, and Rhode Island, grant supreme court judges life terms. Life terms are intended to reduce political influence in the court system but given the increasing politicization of the federal and state court systems, this has not occurred.

During the past several decades, state judicial selection methods have relied more heavily on elections, and those elections have become more expensive and polarized. Thirty-nine states use elections for at least part of their judicial selection method. Fair and impartial judges are a bedrock foundation of independent courts. Scholars, former judges, and advocates have argued that using elections for judicial selections politicizes state court systems. In the 2018 election cycle, nearly 40 million dollars was spent on state supreme court elections alone (Keith et al., 2019). Special interests and dark money groups have accounted for 27% of all spending in those campaigns, far outpacing their share in congressional elections. The influence of money in the state judicial selection system has undercut the ability of these vital institutions to be fair and independent arbitrators of justice.

Judicial branch state courts are limited in their power to influence education policy because of several constraints. First, state courts can only make judicial decisions on cases that are before the courts. They cannot proactively seek out cases. Second, in the separation of powers system, the state courts maintain a check on the policymaking branches through their ability to rule on the constitutionality of laws and regulations. However, when the policy preferences of the courts differ from those of the state legislature and governor, the policymaking branches typically win. The state court can rule on a matter, but the state legislature and the governor have the constitutional authority to write and sign legislation or make constitutional changes to negate the court decision. Third, state courts lack enforcement authority.

A state court can decide a case that calls for a change in education systems, but courts lack the capacity to make changes without action by the state legislature or executive branch bureaucracies. Despite these power asymmetries, state courts can have dramatic impacts on state education systems through rulings on constitutional and statutory responsibilities. As will be discussed in more detail in Chapter 9, state court rulings on education finance issues can have far-reaching impacts on state education systems.

Informal Actors

A wide range of organized interests attempt to influence government policy. The term *interest group* refers to a group of people who seek to influence public policy based on a common interest or concern. The term also refers to organized interests that are required to register in states for official lobbying activities; states vary in lobbying requirements and interest group registration. Not all interest groups are the same. *Institutional interests*, the most common type, are nonmembership organizations such as businesses, local governments, and post-secondary institutions (Gray & Lowery, 2001). *Associations* are interest groups composed of organizations such as business groups. For instance, all states have a state chamber of commerce that represents business interests. *Traditional membership groups* are composed of individual members who voluntarily join, pay dues, and share specific policy goals. Professional organizations, including teachers unions, fall into this interest group category.

The number of state interest groups has grown dramatically in recent decades, from 15,000 in 1980 to 57,920 in 2015 (Garlick & Cluverius, 2020). This growth was caused by the devolution of policy responsibilities from the federal to state governments. During the past 40 years, federal programs including Temporary Assistance to Needy Families, the Safe Drinking Water Act, and the ESSA devolved responsibilities, which increased lobbying efforts. Interest group growth is also a product of more government regulation of an increasingly complex economy and society. Finally, interest group growth is a result of the development of new technologies and innovations, from cell phones to stem cell research to online education.

Research indicates that interest groups influence state education policy and spending (Brower et al., 2017; Gray & Lowery, 1999; Tandberg, 2010; Tandberg & Wright-Kim, 2019). The composition and strength of the interest group community in a state can explain policy and spending priorities, illustrating the influence of these nongovernmental actors on government institutions. Interest group power has three components: money, membership, and leadership. Interest groups that attract large memberships can wield more influence over policy leaders as potential voters and as advocates. Interest groups that can raise large sums of money can finance their organization and donate to political campaigns. Leadership is central to interest group influence because organizations like teachers unions are large and complex, with millions of members, thousands of staff, and countless local chapters. Leadership is also necessary to develop and implement effective advocacy campaigns. Interest groups influence government actors and institutions through lobbying, acting to influence current government decisions, or creating relationships conducive to shaping future government decisions.

Teachers Unions

Teachers unions and business groups are the most influential interest groups in state government. The two largest teachers unions in the country are the National Education Association, with more than three million members, and the American Federation of Teachers, with 1.7 million members. In the 2016 election cycle, teachers unions donated more than $40 million to state campaigns, $30 million to federal campaigns, and tens of millions of dollars to advocacy organizations. Teachers union leaders are highly skilled at influencing election outcomes through campaign donations, campaigning, and advocacy. In recent years, teachers unions have successfully advocated for higher teacher pay, better working conditions, employment protections, and more education resources. Teachers union support is not bipartisan. Ninety-five percent of teachers union campaign donations go to Democratic candidates, making them highly influential with one political party.

Business Interest Groups

The U.S. is *pluralistic*, a political philosophy recognizing and affirming that a diversity of interests within a political body can ensure no single interest becomes dominant. Political scientists have long argued that pluralism has a bias in favor of moneyed interests, namely businesses (Dahl, 1956). Nearly 85% of lobbying expenditures nationwide are from business interests (Baumgartner & Leech, 2001). The lobbying assets of business organizations provide them with an advantage in achieving their desired policy objectives. The policy environment can limit their influence when the issue is salient and public opinion is strongly opposed to business objectives.

Foundations

Philanthropy's influence on education policy has grown significantly during the past two decades as well-resourced foundations increased in number, the global economy created an international job market, and the United States fell behind other industrialized nations in secondary and postsecondary educational attainment measures. The power of foundations in the public policy arena is directly tied to their financial resources. In 1995, just 16 foundations held more than $1 billion in assets and 164 held more than $100 million (Tompkins-Stange). By 2021, 140 foundations had more than $1 billion in assets and approximately 45,000 held more than $100 million.

When do interest groups wield power and when do they succeed? Research indicates interest groups, particularly business interests, prevail only under specific environmental conditions (Lowery & Gray, 2004). Interest groups rarely succeed if public opinion is strongly against their policy goals. Elected representatives have a reelection incentive that requires them to maintain a plurality of support among likely voters. If their constituents are strongly against a legislative action, no level of interest group funding or lobbying is likely to incentivize them to risk reelection. For low-salience issues, issues of minor concern to the public at large, interest groups can influence public policy change. Interest groups are more adept at negative than positive power. In other words, interest groups are better positioned to protect the status quo than to enact new policies.

Interest group power is based partially on the level of state regulation. Most states require interest groups to register as lobbyists, but the definition of lobbying varies widely. States with broader definitions have more control over lobbying activities. Disclosure laws require lobbyists to make public any expenditures they make to government officials, specifically gifts and campaign contributions. Interest group regulations are effective at altering lobbyist behavior by limiting the ability of these organizations to fully utilize their power in terms of campaign contributions (money) and lobbying relationships (tactics). Despite these regulatory efforts, interest groups, particularly teachers unions and business interests, continue to wield significant power in state education policy.

Informal actors use money, influence with voters, and campaign tactics to influence elected officials' reelection incentives. Therefore, they have tremendous influence with elected leaders. Teachers unions almost exclusively support Democratic candidates and typically are their largest donors. While teachers unions dictate much of Democratic candidates' education agenda, business leaders dictate much of the Republican education agenda. State partisan control drives whether the education policy agenda of teachers unions or of business interest groups receives majority legislative support. Educational leaders can better understand the political and policy dynamics of an education issue by understanding the policy agenda and resources of informal actors.

Pennsylvania State Curriculum Standards Case Study

This chapter began with a summary of Pennsylvania's fight over the establishment of state curriculum standards. It asked who ultimately determines education policy outcomes. Considering the powers discussed in this chapter for formal actors in the legislative, executive, and judicial branches and informal actors including interest groups, political parties, and the public, the answer depends on the policy and political context. This section applies the Chapter 1 theoretical principles to this chapter's content to answer these questions.

Institutions

The first principle is that the power dynamics of institutions varies from state to state depending on constitutional and statutory authority and the political environment. In a vacuum, the state legislature is the first branch of state government and the most powerful institution. If the state legislature is united in favor of a particular policy outcome, typically it has the authority to change the law or even the state constitution. However, its power is predicated on several factors discussed throughout this chapter. First, more professionalized legislatures have more power than citizen legislatures because of the additional resources, time, and opportunity they can use to consider and enact legislative policy. Pennsylvania had one of the most professionalized legislatures in the country, and therefore it had the resources and opportunity to determine the state curriculum standards issue if it was united.

However, the Pennsylvania state legislature was not united. The political environment matters. States with one-party control have greater ability to concentrate power in state legislative majority coalitions. Since 1994, the Pennsylvania Senate has been under Republican control; however, its House of Representatives was under Democratic control between 2006 and 2010, and a Democratic governor was in power 14 of the previous 18 years. Divided government limited the ability of majority coalitions to dominate the policy space and led to instability in education policy, such as consistent curriculum standards. Despite numerous legislators introducing bills to remove the Common Core standards, the state legislature failed to act because members were unable to build majority coalitions in the House and Senate. Other than the House and Senate leaders, the Education Committee members were the most influential legislators on the issue of education standards. The state legislature could not overcome collective action problems and build a broad consensus on Common Core standards. The state legislature has the most institutional power over legislative policy issues, but it also faces the greatest barriers to acting, with numerous veto points throughout the legislative process.

Given the state legislature's inability to solve the state curriculum issue, the responsibility fell to the executive branch. Pennsylvania has a Model 4 education governance structure in which the governor appoints both the SBE and the CSSO. This provided Governor Corbett with centralized power to determine the policy outcome. While the SBE typically has policy jurisdiction over curriculum standards, the centralized governance model empowered the governor to make the ultimate decision.

In the 2010 elections, Republicans won the Pennsylvania House and governor's office, paving the way for conservative policy shifts. Following the 2010 elections, Pennsylvania's Senate was split 27 Republicans to 24 Democrats and the House of Representatives was split 112 Republicans to 92 Democrats. However, 45 states had signed onto the Common Core standards and Pennsylvania business, military, and higher education interest groups had supported the Common Core standards, incentivizing conservatives' support. Beginning in late 2013, conservative support for Common Core standards began to change as conservative interest groups including home schoolers, evangelicals, and conservative think tanks called for their repeal (Jochim & Lavery, 2015). In Pennsylvania, the interest group Pennsylvania Against Common Core, after hearing conservative radio and TV host Glenn Beck claim that Common Core was a federal takeover of American education, organized against the standards. Americans for Prosperity, a conservative advocacy interest group founded and funded by billionaires Charles and David Koch, spent over $200 million nationwide during the 2014 midterm elections on political advertising, including efforts to turn public opinion against the Common Core. The impact of conservative group advocacy had the intended impact. EdNext, an education research organization, found that support for the Common Core standards declined from 76% to 46% between 2013 and 2014 and opposition increased from 13% to 40%. Research indicates that conservative interest group efforts successfully moved public opinion on one of the most contentious education policy issues in the U.S. by 2014 (Supovitz & McGuinn, 2019).

The policy tool being used matters. State standards are a regulatory issue that Pennsylvania delegates to its SBE. Although the legislative branch has sole authority to pass laws, executive branch agencies are granted authority to write, implement, and enforce regulations. If it needed to pass legislation to revise curriculum standards, the power dynamic would shift toward the legislative branch and increase the likelihood of status quo – no change in the state standards.

History matters. States have pushed back against national education standards for decades. In 1989, the George H.W. Bush administration adopted national education goals that included content standards. In 1994, the reauthorization of ESSA required all states to establish rigorous education standards. Conservative elected leaders and interest groups have long fought against adoption of national academic standards as an example of government overreach in violation of states' rights. Despite the initiative from state political leaders, including members of the National Governors Association and the CCSSO, conservative pushback was inevitable and predictable, especially after the Barack Obama administration provided funding to support the initiative. In Pennsylvania, the political history of conservative opposition mattered in quickly mobilizing conservative opposition to the Common Core standards.

How Educational Leaders Identify Formal and Informal State Policy Actors

In a democracy, voters decide elections, but those who involve themselves in the policy-making process determine policy outcomes. Educational leaders can influence state education policy subsystems, but that requires knowing who to contact and how to get involved. Chapter 4 discussed how to identify and define a problem, how to gather information to persuade policymakers, and how to identify who in federal government can help fix your problem. This chapter focused on identifying state-level actors that can fix the problem, building support for the cause, and techniques for persuading decision makers.

Once one determines a problem requires a state-level policy change, one must identify the specific institutions that can solve it. Table 5.13 identifies the typical jurisdictions of policy issues. These policy jurisdictions vary by state, so it is necessary to determine whether these apply in one's state. Policy jurisdictions can also change based on the context of the policy change. For example, in 2018, Massachusetts adopted new history and social studies curriculum standards, which would typically fall under SBE jurisdiction. The Massachusetts Board of Education did work with educators, scholars, and policymakers to develop the updated standards and vote to adopt them; however, the state legislature also voted to pass the curriculum standards in authorizing legislation because of the broad impacts and specific civic

Table 5.13 Education Policy Jurisdictions of State Government Institutions

Institution	Policy jurisdiction
State legislature	Lawmaking
	State budgets
	Represent constituents
	Executive oversight
Governor	Implement laws
	Develop executive budget requests
	Influence legislation
	Appoint board members and chief state school officers
	Set policy agenda
	Oversight of education department
Education department	Administration of statewide special services (e.g., teacher placement, financial services, statewide testing)
	Provide information on education status
	Conduct long-range studies for planning the state program of education
	Encourage public support and participation in the education system
	Education operations (e.g., disability services)
	Regulate the administrative duties and responsibilities of local schools in compliance with state and local laws
	Oversight of use of local public school funds
	Enforce school health and safety rules
	Determine the proper qualifications and licensing of teachers
	Oversight of compulsory and child labor laws
State board of education	Adopt short- and long-term goals for the public education system
	Adopt policies, rules, and regulations to perform duties delegated by law
	Maintain administrative organization for personnel of the board
	Determine high school graduation standards
	Provide general supervision of public school system
	Submit budget requests to the state legislature and governor
	Oversight of teacher licensure
	Adopt curriculum standards
	Supervise the certification of instructors
	Provide annual reports of the quality and status of public education
Chief state school officer	Enforce all laws, rules, and regulations of the state
	Oversight of the state department of education
	Serve as the head administrative officer of state education
	Advise on the current status of the public school system
	Oversee public school data systems
	Oversee ongoing training and professional development
	Design and implement a statewide system of educational assessment
	Provide assistance to local school districts

service graduation requirements. It also voted on appropriations legislation to fund their implementation.

To identify who can solve a problem, one place to start is www.USA.gov, an interagency government resource administered by the General Services Administration. Its state government page, www.usa.gov/state-tribal-governments, has links to all state legislatures, governors, education departments, elected officials, and additional state agencies. The CCSSO has links to all CSSOs at https://ccsso.org/chiefs. The National Association of State Boards of Education has profiles of all state board governance structures and policy issues before the state boards on their website at https://stateboardinsight.nasbe.org. The U.S. Department of Education has links to all state education departments, higher education agencies, and adult education agencies at https://www2.ed.gov/about/contacts/state/index.html.

How to Build Support for a Policy Issue

Those who seek to change public policy need to determine the level of public support for the issue; identify arguments that resonate with the public; and target specific interest groups, citizens, and policymakers with a policy campaign (Graham & Hand, 2010). Public support for a policy issue does not guarantee success, but change is nearly impossible without public support. Many educators make the mistake of assuming their cause will garner widespread support because it is righteous. Public resources are finite, so policy choices are a zero-sum game in which a win for one group leaves fewer resources for another. As a result, policy decisions almost always face significant opposition. It is incumbent upon policy entrepreneurs to identify the level of public support for a policy issue. If the policy issue has issue expansion, meaning it moves beyond the policy subsystem into the broader public consciousness and deliberation, then public support for the policy issue becomes central to the prospects for change. If the policy issue remains within the policy subsystem, then public opinion is less determinative of its prospects. In some cases, educational leaders can identify public opinion through publicly available polls. In other cases, it will require talking with a wide range of experts, including policy subsystem actors. For example, the legislative staff of education committee members is a prime source for understanding support for and opposition to a policy issue.

Next, educational leaders need to identify arguments that will resonate with policy subsystem actors to convince them that precious public resources and time should be expended on a policy issue. This requires collecting information through research and speaking with policy subsystem actors to understand the arguments for and against the policy change. To understand the motivation of various public stakeholders, one must explore their incentive structure. For example, why might business groups, teachers unions, or higher education administrators support or oppose a particular policy? Rather than assuming, talk to various stakeholders and understand their reasons for supporting or opposing an issue. If they oppose the policy change, determine how the policy proposal may be adjusted to gain their support.

Finally, educational leaders need to build coalitions of support by using research and making clear arguments. Different evidence and arguments will convince different subsystem actors, interest groups, and citizens. For example, to convince a governor to support an educational policy change, one should appeal to the economic impact the change would garner, particularly as it relates to an increase in employment. To appeal to state legislators worried about balancing the state budget, cite potential long-term cost savings of the policy change. Ultimately, understanding the key formal and informal actors, the power dynamics of the policy subsystem, and how to build coalitions of support are all foundational elements to influencing state education policy decisions.

Key Terms

administrative oversight
appointment power
appropriations
associations
authorization
budget authority
bureaucracy
chief state school officer
conference committee
conformity costs
constitution
constitutional commission
constitutional convention
constitutions
coordinating board
direct democracy
direct initiative
education department or agency
foundations
general jurisdictional courts
governing board
governor
higher education governance models
indirect initiative
institutional interests
interest groups
intermediate appellate courts
joint committee
K–12 education governance models
legislative professionalism
limited jurisdictional trial courts
majority leader
minority leader
pluralistic system
power of the purse
senate president pro tempore
speaker of the house
special committee
standing committee
state board of education
state judiciary
state legislature
state supreme court
statutory law
traditional membership groups
transaction costs
veto power

Discussion Questions

1. What education language is in your state constitution? What is the statutory language for education in your state? Do your state constitution and statutory laws exceed minimum education requirements? Does your state establish a strong or weak legal justification for K–12 or postsecondary education?
2. What education laws has your state legislature passed in the past 10 years? What is the composition of its education committees? What is its leadership structure? How involved is the state legislature in education in your state?
3. What state education governance structure does your state utilize? How much power does your governor have within this governance structure?
4. What are the composition and responsibilities of your state board of education?
5. What are the responsibilities of your chief state school officer?
6. Has your state supreme court decided any education finance or higher education cases?
7. What are the most influential education interest groups in your state?

Activities and Assignments.

1. Identify a state policy issue closely related to your research. Provide an overview of the policy issue. Utilize state website resources from the textbook website and newspaper articles to discuss who was involved with the creation of the policy issue.
2. Choose either elementary and secondary education or postsecondary education in your state. Discuss the power relationships in your state governance structure. Who has the power related to your policy issue?
3. Use resources from the textbook website to identify which interest groups have contributed to members of your state's legislative leadership and the leadership of its house and senate education committees.

References

American Bar Association. (2008). *Judicial selection: The process of choosing judges.* Coalition for Justice.

Arceneaux, K. (2001). The gender gap in state legislative representation: New data to tackle an old question. *Politics Research Quarterly, 54*(1), 143–160.

Baker v. Carr, 369 U.S. 186 (1962).

Barrett, E. J. (1995). The policy priorities of African American women in state legislatures. *Legislative Studies Quarterly, 20*(2), 223–247.

Baumgartner, F. R., & Leech, B. L. (2001). Interest niches and policy bandwagons: Patterns of interest group involvement in national politics. *Journal of Politics, 63*(4), 1191–1213. https://doi.org/10.1111/0022-3816.00106

Blume, H., & Ceasar, S. (2014, June 10). California teacher tenure and seniority system struck down. *Los Angeles Times.*

Blume, H., Resmovits, J., & Kohli, S. (2016, April 14). In a win for unions, appeals court reverses ruling that threw out teacher tenure in California. *Los Angeles Times.* www.latimes.com/local/lanow/la-me-ln-court-rejects-bid-to-end-teacher-tenure-in-california-marking-huge-win-for-unions-20160414-story.html

Bowman, A. O., & Kearney, R. C. (2008). *State and local government.* Houghton Mifflin.

Bratton, K. A. (2002). The effect of legislative diversity on agenda setting evidence from six state legislatures. *American Politics Research, 30*(2), 115–142.

Bratton, K. A., & Haynie, K. L. (1999). Agenda setting and legislative success in state legislatures: The effects of gender and race. *The Journal of Politics, 61*(3), 658–679.

Brower, R., Jones, T. B., Tandberg, D., Hu, S., & Park, T. (2017). Comprehensive developmental education reform in Florida: A policy implementation typology. *The Journal of Higher Education, 88*(6), 1–26. https://doi.org/10.1080/00221546.2016.1272091

Brown, C. G., Hess, F. M., Lautzenheiser, D. K., & Owen, I. (2011). *State education agencies as agents of change: What it will take for the states to step up on education reform*. American Enterprise Institute for Public Policy Research.

Carmichael, S. B., Martino, G., Porter-Magee, K., & Wilson, W. S. (2010). *The state of state standards – and the common core – in 2010*. Thomas B. Fordham Institute.

Casellas, J. P. (2009). Coalitions in the house? *Political Research Quarterly*, *62*(1), 120–131. https://doi.org/10.1177/1065912908315335

Clark, C. J. (2019). *Gaining voice: The causes and consequences of Black representation in the American states*. Oxford University Press.

Council of Chief State School Officers. (2017). *Council of chief state school officers 2017–2020 strategic plan*. https://ccsso.org/sites/default/files/2018-01/2017-2020%20Strategic%20Plan-Online Version.pdf

Dahl, R. A. (1956). *A preface to democratic theory*. University of Chicago Press.

Dallman, S., & Nath, A. (2020). *Education clauses in state constitutions across the United States*. Federal Reserve Bank of Minneapolis.

Darcy, R., & Choike, J. R. (1986). A formal analysis of legislative turnover: Women candidates and legislative representation. *American Journal of Political Science*, *30*(1), 237–255. https://doi.org/10.2307/2111303

Dinan, J. (2016). *The American state constitutional tradition*. University of Kansas Press.

Erickson, B. (2019, November 17). *Your state's constitution: The people's document*. National Conference of State Legislatures. www.ncsl.org/blog/2017/11/17/your-states-constitution-the-peoples-document.aspx

Ferguson, M. (2018). Governors and the executive branch. In V. Gray, R. Hanson, & T. Kousser (Eds.), *Politics in the American states: A comparative analysis* (7th ed., pp. 235–274). CQ Press.

First, P., & Quaglia, J. (1990). *The evolving roles of the state boards of education, state education agencies, and chief state school officers (occasional paper series no. 8)*. University of Maine, College of Education.

Frymer, P. (1999). *Uneasy alliances: Race and party competition in America*. Princeton University Press.

Fulton, M. (2019). *An analysis of postsecondary governance structures*. Education Commission of the States.

Garlick, A., & Cluverius, J. (2020). Automated estimates of state interest group lobbying populations. *Interest Groups & Advocacy*, *9*(3), 396–409.

Goelzhauser, G. (2019). *Judicial merit selection: Institutional design and performance for state courts*. Temple University Press.

Graham, S. B., & Hand, C. (2010). *America the owner's manual: Making government work for you*. CQ Press.

Gray, V., & Lowery, D. (1999). *The population ecology of interest representation: Lobbying communities in the American states*. University of Michigan Press.

Gray, V., & Lowery, D. (2001). The institutionalization of state communities of organized interests. *Political Research Quarterly*, *54*(2), 265–284. https://doi.org/10.1177/106591290105400202

Heniff, B., Jr. (2012). *Overview of the authorization-appropriations process*. Congressional Research Service.

Henig, J. R. (2009). Mayors, governors, and presidents: The new education executives and the end of educational exceptionalism. *Peabody Journal of Education*, *84*(3), 283–299. https://doi.org/10.1080/01619560902973449

Henig, J. R. (2013). *The end of exceptionalism in American education: The changing politics of school reform*. Harvard Education Press.

Hutchens, N. H. (2008). Preserving the independence of public higher education: An examination of state constitutional autonomy provisions for public colleges and universities. *JC & UL*, *35*, 271.

Jochim, A., & Lavery, L. (2015). The evolving politics of the common core: Policy implementation and conflict expansion. *Publius: The Journal of Federalism*, *45*(3), 380–404. https://doi.org/10.1093/publius/pjv015

Johnson, H., & Mejia, M. C. (2019). *California's higher education system*. Public Policy Institute of California. www.ppic.org/wp-content/uploads/higher-education-in-california-californias-higher-education-system-october-2019.pdf

Keith, D., Berry, P., & Velasco, E. (2019). *The politics of judicial elections, 2017–18*. Brennan Center. www.brennancenter.org/our-work/research-reports/politics-judicial-elections-2017-18

Kraft, R. (2019). *Quarrel over common core: A Pennsylvania primer*. WFMZ. www.wfmz.com/news/quarrel-over-common-core-a-pennsylvania-primer/article_c3a035d1-6ff9-51eb-8fc4-a2f1a1e31254.html

Lasswell, H. D. (1936). *Politics: Who gets what, when, how*. Whittlesey House.

Levy, L. W. (1995). *Seasonal judgments: The American constitution, rights, and history*. Transactions Publishers.

Loeb, S., Miller, L. C., & Strunk, K. O. (2009). The state role in teacher professional development. *Education Finance and Policy, 4*(2), 212–228.

Louis, K. S., Leithwood, K., Wahlstrom, K. L., & Anderson, S. E. (2010). *Investigating the links to improved student learning*. The Wallace Foundation.

Lowery, D., & Gray, V. (2004). A neopluralist perspective on research on organized interests. *Political Research Quarterly, 57*(1), 164–175. https://doi.org/10.1177/106591290405700114

Mayhew, D. (1974). *Congress: The electoral connection*. Yale University Press.

Mills, M. R. (2016). Stories of politics and policy: Florida's higher education governance reorganization. *The Journal of Higher Education, 78*(2), 162–187. https://doi.org/10.1080/00221546.2007.11780872

Moe, R. C. (1988). *Prospects for the item veto at the federal level: Lessons from the states*. National Academy of Public Administration.

Mooney, C. Z. (2013). Explaining legislative leadership influence. *Political Research Quarterly, 66*(3), 559–571. https://doi.org/10.1177/1065912912458369

Murphy, J. (2013, May 20). Corbett orders delay in Common Core academic standards' implementation. *Patriot-News*. www.pennlive.com/midstate/2013/05/corbett_orders_delay_in_common.html

National Center for State Courts. (2014). *Court statistics project*. www.courtstatistics.org/

National Center for State Courts. (2020). *Methods of judicial selection*. www.ncsc.org/consulting-and-research/areas-of-expertise/court-leadership/judicial-selection

National Conference of State Legislatures. (2020). *Roles and responsibilities of selected leadership positions*. www.ncsl.org/legislators-staff/legislators/legislative-leaders/leadership-positions-roles-and-responsibilities.aspx

Orey, B. D., Smooth, W., Adams, K. S., & Harris-Clark, K. (2006). Race and gender matter: Refining models of legislative policy making in state legislatures. *Journal of Women, Politics & Policy, 28*(3–4), 97–119. https://doi.org/10.1300/j501v28n03_05

Parker, E. (2016). *50 state review: Constitutional obligations for public education*. Education Commission of the States.

Reid, D. (2016, April 20). *The role of the courts in shaping education policy*. Michigan State University, College of Education. https://education.msu.edu/green-and-write/2016/the-role-of-courts-in-shaping-educational-policy/

Renter, D. S., Tanner, K., Braun, M., & Kober, N. (2019). *Number of low-performing schools by state in three categories (CSI, TSI, and ATSI), school year 2018–19*. Center on Education Policy; The George Washington University Graduate School of Education and Human Development.

Shober, A. F. (2012). Governors make the grade: Growing gubernatorial influence in state education policy. *Peabody Journal of Education, 87*(5), 559–575. https://doi.org/10.1080/0161956x.2012.723494

Squire, P., & Hamm, K. E. (2005). *101 chambers: Congress, state legislatures, and the future of legislative studies*. Ohio State University Press.

Squire, P., & Moncrief, G. (2019). *State legislatures today: Politics under the dome*. Rowan & Littlefield.

Sunderman, G. L., & Orfield, G. (2007). Do states have the capacity to meet the NCLB mandates? *Phi Delta Kappan Magazine, 89*(2), 137–139. https://doi.org/10.1177/003172170708900209

Supovitz, J., & McGuinn, P. (2019). Interest group activity in the context of common core implementation. *Educational Policy, 33*(3), 453–485. https://doi.org/10.1177/0895904817719516

Tandberg, D. A. (2010). Politics, interest groups and state funding of public higher education. *Research in Higher Education, 51*(5), 416–450. https://doi.org/10.1007/s11162-010-9164-5

Tandberg, D. A., & Wright-Kim, J. (2019). State higher education interest group densities: An application of the energy-stability-area model to higher education. *The Review of Higher Education, 43*(1), 371–402. https://doi.org/10.1353/rhe.2019.0099

Timar, T. B. (1997). The institutional role of state education departments: A historical perspective. *American Journal of Education, 105*(3), 231–260.

Weber, M. (1948). *From Max Weber: Essays in sociology* (C. W. Mills & H. H. Gerth, Trans.). Routledge; Keegan Paul.

Weiss, J., & McGuinn, P. (2017). *The evolving role of the state education agency in the era of ESSA and Trump: Past, present, and uncertain future*. The Consortium for Policy Research and Education. https://search.issuelab.org/resources/31435/31435.pdf

Wirt, F., & Grove, S. (1990). Education. In V. Gray, H. Jacob, & R. B. Albretton (Eds.), *Politics in the American states: A comparative analysis* (5th ed., pp. 445–456). Scott Foresman & Co.

6 Local Education Governance

Power and Local Control

The United States has a tradition of strong local government, dating back to the first town hall meeting held in Dorchester, Massachusetts, in 1633. During the colonial period, the American colonies had only 2.5 million people, with the largest city, Philadelphia, having only 40,000 people. The agrarian, low-density communities were deeply rooted in the concept of local self-government. The American Revolution was caused by colonial opposition to British centralized control and taxation. The concepts of local self-government and mistrust of centralized power are founding principles of American culture. These founding principles are manifest in Americans' preference for local government today. According to a 2021 Gallup poll, Americans' trust in the federal government was 39%, while trust in state governments was 57% and local government 66% (Brenan, 2021). Local governments are perceived as closer and more responsive to people's daily lives than state or federal governments are.

Given Americans' preference for local government, it is ironic that state and federal governments have more power than local governments. The relationship between the federal and state governments is fundamentally different from the relationship between state and local governments. Unlike federal and state governments, local governments are not sovereign, meaning their power derives from state governments rather than from the people they serve. This means states vary widely in the political power and authority they delegate to local governments. Political power delegated from the state to local governments includes structural, functional, fiscal, and personnel (United States Advisory Commission on Intergovernmental Relations [USACIR], 1993). Structural power refers to the power to choose the form of government and enact or revise local government charters, the equivalent of a state constitution for local government. Functional power refers to the ability of local governments to exercise self-government. Fiscal power denotes the authority to tax, borrow, and engage in other financial activities. Personnel power is the authority to set employment rules, employment conditions, and collective bargaining. Historically, states afford local governments the broadest discretion in structural powers and the least discretion in financial powers (Zimmerman & United States Advisory Commission on Intergovernmental Relations, 1981).

Historically, two principles have guided states' application of local government authority: Dillion's rule and home rule. Dillion's rule holds that local governments only exercise the powers expressly granted by the state, the grant of power must be explicitly conferred by the state constitution or a state statute, and the power must be essential to the local government's existence (Krane et al., 2001). Dillion's rule provides states with broad authority over local government structures, functions, and fiscal authority. Dillion's rule was named after Iowa Supreme Court Justice John Dillon for his decision in *The City of Clinton v. The*

DOI: 10.4324/9781003231561-8

Cedar Rapids & Missouri River Railroad Co. (1868), which affirmed that local governments are considered an extension of the state government and bound by the state constitution. In 1907, the United States Supreme Court upheld the decision in *Hunter v. Pittsburgh*. Thirty-nine U.S. states now employ Dillion's rule. Dillion's rule provides states with control over local governments and limits local governments' ability to respond to crisis.

Home rule grants local governments greater autonomy, if they obey the state constitution and laws, in areas including the ability to pass laws and local government charters. Ten states apply home rule: Alaska, Iowa, Massachusetts, Montana, New Jersey, New Mexico, Ohio, Oregon, South Carolina, and Utah (Krane et al., 2001). Several states employ both Dillion's and home rules. In these circumstances, Dillion's rule applies to all local governments except those explicitly provided home rule status in the state constitution or statutes.

Despite their relative lack of sovereignty and power, local governments play an outsized role in the day-to-day lives of most Americans (National League of Cities [NLC], n.d.). According to the Census Bureau (2019), local governments employ 14.2 million people, compared to 5.5 million state employees and fewer than 3 million federal employees. Local government services typically include education, fire protection, police protection, public maintenance, public utilities, recreation, social services, transportation, and zoning regulations. Different types of local governments provide different services.

Types of Local Governments

County Governments

There are four types of local government: counties, municipalities, special districts, and school districts. County governments are the largest units of local government. According to the Census Bureau, the United States has 3,143 counties. All states divide their geographic boundaries into counties except Louisiana, where equivalent subunits are called parishes, and Alaska, where the equivalent subunits are called boroughs. The functions of county governments vary widely across the states.

Counties were created to serve as administrative extensions of state governments (NLC, n.d.). Population growth and expanding suburbs following World War II increased the need for local governments to provide services. The additional responsibilities delegated to county governments came with additional autonomy from state government and political accountability. In 1952, only six states allowed county government charters; today, 32 do and six others allow limited charters (DeSantis & Renner, 1993; Sokolow, 2004). The charter reform movement increased local autonomy and decreased local government corruption, inefficiency, and partisanship (DeSantis & Renner, 1993; Martin, 1993).

Counties utilize three primary government structures: commission, council-executive, and commission-administrator. The most common form of county government is commission. This type of government has an elected board of commissioners that exercises both executive and legislative functions. County commissions' legislative functions typically include passing county ordinances and budgets, and their executive functions include control over administrative offices and implementation and oversight of county services.

Commission-administrator governments are a reform of county commissions. Commission-administrator governments divide the legislative and executive functions between a council and an executive, much like federal and state governments. The elected commission, as in the commission form of government, maintains authority over legislative and executive functions, but it selects an administrator to run the government. The commission maintains control over all decisions, hires the administrator, and retains political accountability.

Council-executive governments have an independent officer who has the authority to carry out executive functions. The county executive's powers are equivalent to a county-level governor or president, including veto authority over council ordinances, appointment of executive department staff, and oversight of daily operations. The separation of powers between the elected council and the elected executive divides political accountability between the government branches.

Municipalities

Municipalities are political subdivisions of a state for which a municipal corporation has been established to provide general local government for a specific population within a defined geographic area. They include cities, boroughs, villages, and towns (Simone, 2021). The main difference between municipalities and counties is that municipalities are the source of the local government. Counties are established by the state constitution or statute in a top-down approach, but municipalities are established in a bottom-up approach in which a community incorporates as a legal entity for self-government. Municipalities are not simply subunits of the state government.

Geographically, municipalities are generally established within counties. Municipalities are organized under state constitutions and laws with powers exercised by elected governments. Historically, local government structures distinguished a city from a town, with cities being governed by representatives and towns allowing direct democratic deliberation. Today, the defining characteristics of cities and towns differ by state but more often are based on population size rather than government structure.

The terms city and urban are often used interchangeably, but they are not the same. According to the Census Bureau, urban areas have a minimum population of 5,000 people or 2,000 housing units. Rural areas fall below these thresholds. Cities are defined as an area of at least one square mile, population of at least 1,000 people, and a population density of 500 people per square mile (Census Bureau, 2019). Urban areas include cities and suburbs. Rural areas include all population, housing, and territory not included within an urban area.

Townships are a geographic and political subdivision of a county and are generally located in rural areas. Townships, unlike municipal towns, establish local governments in areas without a minimum population concentration. These political subdivisions are established by groups of citizens for the distribution of general government services and to resolve political issues.

Municipality governance systems fall into four categories: mayor-council, council-manager, commission, and town meeting. These systems rank from high conformity costs/low transaction costs to low conformity costs/high transaction costs. Transaction costs are the time and effort required to compare preferences and negotiate compromises. Conformity costs are the difference between what individuals would ideally prefer and what political leaders decide to do. Strong executives with a weak or absent legislative body epitomize a low transaction cost governance system. The advantages of strong executives are their ability to make quick, efficient decisions. The disadvantage of strong executive systems is they can impose high conformity costs on their constituents because they have the authority to make decisions with little input from political or civic actors. Strong mayor systems are the local governance model with the lowest transaction costs. Town meetings are the other end of the governance spectrum. Town meetings allow all members of the community to have a say in local governance decisions. The advantage of this system is low conformity costs, as all in the community have their voices heard. The disadvantages are high transaction costs, making it difficult for local governments to make efficient decisions. This subsection discusses each of the local governance systems and their advantages and disadvantages.

Mayor-Council

The mayor-council governance system has a separation of legislative and executive responsibilities. According to a 2018 International City/County Management Association (ICCMA) survey, 38.2% of municipalities nationwide employ a mayor-council form of government (ICCMA, 2019). The distribution of powers and responsibilities between the mayor and council vary considerably across the municipalities utilizing this system.

Mayor-council systems that provide more authority and responsibilities to the mayor than the council are called strong mayor systems, and those that provide more authority and responsibilities to the council are called weak mayor systems. Strong mayors exercise authority comparable to a state governor. Typical strong mayor responsibilities include broad appointment powers, veto authority over council legislative actions, budget authority, and oversight of day-to-day government operations. In weak mayor systems, the mayor presides over the council but has no formal executive authority. The council has both executive and legislative powers. In weak mayor systems, the mayor must utilize informal powers to influence the council. The influence of the mayor varies with the informal powers wielded by the mayor.

The city councils in both strong and weak mayor systems retain legislative authority including reviewing and approving budgets; passing ordinances and resolutions; establishing long- and short-term priorities; oversight of employee performance; establishing tax rates; modifying the local government charter; and regulating business, land use, and zoning laws (NLC, n.d.). According to the ICCMA (2019), 20% of municipalities list political parties on ballots for city council seats. Council sizes range from five to 51, with a national average of six. Typically, as the population size increases, the number of council seats increases. For example, the New York City Council is comprised of 51 elected members, while the Springfield, MA, City Council is comprised of five elected members. Similar to Congress and state legislatures, municipal councils utilize committee systems to allow policy specialization, improve organizational efficiency, and increase citizen participation.

Council-Manager System

The council-manager system differs from the mayor-council system by separating political and administrative government functions rather than separating executive and legislative functions (Smith et al., 2008). In this governance system, the council performs political and policy decisions including passing ordinances and resolutions; approving budgets; and regulating business, land use, and zoning laws. The manager implements the policy directives of the council and runs the day-to-day operations of the municipal government. According to the ICCMA (2019), approximately 48.2% of municipalities employ a council-manager system.

The council-manager system was a progressive response to a long history of local government corruption. In 1915, the mayor-council system was founded by the National Civic League (NCL), ICCMA, and other civic organizations to reduce local government corruption and partisanship (NCL, 2021). The largest cities with a council-manager system are Phoenix, AZ; San Antonio, TX; Dallas, TX; and San Jose, CA.

Commission Systems

Municipal commissions are local governance systems endowed with executive and legislative powers. Each commissioner is elected to run an executive department such as finance, health, police, or public works. In addition to serving as executive department leader, they also play a legislative role as a member of the commission. The advantage of the commission system is that the lack of checks and balances allows the governance system to work efficiently. The simple organizational system, in theory, allows for direct, efficient policy implementation. This form of local government originated in Galveston, TX, in 1901 following the hurricane that destroyed the city. The breadth of the disaster required an efficient governing system to deal with the emergency and rebuild the city. The disadvantages of the governance system are that department leaders make decisions that best serve their department rather than the local government and constituents. Given the practical limitations of the government outside of emergency situations, the commission system is only employed by 3% of local governments (ICCMA, 2019).

Town Meetings

Town meetings exemplify the oldest and most democratic local governance system. During the colonial period, small New England communities utilized the town meeting system to ensure consensus decision making. Town meetings came to signify the principles of self-government and local decision making that would become part of the American political tradition. This governance structure is a form of direct democracy that places a premium on low conformity costs by having the whole town act as the legislative body. Town meetings have the distinct disadvantage of high transaction costs. Because all community members have a voice, decisions are difficult to reach. This is the primary reason only 2% of local governments still use this governance system, most of them small New England towns.

An open town meeting refers to town meetings where all registered voters comprise the town's legislature and are eligible to vote. Article LXXXIX of the Massachusetts Constitution requires all towns with fewer than 6,000 residents to adopt an open town meeting form of government. Representative town meetings require registered voters to elect representatives by precinct to represent them in the town meeting. The representatives, rather than all registered voters, have town meeting voting authority.

Special Districts

Municipalities and county governments discussed in this chapter are general purpose governments that deliver a broad range of public services. In contrast, special districts are governmental subunits created for a specific purpose that have administrative and fiscal independence from other local governments. Special districts can extend through multiple municipalities or counties and offer a specific service over a larger geographic area. The United States has more than 38,000 special districts. According to the Census Bureau (2019), special district functions include air transportation, corrections, education, electric power, fire protection, gas supply, health, highways, hospitals, house and community development, industrial development, libraries, natural resources, parking facilities, parks and recreation, sewerage, solid waste management, transit, and water supply. The Census Bureau excludes school district governments from the category of special districts. Special districts are the most common local government type in the United States.

Municipalities and counties have limited tax bases and provide a broad range of public services, making it difficult to deliver all services citizens need. A special district has the advantage of administering new or expanding public services and paying for those services independently of the general government. Special districts allow local governments to provide additional services without directly impacting the local tax rates or tax base. These malleable and nimble local government systems allow local governments to provide public services, respond to changing local environments, and combat emergencies in ways other local systems cannot.

School Districts

Public school districts are another type of special purpose government. They administer elementary and secondary schools within a geographic area. Public school systems are classified as independent or dependent. Dependent school systems are under the control of another local or state government and are not independent of them. School districts, like municipalities and county governments, are local governments. The United States has more than 13,000 public school districts functioning as independent special purpose governments and more than 1,000 dependent school districts (Census Bureau, 2019).

States use different school district definitions. Consolidated school districts are formed from the merger of two or more school districts. Independent school districts typically operate independently of county or municipal governments and under the supervision of a state government authority. A unified school district provides elementary and secondary education services and instruction. Elementary school districts and secondary school districts only serve specific grade levels.

School districts were designed as political and administrative units to manage the massive growth, particularly in secondary schooling, that occurred throughout the late 19th and early 20th centuries (Tyack, 1974). During the 20th century, as states acquired more control over local public schools, a school consolidation movement dramatically reduced the total number of school districts. School consolidation refers to combining school districts and their functions under a single administration. Between 1940 and 2020, the number of school districts decreased **89%**, from **117,000** to **13,187**. Between 1930 and 1970, the main period of school consolidation, average district size increased from 170 to 2,300 students through the elimination of **120,000** schools and 100,000 districts (Berry & West, 2008). This institutional evolution transformed school districts from one-room schoolhouses into large professional bureaucracies. The consolidation movement coincided with the professionalization of elementary and secondary education. The professionalization movement reduced the influence of urban political machines and the parochialism of rural one-room schoolhouses (Tyack, 1974).

School consolidation was driven by claims of economic efficiency, specialized instruction, and improved school infrastructure. Smaller school districts are more expensive to operate than larger ones due to economies of scale, factors that cause the average cost of production to decline as volume increases. All school districts require certain minimum overhead costs, regardless of size. Larger schools distribute those overhead costs across more students, lowering the average cost. Larger districts and school sizes increase the number of faculty, allowing greater specialization of the curriculum. Larger school districts also increase the economies of scale for building construction. As the percentage of the population receiving secondary education rose throughout the 20th century, the cost of public education rose. Consolidation provided an opportunity to moderate the capital and human labor costs of this educational expansion.

Opponents of school district consolidation argue these reorganizations harm communities. Consolidation eliminates or combines schools or districts to form a larger school system. Schools often serve as a community hub; the loss of these institutions can damage the social fabric. Larger schools can reduce parent and student school involvement, both of which are associated with student academic achievement. Larger school districts can also increase the average distance of students from the school buildings and thus transportation costs (Duncombe & Yinger, 2007). School consolidation can increase administrator and teacher salaries and benefits when small, rural schools combine with school systems that have higher personnel costs (Duncombe & Yinger, 2007).

School district sizes vary greatly across and within states. Table 6.1 depicts the number of districts by state, ranging from the over 1,000 districts in Texas to the single districts in Hawaii and the District of Columbia. Average student enrollment also varies widely across states, from a high of nearly 40,000 students per district in Florida to a low of 500 in Montana (excluding the single-district states). Generally, more rural states have smaller student enrollments per district. Rural population density and distances between population centers increase the number of districts required and reduces the number of students served by each district.

Most educational policy reform initiatives focus on the state or school levels rather than the district level (Spillane, 1996). Many states' school funding formulas continue to incentivize school district consolidation. Research indicates district consolidation has already maximized fiscal efficiency for most moderate and large school systems (Howley et al., 2011).

Local School Boards

The nation's nearly 14,000 local school boards administer education to the more than 50 million children in the American public education system. A local board of education may also be called a board of directors, school board, or school committee. School board members are the closest policymakers to school children. Local school board authority derives from the state constitution and laws. Like any local government entity, school boards are ultimately an extension of state government. The state legislature delegates power to local school boards to develop policies, rules, and regulations to oversee school operations. The school board is considered a corporate body, meaning it must conduct official meetings prior to official action. School board members are technically state officers who act on behalf of the state in fulfilling their duties and responsibilities.

Local school boards govern education policy and administrative procedures for school districts. School board responsibilities include establishing district goals; overseeing central administration, school administrative staff, and teachers to achieve goals; allocating district funds; and representing the broader community. School boards typically are responsible for the appointment and oversight of the district superintendent. Most school boards hold open meetings to meet requirements for public access and participation.

Ninety-six percent of school board members are elected (Hess, 2002). School board members can be elected at-large by all members of the district or by voters within a particular geographic section of the district. School board elections are primarily nonpartisan. Hawaii is the only state that does not utilize local school boards. Mayors and other executive branch officers appoint 4% of school board members. Cities where the mayor appoints all or part of the local school board include Baltimore, MD; Boston, MA; Cleveland, OH; Washington, DC; Jackson, MS; New York, NY; Oakland, CA; Philadelphia, PA; and Providence, RI. School boards are typically composed of between five and 15 members who are uncompensated volunteers. Local school board elections are plagued by a lack of candidates and low voter

Table 6.1 School Districts, Enrollment, and Average District Enrollment by State, 2020

State	Number of districts	Enrollment	Average district enrollment
Alabama	138	725,900	5,260
Alaska	53	136,700	2,579
Arizona	230	1,168,800	5,082
Arkansas	237	493,700	2,083
California	977	6,215,200	6,362
Colorado	178	936,900	5,263
Connecticut	138	502,100	3,638
Delaware	19	142,600	7,505
District of Columbia	1	98,600	98,600
Florida	73	2,919,000	39,986
Georgia	180	1,817,000	10,094
Hawaii	1	193,300	193,300
Idaho	117	293,900	2,512
Illinois	853	2,003,100	2,348
Indiana	291	1,020,800	3,508
Iowa	328	514,500	1,569
Kansas	287	503,400	1,754
Kentucky	171	708,400	4,143
Louisiana	72	729,100	10,126
Maine	192	171,800	895
Maryland	24	917,300	38,221
Massachusetts	316	937,600	2,967
Michigan	539	1,440,800	2,673
Minnesota	331	892,500	2,696
Mississippi	137	475,700	3,472
Missouri	518	911,700	1,760
Montana	302	151,100	500
Nebraska	244	325,200	1,333
Nevada	20	492,700	24,635
New Hampshire	162	170,000	1,049
New Jersey	546	1,365,600	2,501
New Mexico	129	338,300	2,622
New York	686	2,757,500	4,020
North Carolina	120	1,589,400	13,245
North Dakota	179	124,900	698
Ohio	615	1,688,900	2,746
Oklahoma	512	711,700	1,390
Oregon	175	623,100	3,561
Pennsylvania	499	1,684,700	3,376
Rhode Island	34	139,200	4,094
South Carolina	79	793,900	10,049
South Dakota	169	140,900	834
Tennessee	141	1,008,400	7,152
Texas	1,022	5,594,600	5,474
Utah	42	688,200	16,386
Vermont	98	82,600	843
Virginia	132	1,308,100	9,910
Washington	306	1,133,800	3,705
West Virginia	55	274,900	4,998
Wisconsin	423	854,700	2,021
Wyoming	49	100,000	2,041
United States	13,140	51,737,900	3,937

turnout (National School Board Association [NSBA], 2018). Historically, local government election voter turnout in the United States is less than 10%.

The expansion of the federal and state role in American education since the 1960s has come at the expense of local school board authority. The federal government has expanded its authority to equalize school funding gaps, achievement gaps, civil rights, and disability rights. State governments have expanded their role in order to improve funding equity and their ability to administer federal funding resources. Education policymaking roles historically delegated to local school boards have increasingly become driven by state governments, including the development of academic standards, curriculum development, and professional teacher preparation. The school consolidation movement also transferred authority from locally elected school boards to educational bureaucracies (Tyack, 1974).

Local school board duties and responsibilities continue to include administrative oversight, developing curriculum, adopting an annual budget, and meeting federal and state mandates for public schools. School boards also represent the community, advocate for the educational needs of children, and provide leadership in the selection of school staff. Researchers have identified three key roles that local school boards play: policymaking, administration, and leadership.

Policymaking. Local school boards are required by state law to approve district budgets and curriculum frameworks and to develop educational standards and assessment systems. Although school board members prefer to focus on long-term planning and broad policy-making goals, daily operations take up most of their time. School board members operate in a complex environment of state and federal mandates, teachers unions, and community disagreement over educational goals and priorities.

Administration. In theory, the local school board is a legislative branch responsible, like state legislatures and Congress, for enacting policy and appropriating funding, and the school superintendent is responsible for executive functions including implementing policy decisions and carrying out daily operations. In practice, school board members often get involved in the daily operations of schools to determine whether their policy prescriptions are being implemented as desired. According to the National School Board Association (NSBA), there are at least eight characteristics of effective school boards, including:

- **high expectations and clear goals**: Effective school boards commit to a vision of high expectations for student achievement and quality instruction and define clear goals toward that vision.
- **shared belief in all children's ability to learn**: Effective school boards have strong shared beliefs and values about what is possible for students and their ability to learn and of the system and its ability to teach all children to high levels.
- **accountable for student achievement**: Effective school boards are accountability driven, spending less time on operational issues and more on policies to improve student achievement.
- **collaborative relationship with the community**: Effective school boards have a collaborative relationship with staff and the community and establish a strong communications structure to inform and engage both internal and external stakeholders in setting and achieving district goals.
- **data driven for continuous improvement**: Effective boards are data savvy; they embrace and monitor data, even when the information is negative, and use it to drive continuous improvement.
- **develop and align resources**: Effective school boards align and sustain resources, such as professional development, to meet district goals.

- **strong internal teamwork with superintendent**: Effective school boards lead as a united team with the superintendent, each from their respective roles, with strong collaboration and mutual trust.
- **continuous improvement**: Effective school boards take part in team development and training, sometimes with superintendents, to build shared knowledge, values, and commitments for their improvement efforts.

School board membership. In 2017, more than 50% of local school board members were women (NSBA, 2018). This made local school boards the only U.S. elected institution with a female membership equaling the U.S. average. By comparison, 27% of the 117th Congress and 30% of state legislators are women. According to the NSBA's 2018 survey, gender equity has improved steadily. The percentage of female school board members nationwide has increased from 39.9% in 1992 and 44% in 2010. School boards are the most progressive political institutions in terms of gender equity in America.

Unfortunately, local school board membership does not reflect U.S. racial and ethnic diversity. Local school board members are 78% White, compared to 48% of public school children (NSBA, 2018). African Americans comprise 10% of local school board members and 16% of public school students. Hispanic and Latinos comprise only 3% of local school board members and 27% of public school students. Research indicates local school board diversity results in tangible differences in school policy and outcomes (Samuels, 2020).

Superintendents

Local school boards delegate executive functions to the superintendent of the public school system. Superintendents implement school board policy directives and manage daily school operations. Superintendents are usually selected by the school board and in many states also serve as nonvoting board members. Both the school board and the superintendent are held accountable for each school's academic achievement. In 1837, Buffalo, NY, became the first school district to appoint a superintendent (Callahan, 1966). Increases in school district size and complexity in the late 19th century and early 20th century required additional accountability and oversight. As the position of superintendent and other school leadership positions became more complex in the latter half of the 20th century, state governments increased school administrator licensure and professional training requirements. Table 6.2 identifies state requirements for local school superintendents. Most states now require teacher licensure, a master's degree from an approved graduate program, a minimum of 3 years of teaching experience, and passing a school administrator exam.

Scholars have identified five superintendent responsibilities and duties: teacher-scholar, statesperson, communicator, business manager, and social scientist (Kowalski & Brunner, 2011). The role of teacher-scholar refers to the responsibility to implement state curricula and supervise teachers and instruction. As the roles of administrators and teachers became increasingly different, the superintendent became less of an instructional supervisor (Callahan, 1964). The role of superintendent as manager developed because of the skills required to run increasingly sophisticated organizations. Superintendents' managerial responsibilities grew to include budget development and administration, personnel management, and facilities management (Kowalski & Brunner, 2011). Although debates have occurred about the challenge of superintendents functioning as a business manager and instructional leader, educational leaders advocated for retaining both sets of responsibilities. Higher education institutions began to include management courses in educational leadership graduate training to prepare superintendents for both roles. The Great Depression and the budgetary

Table 6.2 State Requirements for School Superintendents

State	Teacher licensure	Master's degree	Approved graduate program	Teaching experience (years)	School administrator exam	Additional training
Alabama	Y	Y	Y	3	Y	Y
Alaska	Y	Y	Y	3	N	Y
Arizona	Y	Y	Y	3	Y	Y
Arkansas	Y	Y	Y	3	Y	Y
California	Y	Y	Y	3	Y	Y
Colorado	Y	Y	Y	3	Y	Y
Connecticut	Y	Y	Y	3	Y	Y
Delaware	Y	Y	Y	3	Y	Y
Florida	Y	Y	Y	3	Y	Y
Georgia	Y	Y	Y	3	Y	Y
Hawaii	Y	Y	Y	3	Y	Y
Idaho	Y	Y	Y	3	Y	Y
Illinois	Y	Y	Y	3	Y	Y
Indiana	Y	Y	Y	3	Y	Y
Iowa	Y	Y	Y	3	Y	Y
Kansas	Y	Y	Y	3	Y	Y
Kentucky	Y	Y	Y	3	Y	Y
Louisiana	Y	Y	Y	3	Y	Y
Maine	Y	Y	Y	3	Y	Y
Maryland	Y	Y	Y	3	Y	Y
Massachusetts	Y	Y	Y	3	Y	Y
Michigan	Y	Y	Y	3	Y	Y
Minnesota	Y	Y	Y	3	Y	Y
Mississippi	Y	Y	Y	3	Y	Y
Missouri	Y	Y	Y	3	Y	Y
Montana	Y	Y	Y	3	Y	Y
Nebraska	Y	Y	Y	3	Y	Y
Nevada	Y	Y	Y	3	Y	Y
New Hampshire	Y	Y	Y	3	Y	Y
New Jersey	Y	Y	Y	3	Y	Y
New Mexico	Y	Y	Y	3	Y	Y
New York	Y	Y	Y	3	Y	Y
North Carolina	Y	Y	Y	3	Y	Y
North Dakota	Y	Y	Y	3	Y	Y
Ohio	Y	Y	Y	3	Y	Y
Oklahoma	Y	Y	Y	3	Y	Y
Oregon	Y	Y	Y	3	Y	Y
Pennsylvania	Y	Y	Y	3	Y	Y
Rhode Island	Y	Y	Y	3	Y	Y
South Carolina	Y	Y	Y	3	Y	Y
South Dakota	Y	Y	Y	3	Y	Y
Tennessee	N	N	Y	3	Y	N
Texas	Y	Y	Y	2	Y	N
Utah	Y	N	Y	1	Y	N
Vermont	Y	Y	Y	3	Y	Y
Virginia	Y	Y	Y	3	Y	Y
Washington	Y	Y	Y	3	Y	Y
West Virginia	Y	Y	Y	3	Y	Y
Wisconsin	Y	Y	Y	3	Y	Y
Wyoming	Y	Y	Y	3	Y	Y

problems that followed forced superintendents to be lobbyists, advocates, and democratic leaders (Kowalski, 1995). In the mid-20th century, school administration developed into an academic discipline aligned with other social science disciplines. Social science training elevated the status of the profession and applied scientific practices to educational practice (Cooper & Boyd, 1987; Kowalski, 2003). Superintendents have come to play a central role in school reform and improvement efforts in the 20th century. In this role, the superintendent as communicator collaborates with school, community, and political stakeholders to build and maintain school culture (Kowalski & Brunner, 2011).

According to the American Superintendent 2020 Decennial Study, **26.7%** of local school superintendents were female and **72.9%** were male. In its 2000 study, only **13.1%** of superintendents were female, meaning the percentage of female superintendents doubled in 2 decades (Tienken, 2020). Despite these gains, a significant gap in gender equity persists at the highest levels of local school leadership. The superintendent gender gap is even more alarming when one considers that the public teaching force, the primary applicant pool of administrative positions, has the opposite gender split: **74.3%** are women.

Superintendents are also predominantly White, with more than **91%** of them identifying as White compared to **58.9%** of the U.S. population (Mountford & Richardson, 2021). African Americans comprise **13.6%** of the population, but only **3.48%** of superintendents. Hispanics comprise **19.1%** of the population and only **2.4%** of superintendents. All other racial categories – Native American or Native Alaskan, Asian, Native Hawaiian, Pacific Islander, or other races – accounted for less than **1%** of superintendents. While the percentage of non-White superintendents has increased since 2000, from **5%** to **8.26%**, the increase has not kept pace with the increase in student and population diversity. According to the American Association of School Administrators, local superintendents have an annual turnover rate of **14%–16%**. In the 2022–23 academic year, the turnover rate jumped to **25%**.

Principals

Elementary and secondary school principals oversee all school operations, coordinate curriculums, manage staff, and build safe and beneficial learning environments for students (Bureau of Labor Statistics, 2024). The National Association of Elementary School Principals (2019) identified three pillars of effective principals: empowering people, building culture, and optimizing systems. Research indicates that principals produce positive outcomes by developing schoolwide instructional leadership, a positive school environment, and collaborative learning communities to improve teacher practice and by managing personnel and resources strategically.

During the past 3 decades, more principals have been women, but their ranks have not become much more ethnically diverse (Grissom et al., 2021). According to the National Center for Education Statistics (NCES, 2022), public school principals remain predominantly White, **78%** compared to **45%** of public school students. Table 6.3 depicts the demographic characteristics of public school principals. During the past 20 years, Hispanic principals increased from **5%** to **9.3%** while Hispanic public school students increased from **16%** to **28%**. Keeping pace with Hispanic student enrollment would require tripling Hispanic principal recruitment and retention. Women now are a majority of public school principals for the first time. The distribution of women continues to skew toward younger grades. While women are **68.6%** of elementary school principals, they account for only **43.7%** of middle school principals and **35.5%** of high school principals (Taie & Lewis, 2022). Because

Table 6.3 Characteristics of Public School Principals

Characteristic	Public school principals		Public school students	
	1999–2000	*2020–2021*	*1999–2000*	*2020–2021*
Female	44%	56%	48.6%	48.6%
Male	56%	44%	51.4%	51.4%
African American	11%	10.4%	17%	15%
Asian	1%	1%	5%	5%
Hispanic	5%	9.3%	16%	28%
White	82%	77.1%	61%	45%

the average high school principal's salary is considerably higher than the pay of elementary school principals, this disparity exacerbates the pay equity gap.

Public and Private School Options

Historically, public education has been intertwined with residential zoning policies that assign homes to schools based on geographic proximity (Calder, 2019). School quality is reflected in housing and rental prices due to people's willingness to pay for improved government services including school quality (Black, 1999). Low-income households face substantial barriers to accessing effective schools because the high cost of housing limits equal educational opportunities. Selecting a neighborhood based on school quality is considered a form of residential school choice (Egalite & Wolf, 2016). Options for families within the public schools include open enrollment, magnet schools, and charter schools.

Intradistrict Open Enrollment

Intradistrict open enrollment is a form of public school choice that allows students to transfer from their neighborhood or residentially assigned school to another public school within the same school district. Intradistrict open enrollment is considered a form of school choice because families can choose a school other than their neighborhood school. Twenty-seven states and the District of Columbia permit intradistrict open enrollment. Nineteen of these states and the District of Columbia require intradistrict open enrollment, and 11 states have voluntary programs in which districts can choose to allow intradistrict transfers. Intradistrict state policies are often designed to increase access to high-performing schools and improve school integration.

State policies vary considerably in the criteria used to determine eligibility and priority for intradistrict transfers. Broad open enrollment policies have limited or no eligibility criteria for intradistrict transfers beyond limited capacity, while limited open enrollment policies require specific eligibility criteria including school performance, school demographics, and socioeconomic factors. Many states require districts to give priority to students seeking transfers from low-performing schools or high-poverty schools. There also is considerable variability across states in the transparency of open enrollment student transfer decisions including the public reporting of open enrollment data. The lack of publicly reported open enrollment data can make it difficult for school leaders, researchers, and policymakers to access the effectiveness and impact of open enrollment policies.

Interdistrict Open Enrollment

Interdistrict open enrollment policies allow students to transfer from their residentially assigned school district to another school district in the state. Twenty-four states require interdistrict open enrollment, while another 28 states allow districts to choose to participate in interdistrict open enrollment. Some states, including California and Colorado, prioritize students enrolled in low-performing or high-poverty districts for interdistrict transfers.

Magnet Schools

Magnet schools are public schools subject to the same regulations as other public schools in the district in which they operate. Student recruitment and school curriculum distinguish magnet schools from neighborhood public schools. Magnet schools recruit students from multiple districts. They also offer a specialized curriculum focusing on a particular area of study such as the arts, world languages, technology, social studies, STEM, or physical education. Magnet schools operate under standard public school regulations, distinguishing them from charter schools that operate under charters that provide additional autonomy.

According to the NCES (2022), the U.S. had approximately 2.7 million students enrolled in magnet schools in the 2019–2020 school year. Nearly half of them, 1.2 million, were secondary school students, while the other 55% were elementary or middle school students. Magnet schools typically use a lottery system, and approximately 25% use academic criteria for admission. Table 6.4 shows public school options in the various states.

Private School Options

Vouchers

School voucher programs provide public funds for students attending participating private schools. Student eligibility varies across state and local jurisdictions, but it generally requires an income threshold, student disability diagnosis, or enrollment in a "failing" public school (Frendeway et al., 2015). Voucher programs limit eligibility to specific geographic areas ranging from a single school district to an entire state. Some programs limit student eligibility to a targeted population, typically based on socioeconomic status, and others provide universal access. State regulations determine the financial value of the voucher, total number of vouchers awarded, and which schools are eligible to receive school voucher funding.

Education Savings Accounts

Education savings accounts (ESAs) provide parents with public funds deposited into a savings account. The funds can be used for a wide range of approved educational purposes including private school tuition, tutors, homeschooling supplies, and online education. ESA eligibility requirements vary by state but are typically based on income level, disability status, or public school performance level. Eleven states have established ESA programs: Arizona, Arkansas, Florida, Indiana, Iowa, Mississippi, New Hampshire, North Carolina, Tennessee, Utah, and West Virginia.

The implementation of ESAs has become controversial. Unlike school choice vouchers, ESA funding can be used for a broad array of educational expenses. What constitutes an eligible expense is often unclear. Most programs provide funding for private school tuition, public transportation, and supplemental materials, but the lack of clear guidelines has led to calls for additional safeguards for the use of public funds. Unlike 529 college plans that are funded by individuals, ESAs

Table 6.4 Types of Public-School Options by State

State	Intradistrict open enrollment	Interdistrict open enrollment	Charter schools	Magnet schools	Virtual schools
Alabama	No	Yes	Yes	Yes	5
Alaska	No	Yes	Yes	Yes	186
Arizona	Yes	Yes	Yes	Yes	67
Arkansas	Yes	Yes	Yes	Yes	516
California	Yes	Yes	Yes	Yes	1,284
Colorado	Yes	Yes	Yes	Yes	63
Connecticut	Yes	Yes	Yes	Yes	0
Delaware	Yes	Yes	Yes	Yes	0
District of Columbia	Yes	Yes	Yes	Yes	1
Florida	Yes	Yes	Yes	Yes	219
Georgia	Yes	Yes	Yes	Yes	5
Hawaii	Yes	Yes	Yes	Yes	1
Idaho	Yes	Yes	Yes	Yes	17
Illinois	Yes	Yes	Yes	Yes	2
Indiana	Yes	Yes	Yes	Yes	9
Iowa	No	Yes	Yes	Yes	448
Kansas	No	Yes	Yes	Yes	16
Kentucky	No	Yes	Yes	Yes	456
Louisiana	Yes	Yes	Yes	Yes	6
Maine	No	Yes	Yes	Yes	2
Maryland	No	Yes	Yes	Yes	2
Massachusetts	No	Yes	Yes	Yes	2
Michigan	Yes	Yes	Yes	Yes	226
Minnesota	No	Yes	Yes	Yes	33
Mississippi	No	Yes	Yes	Yes	14
Missouri	Yes	Yes	Yes	Yes	2
Montana	No	Yes	No	No	192
Nebraska	No	Yes	No	Yes	4
Nevada	No	Yes	Yes	Yes	5
New Hampshire	Yes	Yes	Yes	Yes	2
New Jersey	No	Yes	Yes	Yes	0
New Mexico	Yes	Yes	Yes	Yes	7
New York	No	Yes	Yes	Yes	0
North Carolina	No	Yes	Yes	Yes	337
North Dakota	No	Yes	No	No	0
Ohio	Yes	Yes	Yes	Yes	14
Oklahoma	No	Yes	Yes	Yes	11
Oregon	No	Yes	Yes	Yes	442
Pennsylvania	No	Yes	Yes	Yes	17
Rhode Island	No	Yes	Yes	Yes	1
South Carolina	No	Yes	Yes	Yes	654
South Dakota	Yes	Yes	Yes	No	153
Tennessee	Yes	Yes	Yes	Yes	172
Texas	Yes	Yes	Yes	Yes	8
Utah	Yes	Yes	Yes	Yes	18
Vermont	Yes	Yes	Yes	Yes	78
Virginia	Yes	Yes	Yes	Yes	370
Washington	Yes	Yes	Yes	Yes	410
West Virginia	Yes	Yes	Yes	Yes	0
Wisconsin	Yes	Yes	Yes	Yes	2,063
Wyoming	No	Yes	Yes	No	0
United States	29 states	42 States			8,547

Note: Virtual schools data from NCES (https://nces.ed.gov/ccd/tables/201819_Virtual_Schools_table_1.asp).

are funded by states. Proponents argue the funds expand opportunities, particularly for nontraditional students. Opponents argue ESAs shift funding away from the public schools that serve all children and toward private schools that can discriminate in their enrollment decisions.

Homeschooling

According to the U.S. Department of Education (DOE), homeschooling requires three conditions: parents reporting their kids being schooled at home instead of at a public or private school, student enrollment in public or private school does not exceed 24 hours a week, and the student is not being temporarily homeschooled due to illness. During the 2020–2021 school year, nearly 3 million (5.4%) elementary and secondary students were homeschooled. This represented a doubling of homeschooled students since before the COVID-19 pandemic: It was 1.5 million (2.8%) in 2019. Whites (4%) homeschool at more than double the rate of Hispanic (1.9%) or Black students (1.2%). Children are more likely to be homeschooled if they reside in a household with three or more children, have at least one parent not in the workforce, and live in a rural area (NCES, 2022). According to the NCES 2021 Household Pulse Survey, the primary reasons parents selected as a reason for homeschooling their children included "concern about school environment such as safety, drugs, or negative peer pressure" (80%), "a desire to provide moral instruction" (74.7%), "emphasis on family life together" (74.6%), "dissatisfaction with the academic instruction at other schools" (72.6%), and "a desire to provide religious instruction" (58.9%).

The federal government does not provide homeschooling requirements, deferring that responsibility to the states. As discussed in Chapter 2, each state's compulsory education laws require all children to attend school until a particular age. Homeschooling qualifies as meeting the compulsory education requirement in all 50 states, but the level of regulation varies widely. Most states require parents to notify their local school district or the state department of education of their intent to homeschool their children. Twenty-three states require instruction equivalent to the amount of instruction required in public school. Twenty-nine states require homeschool instruction in particular subjects typically including math, English language arts, science, and social studies. Twenty states require a homeschool assessment, with 12 of those states requiring standardized testing. Twenty-six states allow homeschooled students to attend public school part-time and participate in extracurricular and cocurricular activities. The expansion of state online schools and the increasing number of homeschooled student participation in state-sponsored online education has muddled the distinction between homeschooling and public schooling.

Education Levels

The United Nations Educational, Scientific, and Cultural Organization developed the International Standard Classification of Education (ISCE) framework to characterize education by programs and fields, allowing for comparisons across nations. Table 6.5 describes the nine levels from early childhood education to doctorate degrees. Levels 0–4 refer to early childhood, primary and secondary education.

Preprimary Education

The first category, preprimary education, refers to early childhood education programs that support children's early cognitive, physical, social, and emotional development and prepare them for primary education. Early childhood programs provide formal and informal teaching of children before entering kindergarten, including public programs such as Head Start and private preschools and childcare. According to the NCES (2023), **63%** of 3- to 5-year-olds were enrolled in a prekindergarten program. Among 5-year-olds, the enrollment rate was **86%** for the 2021–2022 school year. Table 6.6 identifies the percentage of 3-, 4-, and 5-year-olds in preprimary education by race.

Prekindergarten, also known as pre-K, is a publicly funded early childhood education program for children from as early as 3 years old through kindergarten (Couchenour & Chirsman, 2016). Prekindergarten is designed to provide children with academic and social learning experiences to be successful in elementary school. In 1965, the Elementary and Secondary Education Act established the Head Start program, which was designed to meet the academic, emotional, social, health, nutritional, and psychological needs of low-income children so all children would enter elementary school equally ready to learn.

Primary Education

Primary education typically includes children aged 6–11 or kindergarten through fifth or sixth grade. Children begin primary education in kindergarten. Table 6.7 identifies state

Table 6.5 International Standard Classification of Education Framework

Level	Label	Description
0	Early childhood education	Designed to support children's early cognitive, physical, social, and emotional development. Children develop the social-emotional and academic skills necessary for primary education and society.
1	Primary education	Designed to provide students with fundamental skills in reading, writing, and mathematics and establish a foundation for learning and understanding core areas of knowledge, personal, and social development.
2	Lower secondary education	Designed to build on primary education organized around a subject-oriented curriculum.
3	Upper secondary education	Designed to complete secondary education in preparation for tertiary education and provide skills for employment.
4	Postsecondary nontertiary	Designed to build on secondary education to prepare students for the labor market or tertiary education, including vocationally oriented education.
5	Short-cycle tertiary education	Designed to build on secondary education to prepare students for the labor market or tertiary education, including practice-oriented and occupation-specific education.
6	Bachelor's	Designed to provide students with intermediate academic or professional knowledge, skills, and competencies leading to a first postsecondary degree.
7	Master's	Designed to provide students with advanced academic and professional knowledge, skills, and competencies.
8	Doctorate	Designed to provide students with an advanced research qualification based on original research.

Table 6.6 Percentage of 3- to 4-Year-Olds and 5-Year-Olds Enrolled in School, by Race and Ethnicity

Race/ethnicity	3- to 4-year-olds	5-year-olds
Asian	59	92
Black	48	90
Hispanic	42	82
White	55	86
Two or more races	48	97

Table 6.7 State and District Kindergarten Entrance and Attendance Requirements

State	Compulsory school age	Kindergarten entrance age	Required full-day kindergarten	Required half-day kindergarten	Kindergarten attendance required
Alabama	6	5 on or before 9/1	Yes	No	No
Alaska	7	5 on or before 9/1	No	No	No
Arizona	6	5 on or before 8/31	No	Yes	No
Arkansas	5	5 on or before 9/1	Yes	No	Yes
California	6	5 on or before 9/1	No	Yes	No
Colorado	6	5 on or before 10/1	No	No	No
Connecticut	5	5 on or before 1/1	No	Yes	Yes
Delaware	5	5 on or before 8/31	Yes	No	Yes
District of Columbia	5	5 on or before 9/30	Yes	No	Yes
Florida	6	5 on or before 9/1	No	No	No
Georgia	6	5 by 9/1	No	Yes	No
Hawaii	5	5 on or before 7/31	Yes	No	Yes
Idaho	7	5 on or before 9/1	No	No	No
Illinois	6	5 on or before 9/1	Yes	Yes	No
Indiana	7	5 on or before 8/1	Yes	Yes	No
Iowa	6	5 by 9/15	No	Yes	No
Kansas	7	5 on or before 8/31	No	Yes	No
Kentucky	6	5 on or before 7/31	No	Yes	No
Louisiana	7	5 by 9/30	Yes	No	Yes
Maine	6	5 on or before 10/15	No	Yes	No
Maryland	5	5 by 9/1	Yes	No	Yes
Massachusetts	6	Each district determines age requirements	No	Yes	No
Michigan	6	5 by 9/1	No	No	No
Minnesota	7	5 on or before 9/1	No	No	No
Mississippi	6	5 on or before 9/1	Yes	No	No
Missouri	7	5 on or before 7/31	No	Yes	No
Montana	7	5 on or before 9/10	Yes	Yes	No

(Continued)

Table 6.7 (Continued)

State	Compulsory school age	Kindergarten entrance age	Required full-day kindergarten	Required half-day kindergarten	Kindergarten attendance required
Nebraska	6	5 on or before 9/30	No	Yes	Yes
Nevada	7	5 on or before 9/30	No	Yes	Yes
New Hampshire	6	Not specified	No	No	No
New Jersey	6	Local education agency option	No	No	No
New Mexico	5	5 on or before 9/1	No	Yes	Yes
New York	6	Local education agency option	No	No	No
North Carolina	7	5 on or before 8/31	Yes	No	No
North Dakota	7	5 on or before 7/31	No	Yes	No
Ohio	6	Local education agency option	No	Yes	Yes
Oklahoma	5	5 on or before 9/1	Yes	No	Yes
Oregon	6	5 on or before 9/1	No	Yes	No
Pennsylvania	6	Local education agency option	No	No	Yes
Rhode Island	5	5 on or before 9/1	Yes	No	Yes
South Carolina	5	5 on or before 9/1	Yes	No	Yes
South Dakota	5	5 on or before 9/1	No	Yes	Yes
Tennessee	6	5 on or before 8/15	Yes	No	Yes
Texas	6	5 on or before 9/1	Yes	Yes	No
Utah	6	5 on or before 9/1	No	Yes	No
Vermont	6	5	No	Yes	No
Virginia	5	5 on or before 9/30	Yes	No	Yes
Washington	8	5 on or before 8/31	Yes	No	No
West Virginia	6	5 on or before 8/31	Yes	No	Yes
Wisconsin	6	5 on or before 9/1	No	Yes	Yes
Wyoming	7	5 on or before 9/15	No	Yes	No

Note: Data from NCES (https://nces.ed.gov/programs/statereform/tab1_3-2020.asp).

requirements for kindergarten entrance age. Most states require children to enter kindergarten when they have turned 5 years old by a certain date, most commonly September 1. Forty-four states require that school districts offer at least half-day kindergarten. However, only 17 states and the District of Columbia require children to attend full-day kindergarten, and another 16 require half-day kindergarten.

In the U.S., grades through 5 or 6 are referred to as elementary schools. Elementary schools assign students to a teacher or classroom for an entire school year. All U.S. states require school attendance between the ages of 5 and 8 years old. Table 6.7 also notes each state's compulsory school age, the age at which all children are required to attend school. State compulsory school laws can be fulfilled through attendance at a public school, a state-certified private school, or an approved homeschool program.

Lower Secondary School

Early 20th century education and political leaders decided to develop a lower and upper secondary school structure to improve the preparation of students for high school and college, while respecting maturity differences by schooling these students in a separate building from high school students. ISCE's second-level classification is lower secondary school. In the U.S. context, lower secondary schools may be middle schools or junior high schools. Middle schools typically have students in Grades 6–8. Junior high schools have students in Grades 7–9. Junior high schools are academically focused as rigorous preparation for high school and college. The goal of middle schools is to develop the whole student by prioritizing social, emotional, and academic growth.

Between 1970 and 2020, the number of U.S. middle schools increased from **2,100** to nearly **16,000**, a **660%** growth rate. During that same period, junior high schools decreased from **7,800** to **2,500**, a **68%** decrease. Both social and demographic forces influenced the expansion of lower secondary schools, particularly middle schools. Middle school expansion often resulted from overcrowding of elementary schools as school-age populations increased.

Upper Secondary School

The ISCE defines upper secondary school as preparation for tertiary education and providing skills for employment. Tertiary education refers to postsecondary school education including college, universities, and trade schools. In the U.S., upper secondary schools are called high schools. They generally include Grades 9–12 and serve students aged 13–18. High schools include subject-based classes. In 1906, the Carnegie Foundation for the Advancement of Teaching defined admissions criteria for colleges and universities as requiring 4 years of high school. A total of 120 hours of study with an instructor in a single subject meeting five times a week for 40 to 60 minutes for 24 weeks each year equals one unit of high school credit. Most public high school students earn six to seven credits per year.

Forty-six states require a minimum number of high school credit requirements to earn a diploma, with 24 credits the most common requirement. All states have course requirements in English, math, science, and social studies, though they vary in the total credits required in each subject. Some states' graduation requirements include credits in additional subjects including career preparedness or career and technical education, civic education, financial literacy, fine arts, humanities, languages, oral communication, physical education and health, and visual and performing arts. Thirty-four states also include a high school assessment as a graduation requirement.

Higher Education Organizational Structure

American higher education institutions award four types of degrees: associate, bachelor's, master's, and doctoral. According to the DOE, 2-year institutions are legally authorized to offer at least a 2-year program of college-level studies leading to an associate degree or creditable toward 4-year postsecondary institutions. Associate degrees typically require 60 semester credits and can be a terminal degree in a vocational field or prepare students for a bachelor's degree. Bachelor's degrees typically require 4 years of study and prepare students for employment or graduate degrees. Master's degrees generally require an additional 1 or 2 years of study beyond the bachelor's degree. Characteristically, master's degrees require an original master's thesis or a field experience for professional degrees. A doctoral degree requires anywhere from 60 to 120 credits beyond the bachelor's degree, and time to completion can range from 2 to 7 years. Doctoral degrees require a major research project called a dissertation. Doctoral degrees can be research focused (PhD) or practitioner focused in fields including dentistry (DDS), divinity (DD), education (EdD), law (JD), and medicine (MD).

Postsecondary Education Sectors

American higher education institutions emanate from several different sectors of the economy including public, private nonprofit, and private for-profit (McKeown-Moak & Mullin, 2014). For postsecondary students to be eligible for federal assistance, they must attend a Title IV institution. This requirement provides the DOE significant authority to determine the eligibility of institutions of higher education (IHEs). Title IV of the Higher Education Act (HEA) authorizes federal aid for postsecondary institutions, students, and families and establishes postsecondary eligibility criteria and participation requirements. The DOE recognizes approximately **6,000** postsecondary institutions, **1,892** of which are public (**32%**), 1,754 are private nonprofit (**30%**), and 2,270 are private for-profit (**38%**).

Title IV, Section 101 of the HEA defines public and private nonprofit educational institutions and articulates their eligibility requirements. According to the NCES, public institutions are operated by state or other government entities and are primarily supported by public funds. Private nonprofit institutions are owned and operated by one or more nonprofit corporations or associations, authorized by the Internal Revenue Service to be a tax-exempt organization under Section 501(c)(3) of the Internal Revenue Code, and are legally authorized to operate by the state in which they are physically located. Title IV also requires IHEs to (a) admit only students with a high school diploma or the equivalent; (b) offer an associate, bachelor's, graduate, or professional degree; and (c) receive accreditation by an agency recognized by the DOE (Hegji, 2023).

Title IV, Section 102 of the HEA includes both the Section 101 institutions and proprietary, postsecondary vocational, and foreign institutions. Proprietary institutions are those that are neither public nor private nonprofit institutions. The eligibility criteria for a proprietary IHE include (a) providing an eligible program of training, (b) providing a liberal arts program that leads to a baccalaureate degree, and (c) being legally authorized for 2 consecutive years to provide the educational program. Postsecondary vocational institutions are defined as public or private nonprofit institutions that prepare students for gainful employment in a recognized occupation. Foreign institutions refer to foreign-based postsecondary institutions if they are a public or private nonprofit institution and have been approved by the DOE. Table 6.8 shows the number of different types of postsecondary institutions.

Table 6.8 Number of Postsecondary Institutions by Level and Control, 2020–2021

Level and control of institution	Number of institutions
Title IV institutions	5,916
Public	1,892 (32%)
Private nonprofit	1,754 (30%)
Private for-profit	2,270 (38%)
Title IV nondegree-granting institutions	1,985
Title IV degree granting institutions	3,931
2-year colleges	1,294
4-year colleges	2,637

U.S. Framework for Quality Assurance in Higher Education: The Program Integrity Triad

How do the federal and state governments ensure the quality of higher education institutions and programs? Although the U.S. higher education system has long had a reputation as the best in the world, its decentralized nature has caused multiple challenges including consistent educational standards, distinctions between secondary and postsecondary educational offerings, and transferability of credentials (Hegji, 2017). The U.S. higher education system developed with limited federal or state government oversight, posing systemic challenges and opportunities. Colleges and universities established a voluntary system of accrediting associations to evaluate peer institutions to improve their academic reputation, distinguish less qualified academic institutions, and establish common standards to allow institutional credential transfers. In 1944, the GI Bill, or the Serviceman's Readjustment Act, provided financial aid to veterans. This increased the federal role in postsecondary education and the number of higher education institutions seeking federal funds. The 1952 Readjustment Assurance Assistance Act required that institutions receiving federal funds be accredited by an approved accrediting and state agency. Growing disparities in the U.S. higher education system outcomes, increasing costs, and a lack of oversight motivated Congress to develop a more rigorous shared accountability system. In 1992, Congress reauthorized the HEA, which established a program integrity triad that required postsecondary institutions to receive state authorization, accreditation, and certification. The USDOE, state authorizing agencies, and accrediting agencies collaboratively oversee U.S. higher education institutions and programs.

DOE Certification

In 2023, the federal government budgeted approximately $174 billion for higher education funding, almost all of it for student financial aid. The USDOE has authority to certify the accrediting agencies that determine IHEs' eligibility for federal funds and administers financial aid programs (Bruckner, 2020). Higher education institutions rely on federal student financial aid, which gives the DOE considerable financial leverage. Critics argue the DOE has had limited incentives to regulate higher education institutions and abdicates that role to private institutions. They claim accrediting agencies are compensated by the institutions they are regulating, making member evaluators reluctant to revoke accreditation. Proponents argue the accreditation process allows educators to determine academic standards and state authorization allows states to share oversight of higher education systems.

State Authorization

State authorization refers to the formal act of authorizing or chartering to offer legally recognized degrees. This process requires the state government to authorize postsecondary institutions to operate through a charter, statute, or constitutional provision and establish a review process to address complaints (Hegji, 2023). The level of rigor and bureaucratic oversight of the state authorization processes varies considerably. The DOE also requires state authorizers to make their process available and report postsecondary institutions that commit fraud in the administration of Title IV programs or have their postsecondary operation authorization revoked. State authorizers safeguard consumers from unfair business practices to ensure a minimum level of educational quality (Bruckner, 2020).

Public and private colleges and universities require state authorization, a process with significant state variation that may include state licensure, budget, policy, and performance reviews. Private higher education institutions must be licensed in the state in which they are physically located. Public institutions require state legislative authorization. Some states require a review conducted by state postsecondary and vocational agencies, and others accept independent accreditation in lieu of a state review.

Between 1980 and 2010, private for-profit degree granting postsecondary student enrollment increased from 111,714 to 2,022,785, a 1,700% increase (https://nces.ed.gov/programs/digest/d19/tables/dt19_304.22.asp). Multiple government investigations have confirmed state regulators' lack of oversight of higher education institutions, particularly in for-profit and distance learning (GAO, 2010). In 2010, the Obama administration issued new regulations that expanded Title IV state authorization system requirements to include institutional complaint systems, clarified accreditation versus licensure, and defined institutional charitable status. In 2016, state authorization regulations were expanded to include distance education and foreign branch campuses. The DOE's Office of Postsecondary Education issued both regulatory updates to improve consumer protection against predatory higher education practices that had proliferated among for-profit expansion.

Accreditation

The DOE governs the higher education accreditation system but does not directly accredit educational institutions or programs. The DOE reviews and approves private organizations through an accreditor recognition process and publishes a list of nationally recognized accrediting agencies. The DOE also recognizes state agencies of vocational and nursing educational institutions. The National Advisory Committee on Institutional Quality and Integrity (NACIQI) advises the DOE's process for accrediting agencies to establish eligibility to participate in Title IV programs. Accrediting organizations are required to complete a rigorous application process to receive federal recognition. The secretary of education makes the final determination on accrediting recognition based on DOE and NACIQI recommendations.

Accreditation is a voluntary evaluation process designed to assess the quality of postsecondary programs. The Council of Higher Education Accreditation (CHEA), a nongovernmental higher education membership organization that evaluates the quality of higher education accrediting agencies, identifies purposes of accreditation including assuring college and university academic quality, access to federal and state funds, signaling quality standards, and transferring courses and programs among colleges and universities (Accreditation, 2024). Accreditation is a peer review process designed to ensure a minimum level of academic quality. Higher education institutions maintain access to federal and state funds by voluntarily participating in the accreditation process. Accreditation also signals to external stakeholders, including employers, prospective students, and the public, that college and university credentials provide potential employees with necessary knowledge and skills. Higher education institutions support accreditation as a means of improving their reputation and brand within a competitive education market. Accreditation also ensures standards across the decentralized higher education system, ensuring students can transfer courses, credits, and programs among colleges and universities.

Postsecondary accrediting agencies fall into three categories: regional, national, and specialized or programmatic. There are seven regional accrediting agencies across six regions. Table 6.9 shows the region each accrediting agency oversees and the number and student population of higher education institutions. The institutions and student population size range from the New England Commission of Higher Education, covering six states with 215 institutions serving 863,276 students, to the Southern Association of Colleges and Schools Commission, covering 11 states with 780 institutions serving 6,593,228 students. Regional accrediting agencies grant accrediting status to the entire institution but do not guarantee the quality of the individual programs. Table 6.10 describes programmatic accrediting topics.

National accrediting agencies fall into two categories, faith related and career related. Faith-based accreditors review the 241 religiously affiliated higher education institutions. National career-related accrediting agencies review approximately 2,800 primarily single-purpose higher education institutions including business, health, and technology. Regional, faith-related, and career-related accrediting agencies typically certify higher education institutions. Table 6.11 lists these types of agencies.

Table 6.9 Regional Accrediting Agencies Institutions, Student Population and Region

Regional accrediting organization	Number of institutions accredited	Student population	Region
Accrediting Commission for Community and Junior Colleges	136	1,405,550	California, Hawaii, the Territories of Guam and American Samoa, the Commonwealth of Northern Mariana Islands, the Republic of Palau, the Federated States of Micronesia, and the Republic of the Marshall Islands
Higher Learning Commission	963	4,977,819	Arizona, Arkansas, Colorado, Illinois, Indiana, Iowa, Kansas, Ohio, Oklahoma, Michigan, Minnesota, Missouri, Nebraska, New Mexico, North Dakota, South Dakota, West Virginia, and Wyoming
Middle States Commission on Higher Education	526	4,125,999	Delaware, the District of Columbia, Maryland, New Jersey, New York, Pennsylvania, Puerto Rico, and the Virgin Islands
New England Commission of Higher Education	215	863,276	Connecticut, Maine, Massachusetts, New Hampshire, Rhode Island, Vermont, and internationally
Northwest Commission on College and Universities	154	3,324,978	Alaska, Idaho, Montana, Nevada, Oregon, Utah, Washington, internationally, and distance education
Southern Association of Colleges and Schools Commission	780	6,593,228	Alabama, Florida, Georgia, Kentucky, Louisiana, Mississippi, North Carolina, South Carolina, Tennessee, Texas, Virginia, Latin America, and internationally
WASC Senior College and University Commission	214	1,399,418	California

Table 6.10 Programmatic Accrediting Categories

Academics and resources	Licensure and governance	Consumer protection
Instructor qualifications	Governing board and organizational structure	Student grievance policies
Facility and equipment	Advertising, marketing, and recruiting practices	Tuition recovery fund
Mission and vision	Articles of incorporation	School closure/teach out plan
Curricula	Accreditation information	Surety bond
Credit-hour requirements	Licenses from other boards, agencies, or commissions	Audited financial statements
Student support services	Business licenses	Multiyear budget and financial projections
Course catalogue		Tuition refund policy
Student handbook		Student record procedures
Tuition and fee schedule		
Admissions requirements		
Graduation requirements		

Note: Data from source (https://sheeo.org/wp-content/uploads/2019/07/SHEEO_StateAuth.pdf).

Programmatic accrediting agencies operate nationwide and review programs and single-purpose institutions. Programmatic accreditation validates that a specific program or department meets established standards in a field of study. A college or university would be accredited by a regional or national accrediting organization, while the schools and program within an institution are accredited by programmatic accrediting agencies. For example, education preparation programs are accredited by the Council for the Accreditation of Educator Preparation and law schools are accredited by Council of the Section of Legal Education and Admissions to the Bar, American Bar Association. The DOE and the CHEA combined recognize 77 total programmatic accreditation organizations.

Table 6.11 National Faith-Related, National Career-Related, and Institutional Accrediting Agencies

Type of accrediting agency	Accrediting agencies
National faith-related	Association for Biblical Higher Education Commission on Accreditation
	Association of Institutions of Jewish Studies
	Association of Advanced Rabbinical and Talmudic Schools Accreditation Commission
	Commission on Accrediting of the Association of Theological Schools
	Transnational Association of Christian Colleges and Schools Accreditation Commission
National career-related	Accrediting Council for Continuing Education and Training
	Accrediting Bureau of Health Education Schools
	Accrediting Commission of Career Schools and Colleges
	Council on Occupational Education
	National Accrediting Commission of Career Arts and Sciences
	New York State Board of Regents
Institutional	Distance Education Accrediting Commission

How does the accreditation process work? First, institutions and programs conduct a self-study providing a summary of performance based on accrediting agency standards (CHEA, 2002). Second, a peer review committee composed of faculty and administrators from peer and aspirant higher education institutions reviews the self-study. Third, the accrediting organization sends a review team, typically a subset of the peer review committee, to the institution or program for a site visit to confirm elements of the self-study. Typically, the review team prepares a report identifying institution or program strengths and areas in need of improvement. Fourth, the accrediting agency decides about the institution's or program's accrediting status by granting approval, renewal, denial, deferral, a probation order, or a notice of warning. Fifth, accrediting agencies monitor institutions and programs and may require additional information between accreditation reviews. Institutions and program are required to participate in the full accreditation process every 5 to 10 years. Critics have argued that the accreditation process is a rubber stamp. Research indicates that in 1 year, DOE- and CHEA-recognized accrediting agencies reviewed 5,276 institutions and programs and denied accreditation only 42 times, a 0.7% denial rate (Hegji, 2017).

U.S. Higher Education Classifications

In 1973, the Carnegie Classification system for U.S. postsecondary education was published by the Carnegie Commission on Higher Education to categorize institutions based on common characteristics. The classification system divides colleges and universities into categories based on their function, mission, instructional program, enrollment profile, size, and degree-granting programs (see Table 6.12). The classification system was developed to aid higher education research. Proponents argue the simple, objective classification system provides a basis for a shared language for characterizing institutions and planning and interpreting research. Critics argue the system oversimplifies the higher education landscape and values research over teaching and service. The widespread acceptance of the classification system has consequences for access to human and fiscal resources (McCormick, 2000).

In 2021, Carnegie Foundation and the American Council of Education partnered to improve the methodological transparency of American college and university classifications to reflect the increasingly diverse higher education landscape. Doctoral universities include institutions that award at least 20 research doctoral degrees, degrees geared toward training researchers, or at least 30 professional practice doctoral degrees, degrees geared toward practical or professional practice in the field, in at least two programs. Doctoral universities are divided into three categories: Research 1 doctoral universities (R1), Research 2 doctoral universities (R2), and doctoral/professional universities. In 2025, the updated Carnegie Classification will designate doctoral degree-granting institutions as R1 if they achieve $50 million dollars in research spending and award at least 70 research doctorates. The R2 classification will require $5 million in research spending and 20 research doctorates. A third category, research colleges and universities, will be for postsecondary institutions spending at least $2.5 million on research regardless of the awarding of doctoral degrees.

Master's colleges and universities include institutions that award at least 50 master's degrees and fewer than 20 doctoral degrees. The master's colleges and universities classification also has three categories: Masters 1 (M1), Masters 2 (M2), and Masters 3 (M3). The M1 classification includes colleges and universities awarding at least 200 degrees, M2 includes institutions awarding 100–199 master's degrees, and M3 includes those awarding 50–99 master's degrees. Institutions that award fewer than 50 master's degrees but enroll exclusively graduate and professional students or award more graduate and professional degrees than undergraduate degrees also receive the M3 designation.

Table 6.12 Carnegie Classification System for U.S. Postsecondary Education

Category	Subcategory classification
Doctoral universities	R1: Doctoral universities – very high research activity
	R2: Doctoral universities – high research activity
	D/PU: Doctoral/professional universities
Master's colleges and universities	M1: Master's colleges and universities – larger programs
	M2: Master's colleges and universities – medium programs
	M3: Master's colleges and universities – small programs
Baccalaureate colleges	Arts & science focus
	Diverse fields
Baccalaureate/associate's colleges	Mixed baccalaureate/associate's colleges
	Associate's dominant
Associate's colleges	High transfer – high traditional
	High transfer – mixed traditional/nontraditional
	High transfer – high nontraditional
	Mixed transfer/career & technical – high traditional
	Mixed transfer/career & technical – mixed traditional/nontraditional
	Mixed transfer/career & technical – high nontraditional
Special focus 2-year institutions	Health professions
	Technical professions
	Arts & design
	Other fields
Special focus 4-year institutions	Faith-related institutions
	Medical schools & centers
	Other health professions schools
	Research institution
	Engineering and other technology-related schools
	Business & management schools
	Arts, music, & design schools
	Law schools
	Other special focus institutions
Tribal colleges and universities	

The baccalaureate colleges classification includes institutions where more than 50% of degrees awarded are undergraduate. Institutions that award at least half of their bachelor's degrees in arts and science fields are classified in the arts and science group and in the diverse fields classification if they do not meet that threshold. The baccalaureate/associate's colleges classification includes 4-year colleges that confer more than 50% of degrees at the associate level. Its subcategories include mixed baccalaureate/associate's colleges, classified by conferring more than 10% of degrees at the baccalaureate level, and associate's dominant, classified as institutions conferring less than 10% of their degrees at the baccalaureate level.

Associate's colleges are institutions that exclusively award associate degrees. The category includes nine subcategories based on the disciplinary focus and dominant student type. The disciplinary focus criteria distinguish between programs designed to lead to immediate employment and those that require further education to obtain employment. The disciplinary focus criteria classify institutions with 35.7% or less of degrees in career and technical disciplines as high transfer programs, those with at least 53.8% of degrees in career and technical disciplines as high career and technical, and those with between 35.7% and 53.8% in career and technical disciplines as mixed transfer/career and technical programs. The student mix criteria is based on the ratio of degree-seeking to nondegree-seeking students, with ratios above .628 designated as high traditional, those lower than .533 as high nontraditional, and those in between as mixed traditional/nontraditional.

The Carnegie Classification system has an additional category called special focus for institutions that award 75% of degrees in a single field; it has two subcategories, 2-year and 4-year institutions. The 2-year categories include health professions, technical professions, arts and design, and other fields. The 4-year subcategories include faith-related institutions; medical schools and centers; other health professions schools; research institutions; engineering and other technology-related schools; business and management schools; arts, music, and design schools; law schools; and other special focus institutions. The final higher education category is the 37 tribal colleges and universities of the American Indian Higher Education Consortium.

Functional Areas of Higher Education Institutions

The National Association of College and University Business Officers (NACUBO) created a classification system to standardize reporting expenses. These classifications provide insight into functional areas across U.S. higher education institutions. Table 6.13 includes college and university major functions and subcategories.

The National Association of Student Personnel Administrators (NASPA) identifies 39 functional areas that are housed within student affairs divisions. The broad range of student affairs functional areas illustrates the growth of higher education services and the complexity

Table 6.13 NACUBO Functional Classifications

Major function	Description	Subcategories
Auxiliary enterprises	Auxiliary enterprises are operations that provide goods or services to students, faculty, or staff and that charge a fee for those services, including food service, residence halls, bookstores, student unions, and intercollegiate athletics.	Auxiliary enterprises – student Auxiliary enterprises – faculty/staff Auxiliary enterprises – other Auxiliary enterprises – information technology
Academic service support		Libraries Museums and galleries Education media services Academic computing services Ancillary support Academic administration Academic personnel development Course and curriculum development
Hospitals		Direct patient care Health care support services Administration of hospitals Physical plant operations for hospitals Hospital information technology Academic support information technology

(Continued)

Table 6.13 (Continued)

Major function	Description	Subcategories
Independent operations		Independent operations/ institutional
		Federally funded research
Institutional support		Executive management
		Fiscal operations
		General administrative
		Public relations and development
		Administrative information technology
Instruction	This category includes all activities that are part of an institution's instructional program. Included are credit and noncredit courses for academic, vocational, and technical instruction; remedial and tutorial instruction; regular, special, and extension sessions; and community education. Includes departmental research and sponsored instruction.	Academic instruction
		Vocational and technical instruction
		Special session instruction
		Community education
		Preparatory/remedial instruction
Operations and maintenance plant	This category includes all expenses for activities specifically organized to produce research, whether commissioned by an agency external to the institution or separately budgeted for within a unique accounting string by an organizational unit within the institution.	Physical plant administration
		Building maintenance
		Custodial services
		Utilities
		Landscape and grounds maintenance
		Major repairs and renovations
		Security and safety
		Logistical services
		Operations and maintenance information technology
Public service		Community services
		Cooperative extension service
		Public broadcasting services
		Public service information technology
Research		Institutes and research centers
		Individual and project research
		Research information technology
Scholarships, fellowships, and student prizes and awards		Scholarships
		Fellowships
		Student prizes and awards
Student services		Student services administration
		Social and cultural development
		Counseling and career guidance
		Financial aid administration
		Student admissions and recruiting
		Student records
		Student health services
		Student services information technology

of college and university administrations. Table 6.14 includes all 39 student affairs functional areas, from academic advising to student conduct.

Higher Education Administration

American colleges and universities, like other complex organizations, require a broad range of administrators. The U.S. standard higher education administrative hierarchy includes governing boards or boards of trustees; senior administration including presidents, vice presidents, provosts, and deans; and faculty. This section explores the roles and responsibilities and hierarchical structure of college and university administration.

Governing Boards

American colleges and universities are governed by a board of trustees. In private colleges and universities, trustees are selected by the board members. In public colleges and universities, trustees are primarily appointed by the governor or the state legislature. Most higher education institutions are corporations under state law. Board members maintain legal authority and fiduciary responsibility for the corporation. According to the Association of Governing Boards of Universities and Colleges, women constitute 37% of college and university trustees (Colleges, 2021). Board members from minority groups constitute approximately 20% of public boards and 16% of private boards. College and university governing boards, like most government and educational institutions, are less diverse than the broader U.S. population.

President (Chancellor)

Presidents typically are the highest-ranking executive officer or administrator at a college or university. The president liaises with the board of trustees to implement its strategic direction for the institution. Presidents' internal institutional responsibilities include financial management, administrator and faculty recruitment, and oversight of university administration.

Table 6.14 NASPA Student Affairs Functional Areas

Academic advising	Enrollment management	Recreational sports
Admissions	Financial aid	Registrar
Alumni programs	GLBT student services	Spiritual life/campus safety
Campus activities	Graduate and professional student services	Student affairs assessment
Campus safety	Greek affairs	Student affairs fundraising and development
Career services	Intercollegiate athletics	Student affairs research
Civic learning and democratic engagement	International student services	Student conduct and academic integrity
Clinical health programs	Learning assistance/academic support services	Student conduct and behavioral case management
College union	Multicultural services	Student media
Community service/service learning	Nontraditional student services	TRIO and educational opportunity
Commuter student services	On-campus dining	Veterans' services
Counseling services	On-campus housing	Wellness programs
Disability support services	Orientation	Women's center

Presidents' external-facing responsibilities include improving the institution's public image and rankings, liaising with other institutions, and increasing institutional resources. Resource development includes lobbying governments; securing external research and program funding; and fundraising from graduates, businesses, and other internal and external stakeholders.

When a state university system has several campuses, it may designate chancellors to oversee the entire system. State university systems created by grouping existing higher education institutions like those in California (the California State University system) and New York utilize this organizational structure. In states with this structure, the chancellor manages the operations of the university system. The chief administrator of each campus is often referred to as the president. State university systems that established or delegated authority to campuses in the 20th century, like Arkansas, California (the University of California system), Illinois, Massachusetts, Missouri, North Carolina, and Wisconsin, designate systemwide chiefs as presidents and individual institution chief executives as chancellors. In this system, chancellors are the chief administrators for individual university campuses and report to the system president.

Provost

The provost is the chief academic officer. Their portfolio of responsibilities typically includes supervision of deans, associate provosts, department chairs, and faculty to support academic research and scholarship, curriculum research, and assessments of academic program effectiveness. The provost leads academic planning and establishes policies and practices. Provosts typically also lead academic-related resource allocation processes and administrative practices related to academic functions including enrollment, curriculum, and standards.

Vice Presidents

In U.S. colleges and universities, a vice president is the highest-ranking administrator within a functional area of the institution. These functional areas can comprise both academic and nonacademic divisions including academic affairs, administration, admissions, athletics, campus life, diversity, enrollment management, equity and inclusion, finance, human resources, information technology, research and engagement, student affairs, and university relations.

Deans

College and university deans are the ranking administrators of an academic college within a university. Dean responsibilities include supervising faculty and academic staff, coordinating activities within specific divisions or departments, employee recruitment and retention, and budgetary oversight. College deans typically transition from faculty positions or lower level administrators. Senior leadership positions that supervise an administrative rather than an academic unit of the college or university may also carry the title of dean. For example, dean of students is typically the title for an administrator overseeing an academic affairs division. Deans of administrative units often have a higher education administration background rather than an academic one.

Faculty

According to the NCES, U.S. degree-granting colleges and universities employed 1.5 million faculty during the 2021–2022 academic year. Fifty-six percent of faculty were full-time and

Table 6.15 Faculty Rank and Titles

Category	Position
Full-time, tenure-track	Assistant professor
	Associate professor
	Professor
	Distinguished professor
Full-time, nontenure-track	Lecturer
	Instructor
	Teaching assistant professor
	Teaching associate professor
	Teaching professor

44% were part-time. The racial composition of full-time faculty included a higher percentage of Whites and Asians and a lower percentage of other minority groups than overall U.S. demographics. Seventy-three percent of faculty were White; 12% were Asian, 6% were Black, 6% were Hispanic, and less than 1% were American Indians, Native Alaskans, or Pacific Islanders.

Shared governance refers to the role of faculty in the responsibility of leading colleges and universities. The faculty role in higher education governance expanded through the rise of American research universities (1876–1920), higher education expansion (1920–1940), and the golden age of American higher education (1940–1975; Gerber, 2014). Since the 1970s, faculty de-professionalization shifted higher education toward a market-based model that emphasizes nontenure-track faculty and empowers administrators to maximize institutional profits (Gerber, 2014). Faculty have primary responsibility for curriculum, pedagogical methods, research, and faculty status. Table 6.15 identifies faculty rank and titles.

During the 2021–2022 school year, approximately 24.9 million students were enrolled in the 5,775 U.S. postsecondary institutions. This enrollment was down from an all-time high of 29.5 million students in 2010–2011. Table 6.16 illustrates postsecondary enrollment by institutional level and control. Approximately half of all students enroll in 4-year public institutions. Private, for-profit, 4-year institutions enroll more than 3.5 million, nearly a quarter of all students. Private, for-profit institutions enroll three quarters of a million students. Two-year institutions enroll 3.4 million students, or 22% of all U.S. postsecondary students.

Table 6.16 Postsecondary School Enrollment by Level and Control of Institution, 2020–21

Level of control of institution	All students	Undergraduate	Graduate
All institutions	15,188,908	12,943,778	2,245,130
4-year public	7,497,287	6,392,831	1,104,456
4-year private for-profit	3,509,532	2,560,796	948,736
4-year private nonprofit	751,901	559,963	191,938
2-year public	2,819,269	2,819,269	0
2-year private nonprofit	47,587	47,587	0
2-year private for-profit	262,336	262,336	0
>2-year public	46,240	46,240	0
>2-year private nonprofit	8,312	8,312	0
>2-year private for-profit	246,444	246,444	0

Key Terms

accreditation
accrediting agencies
associate degree
associate's colleges
at-large elections
baccalaureate colleges
bachelor's degree
board of trustees
Carnegie Classification system
chancellors
city councils
commission
commission administrator
council-executive
council-manager
Council of Higher Education Accreditation
county government
deans
Dillion's rule
doctoral degree
doctoral universities
education savings accounts
elementary school
faculty
fiscal power
functional power
governing boards
high school
home rule
home schooling
interdistrict open enrollment
intradistrict open enrollment
junior high school
kindergarten
local school boards
magnet schools
master's colleges and universities
master's degree
mayor-council
middle school
municipalities
National Advisory Committee on Institutional Quality and Integrity
open town meeting
personnel power
prekindergarten
presidents

principals
private for-profit institutions
private nonprofit institutions
proprietary institutions
provost
public institutions
Research 1 universities
school consolidation
school districts
school vouchers
self-study
shared governance
sovereign
special districts
state authorization
superintendents
town meetings
tribal college and universities
undergraduate institutions
vice presidents
weak mayor systems

Discussion Questions

1. What education language is in your state constitution? What is the statutory language for education in your state? Do your state constitution and statutory laws exceed minimum education requirements? Does your state establish a strong or weak legal justification for K–12 or postsecondary education?
2. What education laws has your state legislature passed in the past 10 years? What is the composition of its education committees? What is its leadership structure? How involved is the state legislature in education in your state?
3. What state education governance structure does your state utilize? How much power does your governor have within this governance structure?
4. What are the composition and responsibilities of your state board of education?
5. What are the responsibilities of your chief state school officer?
6. Has your state supreme court decided any education finance or higher education cases?
7. What are the most influential education interest groups in your state?

Activities and Assignments

1. Identify a local policy issue closely related to your research. Provide an overview of the policy issue. Utilize local and institutional resources online resources and newspaper articles to discuss who was involved with the creation of the policy issue.
2. Discuss the power relationships in your local and institutional governance structure. Who has the power related to your policy issue?
3. Identify which interest groups have the most influence over local and institutional policy decisions.

References

Association of University and College Governing Boards. (2021). *Policies, practices, and composition of governing boards of colleges and universities, and institutionally related foundations.* https://agb.org/product/policies-practices-composition-2021/

Berry, C. R., & West, M. R. (2008). Growing pains: The school consolidation movement and student outcomes. *Journal of Law, Economics, and Organization, 26*(1), 1–29. https://doi.org/10.1093/jleo/ewn015

Black, S. E. (1999). Do better schools matter? Parental valuation of elementary education. *The Quarterly Journal of Economics, 114*(2), 577–599. https://doi.org/10.1162/003355399556070

Brenan, M. (2021, September 30). *America's trust in government remains low.* Gallup. https://news.gallup.com/poll/355124/americans-trust-government-remains-low.aspx

Bruckner, M. A. (2020). The forgotten stewards of higher education quality. *UC Irvine Law Review, 11*, 1.

Bureau of Labor Statistics. (2024). *U.S. department of labor occupational outlook handbook.* www.bls.gov/ooh/about/ooh-faqs.htm

Calder, V. B. (2019). *Zoned out: How school and residential zoning limit educational opportunity (SCP report no. 6–19).* Joint Economic Committee. www.jec.senate.gov/public/_cache/files/f4880936-8db9-4b77-a632-86e1728f33f0/jec-report-zoned-out.pdf

Callahan, R. E. (1964). *Education and the cult of efficiency: A study of the social forces that have shaped the administration of public schools.* The University of Chicago Press.

Callahan, R. E. (1966). *The superintendent of schools: A historical analysis.* Washington University Graduate Institute of Education.

Census Bureau. (2019). *2017 census of governments, individual state descriptions: 2017.* www.census.gov/content/dam/Census/library/publications/2017/econ/2017isd.pdf

The City of Clinton v. The Cedar Rapids & Missouri River Railroad Co., 24 Iowa 455 (1868).

Cooper, B. S., & Boyd, W. L. (1987). The evolution of training for school administrators. In J. Murphy & P. Hallinger (Eds.), *Approaches to administrative training in education* (pp. 3–27). SUNY Press.

Couchenour, D., & Chirsman, J. K. (Eds.). (2016). Prekindergarten. In *The SAGE encyclopedia of contemporary early childhood education.* Sage.

Council for Higher Education Accreditation. (2002). *The fundamentals of accreditation: What do you need to know?* www.chea.org

Council for Higher Education Accreditation. (2024). *Almanac of external quality review.* https://almanac.chea.org/

DeSantis, V. S., & Renner, T. (1993). Governing the county: Authority, structure, and elections. *Contributions in Political Science, 314*, 15–15.

Duncombe, W., & Yinger, J. (2007). Does school district consolidation cut costs? *Education Finance and Policy, 2*(4), 341–375. https://doi.org/10.1162/edfp.2007.2.4.341

Egalite, A. J., & Wolf, P. J. (2016). A review of the empirical research on private school choice. *Peabody Journal of Education, 91*(4), 441–454. https://doi.org/10.1080/0161956x.2016.1207436

Frendeway, M., Sawatka, K., Mareavage, W., Martinez, K., & Dauphin, P. (2015). *School choice yearbook 2014–15: Breaking down barriers to school choice.* Alliance for School Choice.

Gerber, L. G. (2014). *The rise and decline of faculty governance: Professionalization and the modern American university.* Johns Hopkins University Press.

Grissom, J. A., Egalite, A. J., & Lindsay, C. A. (2021). *How principals affect students and schools: A systematic synthesis of two decades of research.* The Wallace Foundation. www.wallacefoundation.org/knowledge-center/Documents/How-Principals-Affect-Students-and-Schools.pdf

Hegji, A. (2017). *An overview of accreditation of higher education in the United States (ED59787).* ERIC. https://files.eric.ed.gov/fulltext/ED597874.pdf

Hegji, A. (2023). *Institutional eligibility for participation in title IV student financial aid programs.* Congressional Research Service. https://crsreports.congress.gov

Hess, F. M. (2002). *School boards at the dawn of the 21st century: Conditions and challenges of district governance.* National School Boards Association. https://web.archive.org/web/20120912135309/www.aei.org/files/2002/02/01/20060228_SchoolBoards.pdf

Howley, C., Johnson, J., & Petrie, J. (2011). *Consolidation of schools and districts: What the research says and what it means.* National Education Policy Center. http://nepc.colorado.edu/publication/consolidation-schools-districts

International City/County Management Association. (2019). *Municipal form of government survey: Summary of survey results.* https://lims.minneapolismn.gov/Download/File/4673/2018%20ICMA%20Municipal%20Form%20of%20Government%20Survey%20Report.pdf

Kowalski, T. J. (1995). *Keepers of the flame: Contemporary urban superintendents.* Corwin.

Kowalski, T. J. (2003). *Contemporary school administration* (2nd ed.). Allyn & Bacon.

Kowalski, T. J., & Brunner, C. C. (2011). *The school superintendent: Roles, challenges, and issues.* Educational Leadership Faculty Publications. https://ecommons.udayton.edu/eda_fac_pub/43

Krane, D., Rigos, P., & Hill, M. B. (2001). *Home rule in America: A fifty-state handbook.* CQ Press.

Kutz, G. D. (2010). For-Profit Colleges: Undercover Testing Finds Colleges Encouraged Fraud and Engaged in Deceptive and Questionable Marketing Practices. Testimony before the Committee on Health, Education, Labor, and Pensions, US Senate. *GAO-10-948T.* US Government Accountability Office.

Martin, L. (1993). American county government: An historical perspective. In D. R. Berman (Ed.), *County governments in an era of change* (pp. 1–13). Greenwood Press.

Massachusetts Constitution, Article LXXXIX.

McCormick, A. C. (2000). Bringing the Carnegie classification into the 21st century. *AAHE Bulletin, 52*(5), 3–6.

McKeown-Moak, M. P., & Mullin, C. M. (2014). *Higher education finance research: Policy, politics, and practice.* Information Age Publishing.

Mountford, M., & Richardson, J. W. (2021). Promoting equity in the modern superintendency. *AASA Journal of Scholarship and Practice, 18*(3).

National Association of Elementary School Principals. (2019). *Leading learning communities: Pillars, practices, and priorities for effective principals.* NAESP Publishers. www.naesp.org/sites/default/files/Leading%20Learning%20Communities%20Executive%20Summary.pdf

National Center for Education Statistics. (2022). *Homeschooled children and reasons for homeschooling: Condition of education.* https://nces.ed.gov/programs/coe/indicator/tgk

National Center for Education Statistics. (2023). *Enrollment rates of young children. Condition of education.* U.S. Department of Education, Institute of Education Sciences. Retrieved May 24, 2024, from https://nces.ed.gov/programs/coe/indicator/cfa

National Civic League. (2021, April 26). *Assault on city management undermines local integrity.* www.nationalcivicleague.org/assault-on-city-management-undermines-local-integrity/

National League of Cities. (n.d.). *Local government authority.* Retrieved May 18, 2022, from https://web.archive.org/web/20160804131854/www.nlc.org/build-skills-and-networks/resources/cities-101/city-powers/local-government-authority

National School Board Association. (2018). *Today's school boards & their priorities for tomorrow: 2018 survey conducted by the national school boards association in partnership with K12 Insight.* https://cdn-files.nsba.org/s3fs-public/reports/K12_National_Survey.pdf

Samuels, C. (2020). *Why school board diversity matters.* Education Week.

Simone, B. (2021). Municipal reparations: Considerations and constitutionality. *Michigan Law Review, 120*, 345. https://repository.law.umich.edu/mlr/vol120/iss2/5

Smith, K. B., Greenblatt, A., & Mariani, M. (2008). *Governing states & localities* (2nd ed.). CQ Press.

Sokolow, A. D. (2004). The limited and contrary uses of county charter reform: Two California cases. *State and Local Government Review, 36*(1), 7–19. https://doi.org/10.1177/0160323x0403600101

Spillane, J. P. (1996). School districts matter: Local educational authorities and state instructional policy. *Educational Policy, 10*(1), 63–87. https://doi.org/10.1177/0895904896010001004

Taie, S., & Lewis, L. (2022). *Characteristics of 2020–21 public and private K–12 school principals in the United States: Results from the national teacher and principal survey first look (NCES 2022–112).* National Center for Education Statistics. https://nces.ed.gov/pubsearch/pubsinfo.asp?pubid=2022112

Tienken, C. H. (2020). *The American superintendent 2020 decennial study.* American Association of School Administrators. www.aasa.org/publications/publication/the-american-superintendent-2020-decennial-study

Tyack, D. (1974). *The one best system: A history of American urban education.* Harvard University Press.

United States Advisory Commission on Intergovernmental Relations. (1993). *State laws governing local government structure and administration.* U.S. Advisory Commission on Intergovernmental Relations.

United States Government Accountability Office. (2010). *For-profit colleges: Undercover testing finds colleges encourage fraud and engaged in deceptive and questionable marketing practices. Testimony before the committee on health, education, labor, and pensions.* U.S. Senate Committee.

Zimmerman, J. F., & United States Advisory Commission on Intergovernmental Relations. (1981). *Measuring local discretionary authority.* Advisory Commission on Intergovernmental Relations.

Part III

The Policy Process

7 Issue Definition, Agenda Setting, and Policy Formulation

The *policy process* includes five stages: issue definition, agenda setting, policy formulation, implementation, and evaluation. The policy process begins with the identification of a problem negatively impacting the broader public. A *policy problem* is a condition that produces dissatisfaction among society and requires government action to address. *Agenda setting* is the process by which policy issues gain or lose public and policymaker attention. If the public and governmental actors give the problem attention and define the issue, then it gains prominence on the public agenda. *Policy formulation* involves governmental and nongovernmental actors developing a policy solution. The process of putting policy into effect is called *implementation. Policy evaluation* is the final stage, in which process and outcomes are compared to policy goals to determine the policy's effectiveness, informing the next policy cycle. This chapter explores the first three stages of the policy process: issue definition, agenda setting, and policy formulation. Although these policy process stages are relatively unfamiliar to educational leaders, they determine policy substance and the political feasibility of policy change. This chapter answers these questions: How do policymakers and the public decide which problems require government attention? How do governmental and nongovernmental actors formulate policy? How do educational leaders influence the issue definition, agenda setting, and formulation stages?

Policy Problems and Issue Definition

What factors determine whether a problem is a private or public issue? If the problem is a public issue, what factors determine whether it deserves a government response? The policy process begins as a direct response to an issue that policy actors have defined as a problem. Public understanding of public versus private issues has changed over time. With some notable exceptions, the range of public issues has grown. As discussed in Chapter 2, education, notably higher education, was considered primarily a private issue for much of American history. As the connection between education and its civic, economic, social, and political benefits became more apparent, education slowly shifted from a private to a public issue.

How do problems get defined? Policy problems are conditions the public finds unacceptable and wants to change or mitigate. Scholarship places issue definition at the center of policy subsystem creation and destruction (Baumgartner & Jones, 1993, 2002; Jones & Baumgartner, 2005; Rochefort & Cobb, 1993). Policy subsystems are networks of formal and informal actors revolving around a defined policy issue area. Enthusiasm over a policy issue generates political attention and creates policy subsystems that endure after attention declines. Policy subsystem stability is diminished by increasing criticism of the existing policy

DOI: 10.4324/9781003231561-10

structure's ability to mitigate problems. Interest groups, media attention, and policy entrepreneurs combine to bring attention to change the existing policy subsystem.

Problem identification is inherently political, as policy problems presume a governmental response. The political process of problem identification is a struggle over alternative realities and framing the issues and conditions. According to Rochefort and Cobb (1993), cultural values, interest group advocates, scientific information, and professional advice all contribute to defining an issue or problem. Political actors seek to maintain or redefine policy issues to their advantage. This political struggle to define policy issues begins at the problem identification stage and continues throughout the policy process's formulation, implementation, and evaluation stages.

Political institutions increasingly influence problem definitions by utilizing mass media to shape public opinion. Public acceptance of a policy definition is a prerequisite to agenda setting. Problem definition and framing determine which problems receive public and government attention and which do not. Political attention is a scarce resource. Political institutions and actors need more time, money, and expertise; this *carrying capacity* constrains the policy issues that can be considered (Jones & Baumgartner, 2005). The number of problems requiring political attention is boundless, so issue selection is critical in the policy process (Green-Pedersen & Walgrave, 2014). Political actors' limited carrying capacity motivates them to advocate for allocating attention to their preferred policy issues. Ideology, political party platforms, and personal experiences influence the political elite's preferences.

Issue definition is the process by which a problem is transformed into a policy issue the government can address. Issue definition is inherently political, as groups for and against a policy issue compete to define the issue. Supporters seek to define the policy issue in broad, favorable terms, illustrating how a solution will positively impact them. In contrast, the opposition aims to define the solutions negatively and highlight their downsides. The public perceives a broad set of conditions as requiring public attention. While the constellation of issues the public considers problems remains relatively constant, the priority of issues rises and falls over time. Gallup's historical public satisfaction with public education from 2000 to 2022 indicates public dissatisfaction fluctuates over time, with a high of 53% in 2004 and a low of 36% in 2023. Following the NCLB's enactment, public satisfaction with education policy returned to historical levels and continued in equilibrium for a significant period. Public and elite attention to policy issues has been given substantial consideration by scholars as they try to understand the theoretical mechanisms that drive policy agenda setting.

Anthony Downs (1972) proposed the issue attention cycle to describe how elite and public attention rises and falls on an issue, analogous to the media news cycle (see Figure 7.1). The theory holds that attention is a fleeting thing and that issues rise in attention, remain there briefly, and gradually fade from attention. This issue attention process is independent of the success of a policy solution. A particular issue receives attention for a short period, irrespective of whether the issue is mitigated or resolved. The issue attention cycle has five stages: pre-problem, alarmed discovery and euphoric enthusiasm, realizing the cost, gradual decline of intense public interest; and post problem. The pre-problem stage occurs when a highly undesirable social condition exists that has failed to garner widespread public interest. Alarmed discovery and euphoric enthusiasm occur due to dramatic events that make the broader public aware of the problem. The policy network seeks a solution to mitigate the problem. Public and elite engagement and increased policy knowledge lead to realization of the costs associated with solving the problem.

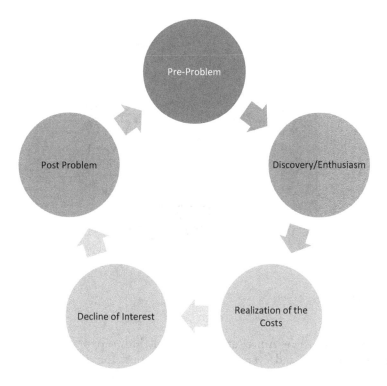

Figure 7.1 Issue Attention Cycle

Agenda Setting

Birkland stated, "Agenda setting is the process by which problems and potential solutions gain or lose public attention." National, state, and local government policymakers have finite time, resources, and capacity. Groups seeking to have their preferred problem addressed must struggle for their issue to receive collective attention and support. Conflict is inherent in any system where the demand for resources exceeds the supply. This is true of the policy process as groups vie for limited resources and public attention.

The agenda refers to problems and potential solutions that come to the attention of the broader public and their government representatives. Public agendas are so ubiquitous that they are helpful for differentiating policy issues from their proximity to the institution deciding to accept or reject a proposed solution. Cobb and Elder (1983) developed a typology of agenda levels to explain the proximity of policy issues to institutional decision making. Figure 7.2 illustrates agenda levels analogous to a target with concentric circles. The closer one moves toward the bullseye, the closer one moves toward institutions considering the policy issue.

The *agenda universe* is the broadest and most distant level of the public agenda. It includes all ideas considered by the public or the political system. The agenda universe would consist of all policy solutions irrespective of the level of public or elite support the solution would garner. For example, solutions as broad as providing free postsecondary education to all Americans and dissolving American higher education would be included

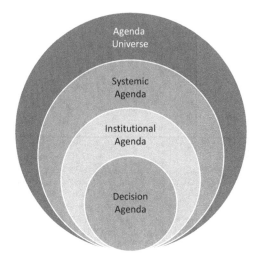

Figure 7.2 Agenda-Setting Levels

in the agenda universe. Few Americans or political elites support free postsecondary education for all Americans, and even fewer would support the dissolution of the American postsecondary system. Still, both are part of the broad array of ideas included in the agenda universe. Although students often snicker or sneer at very unpopular policy issues in the agenda universe, such as privatizing all U.S. education, it is vital to remember that ideas that seem unbelievable today can be legitimate options for future generations. As discussed in Chapter 2, educating women and minority groups existed only in the agenda universe for too much of American history.

The *systemic agenda* is the next closer agenda level. It includes all issues commonly perceived by the public and political elites as meriting public attention and legitimately within the jurisdiction of government (Cobb & Elder, 1983). The issue of free college education has risen to the level of the systemic agenda in recent years, but the termination of the American postsecondary system has not. Neither the public nor political elites consider dismantling the American higher education system as meriting public attention. Government institutional actors consider public agenda items when they rise to the institutional agenda. The *institutional agenda* includes all policy issues being officially considered by local, state, or national government institutions or actors, irrespective of their likelihood of being enacted.

The goal of any political group is to get their policy issue to the final agenda level, the bullseye of the agenda levels: the decision agenda. The *decision agenda* signifies policy issues being acted upon by governmental institutions. Being acted upon does not mean the policy will be successful. Government actors may consider the issue and then maintain the status quo. The level of conflict characteristically increases as a policy issue moves closer to the decision agenda (Birkland, 1997, 1998). Interest groups and political elites need not worry about issues in the agenda universe that are unable to receive broad public support or political elite attention. On the other hand, policy issues on the decision agenda are topics on the daily news, social media, political debates, government briefings, and election commercials.

Policy Windows

Policy windows are agenda-setting opportunities. Policy windows open and close based on the interaction of political institutions, policy actors, and proposed policy solutions (Kingdon, 1984). Public problems typically arise on the agenda due to sudden events or crises. Policy experts propose solutions to mitigate problems in the policy stream. The *policy stream* comprises factors influencing the political environment, including elections, political control, and social and economic conditions. Policy streams converge at critical junctures when problems connect with solutions under favorable political conditions.

Kingdon identified four types of policy windows: routinized, discretionary, spillover, and random (Kingdon, 1984). The policy window types exist on a continuum of institutionalization and predictability. *Routinized political windows* arise from regularly occurring political or procedural events, including annual budget and bill reauthorizations. *Spillover windows* arise when related issues are drawn into existing open windows, including omnibus and budget bills. Individual political actor preferences drive *discretionary windows. Random windows* result from crisis events. Political actors can configure institutional rules to keep policy windows closed for extended periods. A limited group of leaders, politicians, and bureaucrats who govern a policy sector for an extended period constitutes a policy monopoly. Limited elite and public attention to an issue can lock in the existing policy monopoly.

Policy Subsystems

Policy subsystems are substantive policy issue areas composed of official and unofficial stakeholder networks that influence the design of policy solutions (Sabatier & Jenkins-Smith, 1999). Substantive policy issues unite stakeholders across government branches, agencies, and interest groups. Policy subsystems recognize that political dynamics differ across policy issues based on the level of public interest, subsystem stability, and the history of policy outputs.

According to Thurber (1996), policy subsystems range from macro to micro. Table 7.1 depicts the policy subsystems typology. Policy decisions with high levels of public interest and media coverage characterize macro subsystems. *Macro policy systems* are typically highly controversial issues that impact electoral politics. Political elites, incentivized by reelection goals, focus on macro policy issues because their public visibility means they may impact elections. Economic, political, and social events elevate policy issues to the macro policy system by expanding public attention and political saliency, incentivizing higher level decision makers to dominate political processes and policy decisions. Crises can centralize power in the hands of a small group of elite decision makers. Annual federal and state budget negotiations or the reauthorization of significant education bills such as the Elementary and Secondary Education Act are examples of macro education policy systems.

Table 7.1 Policymaking System Typology

Policymaking system	Visibility of decision	Scope of conflict	Level of conflict	Number of participants
Macro policy system	High	Wide	High	Many
Policy subsystem	Low	Narrow	Low	Few
Micro policy system	Invisible	Very narrow	Low and personalized	Few

Micro policy systems are characterized by elite government actors' complex or highly technical decisions. The public typically has limited interest in micro policy issues. The relatively low public attention paid to micro policy issues makes them less significant from an election perspective. The hidden nature of micro policy systems provides political actors autonomy to legislate without fear of electoral reprisal. Public opinion has less impact on micro policy systems due to the lack of public knowledge and electoral impacts. Policy subsystems are fluid and can shift along the – micro spectrum over time. Economic, political, and social events can change a micro policy subsystem to a macro one, increasing its saliency and shifting the influence of political stakeholders. Policy subsystems also range from open to closed. Closed subsystems provide less access to the broader public, as a small group of elite government actors dominates them. See Table 7.1 for an overview of the different policymaking systems.

Focusing Events

Policy issues rise and fall on the public agenda for countless reasons. Changes in indicators and focusing events are two critical influences on agenda setting (Birkland, 1997; Kingdon, 1984; Lawrence & Birkland, 2004). *Indicators* are measures of underlying policy problems. Changes in measures over time can lead to increased attention to the policy issue. For example, the Program for International Student Assessment (PISA) measures 15-year-old students' reading, mathematics, and science literacy across all Organisation for Economic Cooperation and Development (OECD) countries. The U.S. decline in international rankings has increased attention on American educational investments and reforms. Indicator changes lead to discussions about the scope of the problem and the necessity of government action.

Focusing events are exogenous events highlighting a problem that led to increased attention and possible policy change (Atkinson, 2019). Defining characteristics of focusing events are that they are sudden, rare, and harmful now or in the future (Birkland, 1997). Focusing events can develop into symbols that amplify their power. The 9/11 terrorist attacks were a focusing event that altered American political dynamics across several policy issues. In 2002, the NCLB reauthorization occurred after 9/11 incentivized bipartisan collaboration that would not have otherwise been possible. The COVID-19 pandemic is another example of a focusing event for K–12 and higher education. The pandemic led to widespread disruptions in education systems and negative student, faculty, and staff outcomes. It prompted extensive budgetary and policy changes in elementary, secondary, and postsecondary education systems.

Policy Entrepreneurs

Policy entrepreneurs deploy resources, including knowledge, time, energy, money, and reputation, to change policy in their preferred direction at critical junctures (Kingdon, 1984). *Policy entrepreneurs* can be stakeholders in elected government, appointed positions, interest groups, research organizations, or foundations (Mintrom & Norman, 2009). According to Mintrom and Norman (2009), policy entrepreneurship involves four elements: displaying social acuity, defining problems, building teams, and leading by example. Policy entrepreneurs display social acuity by engaging policy networks, understanding their motives and goals, and strategically responding to those motives. Problem or network brokers act as nexuses or connectors between individuals and organizations in a policy network.

Policy Formulation

Agenda setting focuses attention on a public problem in order to move a policy solution from the agenda universe to the decision agenda. When policymakers in the legislature or bureaucracy take up the issue, it enters the formulation stage. Policy formulation consists of policymakers discussing a problem and potential solutions and weighing alternatives to choose a policy solution from among the alternatives. Policymakers and bureaucrats create legislative, regulatory, or programmatic solutions to mitigate a problem. Policy formulation occurs within political institutions including the legislative, executive, and judicial branches of federal, state, and local governments.

Legislative Branch

Congress's organizational structure enables it to overcome collective action problems by building majority coalitions to enact legislation. The authority to enact legislation is Congress's preeminent power. The legislative process has numerous *veto points*, points in the policymaking process at which opposition can block policy change. This makes the enactment of legislation difficult. Congress passes only 1%–3% of all bills introduced. The rules of congressional procedure govern the process by which a bill becomes a law.

The legislative process begins with the introduction of a bill to Congress. While anyone can draft a bill, only members of Congress can submit one to the clerk for consideration. Even the president, who proposes many bills, must have a member of the House or Senate introduce them. Once introduced, the bill is assigned a number and referred to the committee of jurisdiction. For most education bills, that is the House Education and Labor Committee or the Senate Health, Education, Labor, and Pensions Committee. Bills are sometimes referred to multiple committees when the legislation extends across committee jurisdictions.

Hearings

The committee typically refers the bill to one of its subcommittees. The subcommittee can hold hearings, amend the legislation, and refer the bill to the full committee. The committee can also hold hearings, amend the legislation, and vote the bill out of committee to the floor. A *hearing* is a meeting or session of a congressional committee used to obtain information on proposed legislation, investigate, or evaluate government activities. Table 7.2 provides a list of education-related hearings in the House Committee on Education and Labor during the 116th Congress. The committee considered elementary, secondary, and higher education and social and economic issues facing students. The topics discussed included the impact of COVID-19 on elementary, secondary, and postsecondary education, for-profit higher education, educational equity, Pell grants, child homelessness, and foster care.

The House Committee on Education and Labor also held a hearing on the U.S. Department of Education's policies and priorities. This hearing provides an example of Congress conducting its oversight role of executive branch agencies. Members of Congress are incentivized to conduct government oversight only when they reap political rewards. If a congressional chamber is controlled by the party opposing the president, majority members have greater political incentives to fulfill their oversight role to improve their party's reputation and harm the president's party's reputation.

Table 7.2 116th Congress House Committee on Education and Labor Education Related Hearings

Date	Hearing Title
March 17, 2021	Rising to the Challenge: The Future of Higher Education Post COVID-19
March 25, 2021	Lessons Learned: Charting the Path to Educational Equity
April 20, 2021	For-Profit College Conversions Examining Ways to Improve Accountability and Prevent Fraud
April 28, 2021	Building Back Better: Investing in Improving Schools, Creating Jobs, and Strengthening Families
May 6, 2021	Addressing the Impact of COVID-19 on Students With Disabilities
May 19, 2021	Picking up the Pieces: Strengthening Connections With Students Experiencing Homelessness and Children in Foster Care
June 24, 2021	Examining the Policies and Priorities of the U.S. Department of Education
July 29, 2021	Keeping the Pell Grant Promise: Increasing Enrollment, Supporting Success

Floor Debate

The committee reporting a bill to the House or Senate floor must request from the Rules Committee a *rule*, a resolution specifying the procedures and time limit for floor debate. A *closed rule* is a Rules Committee provision that prohibits the introduction of amendments and places severe limits on floor debate. An *open rule* is a Rules Committee provision that permits extended floor debate and the addition of amendments. The House speaker and the Senate majority leader control who speaks during debate. Closed rules help the majority party pass legislation by limiting debate and the minority party's ability to obstruct progress.

The House and the Senate differ in the level of party leadership control over legislative debate. The House of Representatives, given its size and resulting higher collective action costs, requires members to concede significant power to the party leadership to limit debate, which empowers the majority. In the House, a simple majority can vote to end debate. In the Senate, each member has the power to block the close of debate. The *filibuster* is a Senate rule that allows members to prevent action on legislation they oppose by continuously holding the floor and speaking until the majority concedes. Overcoming a filibuster requires a cloture vote of three fifths of the Senate, 60 senators. Because one party rarely controls 60 Senate seats, a cloture vote requires substantial bipartisan support, a circumstance increasingly rare as the nation has become more polarized.

Once a bill has been debated on the floor of the House or Senate, the House speaker or Senate majority leader schedules a chamber vote. Congressional leadership rarely brings a bill to the floor for a vote unless they know the outcome. Consequently, party leadership rarely loses floor votes. When one chamber passes a bill, it is sent to the other chamber for consideration. The legislative process requires not only that both chambers pass the bill but that the bills are identical. If the House and Senate both pass a bill, but the legislation contains differences, a conference committee can be established. A *conference committee* is made up of members from both chambers charged with eliminating any differences between the two versions of the legislation. This process is known as *reconciliation*. Party leaders in each chamber appoint members to the conference committee, often from the standing committee or jurisdiction or senior party leaders. If the conference committee members fail to reach agreement, the legislative process requires the chambers to reconsider their bills, or the legislation dies. When the conference committee makes changes to the House or Senate bill, each chamber requires that the revised bill return to the floor for an additional vote. Once a majority of each chamber has approved the reconciled bills, the legislation is sent to the president's desk for signature.

The president has three choices upon receiving a congressional bill: sign it into law, veto it and send it back to Congress, or ignore it. A *presidential veto* is the constitutional power to refuse to approve a bill preventing its enactment into law. Presidential inaction on a bill can become a *pocket veto*. After 10 days, presidential inaction during a congressional adjournment renders the bill vetoed. But if Congress is in session and the president takes no action within 10 days, the bill becomes law.

Congress may *override* a presidential veto by a two-thirds supermajority in both legislative chambers. Presidential vetoes are rarely overridden by Congress. Since 1789, presidents have vetoed 1,484 congressional bills and only 106 of those vetoes (7.1%) have been overridden. A presidential veto override is politically damaging to the chief executive and their party because it demonstrates political weakness. Presidents act strategically in deciding whether to veto a bill. If the president believes Congress will override the veto, they may not veto it for political rather than policy reasons. The president may have political incentives to not veto the bill so their administration and political party do not look weak, which would harm their chances in the next election.

Executive Branch

Administrative Agency Regulatory Rulemaking

Bureaucracies are government agencies where policies passed by Congress and state legislatures are interpreted and implemented. Bureaucratic organizations are established by Congress or state legislatures to achieve policy goals. Bureaucrats are the agents of elected leaders in the executive and legislative branches. The federal government includes more than 2.1 million civilian bureaucrats. State and local governments include 16 million employees. Government bureaucrats implement the laws and programs passed. Although Congress and state legislatures have the power to pass laws, they delegate significant authority to bureaucracies to implement the laws, make and enforce rules, and settle disputes through administrative adjudication. When Congress establishes a new agency, it grants the agency regulatory authority in a specific policy jurisdiction. The agency cannot exceed the authority granted by Congress or state legislatures or violate the U.S. or state constitutions.

Congressional and state laws are nearly universally vague. As described in the previous section, formulating and adopting laws is an arduous process with numerous veto points. Building supermajority coalitions is difficult under the best of conditions. There is an inverse relationship between the specificity of the legislative language and the likelihood of passage. Each specific measure within a law attracts opposition groups. Vague legislation is easier to pass because it draws less opposition. Most laws lack enough specificity to be implemented by federal and state agencies. *Rulemaking* is the process by which federal or state agencies define the substance of public programs. For example, most people strongly agree with the notion that no child should be left behind, meaning the education system should value all children irrespective of race, creed, gender, disability, or income level. In 2001, when Congress was working on the reauthorization of the Elementary and Secondary Education Act, it focused on the legislation's broad goal of testing all subgroups so district-level test scores could not hide that schools were failing to teach minority, disability, or low-income groups. Although these broad education goals received broad support, once NCLB was implemented, the specific testing and accountability measures and penalties and the lack of school resources decreased support for the program.

The regulatory process involves executive branch agencies and independent regulatory commissions issuing binding regulations that are subsidiary to congressional or state legislation. Bureaucratic agencies' rulemaking activities are constrained by the legislation. The Code of Federal Regulations contains all codified U.S. laws and regulations. Title 34 comprises all national education regulations, policy, and programs pertaining to elementary through postsecondary education; adult, vocational, rehabilitative, and special education; bilingual education; and literacy. Title 34, as shown in Table 7.3, has 1,300 parts including rules, regulations, and procedures for the Department of Education, Office for Civil Rights, Office of Special Education and Rehabilitation Services, Office of Vocational and Adult Education, Office of Bilingual Education and Minority Language Affairs, Office of Postsecondary Education, Office of Educational Research and Improvement, National Institute for Literacy, and National Council on Disability.

Principal-Agent Problem

Congress and state legislatures formulate and adopt policy, and the president and governors, except in the case of veto overrides, support the policy. Legislative bodies do not implement policy; they delegate implementation to state bureaucrats. Bureaucrats are considered the agents of elected officials serving as principals. The *principal–agent problem* refers to the conflict when a person or organization (agent) acts on behalf of another (principal). There are inherent difficulties associated with motivating an agent to act in the best interest of a principal. Consider the simple example of parents trying to get their children to do house chores. The parents (principals) seek to receive help cleaning the house and teach their children the virtue of hard work. Children (agents) do not share the parents' goals and priorities. Children do not typically object to an unclean home or believe they require lessons in hard work. The parents have difficulty incentivizing the agent (children) to carry out the principal's (parents') chores.

Bureaucrats' goals and priorities often deviate from those of the principals. Bureaucrats are typically lifelong public servants dedicated to the long-term goals and objectives of their organization and policy area. They often serve across multiple chief executive administrations and legislative elections. Due to their long-term perspective and lack of electoral pressure,

Table 7.3 The Code of Federal Regulations Title 34 Table of Contents

Volume	Chapter	Parts	Regulatory entity
1		1–99	Office of the Secretary, Department of Education
	I	100–199	Office for Civil Rights, Department of Education
	II	200–299	Office of Elementary and Secondary Education, Department of Education
2	III	300–399	Office of Special Education and Rehabilitative Services, Department of Education
3	IV	400–499	Office of Vocational and Adult Education, Department of Education
	V	500–599	Office of Bilingual Education and Minority Languages Affairs, Department of Education
	VI	600–679	Office of Post-Secondary Education, Department of Education
4		680–699	Office of Post-Secondary Education, Department of Education
	VII	700–799	Office of Educational Research and Improvement, Department of Education
	XI	1100–1199	National Institute for Literacy
	XII	1200–1299	National Council on Disability

bureaucrats often have different priorities than chief executives and legislative leaders. Bureaucrats prioritize agency or program resources irrespective of legislative and chief executive priorities. They consistently desire greater authority, funding, and resources. When the agents' (bureaucrats') priorities differ from those of the principal (legislature, chief executive), bureaucratic drift can result. *Bureaucratic* or *policy drift* refers to implementation that produces policy closer to the bureaucrats' preferences than the original intent of the legislation.

What control mechanisms can a principal put in place to increase the probability of agent compliance and reduce policy drift? Congress and state legislatures can use several inducements and incentives to influence bureaucratic behavior, including oversight, budgetary, and legislative hearings. Legislatures can use oversight authority to investigate executive agency behaviors and spending. Legislatures also control bureaucratic agency budgets. The agency actors know their funding is partially dependent on legislative approval, particularly on high-profile program implementation. Legislatures can also hold legislative hearings and call witnesses to testify on agency implementation. These hearings can place significant legislative and public pressure on bureaucratic agencies to maintain the original legislative intent.

Legislatures and chief executives also have authority to shape bureaucratic behavior prior to policy implementation. Chief executives have the authority to appoint bureaucratic agency leaders, and Congress and state legislatures typically retain authority to confirm those appointments. The president and governors appoint agency leaders who share their political, ideological, and policy stances. The alignment of chief executive and agency head policy preferences decreases the probability of policy drift.

Principals (chief executives, legislatures) can also establish pre-implementation control mechanisms through agency rules and standard operating procedures. Procedural controls established by the legislature and the chief executive constrain the bureaucracy's capacity to drift from the original intentions of laws and programs. The Administrative Procedures Act (APA) and the state administrative procedures that followed constitute the foundation of bureaucratic operating procedures in the United States.

The Federal Regulatory Process

The APA is considered the "constitution" for administrative law in that it defines the process by which federal administrative agencies propose and establish regulations (Hickman et al., 2014). Prior to the passage of the APA, the United States had no uniform administrative law for bureaucratic agencies. In 1946, Congress passed the APA to regulate the decision making of administrative agencies. Congressional Democrats supported the APA to prevent Republicans from dismantling New Deal programs and as a means of coping with the growing complexity of federal programs (Elias, 2016). Republicans supported the APA as a means of constraining the expansion of New Deal programs.

According to the APA, rules mean "the whole or part of an agency statement of general or particular applicability and future effect designed to implement, interpret, or apply law or policy." The APA requires agencies to follow an open public process and provide a notice of proposed rulemaking that announces the time, place, and nature of the rulemaking procedures, legal authority, and rules substance. The APA originally provided for three types of rulemaking: formal, informal, and hybrid. In 1990, Congress approved a fourth type of rulemaking process, negotiated rulemaking. All four rulemaking processes require the public receive adequate notice of a proposed rule in the Federal Register and a public comment period when interest groups can submit data and arguments. The final rule must be published in the Federal Register no less than 30 days before the rule goes into effect (Garvey, 2017).

The *formal rulemaking* process includes a formal hearing with oral testimony and legal counsel. Formal rulemaking is applied only for regulatory issues deemed of significant social or economic consequence, due to the time-consuming and cumbersome nature of the process. The agency must allow interest groups to provide information through oral arguments or written documentary evidence. An agency official or administrative law judge presides over the formal hearing, as in a trial, with authority to administer oaths, issue subpoenas, and exclude testimony.

Informal rulemaking requires federal agencies to publish a regulatory plan and agenda outlining rulemaking activities, which is then posted on www.RegInfo.gov and www. Regulations.gov and printed in the Federal Register. The typical public comment period is 30 to 60 days, but for more complex regulations the comment period can extend as long as 180 days. After the public comment period has passed, the agency may issue a draft of the regulation. Agencies may extend or reopen the public comment period if circumstances demand further public feedback. The agency may alter regulations based on public comments, or it may decide the preponderance of the evidence collected supports the original proposed rule. If the agency finds that the data, expert opinions, and facts of the case warrant a final rule but public comments strongly disagree, the agency must decide against public opinion.

In 1990, Congress passed the Negotiated Rulemaking Act to allow an alternative process called negotiated rulemaking. Negotiated rulemaking engages interest groups in the process of developing administrative regulations or rules rather than seeking feedback after the fact. Negotiated rulemaking was established to increase administrative efficiency by engaging interest group actors in the process to avoid the need to rewrite or make significant changes to rules. The agency head is authorized to establish a rulemaking committee typically consisting of a maximum of 25 members with at least one agency representative (Garvey, 2017). The committee issues a report outlining the areas where consensus was achieved. The committee's findings are not binding on the agency – if a full consensus is not achieved, then a formal or informal rulemaking process is used. In 2021, the U.S. Department of Education held negotiated regulatory hearings for revisions of Title IV of the Higher Education Act of 1965, including to affordability and student loans, Pell grants for prison education programs, and institutional and programmatic eligibility (U.S. Department of Education, 2024).

Final rules go into effect no less than 30 days after being published in the Federal Register unless the agency makes the case that it is in the public interest for the rule to become effective sooner. After a final rule is published, agencies may write compliance rules to inform those implementing the rules how to better understand the regulatory requirements. Guidance materials may include interpretive rules, policy statements, and other guidance documents published on the agency's website or in the Federal Register.

The legislative, executive, and judicial branches all have rulemaking oversight authority and mechanisms to hold bureaucratic agencies accountable. Congress can write more specific laws when there is legislative consensus to limit the discretion of bureaucratic agencies (Kerwin & Furlong, 2018). Congress can also limit the methods and timeframes agencies can use to write rules. In recent years, Congress has increased the procedures agencies must follow to restrict agency discretion. Congress also can write into legislation a hammer, a provision that takes effect after a certain period if the agency does not write an alternative rule.

Scholars have distinguished two types of congressional oversight of bureaucratic actions: police patrols and fire alarms. *Fire alarm* congressional oversight refers to a reactive response that only happens when a problem arises, a complaint is made, or an alarm is sounded (McCubbins & Schwartz, 1984). *Police patrols* refer to proactive oversight in which Congress provides funding to monitor bureaucratic action and takes action to solve issues before they become problems. Although police patrols are more effective at reducing public problems before they occur, they have the downside of higher costs and no guarantee of improved performance. Fire alarm oversight provides Congress members with lower oversight costs and the ability to take credit for putting out the fire. Studies of state-level education reform indicate state legislators, like Congress, prefer fire alarm oversight to maximize the electoral benefits of low monitoring costs and high political rewards for solving problems. After an agency has completed the rulemaking process, Congress can penalize it by reducing its budget or passing less favorable statutes.

The State Regulatory Process

State bureaucratic rulemaking generally follows the federal rulemaking process; however, there is a lot of variation across states. In 1946, the same year that the APA was passed by Congress, the National Conference of Commissioners on Uniform State Laws created the State Administrative Procedure Act as a model for states to develop administrative procedures (Broughel et al., 2022). Table 7.4 provides the year each state enacted administrative procedures (Broughel et al., 2022). In 1941, North Dakota was the first of nine states including Connecticut, Indiana, Michigan, Missouri, Nebraska, Ohio, Pennsylvania, and Wisconsin that enacted APA laws prior to the federal enactment. Kentucky was the final state to adopt APA laws in 1984. Although there is evidence that the enactment of APA state laws was motivated by good government reform efforts, studies also suggest partisan motivations. Democratic-controlled legislatures were more likely to adopt APA laws as a means of protecting bureaucratic processes from political manipulation (de Figueiredo & Bergh, 2004).

Forty-seven states utilize informal rulemaking, and only three states (Delaware, Minnesota, and South Carolina) use formal rulemaking. Formal rulemaking employs a hearing supervised by an administrative law judge. Informal rulemaking includes a notice and public comment period. Informal rulemaking is the predominant process utilized at the federal and state levels. Forty-three states, like the federal government, employ executive regulatory review, with the governor authorized with that review power in 28 of them. State legislative regulatory review authority varies widely across states. In seven states, the state legislature has no role in regulatory review. Among state legislatures that have a role in the regulatory review process, 14 allow a full legislative chamber veto of regulations that have the governor's signature, eight allow the full legislative chamber to approve rules, eight allow a legislative committee to veto rules, and eight allow the full chamber to veto rules and regulations that do not have a governor's signature (Broughel et al., 2022).

Judiciary

Federal and state courts do not play a prominent role in policy formulation. Typically, courts lack public accountability due to lifetime appointments. In states where judges are elected by partisan or nonpartisan methods, courts lack the capacity to assess the benefits and harms of policy decisions. Courts are designed to adjudicate whether a policy is legal and consistent with federal and state constitutions. Despite these drawbacks, courts do play a role in education policy formulation. Federal courts adjudicate civil rights cases including school desegregation, gender equity, and special education. State courts have a long history of ruling on school finance litigation. These judicial decisions direct legislative and executive actors to formulate new policies consistent with federal and state constitutions and law. Through this process, judicial systems influence the formulation of education policy.

Table 7.4 APA Adoption Year by State

State	Year adopted	State	Year adopted	State	Year adopted	State	Year adopted
ND	1941	AZ	1952	OK	1963	NC	1973
MI	1943	MA	1954	GA	1964	UT	1973
OH	1943	RI	1956	WV	1964	TN	1974
WI	1943	MD	1957	ID	1965	IL	1975
CT	1945	OR	1957	NV	1965	NY	1975
IN	1945	WY	1957	LA	1966	TX	1975
MO	1945	AK	1959	SD	1966	VA	1975
NE	1945	CO	1959	AR	1967	MS	1976
PA	1945	WA	1959	VT	1967	SC	1977
US	**1946**	DE	1960	NJ	1968	AL	1981
MN	1946	FL	1961	NM	1969	KS	1984
CA	1947	HI	1961	MT	1971	KY	1984
IA	1951	ME	1961	NH	1973		

Note: de Figueiredo and Vanden Bergh (2004).

Influencing Policy Formulation

Educational leaders are critical stakeholders in education policy systems. Most research focuses on teachers' influence on students' academic, cognitive, engagement, and social-emotional success. Educational leaders can become focused exclusively on their students' and institution's needs and priorities to the exclusion of the larger policy system in which their institution operates. Knowledge of the larger policy system is a prerequisite to influencing policy. This textbook provides the knowledge needed to engage and influence the education policy system. This section provides an overview of the policy influence approaches one can use to make the changes. This section draws from the policy evaluation literature to identify the range of policy influence approaches, techniques, and strategies (H. Jones, 2011; Start & Hovland, 2004).

Direct action refers to influencing policy by building relationships with decision makers, staff, allies, and other key stakeholders. Direct contact with policymakers and their staff has the most significant impact on policy ideas and outcomes. *Lobbying*, the act of influencing the actions and decisions of government officials, is a specific example of direct action. Lobbying typically involves face-to-face interactions with key stakeholders. Organizations involved in directly influencing government actors refer to lobbying as government relations. Direct action is predicated on developing relationships with decision makers, having clear policy goals, and understanding incentive structures and windows of opportunities. Figure 7.3 maps policy influence approaches according to whether they cooperatively or confrontationally seek change. Each approach is also distinguished by taking an evidence-based or interest- and value-based approach. Direct action generally utilizes cooperation with decision makers to seek influence and change through shared values and interests.

Educational leaders can lobby government officials and their staff directly through participation in lobbying organizations like teachers unions, professional organizations, and nonprofit and private organizations. Table 7.5 describes the various policy influence approaches. Both advice and lobbying are direct action strategies (H. Jones, 2011; Start & Hovland, 2004). Lobbying or advice begins with having evidence to support policy positions. Building a coalition, particularly of constituents or voters, can have a powerful impact by enabling one to argue policy support will translate into political support. Raising money for elected leaders can also be a powerful tactic for achieving policy change. Lobbying educates policymakers

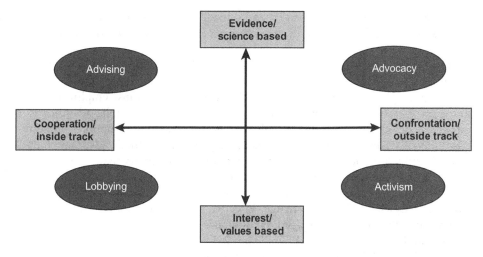

Figure 7.3 Policy-Influencing Approaches
Note: Start and Hovland (2004).

Table 7.5 Policy Influence Approaches

Influence approach	General approach	Definition
Advice	Knowledge dissemination	Occurs through interaction with decision makers, negotiations, and building relationships with stakeholders
Lobbying	Relationship building	Provided through research and advisory support to members, governments, and individuals
Advocacy	Public opinion	Use of public messaging and campaigning to promote and attract attention
Activism	General approach	The initiation of new projects, organizations, and independent activities

and other stakeholders about a problem and the benefits of addressing it. Lobbying is a long-term strategy, not a short-term one. Rarely do policymakers change their policy positions after a single meeting. Consistent, ongoing education and pressure is required, often over multiple years, to achieve policy change.

Advocacy involves the use of public messaging and campaigning to promote and attract attention to influence policy outcomes. Public advocacy involves public messaging to build public support for a policy position and increase pressure on decision makers to yield to policy demands. Advocacy is primarily an indirect influence strategy. Advocacy campaigns include a broad range of activities, such as rallies; circulating petitions; fundraising; marketing; and outreach to the public, decision makers, and voters. Advocacy campaigns are typically waged to persuade the broader public to change the political calculus for elected leaders. Elected leaders are motivated by public demands for policy outcomes. This approach is also called public education, a method of educating the public to change their attitudes and beliefs. Advocacy campaigns also seek to create a network or community of solidarity around a cause and raise awareness about a public problem and policy solutions. Figure 7.3

identifies advocacy as an evidence-based and outside or confrontational influence approach. Rather than working directly with decision makers, advocacy campaigns seek to apply public pressure to force policy change.

Educational leaders can join public and private advocacy campaigns or start their own. The civil rights movement was one of the most successful and broadly recognized public advocacy campaigns in American history. Educational leaders must employ a broad range of strategies to achieve their policy and political objectives. A public advocacy campaign requires clear objectives that a broad coalition can understand and support. Building political coalitions of stakeholders typically is the centerpiece of any public advocacy campaign, to improve its influence and credibility. *Grassroots advocacy* refers to civic activism that allows people directly affected by the problem to take action to achieve a solution. By employing grassroots strategies, educational leaders can diversify their coalitions and build deeper ties to the communities where they seek change. Effective advocacy campaigns use communication strategies and technologies to engage their audience, including email, internet, social media, and television. Facebook (3 billion), YouTube (2.5 billion), Instagram (2 billion), WhatsApp (2 billion), TikTok (1.5 billion), and X (formerly Twitter; 368 million) are the most popular social media platforms in the world. Public advocacy campaigns require a compelling narrative that resonates with the intended audience and generates empathy, support, and action.

Policy influence can also occur through organizations and individuals providing evidence and advice to decision makers. Nonprofits, academic institutions, and businesses conduct research and share the results with decision makers. These organizations can influence decision makers by providing new and compelling evidence to support policy positions. Evidence and advice are both direct and indirect approaches to policy change. Evidence can be used in direct action with decision makers or indirectly in public advocacy campaigns. Evidence and advice are forms of education that seek to influence by sharing compelling data that persuade decision makers to adjust policy.

Educational leaders can use all these policy influence strategies to seek policy change. All policy influence approaches require citizens to move beyond their professional practices and engage the broader policy and political system if they seek change. Many educational leaders avoid politics and policy debates because they feel powerless to make change and are turned off by the caustic nature of public debates. But when educational leaders disengage, policy outcomes lack broad input from those working on the front lines of education. Educational leaders' perspectives are desperately needed in American education policy debates.

Key Terms

administrative agency regulatory rulemaking
Administrative Procedure Act
agenda setting
agenda universe
closed rule
decision agenda
federal regulator process
filibuster
floor debate
focusing events
formal rulemaking
hearings

House Committee on Education and Labor
indicators
informal rulemaking
issue attention cycle
issue definition
legislative override
legislative process
macro policy subsystems
micro policy subsystems
Negotiated Rulemaking Act
open rule
policy drift
policy entrepreneurs
policy formulation
policy problems
policy subsystems
policy windows
presidential or gubernatorial veto
principal-agent problem
problem identification
state regulatory process
systemic agenda

Discussion Questions

1. What are the stages of the policy process? What occurs in each stage?
2. How do issues transition from a condition to a problem?
3. What factors determine whether a problem is a private or public issue?
4. What is agenda setting? What are the types of agendas? How does a policy issue move from one agenda type to another?
5. What is policy formulation? What are the various methods used to formulate policies?
6. How do federal and state legislative processes formulate policy?
7. How do federal and state regulatory processes formulate policy?

Activities and Assignments

1. Explain how your policy issue became identified as a problem. What were the indicators, change in conditions, or focusing events that framed the issue as a problem?
2. Explain how your policy issue made it onto the systemic, institutional, and decision agendas.
3. Explain how your policy was formulated. Who were the key stakeholders that supported and opposed the policy through the formulation process?

References

Atkinson, C. L. (2019). Focus event and public policy. In A. Farazmand (Ed.), *Global encyclopedia of public administration, public policy, and governance* (pp. 1–5). Springer.

Baumgartner, F. R., & Jones, B. D. (1993). *Agendas and instability in American politics.* The University of Chicago Press.

Baumgartner, F. R., & Jones, B. D. (2002). *Policy dynamics*. The University of Chicago Press.

Birkland, T. A. (1997). *After disaster: Agenda setting, public policy, and focusing events*. Georgetown University Press.

Birkland, T. A. (1998). Focusing events, mobilization, and agenda setting. *Journal of Public Policy*, *18*(1), 53–74. https://doi.org/10.1017/s0143814x98000038

Broughel, J., Baugus, B., & Bose, F. (2022). A 50-state review of regulatory procedures. *SSRN Electronic Journal*. https://doi.org/10.2139/ssrn.4093048

Cobb, R. W., & Elder, C. D. (1983). *Participation in American politics: The dynamics of agenda-building*. Johns Hopkins University Press.

de Figueiredo, R. P., & Bergh, R. G. V. (2004). The political economy of state-level administrative procedure acts. *The Journal of Law and Economics*, *47*(2), 569–588.

Downs, A. (1972). Up and down with ecology-the issue-attention cycle. *The Public Interest*, *28*, 38.

Elias, R. A. (2016). The legislative history of the administrative procedure act. *Fordham Environmental Law Review*, *27*(2), 207–224.

Garvey, T. (2017). *A brief overview of rulemaking and judicial review*. Congressional Research Service. https://crsreports.congress.gov/product/pdf/R/R41546

Green-Pedersen, C., & Walgrave, S. (2014). *Agenda setting, policies, and political systems: A comparative approach*. The University of Chicago Press.

Hickman, K. E., Pierce, R. J., & Walker, C. J. (2014). *Federal administrative law: Cases and materials*. Foundation Press.

Jones, B., & Baumgartner, F. R. (2005). *The politics of attention: How government prioritizes problems*. The University of Chicago Press.

Jones, H. (2011). *Background note: A guide to monitoring and evaluating policy influence*. Overseas Development Institute.

Kerwin, C. M., & Furlong, S. R. (2018). *Rulemaking: How government agencies write law and make policy*. CQ Press.

Kingdon, J. (1984). *Agendas, alternatives, and public policies*. Little Brown.

Lawrence, R. G., & Birkland, T. A. (2004). Guns, Hollywood, and school safety: Defining the school-shooting problem across public arenas. *Social Science Quarterly*, *85*(5), 1193–1207. https://doi.org/10.1111/j.0038-4941.2004.00271.x

McCubbins, M. D., & Schwartz, T. (1984). Congressional oversight overlooked: Police patrols versus fire alarms. *American Journal of Political Science*, *28*(1), 165. https://doi.org/10.2307/2110792

Mintrom, M., & Norman, P. (2009). Policy entrepreneurship and policy change. *Policy Studies Journal*, *37*(4), 649–667. https://doi.org/10.1111/j.1541-0072.2009.00329.x

Rochefort, D. A., & Cobb, R. W. (1993). Problem definition, agenda access, and policy choice. *Policy Studies Journal*, *21*(1), 56–71. https://doi.org/10.1111/j.1541-0072.1993.tb01453.x

Sabatier, P. A., & Jenkins-Smith, H. C. (1999). The advocacy coalition framework: An assessment. In P. A. Sabatier (Ed.), *Theories of the policy process*. Westview Press.

Start, D., & Hovland, I. (2004). *Tools for policy impact: A handbook for researchers*. Overseas Development Institute. www.odi.org.uk/resources/download/156.pdf

Thurber, J. A. (1996). Political power and policy subsystems. In A. Editor & Z. Othereditor (Eds.), *Agenda for excellence: Administering the state* (pp. 76–104). Chatham House Publishers.

United States Department of Education. (2024). *Negotiated rulemaking for higher education 2021–22*. https://www2.ed.gov/policy/highered/reg/hearulemaking/2021/index.html?src=rn)

8 Policy Implementation and Evaluation

On January 8, 2002, President George W. Bush signed No Child Left Behind (NCLB) into law. This reauthorization of the Elementary and Secondary Education Act received overwhelming bipartisan support: a 384–45 House vote and an 87–10 Senate vote. Civil rights groups and Democrats led by Massachusetts Senator Ted Kennedy supported the legislation based on its promise to close the achievement gap and provide additional educational resources. Republicans favored the bill to support Bush and for using private sector approaches to education like measuring progress and creating incentives and punitive measures to improve student achievement. The purpose of the legislation was to ensure equitable educational opportunities for all students in America's public education system. The law mandated that states establish state standards, test to measure student progress, and measure adequate yearly progress (AYP) based on disaggregated standardized test scores. Schools that failed to meet AYP thresholds would be subject to increasingly punitive measures.

Despite the laudable goals, bipartisan support, and high expectations, NCLB proved an abject failure by most measures. NCLB never achieved consistent improved student achievement, closed the achievement gap, or expanded federal education resources. The legislation overemphasized standardized testing to the exclusion of all benchmarks of student success. Math and reading were initially the only subjects tested, so it deemphasized all other aspects of the educational experience, including science, social studies, art, music, health, and social and emotional education. The NCLB requirement that teachers be highly qualified, meaning they received training in the subject matter and obtained state certification or licensing, largely bypassed college- and university-based schools of education. Alternative certification routes largely replaced education school training, further delegitimizing the teaching profession. States were allowed to develop their own standards but were required to pass certain student test achievement levels to receive federal funding and avoid punitive measures. Predictably, this led to a race to the bottom as states lowered their standards to ensure students would reach the necessary achievement levels.

State and local officials complained that the U.S. Department of Education failed to consider their concerns when drafting regulations. Those officials also protested that the federal mandates were unrealistic and did not provide sufficient flexibility to achieve achievement benchmarks. Democrats, civil rights groups, and particularly administrators and teachers disapproved of the lack of adequate federal funding. State and local officials argued that the increase in federal funding was not sufficient to pay for the extensive unfunded mandates, let alone improve resources for student achievement (Meier, 2004).

The many failures of the NCLB raise numerous questions. If educational leaders had played a more prominent role in the development of the legislation, would the implementation have been more effective? Did school administrators' and teachers' support for NCLB

DOI: 10.4324/9781003231561-11

goals, but not the policy strategies, predetermine the policy's failure? Could better implementation of the flawed policy have resulted in superior outcomes? To answer these questions, this chapter considers the theory, actors, and key determinants of policy implementation success and failure. This chapter explores the categories and types of policy instruments. The chapter also explores policy evaluation and the role of evaluation in improving policy delivery and revisions.

Policy Typologies

Policy typologies are theoretical constructs that classify public policies based on distinct and predictable patterns of political behavior. Theodore Lowi's groundbreaking typology was based on two foundational concepts (Lowi, 1972). First, policy causes politics. Previous political studies had assumed a reverse causality, with politics causing policy. Lowi argued different types of policy generate different power relationships between interest groups. Lowi also argued coercion is the fundamental government power and that policies should be classified based on the level of government coercion involved in the policy instrument. His policy typology was based upon the degree to which costs and benefits are concentrated for the few or dispersed to the larger public. The policy typology divided policy into three categories: distributive, regulatory, and redistributive.

Distributive Policy

Distributive policies bestow a particular benefit to a specific group or well-defined interest and collect the resources broadly. Distributive policy instruments are characterized by low levels of political conflict and by logrolling or congressional vote trading. Distributive policies generate low levels of conflict because they bestow the benefits of government revenues collected from all citizens on a specific group of actors. Distributive policies are popular with political leaders because they receive credit for the benefits but rarely face reprisal for the incremental increase in government spending. The legislative committee system supports distributive spending because committee members can trade votes with members of other committees to achieve their policy goals. Distributive policies are common in education because they involve the allocation of resources to build infrastructure.

Distributive policy instruments include subsidies, contracts, and nonregulatory licenses. A *subsidy* is a financial grant provided to a private institution or public entity to promote specific activities in the public interest. For example, the U.S. Department of Education delivers more than $130 billion per year in higher education subsidies, including more than $100 billion a year in federal student loans, $30 billion in federal Pell grants, and $3 billion directly to colleges and universities. Each of these policies support the goal of expanding education to improve economic, social, and political outcomes. The costs are paid broadly by taxpayers, but the benefits are directed toward specific social groups.

Regulatory Policy

Regulatory policy imposes costs on a concentrated group and diffuses benefits broadly. Regulatory policies often govern the conduct of business to reduce negative externalities. Scholars distinguish competitive and protective regulatory policy. *Competitive regulatory policy* limits the provision of goods or market participation to a select group. The purpose is to guarantee qualified individuals are conducting professional functions. Teacher and administrator licensure or certification are common examples of competitive regulatory policy. Teacher licensure is an agreement with a state government that a person has fulfilled the minimum education and training requirements to serve as an effective instructor. *Protective regulatory policy* seeks to protect the public and consumers from deceptive advertising and negative externalities. Business interest groups typically resist this type of legislation because it reduces profit margins.

On October 26, 2022, the U.S. Department of Education finalized regulations aimed at protecting veterans and service members from predatory higher education recruitment practices (U.S. Department of Education, 2022). The Higher Education Act had allowed for-profit colleges to recruit veterans and service members without any evidence of the value of their degrees. The new regulation required for-profit colleges to prove their degree would improve employment prospects for veterans and service members. Colleges were required to demonstrate that 10% of their revenue derived from nonfederal sources, but the institutions had been allowed to count G.I. Bill benefits toward the 10% threshold. The regulatory changes no longer allowed higher education institutions to do this. The new regulation further identified which federal benefits no longer counted toward the 10% threshold. The regulatory changes went into effect on January 1, 2023. Bureaucratic agencies typically announce final rules in advance of their effective date to give institutions the opportunity to prepare for the impact of regulatory changes.

Redistributive Policy

Redistributive policies transfer resources from one group to another. A redistributive policy's purpose is to reduce economic, environmental, social, or political inequality. Free market capitalism concentrates wealth, and redistribution systems seek to reallocate resources to broadly improve social well-being and achieve a minimum standard of living for all. Redistributive policies manipulate the allocation of resources and rights between economic or social groups. Redistributive policies concentrate costs and benefits. Redistribution typically occurs from high- and middle-income groups to middle- and low-income groups through taxation and resource redistribution. Redistributive policies, because they shift resources from one social group to another, are the most politically controversial policy category. Redistributive policy is the most contentious and difficult policy to enact because it requires less powerful interests to overcome more powerful groups.

Head Start is a federal program that provides early childhood education, health, nutrition, and parent involvement services to low-income families and children under 5 years old. The goal of the program is to promote these children's school readiness by augmenting their cognitive, social, and emotional development. The program also helps families support their children's holistic well-being. The Head Start program is a classic redistribution policy that transfers general revenues collected from all Americans to low-income families. Other examples of redistributive policies in education include affirmative action programs, desegregation, school finance systems, Title I, Title IX, and Title IV.

Hood and Margetts (2007) developed a policy typology based on nodality, authority, treasure, and organization. Table 8.1 identifies the four instrument categories with examples. *Nodality* refers to information resources or social networks. Federal, state, and local governments exist at the center of a network of organizations and actors. Governments can gather information, shape public opinion, and access their network to develop and implement policy solutions. *Authority* is the official power to prohibit, demand, forbid, or adjudicate a policy solution. Governments have the power to make decisions that other actors must

Table 8.1 Hood Taxonomy of Policy Instruments

Nodality	Authority	Treasure	Organization
Advice	Advisory committees	Grants	Administration
Education	Commissions	Loans	Agencies
Information	Licenses	Subsidies	Departments
Reporting	Regulation	Tax credits	Public corporations
Registration	Self-regulation	User charges	Public enterprises
Training			

accept. Authority within governments includes lawmaking and regulatory powers. Policy instruments in this category include laws, regulations, mandates, and judicial rulings. *Treasure* refers to the government's capacity to raise money through taxes and spend financial resources to fund services, incentivize participation, and provide financial support for organizations or individuals. *Organization* refers to direct government services.

McDonnell and Elmore (1987) identified five policy categories: mandates, inducements, capacity building, system changing, and persuasion. *Mandates* refer to rules governing individual and agency actions, including the required behavior of the target population and a recommended penalty for noncompliance. Mandates seek to achieve widespread behavior change within a population. Mandates require enforcement, which can be challenging, particularly in emergency situations. The enforcement and conformity expenses associated with citizen compliance make mandates a politically costly policy tool. Mandates are typically used only for policy problems with severe consequences or when there is widespread public agreement. A recent ubiquitous example of government mandates is state mask requirements and temporary virtual schooling as a public health response to the COVID-19 pandemic.

Inducements refer to the transfer of money between levels of government, agencies, or individuals for goods or services (McDonnell & Elmore, 1987). Inducement funding can range from transfers for general purposes to specific policy goals detailed in legislation or regulations. Accepting inducements is voluntary, so there is no guarantee school administrators will comply. NCLB is an excellent example of this. Matching grants have been used more often by the federal government. Inducements are most effective when implementers support a policy but lack the resources to achieve proper implementation. Some of the implementation failures of NCLB were due to lack of support for policy inducements.

Capacity building involves investing funding for material, intellectual, or human resource development. These investments are expected to create short- or long-term benefits in support of a desired policy goal. *System changing* is expanding authority to individuals or agencies to alter the institutional structure. Changing the authority to provide a publicly supported service alters the nature of the system. States' development and expansion of charter school authority is a primary example of system changing. The choice of policy instrument category can have far-reaching impacts on the political and policy environment.

Policy Instrumentation

Policy instruments are interventions made by policymakers to achieve policy outcomes. Policy instruments are used to implement an adopted policy. They link the policy formulation and adoption phase to the implementation phase. When asked to name public policy instruments, most people first consider federal and state laws. Although federal and state laws are a fundamental instrument of government power and authority, they are among a broad range of policy instruments. Only Congress and state legislatures have the authority to pass laws. *Laws*, known as *statutes* once passed by a legislature, are second only to the U.S. Constitution and state constitutions. The U.S. Constitution grants citizens many rights that laws cannot take away. However, laws can expand rights beyond those delineated in the U.S. Constitution. For example, Title VI of the Civil Rights Act of 1964 prohibited discrimination based on race, color, or national origin in programs or activities receiving federal financial assistance. That means any educational institution receiving federal assistance must adhere to this extension of rights, including all public elementary and secondary schools and most colleges and universities. These rights are not specifically enumerated in the U.S. Constitution, but the 1964 Civil Rights Act required these protections as an extension of individual rights. Even private schools must adhere to some federal and state laws including accreditation, licensing, teacher certification, school year and school day length, recordkeeping, health and safety, and transportation (Skinner, 2024).

Regulations

Regulations are legal directives that explain how to implement statutes or laws. Regulations are written by executive branch agencies including the U.S. Department of Education and state departments of education. Legislatures give executive branch agencies the authority to set regulations as limited by the authorizing statute. Regulations and rules are published in federal and state codes, books where statutes or regulations on similar subjects are listed for public consumption. State governments maintain regulations and rules for all facets of education systems including administrator certification, compulsory attendance, fire and safety codes, curriculum frameworks, graduation requirements, number of school days, school discipline, and teacher certification and evaluation.

Money

Incentives refers to a set of policy tools used to achieve policy goals, stimulate the economy, solve market failures, or redistribute money. Governments use incentives primarily to encourage or discourage certain behavior. The federal government subsidizes higher education Pell grants and loans to encourage more people to receive postsecondary education. The benefits of higher education include private and public goods. As discussed in Chapter 1, education is a positive externality that is undersupplied in a market economy because the market only responds to the private benefits of the externality, not its public benefits. Education's private benefits are employability and increased present and future earnings potential. The public benefits include the individual's improved role as a productive citizen in democracy, society, and economy due to increased productivity and efficiency. The government uses incentives to encourage education.

Grants

Intergovernmental grants include categorical grants, block grants, and matching grants. Federal grants account for approximately 30% or more than $1.2 trillion of state and local government funding (Dilger, 2015). *Categorical grants* typically use a competitive application process to provide funding for a specific program and are limited to narrowly defined activities. There are four types of categorical grants: formula grants, project grants, formula-project grants, and open reimbursement grants. *Formula grants* are distributed to a jurisdiction based on a formula stipulated in the authorizing legislation (Dilger, 2015). Formula grant distribution categories include enrollment in public schools, population of a state, poverty level, and per capita income of a geographic area. *Project grants* are allocated utilizing a competitive grant application process. *Formula-project grants* combine elements of project and formula grants, including a two-stage grant distribution. First, the federal government distributes funds to the states based on a formula criterion. Second, the states dispense funds to state and local government agencies using a competitive grant application process. *Open reimbursement grants* reimburse recipients for a share of the program costs. The grant is called open because the amount reimbursed depends on the level of spending by the state or local organization or jurisdiction.

Grant types can be depicted on a continuum based on the level of discretion recipients have over how funds are spent (Dilger, 2015). Formula categorical grants, open-ended reimbursement grants, and general revenue sharing grants provide federal administrators with low funding discretion. Block grants provide medium discretion to both federal administrators and recipients. Project categorical grants provide high discretion to federal administrators.

Block grants are multipurpose grants allocated to states through a formula process. Block grants provide state and local governments funding they can use to increase investments in a specific program area. They provide more discretion in the expenditure of funds than categorical grants. Block grants redistribute decision-making authority from higher to lower levels of government, often referred to as the devolution of decision-making authority. In 2015, the Elementary and Secondary Education Act reauthorization established Student Support and Academic Enrichment Block Grants (Shohfi & Tollestrup, 2019). This block grant supports a wide range of educational programs from improving school conditions to digital learning.

Any of these grant categories may include a matching requirement. *Matching grants* require that federal appropriations be combined with state, local, or private funding. Matching grant requirements are a government subsidy to supply more of a public good. Matching grants require the entity receiving the grant to provide funds to supplement the grant award. Matching grants are used to incentivize increased investment by the beneficiary. Typically, matching grants require that state spending meets 20%–50% of the federal appropriation. For example, the federal work-study program provides part-time employment to postsecondary students who meet program eligibility criteria for family income, financial need, previous work-study awards, and the institutional work-study funding available. Students apply through the Free Application for Federal Student Aid (FAFSA) form. Work-study funds are designed to pay for daily needs including food, transportation, and school supplies. Because the program has a matching requirement, the federal government pays 75% of its costs and the higher education institution covers 25%. Studies indicate private institutions are more likely than public institutions to provide work-study to a broader range of students. Matching grants are a popular intergovernmental grant – payments from one level of government to another – used by the federal government to incentivize changes in state government spending and legislative behavior and by state governments to incentivize changes in local government spending and behavior.

Direct Services

Governments also provide direct education services to citizens. Education is the most far-reaching service provided directly by the government. It involves nearly seven million public school employees and 2.5 million employees in public college and universities, equaling nearly 10 million public employees As discussed in Chapters 1–3, education is provided primarily by the government for several reasons, including the market failure of positive externalities in a market economy; ensuring widespread acceptance of common values and a minimum level of literacy and knowledge in a democratic society; and guaranteeing a certain level of educational quality, access, and equity.

Traditional public schools are considered part of local governments. Ninety-four percent of all elementary and secondary public school students attend a school in the neighborhood where they live. The 91,100 traditional public schools are not the only schooling options for students. During the past 50 years, alternatives to traditional public and private school educational opportunities have become more popular. School choice allows public education funds to follow students to schools or services.

Privatization

Privatization is the transfer of production of goods and services from the public sector to the private sector. One argument for privatization is that the free market can provide goods and services more efficiently than the public or nonprofit sectors can. When most people hear the term privatization, they think of selling. If the government sells a corporation or other government service to the private sector, then the organization shifts from public to private ownership. Airport operations, corrections facilities, water and waste utilities, and electric utilities are all examples of government operations that have been transferred to the private sector.

Contracting

Contracts refer to agreements between the government and a private firm to provide a service or product. Contracting is often confused with privatization. Privatization refers to the transfer a business, industry, or service from the public to private sector ownership, and contracting transfers public funding to a private entity that provides the product or service. Contracting is considered a form of quasi-privatization. Public schools contract services like custodial services, management, and transportation. Other contracting examples are cafeteria services, facilities construction, and a textbook company providing exclusive textbook to schools.

Policy Implementation

The passage of a major bill often receives significant press coverage and public attention. Adopting a policy is not the end of the process but rather is the beginning of the real work of putting that policy into practice. *Policy implementation* refers to the effort, knowledge, and resources dedicated to translating policy instruments into action. Turning an education policy into practice is a highly complex process that involves policymakers, bureaucrats, systemwide or districtwide staff, administrators, faculty, the business community, and the local community. In theory, policy implementation alters the education system according to policymakers' policy objectives. In practice, education policy is implemented by millions of bureaucrats, school administrators, teachers, students, and parents who may disagree on the policy objectives. Policy formulation is developing a new state curriculum. Implementation involves identifying whether administrators and teachers have the resources and skills to teach the new curriculum.

Policy formulation and implementation are discussed as separate stages within policy cycles. In practice, the two stages are inexorably connected. Poorly formulated policy results in poor implementation. Well-designed policy still fails if policy formulation did not consider implementation challenges. If policymakers only participate in the formulation and adoption stages, and implementers only participate in the implementation stage, then it is difficult to achieve policy success. Challenges to implementing education policy include vertical and horizontal stakeholder coordination, lack of resources, principal-agent problems, unintended consequences, inadequate resources, coordination issues, and reactions to reforms.

The purpose of passing an education policy is to achieve positive change that improves outcomes for students and their communities. Education practitioners play a central role in this phase of the policy process. Policy implementation is a fundamental responsibility of educational leaders. Education policy implementation is a complex process involving stakeholders at multiple levels of government (*vertical implementation structures*) and coordination among multiple stakeholders (*horizontal implementation structures*). Historically, education policy has attracted a broad range of stakeholders. Federal, state, and local government and nongovernmental actors all play roles in education policy, creating a complex network. Policy implementation occurs within a particular institutional setting, which requires an understanding of institutional culture, power dynamics, and politics. Education policy implementation's complexity derives not only from the many stakeholders involved, but also because it is at the intersection of policy, politics, and the public. Research indicates education systems have grown more complex in recent years as they have shifted from top-down to more horizontal implementation structures (Viennet & Pont, 2017).

Vertical and Horizontal Implementation Structures

The United States federal system disperses power between multiple levels of government and among branches within each level of government. *Multilevel governance* denotes these interactions between government actors within each level and between different levels of government. Vertical implementation structures depict the hierarchy of government and intergovernmental relationships. Federal education policy must be implemented across three levels of government. Coordination across multiple levels of government dramatically increases implementation challenges. Actors at one level of government may have different political or policy priorities and act to thwart rather than support implementation. Horizontal implementation structures are the relationships between organizations across one level of government. Education is not an island. Successful elementary, secondary, and postsecondary students require support.

Policy Implementation Theory

Policy implementation research was born out of failure. In the 1970s, policymakers and scholars were concerned about failures to achieve intended policy outcomes. Implementation studies investigate the process of carrying out government decisions (Berman, 1978). This first generation of implementation research primarily focused on case studies of implementation failure. In 1973, Pressman and Wildavsky published their seminal book *Implementation: How Great Expectations in Washington Are Dashed in Oakland* (Pressman & Wildavsky, 1973). The case study explores implementing an economic development policy in Oakland, California. Previous studies incorporated implementation but had not theorized about the impact of this stage of the policy process. First-generation implementation research expanded the study of public policy formation and adoption to understand the barriers to successful implementation.

Second-generation studies focused on developing theories to identify factors that drive implementation success. This more sophisticated approach focused on vertical integration, the coordination and collaboration process within the government hierarchy within and across levels of government. The field divided into two schools of thought: top-down and bottom-up approaches. The *top-down approach* is a rational management theoretical perspective that views implementation as an administrative problem. Policy success primarily results from administrators' ability and desire to translate elite policy goals into outputs. Administrators are constrained by their authority and their alignment with available resources and policymaker preferences. This perspective views implementation as a process in which high-level administrators achieve policy goals by controlling the actions of bureaucrats.

Critics argue the top-down approach causes many policy implementation failures. The top-down approach should have considered the local context in which implementation occurs and the perspective and preferences of street-level actors. In the U.S. military, failure to follow orders violates the Uniform Code of Military Justice; consequences can include dishonorable discharge, forfeiture of pay, and confinement. A similar code does not constrain complex government bureaucracies. Scholars witnessed a disconnect between policymakers' policy goals and the preferences of government bureaucrats and their environmental realities. The top-down approach should have accounted for the discretion of policy implementers. While policy implementation success requires ongoing interest group support, economic, political, or social factors change after policy formulation. This alters political support and changes the conditions for policy implementation.

The disconnect between the theoretical concept of top-down implementation and the reality of policy implementation failure prompted a second school of implementation, the *bottom-up approach*. This approach identifies the network of actors involved in implementation, beginning with operational-level actors delivering services, and maps back to the top policymakers. In contrast to top-down scholars, bottom-up scholars contend that bureaucratic discretion is a feature, not a bug. Without operational-level bureaucratic discretion to adjust to changing local economic, political, and social conditions, policy implementation is bound to fail (Matland, 1995).

Although the bottom-up approach incorporated critical factors absent from top-down implementation studies, it faced theoretical and practical limitations. Increasing operational-level bureaucrats' discretion improved their ability to adjust to changing local conditions but reduced democratic accountability. Street-level bureaucrats, unlike policymakers, are not accountable to democratic voters. Bottom-up approaches failed to consider the intentional efforts of street-level bureaucrats to promote policy drift and subvert elected officials' policy goals. The bottom-up approach disregards the formulation stage, when policies are characteristically developed in a top-down method. Unintended consequences are difficult to identify in the bottom-up approach because the analysis does not focus on the program or policy goals.

The limitations of the top-down and bottom-up approaches led to a third generation of scholarship that incorporated the complexities of implementation using scientific and game theory methods. Rather than mapping program implementation onto a particular approach, these scholars developed contingency theories that identified different strategies based on local conditions. Game theory, network analysis, and other sophisticated methods were used to understand how implementer discretion influences implementation. Scholars mapped the network of governmental and nongovernmental institutions and organizations that were collaborating to achieve policy goals. Networked organizational structures combine vertical hierarchical intergovernmental relationships with horizontal governmental and nongovernmental partnerships, organizations, and actors to understand the comprehensive policy implementation ecosystem. Implementation networks have increased in complexity as the size of government and nongovernmental actors has grown and diversified.

NCLB illustrates the complex collaboration between federal, state, local, district, and school-level actors that implement education standards and accountability systems, highly qualified teachers, AYP, safe schools, supplemental services, school improvement, and school choice requirements. For example, NCLB required states to set standards for all teachers to be considered highly qualified, districts to communicate with parents on the status of teacher qualifications, and local schools to assist teachers with meeting the state requirements. This provision required the federal government to work with states to implement legislation or regulations defining highly qualified teachers, subject matter competency testing, annual data collection and measurement of highly qualified teachers, and annual teacher professional development. The provision required states to work with school districts to provide the financial and technical support to implement the highly qualified teacher requirements.

State and local implementers organized opposition to what state and local governments referred to as an unfunded mandate, a government regulation imposed on lower levels of government with inadequate financial assistance to help meet the obligation. Pressure mounted for the Bush administration and later the Barack Obama administration to waive key provisions. Every state requested and ultimately received waivers to several key requirements due to mounting political pressure.

Key Determinants of Implementation Success and Failure

Policy outcomes often do not match policy goals and objectives. Policymakers, researchers, and practitioners seek to reduce the gap between policy goals and policy outcomes. In *The Limits of Administration*, Hood (1976) identified five characteristics of an ideal implementation environment (Hood, 1976). First, administration would be unitary, meaning all implementing agents work in unison. Second, the norms and rules of administration would be uniform throughout the organization. Third, there would be no resistance to commands. Fourth, there would be perfect information and communication within the organization. Finally, there would be adequate time to implement the policy as designed.

Unitary Administration

The idealized model rarely exists; this leads to policy implementation failure. Institutions typically lack unity. This is particularly true in the American higher education system, which is highly decentralized with a diverse collection of public, private for-profit, and private nonprofit institutions. These institutions are independent from federal oversight on most issues. The self-regulating accreditation process enables institutional diversity and independence. Postsecondary institutions are also internally decentralized and independent. Elementary and secondary education systems involve a complex combination of federal, state, and local oversight that does not result in unity. Decisions made by federal, state, and district offices are implemented by teachers and staff in colleges, schools, and classrooms. Federal, state, and local government decision makers change during election cycles. Policymaker priorities differ from those of the teachers and staff implementing policies. Educators implementing policy decisions may also disagree with the policy goals and requirements, leading to policy drift.

Uniform Administrative Rules and Norms

Organizations utilize rules and norms to improve the efficiency and consistency of client experiences. Elementary, secondary, and postsecondary institutions develop faculty, staff, and student handbooks and standard operating procedures to improve efficiency and fairness. Institutional rules and norms can create barriers to change.

Street-Level Bureaucrats

Postsecondary, secondary, and elementary faculty and staff implement policy at the street level. Teachers and staff work directly with students on the front lines of policy implementation. These street-level bureaucrats have considerable discretion over the day-to-day implementation of federal, state, or local government policies (Lipinsky, 1980). Street-level bureaucrats may lack precise knowledge of policy goals or may disagree with policy goals and objectives. These divisions lead to a gap between policy goals and street-level bureaucratic decision making, which in turn leads to policy drift and poor policy implementation.

The policymaking process is linear, not cyclical. Policy evaluation is both the final and first stage of the policy process cycle. Figure 8.1 illustrates the stages model phases as originally developed by Lasswell (1936). Once a policy has been formulated and implemented, analysts determine whether it was effective at achieving its goals. Evaluation produces feedback about the effectiveness of policy change that informs the ongoing cycle of policy improvement. Policy evaluation becomes the first step in the next policy cycle by informing problem identification and policy change.

Policy Evaluation

Evaluation of educational policy and programs can range from individual educational institutions to national multiyear, multimillion dollar programs like Head Start or federal loan

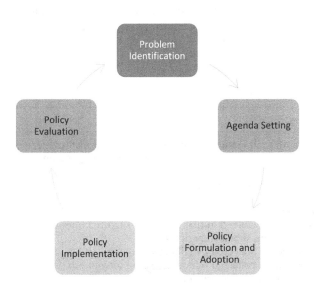

Figure 8.1 The Policy Stages Model

programs. Regardless of context, evaluation begins by defining the policy or program goals. Program goals and objectives are the standard against which evaluators measure impacts. The second step is assessing the educational setting and participants. The educational environment may restrict the indicators or data collection techniques available to evaluators. The third step is to select indicators. Indicators are measurable information used to determine what has changed due to the policy intervention. The choice of indicators is based on the program goals, methods, data analysis, and purpose of the evaluation. Indicators can be qualitative or quantitative data that measure inputs, processes, and outcomes. Federal and state program evaluations typically seek indicators that are specific, measurable, attainable, relevant, and timely. These indicator selection criteria account for the appropriateness and the practical difficulty of collecting data. Evaluators need to weigh the benefits and burdens of collecting evaluation data.

Table 8.2 identifies data collection methods used to evaluate policy. Data collection techniques include quantitative and qualitative data. Interviews, observations, and focus groups are popular qualitative data collection methods used to measure participant experience with a policy or program. Quantitative data collection methods use surveys and existing data sets to analyze numerical data. After data have been collected and analyzed, evaluators use the results to recommend policy or program change and make revisions.

Types of Policy Evaluation

Policy evaluation is conducted to inform decisions that improve policy design, implementation, and revision. *Formative evaluation* is a process of gathering and analyzing feedback during development or implementation to improve how a policy or program is delivered. This type of evaluation occurs while there is still time to improve policy outcomes and understand how to maximize the success of a policy or program. Formative evaluation includes a range of policy evaluation designs including evaluative assessment, implementation evaluation, and process studies. For example, a formative evaluation may be conducted of a pilot study in a particular school district or higher education system to improve policy design and implementation before it is implemented more broadly. Process evaluation is a type of formative assessment used to determine whether policy goals are represented in policy implementation. Process evaluation can identify barriers to policy effectiveness and inform course corrections in policy design and implementation.

Table 8.2 Evaluation Data Collection Methods

Method	Description
Case study	In-depth examination of a program, policy, or institution to understand its context
Document review	Information collected through analyzing existing documents
Existing data sets	Secondary analysis of indicators
Expert review	Information collected through the review of context-specific experts
Focus groups	Information collection that involves structured questioning of a group of people concerning similar experiences
Interview	Information collected by talking with people utilizing structured questions
Observation	Information collected by watching and listening to people using structured or unstructured observation tools
Survey	Survey questionnaires are used to collect standardized, quantitative information

Summative or impact evaluation measures program or policy outcomes. This type of evaluation is a summary of policy outcomes and performance. Summative evaluation assesses an intervention by comparing postintervention participant performance to a standard, benchmark, or preintervention indicator. Summative evaluations identify areas of improvement and inform decisions about policy revisions. Summative evaluations can also promote accountability and transparency by ensuring resources are being used efficiently and effectively.

Key Terms

authority
block grants
bottom-up implementation approach
capacity building
categorical grants
contracting
direct services
distributive policy
formative evaluation
formula grants
horizontal implementation structures
inducements
laws
mandates
matching grants
nodality
organization
policy evaluation
policy implementation
policy implementation theory
policy instrument
policy typologies
privatization
redistributive policy
regulations
regulatory policy
statutes
summative evaluation
system changing
top-down implementation approach
treasure
vertical implementation structures

Discussion Questions

1. What are policy typologies? What are the various categories of policy typologies?
2. How do issues transition from a condition to a problem?
3. What factors determine whether a problem is a private or public issue?

4. What is agenda setting? What are the types of agendas? How does a policy issue move from one agenda type to another?
5. What is policy formulation? What are the various methods used to formulate policies?
6. How do federal and state legislative processes formulate policy?
7. How do federal and state regulatory processes formulate policy?

Activities and Assignments

1. Explain the policy category that define your policy issue. Explain whether your policy issue is distributive, redistributive, or regulatory.
2. Explain the policy instruments used in your policy issue. Explain which policy stakeholders have additional power given the policy instruments utilized.
3. Explain how your policy was implemented. Identify the key implementation stakeholders.
4. Explain how your policy has been evaluated. Explain how the evaluation of your policy will influence future policy revisions.

References

Berman, P. (1978). The study of macro- and micro-implementation. *Public Policy, 26*(2), 155–184.

Dilger, R. J., & Cecire, M. H. (2015). *Federal grants to state and local governments: A historical perspective on contemporary issues.* Congressional Research Service.

Hood, C. (1976). *The limits of administration.* Wiley.

Hood, C., & Margetts, H. (2007). *The tools of government in the digital age.* Macmillan Education.

Lasswell, H. D. (1936). *Politics: Who gets what, when, how.* Whittlesey House.

Lipinsky, M. (1980). *Street-level bureaucracy: Dilemmas of the individual in public services.* Russell Sage Foundation.

Lowi, T. J. (1972). Four systems of policy, politics, and choice. *Public Administrative Review, 32*(4), 298–310.

Matland, R. E. (1995). Synthesizing the implementation literature: The ambiguity-conflict model of policy implementation. *Journal of Public Administration Research and Theory, 5*(2), 145–174.

McDonnell, L. M., & Elmore, R. F. (1987). Getting the job done: Alternative policy instruments. *Educational Evaluation and Policy Analysis, 9*(2), 133–152. https://doi.org/10.3102/01623737009002133

Meier, D. (2004). *Many children left behind: How the no child left behind act is damaging our children and our schools.* Beacon Press.

Pressman, J. L., & Wildavsky, A. B. (1973). *Implementation: How great expectations in Washington are dashed in Oakland.* University of California Press.

Shohfi, K. D., & Tollestrup, J. (2019). Department of education funding: Key concepts and FAQ. *Congressional Research Service Report, 44477.*

Skinner, R., & Sorenson, I. (2024). *Overview of public and private school choice options.* Congressional Research Service.

United States Department of Education. (2022). *Education department unveils final rules to protect veterans and service members, improve college access for incarcerated individuals and improve oversight when colleges change owners.* www.ed.gov/news/press-releases/education-department-unveils-final-rules-protect-veterans-and-service-members-improve-college-access-incarcerated-individuals-and-improve-oversight-when-colleges-change-owners

Viennet, R., & Pont, B. (2017). *Education policy implementation.* https://doi.org/10.1787/fc467a64-en

9 Education Finance Systems

Most countries utilize a centralized system in which the national government maintains administrative and financial authority over education. The United States is among the small minority of countries that maintain a decentralized education system in which each state government maintains administrative and financial control. Decentralized systems transfer administrative and financial authority to a regional or local government. Other countries with decentralized systems include Canada, the Czech Republic, Estonia, Poland, Slovenia, and the United Kingdom. This chapter investigates how the decentralized nature of American education has led to systematic financial inequities and how these inequities provide inequitable opportunities for students based on socioeconomic and racial factors. The chapter also explores financing of higher education expenditures and the role of federal, state, and local governments in the financing of elementary, secondary, and postsecondary education.

Elementary and Secondary Education

American education funding is a complicated combination of federal, state, and local funding called fiscal federalism. State governments provide the largest share of elementary and secondary education funding, 45.3%, followed closely by local funding at 42%. The federal government provides only 12.7% of all education spending. Dependence on local government spending rather than federal sources results in severe funding inequities across school districts. Historically, most public school funding has been drawn from local sources. As late as 1930, 80% of public school funding came from local sources (National Center for Education Statistics, 1993). U.S. education funding's reliance on local property taxes has resulted in lower education funding for low-income and high-minority areas. This means the most disadvantaged students receive the least education resources, and advantaged students receive the most educational resources. Figure 9.1 shows the sources of education funding.

Federal Government

President Joe Biden's Fiscal Year 2024 Department of Education (DOE) budget requested $90 billion in discretionary funding, a $10.8 billion or 13.6% increase from Fiscal Year 2023 (DOE, 2023). The budget request included a $2.2 billion increase in Title I spending, increasing its total to $20.5 billion. The proposal also sought to expand access to high-quality preschool, increased support for children with disabilities, expanded support for community schools, increased investments in teacher recruitment and retention, and supported multilingual learners and diverse schools. The proposal also increased funding for Pell grants, expanded free community college, increased funding for historically Black colleges

DOI: 10.4324/9781003231561-12

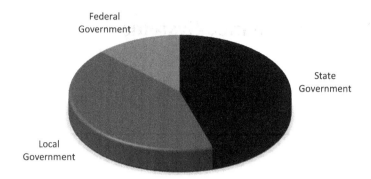

Figure 9.1 Elementary and Secondary Education Funding by Source

and universities, increased career and technical education for adults, and increased support for civil rights enforcement.

If the federal government's appropriations are such a small percentage of total elementary and secondary education spending, how does the federal government have such broad influence over education? The federal government uses funding mechanisms, primarily through the Elementary and Secondary Education Act, to incentivize schools through conditional funding. The federal government provides state and local governments billions of dollars in education funding, conditioned on meeting specific requirements. By incentivizing public schools with much-needed federal funding rather than mandating state action, federal actors can circumvent the Tenth Amendment. Categorical grants are federal grants used to incentivize state and local governments to implement national priorities. Grants-in-aid allow the national government to achieve policy goals that remain the jurisdiction of state and local governments.

Education funding levels are primarily determined by federal and state budgeting processes and local property tax rates. Government budgeting involves legislation that raises revenues and funds programs. The federal government has both authorization and appropriations processes. The authorization process may establish, continue, or modify government agencies or programs. Authorizations are statutory provisions that define the government's authority to act. For example, an authorization act established the DOE, and other acts reauthorized federal programs, including the Elementary and Secondary Education Act, Individuals with Disabilities Act, and the Higher Education Acts. These authorized subsequent appropriations for specific agencies and programs. An authorization may include spending ceilings for agencies and programs, but it does not specify the specific spending allocations – that requires a second process called appropriations.

Article I, Section 8 of the U.S. Constitution assigns the power to levy and collect taxes and the power to borrow money against the credit of the United States to the U.S. Congress. Article I, Section 7 requires that all revenue bills originate in the House of Representatives. Article I, Section 9 states: "No money shall be drawn from the Treasury, but in consequence of appropriations made by law; and a regular statement and account of the receipts and expenditures of all public money shall be published from time to time."

The U.S. Constitution does not prescribe a specific budget process. The Budget and Accounting Act of 1921 created a statutory role for the president by requiring an annual budget submission to Congress in coordination with executive agencies. The 1974 Congressional Budget and Impoundment Control Act established the Congressional Budget Office, which oversees overall fiscal policy. The House and Senate Budget Committees establish a framework for managing the federal budget process.

The federal budget includes both debts from spending and borrowing and receipts of funds collected, primarily from taxes. Appropriation is a statutory provision that provides budget authority or funding to federal agencies and programs. Congress exercises control over budget authority, while the agencies and programs determine outlays or spending. The federal budget consists of discretionary spending, allocated through the annual appropriations process, and mandatory or direct spending, determined outside the appropriations process. The appropriations committees have jurisdiction over discretionary spending, which comprises approximately 30% of total federal spending. Legislative committees have jurisdiction over mandatory or direct spending, which accounts for approximately 63% of total federal spending. Direct spending includes several large programs including Social Security, Medicare, Medicaid, federal military and civilian retirement, and veterans' disability compensation.

The appropriations process in American government consists of a seven-step process that in large part mirrors the legislative process. The appropriations process begins with an executive branch budget recommendation from all executive agencies. These budget requests are based on the previous year's agency budget and commonly include a healthy increase in funding. The Office of Management and Budget reconciles the agency requests with the president's policy priorities to construct a budget recommendation. This recommendation is nonbinding. In other words, Congress is under no obligation to agree with or even consider the budget requests of the executive branch.

The House of Representatives Committee on Appropriations receives the executive branch budget recommendations. This committee is a powerful entity in legislative deliberations; therefore, the House majority leadership assigns a large partisan majority of members to the committee. While the Committee on Appropriations retains some autonomy, the House leadership has numerous ways to keep its members aligned with the preferences of the full House. Once the Committee on Appropriations completes its recommendations and votes on them by majority rule, the appropriations bill goes to the full House. The full House adjusts the bill and puts it to a floor vote.

Once the House of Representatives approves the appropriations bill, the recommendations are forwarded to the Senate Committee on Appropriations. The Senate constructs its own budget bill; however, historically, the Senate bases its recommendations on those passed based by the House. The Senate, much like the House, has several formal and informal ways to ensure the Committee on Appropriations considers the preferences of the full Senate in its budget deliberations. The Senate, however, provides far greater autonomy to individual senators than the House, in keeping with its historical record of independence. The Committee on Appropriations votes the bill out of committee, and it proceeds to the full Senate for a floor vote.

If the House and Senate versions are not identical, a conference committee reconciles the bills. The conference committee includes members of both appropriations committees and House and Senate leadership. The conference committee's approved bill is submitted to the chief executive, at which time it is either signed into law or vetoed. Several states give governors line-item veto authority, the ability to cut specific provisions from appropriations bills. Other states and the national government offer only the ability to veto entire appropriations bills. If the chief executive vetoes the bill, the appropriations process begins again in the House, followed by the Senate. If the chief executive signs the bill, it becomes law. Table 9.1 shows the timetable for this process.

If Congress cannot come to a compromise on an appropriations bill, it can pass a continuing resolution to provide temporary budget authority to agencies and programs. This

Table 9.1 Congressional Budget Process Timetable

Date	Federal budget process stage
First Monday in February	President submits budget
February 15	Congressional Budget Office submits report to budget committees
No later than 6 weeks after president submits budget	Committees submit views and estimates to budget committees
April 1	Senate Budget Committee reports concurrent resolution on the budget
April 15	Congress completes action on concurrent resolution on the budget
May 15	Annual appropriations bills may be considered in the House
June 10	House Appropriations Committee reports last annual appropriations bill
June 15	Congress completes action on reconciliation legislation
June 30	House completes action on annual appropriations bills
October 1	Fiscal year begins

temporary budget authority allows agencies and programs to continue operating until an appropriations bill can be passed. When Congress fails to pass an appropriations bill or a continuing resolution, the government shuts down. The federal government has experienced a partial shutdown 20 times since the Budget Control and Impoundment Act of 1974 established the modern-day budget process. As Congress has become more polarized in recent decades, regular order of the federal budget process has broken down, leading to the use of omnibus bills. In regular order, Congress passes 12 appropriations bills: agriculture, commerce-justice-science, defense, energy and water, financial services, homeland security, interior–environment, labor-HHS-education, legislative branch, military construction-veterans affairs, state-foreign operations, and transportation-HUD. Congress can choose to combine two or more appropriations bills into an omnibus bill that is typically more likely to receive congressional approval because it has provisions that more members of Congress want for their constituents.

State Elementary and Secondary Education Funding

In Fiscal Year 2023, states spent a total of $550.7 billion on elementary and secondary education (National Association of State Board Officers, 2023). Elementary and secondary education is the largest category of total state spending. Total state expenditures include general funds, federal funds, permanent funds, bonds, and other dedicated state funds. Figure 9.2 illustrates total state expenditures by function. Elementary and secondary education is the second highest spending category, 19%, behind only Medicaid's 30%. States provide funding to local school districts to pay for educational costs including school construction, teacher salaries and benefits, instructional materials, and support services. During the past 50 years, state spending as a percentage of total education funding has increased in order to reduce funding inequities.

Figure 9.3 illustrates that elementary and secondary education comprise 33.8% of general fund expenditures. General fund expenditures include all general revenue that does not have specific revenue sources or purposes. Historically, elementary and secondary education has

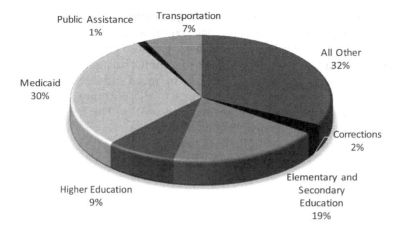

Figure 9.2 Total State Expenditures

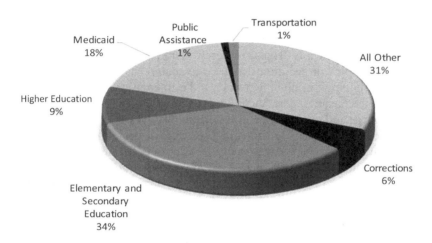

Figure 9.3 General Fund Expenditures

been the largest category of spending, but it has fallen to second behind Medicaid over the past 15 years. The figure depicts total state funding by expenditure function. Elementary and secondary education spending is composed of **45.3%** state funds, **42%** local funds, and **12.7%** federal funds. Most general fund expenditures are approved through a budget process.

State Budget Process

State budget processes resemble the federal budget process. The state budget cycle has a similar seven-step process. Most state budget processes start July 1 rather than October 1: 46 states' fiscal years begin on July 1 and end June 30. The exceptions are Alabama and Michigan (October 1), New York (April 1), and Texas (September 1). The fiscal year begins with state finance agencies producing a revenue forecast. Unlike the federal government, state governments are required to balance their budget, meaning they cannot spend more than they collect in revenue. Forty-nine states have constitutional or statutory balanced budget requirements, the exception being Vermont. State balanced budget requirements vary widely by state. Forty-five states require the governor to submit a balanced budget to the legislature, but only 35 states require the state budget to be balanced at the end of the fiscal year.

In September, state agencies submit requests to the governor based on fiscal revenue projections, spending targets, and the governor's priorities. The state budget office reviews agency requests and makes recommendations to the governor for a budget proposal. The governor revises the proposal and submits the budget to the state legislature in January. The state legislature uses the governor's budget as the basis for legislative deliberations. Legislative committee hearings are held between February and May to review the governor's budget and develop a state legislative budget proposal. The balance of budget authority between the governor and legislature varies widely by state (NASBO, 2021). The state legislature is required to pass a state budget by the end of the fiscal year. The governor may sign or veto the bill. In 44 states, the state provides the governor with line-item veto authority. Line-item veto authority allows the governor to cut specific budget items or provisions from a bill without vetoing the entire budget bill. The state legislature can choose to override gubernatorial vetoes. To override gubernatorial vetoes, 36 states require a two-thirds vote from both legislative chambers, seven require a three-fifths vote, and six require a simple majority vote.

State budgets are comprised of several types of funds. General funds are the major operating fund of state governments. This fund receives state revenues to fund ordinary government operations. Capital project funds are used to acquire and construct major capital assets including public buildings; bridges; highways; and elementary, secondary, and postsecondary school buildings and facilities. Permanent funds are used to generate revenue for government services. Like college and university endowments, only the earnings or investment returns on the principal are used in order to maintain future revenue generation. Special revenue funds dedicate revenue from specific sources to finance certain government activities. Debt service funds account for the payment of principal and interest on short- and long-term government bonds and loans. State education funding is typically determined through funding formulas.

State Education Funding Formulas

State constitutions require policymakers to provide an adequate education for all students. State school finance systems include the rules, regulations, and policies that aggregate state and local revenues and distribute them throughout the state education system. Education costs differ across school districts, based on a wide array of factors including student needs and population characteristics. Students with disabilities, English language learners, and economically disadvantaged students require specialized services that increase instructional costs. School district size, population density, and organizational structures also influence education costs.

State school funding formulas describe the methods by which states distribute state and local funding to school districts. State school finance formulas account for differences in the cost of education across school districts and the resources of local public school districts. The purpose of funding formulas is to reduce socioeconomic disparities in local revenue and adjust school funding based on differences in student and district needs (Picus et al., 2015). According to the (Irwin, 2022), in the 2018–2019 school year, elementary and secondary public school revenues totaled $795 billion. Federal government funding sources totaled $63 billion (8%), state funding sources totaled $371 billion (47%), and local sources totaled $361 billion (45%). Although state funding sources have in the past decade become the highest percentage among the three levels of government, the formulas used to allocate state and local funds vary across the 50 states.

States primarily utilize public school funding formulas to compensate for inequities in the distribution of local funding between school districts with high and low property wealth. Different states have different goals for their public education funding formulas, but all state funding formulas are designed to raise the per pupil funding for low-wealth districts. The percentage of state funding varies widely, from 90% in Hawaii and Vermont to 25% in Illinois.

Foundation Funding Formula. Foundation funding formulas guarantee that school districts will receive a certain level of funding based on the number of students and the property tax rate. When local governments set the property tax rate, they receive a certain level of revenue. The amount of state aid appropriated to each school district is the difference between the guaranteed minimum per-pupil funding level and the amount of funding collected by the local government at the given tax rate. For example, a high-wealth school district may collect $12,000 per student at a given property tax rate, while a low-wealth district may collect $4,000 per student at the same tax rate. If the state has set a minimum foundation level of $12,000 per student, the high-wealth district would not receive any additional funding. In contrast, the low-wealth district would receive $8,000 per student in state aid to reach the minimum foundation level.

Foundation-level spending requires the state legislature to determine both the minimum level of foundation funding and the tax rate required for school districts to receive the guaranteed funding levels. Typically, local school districts can spend more than the foundation level and raise funds beyond the required foundation level. For example, Massachusetts Chapter 70 determines the foundation budget levels for local school districts. The target local contribution, the goal for cities or towns to contribute to the foundation budget, is currently a minimum of 59% and a maximum of 82.5%. The amount spent per pupil in public school districts ranges from more than $44,000 per pupil in Provincetown to less than $13,000 per student in Halifax. Wealthy districts spend well above the foundation level, including Cambridge (124%), Brookline (83%), Wellesley (77%), Newton (70%), Lexington (65%), and Concord (79%), and low-income districts spend below the foundation level, including Springfield (4% below) and Lawrence (4% below).

According to the Education Commission of the States, 34 states used a student-based foundation funding model, 10 used a resource-based allocation, five used a hybrid model, and two used a guaranteed tax base model. A student-based foundation model provides school districts with a base amount of funding per student. The state calculates each district's ability to pay and provides the difference in state funds to reach the foundation minimum. These models often include additional funding or support for students with higher needs and to low-wealth districts.

Resource-Based Funding Formulas. Resource-based funding formulas provide all districts with a minimum base of resources. The funding amount is based on the number of teachers and staff a district requires to serve its students. Alabama, Delaware, Idaho, North Carolina, South Dakota, Tennessee, Virginia, Washington, West Virginia, and Wyoming utilize a resource-based allocation model. To determine the resource allocation, states identify the number of teachers, administrators, and services required per school district and calculate the costs for each district.

Guaranteed Tax Base Model. Guaranteed tax base funding formulas equalize the revenue generated by providing a minimum funding level for each percentage of the property tax rate, regardless of how much revenue is generated. Guaranteed tax base models connect a minimum amount of state funding to the tax effort. Increases in the property tax rate raise the amount for the district (Chingos & Blagg, 2017). This incentivizes districts to increase local taxes to generate additional education revenue because that funding will be matched by the state.

Hybrid Funding Formula. Hybrid funding formulas blend elements of the student-based foundation and resource-based allocation models. For example, Massachusetts utilizes a cost per student formula, like the student-based foundation formula. However, costs are determined by a resource allocation approach. Georgia, Illinois, and Maine also use hybrid models. Few states use hybrid models because of their complexity. Table 9.2 identifies the school funding formula type used in each state and the foundation base amount for states that use that funding type.

Local Government

The primary way local governments fund education is through property taxes. In 2023, state and local governments collected $757 billion in property tax revenue. Local property taxes account for 72.2% of all local government revenue and 32.2% of all state and local tax revenue (Loughead et al., 2022). The property tax a homeowner or business owner pays is based on three factors: the tax rate, the assessment ratio, and the property value. Local governments assess the taxable value of each property in their jurisdiction. The assessed value is typically based on the last sale price, income potential, or size and physical attributes. Property taxes can be assessed on the total or partial value of properties. The assessment ratio represents the portion of the property value subject to the tax. Some states provide statewide caps; others allow property taxes to vary. Table 9.3 identifies the percentage of state and local revenues from property taxes by region. New England and Southwestern states rely most heavily on property tax revenues, and Southeastern states rely on them the least.

Property taxes are regressive, meaning that households with lower incomes spend a larger portion of their budget. All homes in a particular jurisdiction are taxed at the same rate, called a flat tax. Flat taxes are regressive because they take a larger percentage of income from low- than high-income groups. For example, Bridgeport, CT, has a property tax rate of 3.81% and spends $17,616 per student annually, while Charleston, SC, has a property tax rate of 0.5% and spends only $12,426 per student annually. Wealthy jurisdictions with the same property rates generate much higher revenue than low-wealth jurisdictions due to differences in property value. Property tax revenues depend on home values, meaning areas with higher property values collect much more revenue. According to a University of Chicago study, homeowners in the poorest neighborhoods pay effective property tax rates double those in rich neighborhoods (Berry, 2021). Low-income homes are systematically overassessed due to a lack of data to accurately assess market value and wealthier homeowners' efforts to lower their valuation for tax purposes. This results in a transfer of billions of dollars in tax burden from low- to high-income homeowners.

Why does the U.S. rely so heavily on property tax revenue to fund schools, given the funding inequities? Property taxes are more stable than sales and income taxes, which fall with economic downturns. The property tax is also transparent in that potential residents can weigh the costs of the county or municipal property tax against the benefits of government services, including the quality of the education system. Unfortunately, property taxes provide a very unequal distribution of revenue based on the size and socioeconomic wealth of a geographic area. Property values vary significantly across neighborhoods and school districts. High-poverty areas have lower home values and collect less property tax revenue than areas that have high property values. This funding system creates an inequitable distribution of education funding and school resources.

Table 9.2 State School Funding Formulas and Foundation Base Minimums 2021–2022

State	School funding formula type	Foundation base amount
Alabama	Resource-based allocation	
Alaska	Student-based foundation	5,930
Arizona	Student-based foundation	4,390
Arkansas	Student-based foundation	7,349
California	Student-based foundation	9,572
Colorado	Student-based foundation	7,225
Connecticut	Student-based foundation	11,525
Delaware	Resource-based allocation	
Florida	Student-based foundation	4,372
Georgia	Hybrid	2,775
Hawaii	Student-based foundation	4,490
Idaho	Resource-based allocation	
Illinois	Hybrid	
Indiana	Student-based foundation	5,995
Iowa	Student-based foundation	6,323
Kansas	Student-based foundation	4,706
Kentucky	Student-based foundation	4,000
Louisiana	Student-based foundation	4,015
Maine	Hybrid	
Maryland	Student-based foundation	7,991
Massachusetts	Hybrid	
Michigan	Student-based foundation	8,700
Minnesota	Student-based foundation	6,728
Mississippi	Student-based foundation	5,829
Missouri	Student-based foundation	6,375
Nevada	Student-based foundation	6,980
New Hampshire	Student-based foundation	3,786
New Jersey	Student-based foundation	11,775
New York	Student-based foundation	6,835
North Carolina	Resource-based allocation	
North Dakota	Student-based foundation	10,136
Ohio	Student-based foundation	
Oklahoma	Student-based foundation	
Oregon	Student-based foundation	4,500
Pennsylvania	Student-based foundation	
Rhode Island	Student-based foundation	10,310
South Carolina	Student-based foundation	2,489
South Dakota	Resource-based allocation	
Tennessee	Resource-based allocation	
Texas	Student-based foundation	6,160
Utah	Student-based foundation	3,809
Vermont	Guaranteed tax base	
Virginia	Resource-based allocation	
Washington	Resource-based allocation	
West Virginia	Resource-based allocation	
Wisconsin	Guaranteed tax base	
Wyoming	Resource-based allocation	

Table 9.3 Property Taxes Percentages as Total of State and Local Revenues

Region	State	Local	Combined
New England	2.5	97.1	40.2
Midwest	1.1	72.0	32.7
Southeast	1.2	68.4	29.4
Southwest	1.2	78.1	40.3
West	2.1	68.2	30.1

School Funding Inequality

Students in high-poverty neighborhoods face obstacles to learning before they walk through the schoolhouse doors. Poverty creates barriers to learning, including inadequate housing, medical care, and nutrition; literacy and language development deficiencies; and access to material resources including daycare, afterschool, summer school, and student support services. Rather than funding education to ameliorate this problem, the education system is financed to compound it. The highest need students receive the fewest resources, not only per pupil funding but also the distribution of highly qualified teachers, support services, and out-of-school resources.

Interstate funding inequity refers to disparities in per pupil spending across states. State per pupil expenditures range from $30,157 (New York) to $10,709 (Idaho). Disparity in per pupil expenditures results from different state and local tax bases and policy choices. Additional funding disparities occur within states. Differences in property tax revenues result in both interstate and interdistrict funding inequity. Interdistrict funding inequity refers to disparities in per pupil spending across districts within the same state. Intradistrict funding inequity, disparity in funding between schools within a district, further increases funding disparities.

The U.S. civil rights movement occurred primarily in the 1950s and 1960s to win equal rights under the law for African Americans. The movement was a response to the 100 years of racial discrimination and segregation that followed the Civil War and the abolition of slavery. The Reconstruction era (1865–1877) was a period when the United States sought to readmit the former Confederate states and redress the economic, political, and social inequities caused by nearly 250 years of slavery. Between 1865 and 1870, Congress passed and the states approved the Thirteenth, Fourteenth, and Fifteenth Amendments to the U.S. Constitution, also known as the Reconstruction Amendments. The Thirteenth Amendment abolished slavery. The Fourteenth Amendment gave citizenship to all people born in the United States and equal protection under the law to Black people. The Fifteenth Amendment gave Black Americans the right to vote. By the mid-1870s, support for reconstruction began to wane. In 1876, the political parties made a bargain whereby Republican candidate Rutherford B. Hayes would win the disputed presidential election in return for federal troop withdrawal from the South.

By the start of the 19th century, a new racial system had been constructed to disenfranchise African Americans and institute a system of racial segregation. This system consigned African Americans to low-wage employment and used violence to punish those who challenged it. State and local laws were created to legalize racial segregation. Called Jim Crow laws, these lasted for 100 years until the civil rights movement of the 1950s and 1960s.

African Americans' bravery in serving the U.S. military combined with the threat of widespread protest led to President Franklin D. Roosevelt's 1941 executive order requiring national defense jobs and government jobs be selected without regard to race, creed, or national origin and to President Harry Truman's 1948 executive order integrating the U.S. military. In 1954, the Supreme Court in *Brown v. Board of Education* ruled that educational segregation was unconstitutional and ended the separate but equal policy that had served as federal law since the 1890s. Civil rights protests including the boycott of the Montgomery, AL, bus system (1955); the integration of a Little Rock, AR, high school (1957); Woolworth lunch counter sit-ins (1960); Freedom Riders protest of segregated bus terminals (1961); the March on Washington (1963); and the Selma to Montgomery, AL, march to protest the killing of civil rights activists (1965) set the stage for further political, economic, and legal progress.

At the federal level, the civil rights protests led President Lyndon B. Johnson to sign the Civil Rights Acts of 1964, which prohibited discrimination in employment practices based on race, color, religion, sex, or national origin. In 1965, Johnson signed the Voting Rights Act, which eliminated legal barriers at the state and local level that prevented African Americans from exercising their right to vote, including banning all voter literacy tests and providing federal examiners. Despite initial gains in school integration due to the civil rights movement, court decisions restricted mandatory school segregation programs resulting in the resegregation of public schools. Since the 1980's, the percentage of students in highly segregated schools has tripled. According to the Civil Rights Project, more than 40 percent of Black and Hispanic students attend highly segregated schools meaning 90 percent of students are nonwhite (Frankenberg et al., 2019).

A report by EdBuild found that non-White school districts receive $23 billion less in funding than schools in predominantly White districts (EdBuild, 2019). These disparities exist despite the districts serving the same number of students. The United States suffers from a long history of racial bias and segregation in housing policy. Most children in the United States still attend racially segregated school systems. According to the EdBuild report, 27% of students are enrolled in predominantly non-White districts, those where 75% of students are non-White, and another 26% of students are enrolled in predominantly White districts, those where more than 75% of the students are White. Of the approximately 13,800 public school districts, 7,600 are predominantly White, while 1,200 are predominantly non-White. The discrepancy in the number of predominantly White and non-White school districts arises from the concentration of non-White students in larger, primarily urban school districts. This level of educational segregation is extraordinary given the increasing diversity of the U.S. population.

According to the report, the average predominately White school district receives $13,908 and the average predominantly non-White school district receives $11,682 — a $2,226 difference (EdBuild, 2019). There is a financial disparity even when the data considers only poor school districts. Poor, predominately White school districts receive $150 less per student than the national average, but poor, predominantly non-White school districts receive $1,618 less than average.

How much additional investment would be required to provide adequate funding for all students? According to a Century Foundation Report, the United States is underfunding public schools by $150 billion annually (Baker, 2020). Low-income and majority minority school districts, districts with 50% or higher Black or Latino populations, are twice as likely to have funding gaps. The majority minority district funding gap averages more than $5,000 per pupil. Table 9.4 identifies the aggregate state funding gap per year between high- and low-income districts. The funding gap estimates the cost for a student to achieve national average outcomes on reading and math assessments. The states with the highest estimated funding gap as a percentage of current spending are Arizona (89.9%), Nevada (72.2%), Texas (63.3%), New Mexico (60.7%), and Mississippi (54.9%).

Table 9.4 State Aggregate Funding Gaps

State	Total gap	Gap as percentage of current spending
California	$37.52 billion	4.4
Texas	$30.44 billion	63.3
Florida	$10.91 billion	41.8
Arizona	$6.58 billion	89.7
Georgia	$5.20 billion	29.2
North Carolina	$4.77 billion	36.5
Illinois	$4.02 billion	13.8
Nevada	$3.01 billion	72.3
Michigan	$2.87 billion	20.6
Alabama	$2.77 billion	40.0
Indiana	$2.64 billion	26.7
Pennsylvania	$2.49 billion	10.9
Colorado	$2.45 billion	28.0
Oklahoma	$2.41 billion	46.4
Ohio	$2.41 billion	13.1
Mississippi	$2.17 billion	54.9
Washington	$2.09 billion	1.5
New Mexico	$1.90 billion	60.7
Missouri	$1.64 billion	18.5
Arkansas	$1.62 billion	36.3
South Carolina	$1.57 billion	20.1
Louisiana	$1.46 billion	20.4
Oregon	$1.46 billion	23.8
Tennessee	$1.45 billion	18.9
Massachusetts	$1.33 billion	9.4
Kentucky	$1.31 billion	19.1
New Jersey	$1.28 billion	5.4
Virginia	$1.28 billion	8.2
Wisconsin	$1.18 billion	11.6
Utah	$1.17 billion	28.3
Idaho	$812.51 million	37.7
Minnesota	$679.22 million	6.8
Kansas	$611.77 million	12.1
Connecticut	$555.34 million	6.0
Iowa	$544.86 million	9.7
Maryland	$450.03 million	3.3
New York	$427.54 million	0.7
Rhode Island	$297.69 million	14.3
West Virginia	$199.03 million	6.7
Montana	$189.94 million	11.4
Nebraska	$170.79 million	4.4
South Dakota	$118.71 million	8.6
Vermont	$112.78 million	9.3
Maine	$72.22 million	4.3
New Hampshire	$47.41 million	1.7
Alaska	$40.35 million	1.7

School Finance Litigation

How have advocates sought to address the socioeconomic and racial inequalities in the American education finance system? In the 1960s, advocates turned to federal and state courts to combat school funding inequities. School finance litigation is classified into three separate waves of reform. The first wave of school finance litigation focused on federal courts and argued inequities in school funding violated the U.S. Constitution's equal protection clause. In 1971's *Serrano v. Priest*, the Supreme Court ruled that a state school finance system funded primarily by local property taxes violated the equal protection clause. John Serrano, representing public school children and their families, sued California Treasurer Ivy Baker Priest, arguing California's education funding disparities violated the equal rights of students. The petitioners argued California's reliance on local property taxes to fund public schools resulted in funding disparities that led to differences in the quality of educational opportunities. The petitioners also argued educational opportunities were substantially inferior for students in low-wealth districts, in violation of the Fourteenth Amendment's equal protection clause. The California Supreme Court ruled for the plaintiffs, finding significant disparities in school district funding and that education was a fundamental interest. The decision led to California passing legislation to alter the state education finance system to increase equity across districts.

In 1973, only 2 years after *Serrano*, the Supreme Court ruled in *San Antonio Independent School District v. Rodriguez* that the U.S. Constitution does not include a right to equal education. In 1968, Demitrio Rodriguez and a group of San Antonio parents filed a class action lawsuit arguing Texas's inequitable school finance system violated the students' equal protection rights under the U.S. Constitution's Fourteenth Amendment. Rodriguez, filing for students from poor districts, challenged a Texas public elementary and secondary school funding scheme financed by local property taxes that resulted in significant education funding disparities between higher and lower income districts. The suit argued that lower income districts lacked the property tax base of wealthier districts, causing district disparities in per pupil expenditures and unequal education that disproportionately penalized low-income and minority students. A federal district court ruled in favor of the plaintiffs, finding that Texas's public school finance system did not provide equal protection under the law and that education was a fundamental right.

The U.S. Supreme Court ruled the Texas education funding scheme did not violate the Fourteenth Amendment, arguing "the Equal Protection Clause does not require absolute equality or precisely equal advantages." The Supreme Court agreed that significant education funding inequities existed between districts but did not hold education to be a fundamental right. *Rodriguez* has had far-reaching implications by providing legal justification for wide disparities in American education funding and opportunities.

The Supreme Court decision in *San Antonio Independent School District v. Rodriguez* (1973) forced school funding litigants to turn to state courts, leading to the second wave of school finance litigation. In 1973's *Robinson v. Cahill*, the New Jersey Supreme Court found that funding school districts primarily through local property taxes was invalid and required state aid to fill the funding gaps. State cases in the second wave of school finance litigation avoided using the Fourteenth Amendment's equal protection clause and instead focused on state constitutions' equal protection and due process clauses.

The second wave of finance litigation utilized the same approach as the first wave by focusing on equal protection and due process clauses. The second wave focused on state rather than federal constitutional law, but the approach was the same. Both waves focused on horizontal equity, defined as the equal treatment of equals. Horizontal equity is most useful when considering the distribution of educational resources or outputs (Berne & Stiefel, 1999). The concept is more complicated to apply to educational outputs. There is widespread agreement that outputs such as achievement scores and graduation rates should be equitably distributed across student groups. However, one would expect that underserved or disadvantaged students require more resources than their peers to achieve similar outputs. The second wave of school finance litigation encountered limited success in the number of plaintiff victories and adjustments in school finance funding, leading to the third wave.

In the third wave of education finance litigation, plaintiffs shifted their legal strategy from focusing on federal or state equal protection or due process clauses to education clauses in state constitutions. Litigants argued that states had not fulfilled their constitutional obligation to provide an adequate education. They switched from a horizontal to a vertical equity approach, meaning they shifted focus from equal resources to an adequate education for all students. Vertical equity focuses on treating students differently based on their individual educational needs (Underwood, 1995). Like the first two waves, the vertical equity approach focuses on educational inputs rather than educational outcomes. However, vertical equity holds that differently situated children should be treated differently, meaning some student groups require more resources to achieve similar outputs. The challenge is to measure the additional resources disadvantaged students require to achieve given output levels (Berne & Stiefel, 1999).

This approach achieved greater success, with 15 of the first 22 cases resulting in plaintiff victories (Thompson & Crampton, 2002). By focusing on adequacy, courts could provide relief without labeling the poor as a suspect class, a class or group meeting criteria for closer scrutiny by courts when claiming unconstitutional discrimination under a federal or state equal protection claim. When a class or group receives a suspect classification, a strict scrutiny standard is applied. Strict scrutiny is the most stringent of the three judicial review tests (the others are rational basis and intermediate scrutiny) used to evaluate the constitutionality of government policies under legal challenge. Courts are reluctant to apply a suspect class to income classes because the strict scrutiny standard would set a precedent for widespread litigation. The third wave of school finance litigation avoided this Gordian knot by focusing on state education provision clauses that required adequate school funding for all students rather than identifying lower income students as a suspect class. Despite these legal advantages, the third wave of finance litigation has been limited by the degree of interference required to achieve funding changes. The state legislature must act to change the state school funding formula, and it is often reluctant to do so for policy and political reasons.

Elementary and Secondary Education Expenditures

Elementary and secondary education expenditure categories include enterprise operations, food services, general or district administration, instructional staff, operations and maintenance, school administration, support services, and transportation. Salaries, wages, and benefits account for more than 80% of all public education expenditures (Cornman et al., 2022). Expenditures for instruction and instructional staff and support services account for more than 65% of all education expenditures. Purchased services including contracts for food, transportation, janitorial services, and teacher professional development account for 10% of expenditures. Capital outlays including property, building, and alterations account for 10% of education funding.

Postsecondary Education

American exceptionalism is the belief that the United States is distinctive, unique, or exemplary compared to other countries. The U.S. deserves the moniker of exceptionalism in higher education. The United States has boasted the highest rated higher education system in the world through most of the 20th and 21st centuries. The U.S. higher education system is unique in its level of independence from government control, its diversity of institutional types, self-regulation and oversight, and diverse funding system. Postsecondary education is funded by a decentralized system incorporating federal and state governments, families, and philanthropy. Higher education revenue sources include federal and state appropriations, student tuition and fees, private gifts, grants, and contracts.

According to the College Board, in the 2023–2024 academic year, public 4-year out-of-state tuition was $29,150, compared to $11,260 for in-state tuition and $41,540 for private 4-year nonprofit institutions (Ma & Pender, 2023). Public 4-year in-state tuition and fees range from $6,360 in Florida to $17,180 in Vermont. Public 2-year in-district tuition and fees range from $1,440 in California to $8,660 in Vermont. Federal, state, and private grants and college and university grants account for a substantial share of higher education tuition increases (Baum et al., 2013). For example, between 1981 and 2021, federal Pell grants increased from $6.5 to $25.9 billion, with the high of $44.3 billion in 2011.

The United States has the fifth highest percentage of private versus public higher education financing among the OECD countries, 62.5%. The only countries that finance a higher percentage of their postsecondary education through private spending are Australia, Japan, Colombia, and the United Kingdom. In 2020, state and local governments spent $321 billion on postsecondary education, 9% of general spending. In 2020, 89% of state spending financed operational costs, including administrative and faculty.

Higher education institutions have four main sources of revenue: student tuition and fees; state and local government appropriations; federal government appropriations, grants, and financial aid; and gifts and endowments (McKeown-Moak & Mullin, 2014). Tuition and fees are only part of the revenues required to operate a college or university. Government aid from federal, state, and local sources is an additional source of institutional revenue.

Postsecondary Education Revenue by Type of Institution

Higher education funding results from numerous sources, including tuition and fees; investments; government grants, contracts, and appropriations; auxiliary enterprises; and other revenues. The distribution of revenue across types of higher education institutions varies dramatically. Public colleges receive approximately 41% of total revenue from government sources, compared to 12% for private nonprofits and 2% at for-profit institutions. Figure 9.4 illustrates revenue sources by higher education institution type. For-profit institutions receive 93% of revenue from student tuition and fees, compared to 31% for private nonprofits and 20% for public institutions. Investments including endowment interest comprise 46% of private nonprofit institution revenues, compared to 12% at public institutions.

Federal Government

Who should pay for higher education? There is widespread disagreement about whether postsecondary education costs should fall on governments or individuals. Proponents of free or low-cost postsecondary education argue society benefits from higher education through improved economic development and output. Proponents also argue education has a positive externality in that benefits are transferred to third parties as an indirect effect. Positive externalities are underproduced, requiring the government to subsidize them to benefit all society, particularly disadvantaged populations. Opponents argue many of the benefits of higher education go to individuals, so the market should determine the supply.

The United States provides significant federal and state subsidies that vary by higher education sector. The DOE distributes discretionary and mandatory spending to subsidize higher

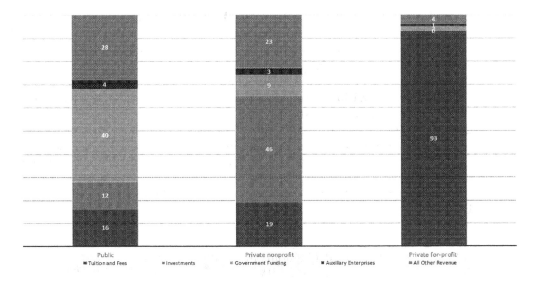

Figure 9.4 Postsecondary Education Revenue by Institution Type and Source of Funds

education. Discretionary spending is budget authority determined by the annual budget appropriations process. Mandatory spending, budget authority controlled by authorizing acts, includes entitlements that require payments to programs, state, or local government if they meet eligibility criteria. Mandatory funding is automatically provided each year without legislative action by Congress.

State and Local Government

In Fiscal Year 2023, states spent $258.7 billion on higher education, making it the third largest category in state budgets after elementary and secondary education and Medicaid. Higher education is 9.2% of state general fund expenditures and 8.7% of total state expenditures. All state governments subsidize the cost of higher education including the public university system, community colleges, and career and technical education institutions. Higher education funding has declined in recent years as a share of general fund expenditures, from 12.9% in 1995 to 9.2% in 2023. During that same period, Medicaid general fund spending increased from 14.4% to 18% (NASBO, 2023).

Incremental Funding. State higher education funding formulas calculate appropriations based on specific inputs including the number of students enrolled, student characteristics, and field of study. Incremental funding is a familiar approach to budgeting. This approach increases or decreases appropriations based on the previous year's funding level. The advantage of an incremental funding approach is its simplicity. Annual funding levels are based on the previous year's budget totals adjusted for cost or revenue changes. The disadvantage of an incremental approach is that it does not account for funding adequacy or the resources required to achieve policy goals. Incremental funding also does not address inequities, resource efficiency, or progress toward policy goals.

Formula Funding. Formula funding accounts for inputs to determine annual appropriations. The base factors most often used to determine higher education funding in state formulas include student enrollment, faculty and staff positions, institutional size, and credit hours. The advantages of funding formulas are they account for institutional needs, provide a simplified method for measuring campus needs, and balance public accountability with institutional autonomy. The disadvantages of funding formulas are they measure the quantity rather than the quality of programs, perpetuate inequities in the system, and poorly adjust for changing institutional needs. Most funding formulas also do not account for adequacy of institutional resources.

Performance-Based Funding. Performance-based funding (PBF) allocates state resources based on institutional outcomes. The approach is different from formula and incremental approaches that focus on inputs rather than outputs. PBF's advantages include incentivizing higher education institutions to achieve desired outputs like increasing the number of degrees conferred in high-needs professions. A disadvantage of PBF is that institutions that use this approach restrict access for disadvantaged youth in favor of students they identify as most likely to graduate (Bell et al., 2018). PBFs are complicated to implement and administer and typically account for a small percentage of higher education institutional funding.

Global Comparative Analysis of Postsecondary Education Finance Systems

The United States can learn much from the higher education finance systems of other countries. The 33 OECD countries fall into four categories of higher education finance systems: low tuition–low subsidy, low tuition–high subsidy, high tuition–high subsidy, and high tuition–low subsidy. Advanced economy countries can be categorized into those that charge tuition and those that charge little or no tuition for higher education (Garritzmann, 2016). Governments can also provide subsidies, payments, tax breaks, or other forms of economic support to economic sectors or industries to lower the service's cost. For example, the U.S. subsidizes postsecondary education through grants to universities, subsidized student loans, and direct scholarship funding. Irrespective of a country's approach to postsecondary tuition, it can provide high or low subsidies to lower the cost of higher education.

As shown in Figure 9.5, most advanced economies require students pay low or no tuition to attend postsecondary institutions. These countries tend to have higher tax rates and pay higher education costs through those taxes. Another approach countries use to finance postsecondary education is the high tuition–high subsidy method. In such countries, students and their families face high tuition costs to attend postsecondary institutions, but the government provides subsidies to lower the cost burden through subsidized loans, scholarships, and direct payments to colleges and universities. The United States squarely falls into the high tuition–high subsidy category. Liberal and social-democratic countries are more likely than those with conservative regimes to spend more on tuition and subsidies (Garritzmann, 2016). The Nordic countries comprise most of the low tuition–high subsidy category, in which the government funds almost all higher education costs.

Higher Education Finance Systems

The U.S. higher education system uses many of these international finance methods. Community colleges, which are public 2-year institutions, follow a low tuition–high subsidy model. In 1946, Truman established the Commission for Higher Education for Our Democracy to recommend policy changes in American higher education. The commission recommended the establishment of a network of community colleges to improve educational access and equal opportunity in postsecondary education. Historically, community colleges were designed to train students for the workforce and increase access to a more socioeconomically

High Tuition–Low Subsidy	High Tuition–High Subsidy
Chile	Australia
Japan	Canada
South Korea	England
	New Zealand
	Netherlands
	United States

Low Tuition–Low Subsidy	Low Tuition–High Subsidy
Austria	Denmark
Belgium	Finland
Czech Republic	Iceland
Estonia	Norway
France	Sweden
Germany	
Greece	
Hungary	
Italy	
Mexico	
Poland	
Portugal	
Slovak Republic	
Slovenia	
Spain	
Switzerland	

Figure 9.5 OECD Country Higher Education Tuition and Subsidy Categories

diverse group of students. Community colleges were also more closely connected to local communities by specializing in preparing students for localized industries and supporting community and economic development. In 1977, the Carnegie Commission on Higher Education recommended the government cover all the costs of attending community college due to their societal benefits. In 2022, Biden's Build Back Better bill included 2 years of free community college nationwide for $45.5 billion. The free community college provision was stripped from the bill during congressional negotiations.

Despite the failure of federal support, Table 9.5 identifies the states with free community college or public 4-year colleges and the states that have proposed some form of free 2-year college programs. In the states requiring students to pay, public community college tuition and fees comprise only about 10% of revenues. Federal and state appropriations, grants, and contracts encompass nearly 80% of revenue.

State public colleges and universities provide a model of moderate tuition-moderate subsidy models. In public 4-year institutions, student tuition and aid are about 20% of total revenue. Federal and state appropriations, grants, and contracts comprise another 40% of revenue, and private gifts, auxiliary enterprises, and other investment returns comprise the final 40%.

Private nonprofit and for-profit colleges and universities use a high-tuition, high-subsidy model. The average private nonprofit institution's annual per student tuition is $35,852, compared to no tuition at public 2-year community colleges in nearly half of U.S. states.

Table 9.5 State Free Community and Public 4-Year Colleges and Proposed Programs

Free or partially free community college statewide	Free public 4-year colleges statewide	Free college programs proposed statewide
Arkansas	Indiana	Alabama
California	New York	Arizona
Connecticut	Washington	Florida
Delaware		Illinois
Georgia		Minnesota
Hawaii		South Carolina
Indiana		Texas
Kentucky		Vermont
Louisiana		Wisconsin
Maine		
Maryland		
Massachusetts		
Michigan		
Mississippi		
Missouri		
Montana		
New Jersey		
New York		
Nevada		
North Carolina		
Oklahoma		
Rhode Island		
Tennessee		
Washington		

Even in states that charge tuition for public community college, the annual average tuition is approximately **$4,000**, or 11% of private school tuition. Table 9.6 shows the array of state funding per student.

Table 9.6 State Support for Postsecondary Education

State	State funding per full-time student equivalent
Alabama	7,243
Alaska	20,190
Arizona	2,509
Arkansas	7,278
California	9,966
Colorado	2,909
Connecticut	13,604
Delaware	6,905
Florida	8,206
Georgia	8,951
Hawaii	20,314
Idaho	8,764

(Continued)

Table 9.6 (Continued)

State	State funding per full-time student equivalent
Illinois	15,585
Indiana	5,979
Iowa	5,605
Kansas	4,999
Kentucky	6,712
Louisiana	5,100
Maine	8,733
Maryland	8,205
Massachusetts	10,430
Michigan	5,515
Minnesota	8,319
Mississippi	5,225
Missouri	5,944
Montana	6,761
Nebraska	8,178
Nevada	7,507
New Hampshire	4,141
New Jersey	7,973
New Mexico	11,564
New York	10,648
North Carolina	9,304
North Dakota	8,953
Ohio	5,601
Oklahoma	5,455
Oregon	6,891
Pennsylvania	5,045
Rhode Island	6,389
South Carolina	5,925
South Dakota	6,782
Tennessee	9,694
Texas	6,020
Utah	8,656
Vermont	5,139
Virginia	7,160
Washington	10,729
West Virginia	6,181
Wisconsin	7,112
Wyoming	16,248

Postsecondary Expenditures

In 2023, higher education institutions spent $702 billion, including $450 billion by public institutions, $239 billion by private nonprofit institutions, and $14 billion by private for-profit institutions. Figure 9.6 illustrates the categories of postsecondary expenses and their distribution by type of institution. Institutions' highest expenditures are academic support, student services, and instructional support, which together account for an average of 50% of all spending (Irwin, 2023). Public 4-year institutions make only 28% of total expenditures in this category, and private 4-year for-profit institutions spend 68%. Instruction varies from a high of 39% of total expenditures at private nonprofits to 27% at private

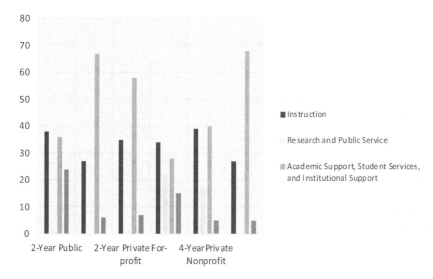

Figure 9.6 Postsecondary Expenditures

for-profits. Public 4-year institutions outspend all other types of higher education institutions by spending 22% of their expenditures on research and public services. Four-year institutions' average cost of attendance was highest at nonprofit institutions ($55,800) and lowest at public institutions ($26,000); private for-profit institutions fell in between ($32,900).

Key Terms

appropriations
assessment ratio
authorization
balanced budget requirements
Budget and Accounting Act of 1921
budget authority
capital project funds
categorical grants
centralized system
Committee on Appropriations, House of Representatives
Committee on Appropriations, Senate
conference committee
Congressional Budget and Impoundment Act of 1974
Congressional Budget Office
continuing resolution
debt service funds
decentralized system
direct spending

federal budget process
foundation funding formula
funding formulas
general funds
grant-in-aid
guaranteed tax-base funding formula
horizontal equity
hybrid funding formula
interdistrict funding inequity
interstate funding inequity
intradistrict funding inequity
mandatory
Office of Management and Budget
omnibus bills
permanent fund
property tax
regressive tax
regular order
resource-based funding formula
San Antonio Independent School District v. Rodriguez
school finance litigation
Serrano v. Priest
special revenue funds
state budget process
strict scrutiny
suspect classification
vertical equity

Discussion Questions

1. How is elementary and secondary education financed?
2. How are financing responsibilities divided between federal, state, and local governments?
3. How is postsecondary education financed?
4. What are the various types of elementary and secondary education funding formulas?
5. How does the use of local property taxes to fund public education increase educational inequalities?
6. How has school finance litigation influenced state education funding?
7. How are postsecondary education financing responsibilities divided between federal, state, and local governments and individual institutions?
8. How do postsecondary education funding and spending vary across by type of institution?
9. What are the various types of postsecondary education funding approaches?
10. How does the federal budget process work? How do state budget processes compare to the federal budget process?

Activities and Assignments

1. Explain how your policy issue is financed. Explain what federal, state, and local government funds are used to finance your policy issue.
2. Explain how you would revise the funding mechanism to mitigate your policy problem.

References

Baker, B. (2020). *Closing America's education funding gap*. Century Foundation.

Baum, S., Kurose, C., & McPherson, M. (2013). An overview of American higher education. *The Future of Children, 23*(1), 17–39. https://doi.org/10.1353/foc.2013.0008

Bell, E., Fryar, A. H., & Hillman, N. (2018). When intuition misfires: A meta-analysis of research on performance-based funding in higher education. In E. Hazelkorn, H. Coates, & A. C. McCormick (Eds.), *Research handbook on quality, performance, and accountability in higher education* (pp. 108–124). Edward Elgar Publishing.

Berne, R., & Stiefel, L. (1999). Concepts of school finance equity: 1970 to the present. In H. F. Ladd, R. Chalk, & J. S. Hansen (Eds.), *Equity and adequacy in education finance: Issues and perspectives* (pp. 7–33). National Academy Press.

Berry, C. (2021). *Reassessing the property tax*. Social Science Research Network. http://dx.doi.org/10.2139/ssrn.3800536

Chingos, M. M., & Blagg, K. (2017). *Making sense of state school funding policy*. Urban Institute.

Cornman, S. Q., Phillips, J. J., Howell, M. R., & Zhou, L. (2022). *Revenues and expenditures for public elementary and secondary education FY20 (NCES 2022-301)*. National Center for Education Statistics. https://nces.ed.gov/pubsearch

EdBuild. (2019). *$23 billion*. EdBuild. https://edbuild.org/content/23-billion/full-report.pdf

Frankenberg, E., Ee, J., Ayscue, J. B., & Orfield, G. (2019). *Harming our common future: America's segregated schools 65 years after Brown*. www.civilrightsproject.ucla.edu.

Garritzmann, J. L. (2016). *The political economy of higher education finance: The politics of tuition feeds and subsidies in OECD countries, 1945–2015*. Palgrave Macmillan.

Irwin, V., De La Rosa, J., Wang, K., Hein, S., Zhang, J., Burr, R., Roberts, A., Barmer, A., Bullock Mann, F., Dilig, R., & Parker, S. (2016). Report on the Condition of Education 2022 (NCES 2022-144). U.S. Department of Education. Washington, DC: *National Center for Education Statistics*. Retrieved [date] from https://nces.ed.gov/pubsearch/ pubsinfo.asp?pubid=2022144.

Irwin, V., Wang, K., Tezil, T., Zhang, J., Filbey, A., Jung, J., Bullock Mann F., Dilig, R., & Parker, S. (2023). Report on the Condition of Education 2023 (NCES 2023-144rev). U.S. Department of Education. Washington, DC: National Center for Education Statistics. Retrieved [date] from https://nces.ed.gov/pubsearch/pubsinfo.asp?pubid=2023144rev.

Loughead, K., Walczak, J., & Koranyi, E. (2022). *Unpacking the state and local tax toolkit: Sources of state and local tax collections (FY 2020)*. Tax Foundation. https://files.taxfoundation.org/20220825103108/Unpacking-the-State-and-Local-Tax-Toolkit-Sources-of-State-and-Local-Tax-Collections-FY-2020.pdf

Ma, J., & Pender, M. (2023). *Trends in college pricing and student aid 2023*. College Board.

McKeown-Moak, M. P., & Mullin, C. M. (2014). *Higher education finance research: Policy, politics, and practice*. Information Age Publishing.

National Association of State Budget Officers. (2021). *Budget processes in the states*. National Association of State Budget Officers.

National Association of State Budget Officers. (2023). *2023 state expenditure report: Fiscal years 2021–2023*. National Association of State Budget Officers.

Picus, L. O., Goertz, M. E., & Odden, A. R. (2015). Intergovernmental aid formulas and case studies. In H. F. Lads & M. E. Goertz (Eds.), *Handbook of research in education finance and policy* (2nd ed., pp. 279–296). Routledge Press.

San Antonio Independent School District v. Rodriguez, 411 U.S. 1 (1973).

Snyder, T. D. (1993). *120 years of American education: A statistical portrait*. US Department of Education, Office of Educational Research and Improvement, National Center for Education Statistics.

Thompson, D. C., & Crampton, F. E. (2002). The impact of school finance litigation: A long view. *Journal of Education Finance, 1*(28), 133–172.

Underwood, J. K. (1995). School finance adequacy as vertical equity. *University of Michigan Journal of Law Reform, 28*(493).

United States Department of Education. (2024). *Fiscal year 2024 budget summary*.

Part IV

Education Policy Issues

10 K–12 Education Policy

Elementary and secondary education faces numerous challenges, from resegregation to teacher turnover to ensuring all students receive the knowledge and skills they need to succeed in college, careers, and life. This chapter explores some of the problems facing American elementary and secondary education and possible ways to solve them. Policy issues that have decreased equity in American education include early education access, school choice, achievement gaps, dropouts, standards and accountability systems, teacher quality, administrator quality, school safety, mental health and wellness, and school discipline. This chapter answers the question: How can policymakers and educational leaders understand equity problems facing American education and develop solutions to mitigate these challenges?

Early Education

Early education focuses on developing language, literacy, and social skills for children from birth to 8 years old. Research indicates early childhood programs improve student academic, economic, health, and social outcomes (Harvard University Center on the Developing Child, 2007). Brain development occurs in early childhood, and lack of proper development opportunities can lead to deficits in cognitive skills, attentiveness, motivation, self-control, and sociability. High-quality early childhood education promotes brain development and provides a foundation in language development, social and coping skills, and learning skills, leading to better short- and long-term outcomes. Children enrolled in high-quality early childhood education programs are less likely to require disability services or commit crimes and more likely to graduate from high school and be employed (Karoly & Bigelow, 2005).

Prekindergarten, also known as preschool, is designed to provide high-quality educational and socialization experiences to enhance school readiness for 4- and 5-year-olds. Federal and state programs including Head Start, Early Head Start, and state pre-K are examples of government-funded programs available mainly to low-income families. The U.S. Department of Health and Human Services operates the Head Start program, an early childhood education, health, and nutrition program for children from birth to age 5 and their families. In 2022, Head Start served 833,000 children, pregnant women, and family members (U.S. Department of Health and Human Services, 2022). Head Start eligibility is limited to families earning less than 100% of the poverty line. In 2023, the federal poverty level was $30,000 for a family of four. Government-funded programs serve only a fraction of the children and families who need high-quality early childhood services.

Unfortunately, children of color and those from low-income families are significantly less likely to attend high-quality early education than their moderate- and high-income peers. Inequitable access to high-quality early education creates knowledge and skill gaps that lead

DOI: 10.4324/9781003231561-14

to opportunity gaps for children throughout their academic careers and beyond. Students who do not attend high-quality early childhood education programs arrive at the school door less prepared to learn, increasing obstacles to their academic, emotional, and social success. Strong political support exists for universal access for all children and families to high-quality, publicly funded prekindergarten education. According to the National Institute for Early Education Research (NIEER), 41% of 4-year-olds and 16% of 3-year-olds participated in a publicly funded pre-K program (Friedman-Krauss et al., 2024).

NIEER, a leader in early education research, developed 10 benchmarks as the minimum standards required for high-quality pre-K programs. Table 10.1 describes the 10 benchmarks that constitute high-quality pre-K. Florida, Georgia, and Oklahoma are the only states with universal pre-K for all 4-year-olds. California, Colorado, District of Columbia, Hawaii, Illinois, Iowa, Louisiana, Maine, New Mexico, New York, and West Virginia have passed or have a multiyear plan to implement universal pre-K. A key obstacle to universal pre-K is funding. During the past 20 years, pre-K enrollment has doubled because of federal, state, and local investments driven by research confirming its widespread benefits. Despite these gains, spending on pre-K was stagnant over that period. Pre-K spending per child is $8,294, compared to an average per child expenditure of $18,426 for K–12 students (Friedman-Krauss et al., 2024). This discrepancy leads to lower teacher salaries, inconsistent quality standards, and lower levels of access.

School Choice

Nearly three quarters of all U.S. elementary and secondary students attend assigned public schools, better known as neighborhood schools. As discussed in Chapter 6, neighborhood schools are ones students are assigned to, for which the district provides transportation, and

Table 10.1 NIEER Benchmarks for High-Quality Pre-K

Policy	Benchmark	Number of the 60 state-funded pre-K initiatives meeting benchmark
Early learning and development standards	Comprehensive, aligned, supported, culturally sensitive	58
Curriculum supports	Approval process and supports	41
Teacher degree	Bachelor's degrees	31
Teacher specialized training	Specialized training in pre-K	47
Assistant teacher degree	Child development associate credential or equivalent	19
Staff professional development	For teachers and assistants: at least 15 hours per year, individual professional development plans, coaching	19
Maximum class size	20 or fewer students	46
Staff-child ratio	1:10 or better	48
Screening and referral	Vision, hearing, and health screenings and referrals	41
Continuous quality improvement system	Structured classroom observations with data used for program development	42

located close to the student's residence. Neighborhood schools are not the only elementary and secondary education option. *School choice* is a term used to define educational alternatives to traditional public schools. School choice options include charter, magnet, vouchers, virtual, private, and homeschooling. The concept holds that parents and students should have the freedom to choose which school option best meets their child's needs. Thirty-two states and the District of Columbia have at least one type of school choice option.

Proponents of school-choice policies intend to instill free market mechanisms into education systems. School choice permits public education funds to follow students to their school of choice. This allows parents, guardians, and students to choose which school to attend. Scholarship on the impact of school choice on the achievement of participating students is mixed. Studies exploring the impact of school choice on the achievement of nonparticipating students, those who remain in the neighborhood school, has predominantly suggested a negative impact on student achievement (Egalite & Wolf, 2016).

School choice opponents argue public funds should be reserved for schools that serve all students. Private schools admit students based on criteria like disability status, English proficiency, gender and sexual identity, and many other factors that public schools are not legally allowed to use to exclude students. Proponents argue this fundamental difference between public and private schools should bar public funding from flowing to private educational institutions. School choice opponents use figures like those in Table 10.2 to argue school choice increases educational inequality and segregation by race and socioeconomic status through the negative impacts on the students who remain in the neighborhood school (Bifulco & Ladd, 2007; Henig, 1994; Kotok et al., 2017).

Achievement Gaps

Children do not arrive at the schoolhouse door equally prepared to learn. There are substantial gaps in kindergarten academic readiness between high- and low-income families. The American dream is based on the egalitarian notion of equality of opportunity. However, the education system is organized to exacerbate academic readiness gaps, not to ameliorate them. The highest need students receive the least resources. According to the Department of Education, the *achievement gap* refers to a group of students that consistently outperforms another group by a statistically significant margin. The achievement gap primarily refers to

Table 10.2 Students Enrolled in Grades 1–12, by School Type and Student's Race/Ethnicity

	Total, all schools	Public school total	Public school type		Public school charter status		Private school
			Assigned	Chosen	Traditional	Charter	
All enrolled students	100.0	90.8	72.8	17.3	84.9	5.0	9.2
White	48.3	46.7	48.7	37.9	47.9	29.5	63.6
Black	13.6	14.0	13	18.3	13.4	24.5	10.1
Hispanic	25.8	26.9	25.6	32.4	26.1	38.3	14.9
Asian	5.7	5.7	5.7	5.9	5.7	4.7	5.4
Pacific Islander	0.3	0.3	0.4	NA	0.3	NA	NA
American Indian or Alaska Native	0.5	0.6	0.6	0.4	0.6	NA	NA
Two or more races	5.8	5.8	6.0	5.0	6.0	2.7	5.6

the persistent disparity in academic performance between underserved and minority students and their White and more affluent counterparts. Achievement gaps also exist between students with disabilities and those without, English language learners and native speakers, and different socioeconomic groups.

In the early 1960s, the National Center for Education Statistics (NCES) commissioned James Samuel Coleman and several other academic researchers to write a report on U.S. educational equality. In 1966, *Equality of Educational Opportunity*, popularly referred to as the Coleman Report, identified an achievement gap between Black and White students. For the next 58 years, the racial achievement gap has been a primary focus of practitioners and researchers who seek to reduce and eliminate it. This achievement gap exists across a broad range of educational measures including standardized tests, grade point average, dropout rates, college enrollment rates, and grade retention (Jeynes, 2015). The National Assessment of Educational Progress (NAEP), also referred to as the nation's report card, is a congressionally mandated assessment program administered by NCES. In 1969, NAEP was first used to measure student achievement nationally. During the more than half a century of NAEP, the achievement gap between White and non-White students has remained alarming and consistent. Research indicates that by eighth grade, the achievement gap indicates a 2-year disparity between White and non-White students (Olneck, 2005).

Socioeconomic status is a leading predictor of educational achievement (Björklund & Salvanes, 2011; Currie, 2009; Kim & Quinn, 2013; White, 1982). Research from all countries confirms a correlation between parental education and socioeconomic status and student educational achievement (Björklund & Salvanes, 2011). Low socioeconomic status children have worse outcomes on a range of health measures that impede academic learning, including fetal and birth conditions, chronic conditions, and mental health (Currie, 2009; Dietrichson et al., 2017). Children from low socioeconomic backgrounds face learning disadvantages because higher socioeconomic families provide a broader language and literacy environment (Hart & Risley, 2003). Research indicates the achievement gap between children of high and low socioeconomic background exists prior to school enrollment and expands during summer breaks (Gershenson, 2013; Heckman, 2006; Kim & Quinn, 2013; Slates et al., 2012).

The University of Colorado Boulder's National Education Policy Center (NEPC) has identified schools throughout the United States that are using evidence-based practices to reduce achievement gaps. NEPC has identified 10 characteristics of schools that reduce achievement gaps (York et al., 2023):

- broaden and enrich learning opportunities, with particular attention to reducing disparities in learning created by tracking and ability grouping;
- create and maintain a healthy school culture, with attention to diversity and to reassessing student discipline practices;
- provide more and better learning time during the school year and summer;
- use a variety of assessments designed to respond to student needs;
- support teachers as professionals;
- meet the needs of students with disabilities in an environment that ensures challenges and support;
- provide students with additional needed services and supports, including mental and physical health services;
- enact a challenging and supported culturally relevant curriculum;
- build on the strengths of language minority students and correctly identify their needs; and
- sustain equitable and meaningful parent and community engagement.

Evidence-based practices begin with traditional academic factors, including high-quality learning opportunities and support for teachers. These practices go beyond these factors to include a holistic approach to education, including ability group tracking, culturally relevant curriculum, school climate, discipline, disability supports, summer learning, and parent and community engagement. These best practices recognize that improving opportunity for all students and closing achievement gaps requires a comprehensive approach.

Dropouts

More than one million students drop out of American high schools each academic year, more than 5,000 students per day of the school year. Nearly one third of all public high school students and half of all Black, Hispanic, and Native American students do not graduate from public high school with their class (Bridgeland et al., 2006). The national graduation rate is at an all-time high of 85.3%. Despite recent improvements in the national graduation rate, high school dropouts continue to be a serious problem for the U.S. public school system.

Increasing demands for an educated workforce to compete in the global knowledge economy mean there are severe economic and social consequences for students who do not complete high school. High school dropouts are more likely than their graduating peers to be in poverty, unemployed, or in prison (Bridgeland et al., 2006). According to the Bureau of Labor Statistics (BLS), high school dropouts earn $606 a week, compared to $749 for high school graduates. This adds up to an annual difference of approximately $7,500 – $50,000 less annually than individuals with advanced degrees. In other words, high school dropouts earn approximately $1 million less than college graduates (Donald, 2001). High school dropouts also have much higher unemployment rates than individuals with high school diplomas.

Dropouts disproportionately are minority, low socioeconomic, urban, single-parent children. The status dropout, a common measure of dropouts, is the percentage of 16- to 24-year-olds who are not enrolled in school and have not completed a high school credential. In 2021, the United States had two million status dropouts between the ages of 16 and 24. Table 10.3 illustrates that the overall rate of status dropouts declined from 8.3% to 5.2%. Notwithstanding this positive trend, dropout rates continue to significantly vary by race and ethnicity. In 2021, Black students (5.9%) dropped out at a rate nearly 50% higher than their White counterparts (4.1%), and Hispanic students (7.8%) dropped out at nearly double the rate of White students. There is also a significant gender gap in dropout rates, with females (4.6%) dropping out at rates significantly lower than males (5.7%).

Students drop out for a broad range of reasons including school environment, lack of connection to the school community, perceptions that school is boring, lack of motivation, academic challenges, and problems outside school (Bridgeland et al., 2006). Risk factors primarily fall into two categories: status and alterable risk factors (Freeman & Simonsen, 2015). Status risk factors refer to demographic or historical factors that are difficult to change, including ability, age, disability, ethnicity, family structure, mobility, parental involvement,

Table 10.3 Status Dropout Rates of 16- to 24-Year-Olds, by Race and Ethnicity 2010, 2021

Year	Total	American Indian or Alaska Native	Asian	Black	Hispanic	Pacific Islander	White	Two or more races
2010	8.3	15.4	2.8	10.3	16.7	4.8	5.3	6.1
2021	5.2	10.2	2.1	5.9	7.8	7.6	4.1	4.9

school size and type, and socioeconomic status. Alterable risks are factors that can be more easily changed over time, including absenteeism, attitudes toward school, disruptive behavior, crisis events, educational supports, grades, and school climate and policies.

Robert Balfanz of Johns Hopkins labeled schools that graduate less than 60% of their students as "dropout factories" (Balfanz & Legters, 2004). Dropout factories are disproportionately concentrated in 50 urban areas with large minority and lower socioeconomic populations. The percentage of African American students enrolled in dropout factories declined from 46% to 19% between 2002 and 2015. What led to the dramatic decrease in dropout factories? Two reasons were the closing of high schools termed dropout factories and other educational reforms.

In 2002, the Department of Education established the What Works Clearinghouse as a federal source of evidence-based information that reviews the quality of research in educational programs, practices, and policies. Evidence-based recommendations for reducing dropout rates in middle and high school include:

- monitor the progress of all students, and proactively intervene when students show early signs of attendance, behavior, or academic problems;
- provide intensive, individualized support to students who have fallen off track and face significant challenges to success;
- engage students by offering curricula and programs that connect schoolwork with college and career success and that improve students' capacity to manage challenges in and out of school;
- for schools with many at-risk students, create small, personalized communities to facilitate monitoring and support.

Standards and Accountability Systems

What are standards and accountability systems? An accountability system is composed of three elements, standards, assessments, and accountability, designed to support student achievement, measure student progress, and hold educational stakeholders accountable. Standards define the knowledge and skills students are expected to learn in specific subjects for each grade level. The purpose of standards is to define what all students need to know to prepare for college, work, and life. Curriculum is the content used to help students meet the standards. Assessments are tests used to see whether students are meeting the standards. Assessments allow education systems to evaluate how students are performing compared to their peers and standards. Assessments are used to measure how schools and districts are performing and to hold them accountable for raising student achievement. Ideally, accountability systems are utilized to reward high-performing schools and provide additional resources and supports to underachieving schools.

Education accountability systems developed over several decades in response to growing frustration with stagnant educational achievement, increasing achievement gaps, and declining international rankings. In 1965, Congress passed the Elementary and Secondary Education Act (ESEA) to promote equal access to education through funding to districts serving disadvantaged students. In 1994, the Improving America's Schools Act, a reauthorization of ESEA, required states to establish reading and math standards and student assessments, make assessment results publicly available by subgroup, and provide interventions in schools not making progress (Martin et al., 2016). The 2002 ESEA reauthorization, No Child Left Behind (NCLB), required testing for reading and math in Grades 3–8 and once in high school. The legislation also required accountability provisions that used sanctions and rewards to incentivize school improvement. NCLB also required states to report results by student characteristics including race, ethnicity, English language learners, disability status, and socioeconomics.

In 2015, the ESEA reauthorization entitled the Every Student Succeeds Act (ESSA) replaced NCLB. ESSA maintained the requirement that states adopt high academic standards but removed federal incentives for raising standards using such tools as the Common Core. ESSA maintained NCLB's testing schedule and annual testing reporting requirements but allowed greater flexibility, such as dividing assessments into smaller components or using alternative assessments. NCLB required states to make adequate yearly progress (AYP) on two indicators, including student proficiency in math and reading and student performance on at least one other indicator. ESSA transferred responsibility for accountability systems from the federal to the state governments.

ESSA eliminated the AYP system, removed the "low-performing" label from underperforming schools, and replaced the system with state intervention in the bottom 5% of schools (Darling-Hammond et al., 2016). ESSA required states to set long- and short-term goals and select performance indicators including the following:

- academic achievement as measured by proficiency on annual assessments in English language arts and math (in each of Grades 3–8, plus one grade in high school);
- another "valid and reliable statewide academic indicator" for elementary and middle schools, which can be a measure of student growth;
- the 4-year adjusted cohort graduation rate for high schools (states may add an extended year adjusted cohort graduation rate if they choose);
- a measure of progress in English language proficiency for English language learners (in each of Grades 3–8, plus one grade in high school); and
- at least one measure of school quality or student success including student engagement, student access to advanced coursework, postsecondary readiness, school climate, and safety.

ESSA provides states with more flexibility to select performance indicators that drive school accountability plans and school improvement efforts. Table 10.4 describes the state performance indicators identified by the Learning Policy Institute (Darling-Hammond et al., 2016). ESSA also supports state efforts to select performance indicators that support underserved schools and students. States can address sources of school inequities by including performance measures that support success for all children, including suspension rates, school climate, chronic absenteeism, extended-year graduation rates, and access to college and career-ready curriculum (Kostyo & Cardichon, 2018). Accountability systems continue to play a central role in state education systems, and improving their performance remains central to improving state educational equity.

Teacher Quality

The U.S. elementary and secondary teaching force comprises 3.8 million full-time and part-time teachers, more than 7% of the labor force (Kraft & Lyon, 2022; Newburger & Beckhusen, 2022). Public elementary schools employ 1.9 million teachers, an increase of 9% over the past decade (NCES, 2023a). Public secondary schools employ another 1.9 million teachers, a 13% increase since the 2011–2012 school year. The elementary and secondary

Table 10.4 Potential State Performance Indicators

Academic outcomes	Opportunities to learn	Engagement
Achievement on assessments • Standardized test results, reported in terms of status and growth for individual students or student cohorts • Performance assessment results from common state tasks • Progress toward English language (EL) proficiency/EL reclassification rates • Students meeting college standard on AP/IB or other college-readiness tests or dual-credit college coursework Graduation/school progress • 4-, 5-, and 6-year adjusted cohort graduation rates • Proportion of 8th graders who progress to 9th grade • Dropout rates Career and college readiness • Students completing college preparatory coursework, approved career technical education (CTE) sequence, or both • Students meeting standard on graduation portfolios, industry-approved certificates, licenses, or badges recognized by postsecondary institutions and businesses	Access to resources • Ratios of students to counselors and specialists to students • Teacher qualifications • Safe, adequate facilities School climate • Evidence from student and staff surveys about school offerings, instruction, supports, trust, and belonging Teachers' opportunities to learn • Access to and participation in professional development and support	Student participation • Average daily attendance/chronic absenteeism rates • Suspension and expulsion rates • Student perceptions of belonging, safety, engagement, and school climate per student surveys Social-emotional learning • Student attitudes towards learning (e.g., academic mindset) • Indicators of social-emotional skills from student assessments • Indicators of social-emotional supports from student surveys Parent/community engagement • Indicators of participation and engagement from parent surveys Teacher engagement • Indicators of participation and engagement from teacher surveys

Note: Darling-Hammond et al. (2016).

teaching profession remains predominantly female – 77% of public school teachers are women. Female teachers are not equally distributed across K–12 schools: 89% of elementary school teachers and 64% of secondary school teachers are women. Elementary and secondary school teachers are also disproportionately White compared to national and public school student demographics: 80% of public school teachers are White, compared with 46% of public school students. Among public school teachers, 9% of them are Hispanic, 6% Black, 2% Asian, and less than 1% American Indian or Native Alaskan. Each of these rates is significantly lower than the public school student population, which is 28% Hispanic, 15% Black, 5% Asian, and 1% American Indian or Native Alaskan. During the past decade, public school teachers have become only slightly more diverse, with a 2% increase in non-White teachers, while student diversity has increased significantly, with the percentage of White students decreasing from 52% to 46%.

During the past decade, American public school teachers' education level has not significantly changed, but the average teacher does have more teaching experience. Teaching certifications are held by 91% of public school teachers, up from 89% in the 2011–2012 academic year. Similar percentages of public school teachers hold advanced degrees, including bachelor's (41%, 38%), master's (48%, 51%), and education specialist degrees or certificates (7.6%, 8.4%). In 2021–2022, 26% of public school teachers had over 20 years of experience, compared to only 23% in 2011–2012.

Before the educational excellence movement of the 1980s, individuals could obtain a teacher certification by graduating from a 4-year college with a major in education or by obtaining a certain number of specified education courses. Due to growing teacher shortages and teacher quality concerns, alternative methods were developed to attract nontraditional teachers to the profession. College and university education schools continue to produce most elementary and secondary teachers. Alternative teacher certifications are programs that train individuals without an education degree or background to pursue a teaching career.

Since 2010, perceptions of teacher prestige have steadily declined (Kraft & Lyon, 2022). According to a Harris Poll survey, teacher prestige declined from 78% to 59% between 1998 and 2022. PDK and Gallup polling asked about perceptions of the teaching profession by asking parents whether they would want their child to become a teacher. Between 2011 and 2022, the percentage of parents who wanted their child to become a teacher declined from 65% to 37%. Data suggest student interest in the teaching profession is also declining. According to a University of Michigan Survey Research Center MTF Survey, the percentage of high school seniors' interest in teaching decreased from 19% to 11% between 1994 and 2020. In the U.S., the elementary and secondary teaching profession has continued to lose prestige, meaning its reputation and social standing (Bleiberg & Kraft, 2022; Kraft & Lyon, 2022). Perceptions of the teaching profession are at their lowest recorded level. During the 2021–2022 school year, teacher turnover increased to 10% nationally (Dilberti & Schwartz, 2023). The loss of prestige has increased teacher turnover rates. Teacher turnover refers to the rate at which teachers exit schools. Teacher turnover is highest in urban, high-minority, and high-poverty districts. Surprisingly, the COVID-19 pandemic did not lead to significantly higher teacher turnover rates.

Research divides characteristics associated with teacher turnover into three main categories: personal, school, and external factors (Carver-Thomas & Darling-Hammond, 2017; Darling-Hammond et al., 2017; Dilberti & Schwartz, 2023; Nguyen et al., 2020). Personal factors include age, gender, race, ethnicity, marital status, and number of children. Personal factors also include teacher qualifications, including university attendance, graduate degree attainment, evaluation ratings, certifications and fellowships, and years of experience. Understanding the impact of personal characteristics and teacher qualifications on teacher turnover can help school leaders and policymakers direct resources to retaining teachers. Research suggests teacher age has a marked influence on teacher turnover. Teachers over 28 are much less likely to leave the teaching profession than younger teachers, suggesting younger teachers are less committed to the profession. Research indicates that teaching certifications and more than 3 years of teaching experience correlate with teachers staying in their schools (Kraft & Lyon, 2022).

School factors include organizational characteristics, school resources, and student body characteristics. School organizational characteristics include size, urbanicity, school type and level, work environment, administrative support, leadership opportunity, and classroom autonomy. School resources refers to the expenditures, classroom material, and classroom assistance afforded to teachers. Student body characteristics refer to student demographic characteristics, including race, socioeconomics, and disability status. Teacher shortages are concentrated in schools serving low-wealth, racially and ethnically diverse, linguistically diverse, and high-needs student populations; urban and rural geographic areas; and high-demand subjects such as foreign language, math, special education, English as a second language, and science. School working conditions determine the level of support and autonomy teachers are provided in the workplace and can influence job performance, satisfaction, and career decisions. Research indicates teachers at middle and charter schools have more turnover than those in elementary and traditional public schools (Kraft & Lyon, 2022; Nguyen et al., 2020). Schools with improved working conditions, higher student achievement, and fewer disciplinary problems are associated with lower teacher turnover. Strong administrative support, teacher induction and mentoring programs, and higher teacher salaries are all associated with lower teacher turnover rates.

External factors, the most recent area of teacher turnover research, refers to external influences including teacher accountability factors and workforce characteristics. Teacher accountability factors include teacher evaluation policies, principal effectiveness, and merit pay. Federal, state, or local policymakers and educational leaders impose these factors on teachers to evaluate their effectiveness. They can provide either positive or negative incentives for teaching employment decisions. Workforce characteristics include retention bonuses, salary, union membership, and employment rates. Workforce conditions can incentivize teachers to stay in the profession through higher pay and benefits and retention bonuses or incentivize teachers to leave the profession when conditions worsen relative to other job market opportunities. According to research, merit pay, more effective teaching evaluations, and higher principal effectiveness scores are all associated with lower teacher turnover rates (Nguyen et al., 2019).

These findings recommend many policies that can improve teacher retention. Reducing teacher shortages requires increasing teacher recruitment and improving teacher retention. Providing salary and benefits that are competitive with other professions with similar educational requirements and are equitable across all districts has been demonstrated to improve teacher retention rates (Carver-Thomas & Darling-Hammond, 2017). Alternative forms of teacher compensation, including loan forgiveness, service scholarships, and bonuses for teaching in hard-to-staff schools and content areas, can also improve teacher retention. Teacher preparation and support programs, including teacher residency, induction programs, and mentoring, have been demonstrated to make a difference in teachers' occupational decisions. School leadership is one of the most critical elements of creating a working environment that encourages teacher retention. Developing principal licensure and training programs, leadership training programs, and principal induction and mentoring programs can improve principal and teacher retention.

Administrator Quality

School leadership ranks as the second most influential school-related factor for student learning, behind only teaching. Research indicates replacing a below average elementary school principal with an above average one provides the equivalent of an additional 2.9 months of math and 2.7 months of reading learning per year per student (Grissom et al., 2021). Principals impact student learning in four primary ways:

- being an instructional leader, coach, and data-driven instructional improver;
- developing a school climate based on norms and values that support all people and emphasize collaboration, safety, respect, and learning;
- creating collaborative learning communities where teachers are supported to improve their practice and student learning; and
- efficiently managing and allocating staffing and resources.

Principals have an outsized impact on vulnerable populations including low-income, underserved, and disabled students.

Public school systems face widespread challenges in recruiting, retaining, and supporting high-quality administrators. First, public school principals have become more diverse in recent decades, but at a much slower rate than public school students. Between 1988 and 2020, the percentage of school principals who were White declined from 87% to 77%. During that same period, the percentage of White students declined from 75% to 45%. The racial gap between public school students and administrators has risen dramatically. Principal diversity matters. Research indicates schools with Black principals increase their share of non-White teachers by an average of 3% per year (Bartanen & Grissom, 2019).

Second, principal turnover rates have been increasing in recent years. According to the 2021–2022 National Teacher and Principal Survey, 20% of public school principals left their school following the 2020–2021 academic year. More than half of those principals left the profession altogether. Principals are more likely to leave the profession if they have 10 or more years of experience, are over age 55, and have lower salaries. Principal turnover was much higher in high-poverty districts, at 23% (Dilberti & Schwartz, 2023). Nearly 75% of principal turnover occurred in high-poverty, rural districts, increasing inequalities in the education system.

Third, state education systems inequitably distribute effective principals across schools. Less qualified principals are disproportionately sorted into schools that serve historically marginalized student populations (Grissom et al., 2019). Principal quality is a difficult concept to define and measure. Researchers use indicators including qualifications, principal and teaching experience, and certification as proxies for principal quality. The unequal distribution of principals is driven by several factors including disproportionate hiring of novice principals, higher principal turnover in high-poverty schools, and principal preferences to work in low-poverty schools (Grissom & Bartanen, 2018).

What can state policymakers do to recruit, retain, and support high-quality principals? Principal standards, like state standards for teaching and learning, are a foundational component of statewide school administrative systems. Forty-seven states and the District of Columbia have adopted leadership standards. Professional administrative standards define principal responsibilities, clarify expectations, and align with other education standards and policies to create a foundation for education success. States can also improve principal recruitment through oversight of principal preparation programs, recruitment pipelines to identify and solicit new principals into the profession, improving and expanding administrator licensing authority, and creating incentives for more equitable distribution of principals into high-needs schools (Grissom et al., 2021). States also can support continuous improvement of school administrators through the development of high-quality principal evaluation systems.

School Safety, Mental Health, and Wellness

According to the Institute of Educational Sciences, nonfatal, violent victimization and theft decreased from 0.05% to 0.01% between 2009 and 2020 (Irwin et al., 2022). Federal school crime and safety statistics also illustrate decreases in bullying, sexual harassment, and student harassment. *School bullying* is defined as the ongoing and deliberate misuse of power in relationships through repeated verbal, physical, or social behavior intended to cause physical, social, or psychological harm. Bullying occurs in schools, out of school, and online through digital media and platforms. According to NCES, 22% of teenage students reported being bullied in 2019, down from 28% in 2009. Student demographic characteristics influence bullying rates. Female, multiracial, and middle school students are bullied at higher rates, as are those in rural and urban school locations and those with disabilities. School crime, including bullying, remains unacceptably high and requires additional interventions.

Gun violence is an epidemic in the United States. According to the Centers for Disease Control and Prevention (CDC), there were **48,000** firearm-related deaths in the United States in 2022, or 132 people per day. In 2020–2021, more children died of firearm-related deaths than any other cause, including motor vehicle, cancer, or other health-related or accidental deaths. According to the Center for Homeland Defense and Security, there have been nearly 300 intentional shootings in K–12 schools since 2015. While K–12 schools remain relatively safe environments for children, school shootings have negative mental health consequences for students, families, teachers, administrators, and community members.

In 2019, the CDC (2022) found one in five children had a mental health issue. In 2021, 42% of students experienced persistent feelings of sadness or hopelessness, compared to 28% in 2011. These alarming rates of poor mental health were more acute for female (**60%**) and LGBTQ+ (**70%**) students. Ten percent of girls and **20%** of LGBTQ+ students reported attempting suicide. Students in every racial and ethnic group reported increased mental health problems. The COVID-19 pandemic exacerbated the already alarming student mental health crisis. In 2022, **69%** of public schools reported increases in student requests for mental health services since the start of the pandemic (NCES, 2023b).

What can schools do to improve student mental health services? According to NCES, nearly all public schools report offering student mental health services, most commonly individual-based interventions, including counseling (**84%**), case management (**70%**), and referrals for out-of-school mental health services (**66%**) (NCES, 2024). State and local leaders can expand supports so all students have access to high-quality mental health services. State and local policymakers and school leaders can also expand mental health service options. Elementary and secondary student mental health services and supports include a range of health promotion strategies. Wellness promotion is a preventive strategy that seeks to educate students to identify mental health challenges early. Identification includes mental health screening and other strategies used to detect students who could benefit from additional support. Intervention and treatment are provided to a subset of students who have been identified as requiring more targeted supports and services. A barrier to providing the necessary supports and services is the lack of mental health professionals, which leads to high staffing ratios. Estimates suggest America's schools had a shortage of **77,000** school counselors, **63,000** school psychologists, and **20,000** social workers. Policymakers and school leaders need to find cost-effective methods to close the gap between student mental health needs and the supply of school-based mental health professionals.

School Discipline

Public fear of school violence, particularly highly publicized gun violence, has led to the criminalization of student behavior. According to the Southern Poverty Law Center, schools suspended less than 4% of students in 1973 (Losen & Skiba, 2010). Between 1995 and 2019, youth confinement rates and arrests declined by 70% (Annie E. Casey Foundation, 2021). Even though juvenile crime rates have plummeted, school suspensions have doubled since the late 1970s. What explains the simultaneous drop in youth crime and increase in school suspensions?

In 1994, as part of the ESEA reauthorization, the Clinton administration expanded the Drug-Free Schools Act and signed the Gun-Free Schools Act (GFSA). The GFSA required states receiving federal funds to require school districts to expel students who brought a firearm to school for at least 1 year and refer them to criminal justice or juvenile delinquency systems. In 1995, the GFSA was amended to change "firearm" to "weapon," expanding the category of weapons students could be expelled for possessing. The GFSA was part of a larger bipartisan effort to get tough on crime efforts that included the Violent Crime Control and Law Enforcement Act of 1994, the Safe Schools Act of 1994, and the Safe and Drug-Free Schools and Communities Act of 1994 (Casella, 2003). These policies collectively enacted mandatory minimum sentencing, three-strikes policies, and the expansion of prison construction (Irby & Coney, 2021). Nearly all states adopted a zero-tolerance policy to comply with GFSA, as required to retain their federal funding under ESEA (Irby, 2013). Surveys indicate 62% of schools still maintain a zero-tolerance policy or mandatory penalties (Perera & Diliberti, 2023). The expansion of zero-tolerance policies has conflated criminal law and student disciplinary policy, criminalizing public schools.

The school-to-prison pipeline refers to policies and practices resulting in increased school suspensions. School resource officers (SROs) are the primary conduit connecting public schools to the criminal justice system. According to the National Association of School Resource Officers, school resource officers have three roles: educator, informal counselor, and law enforcer (Canady et al., 2012). According to NCES, the percentage of public schools with resource officers at least once a week increased from 1% to 48% between 1976 and 2016, and to 65% for secondary schools (Musu-Gillette et al., 2018). The proliferation of resource officers brings the juvenile justice system into school systems. Schools with SROs had five times as many arrests, even after controlling for district poverty level, as schools without them (Justice Policy Institute, 2020). Research indicates SROs do not increase school safety (Gottfredson et al., 2020; James & McCallion, 2013; Na & Gottfredson, 2013).

The criminalization of the public school system disproportionately impacts minority students, especially Black students. In 2019, Black youth were four times as likely to be suspended and incarcerated as their White peers. Black students comprise approximately 15% of the school-age population and nearly 40% of students who receive at least one suspension (Bell, 2021). These racial disparities persist across school sanctions, including office discipline referrals, suspensions, and expulsions (Lehmann et al., 2022). The discipline gap has long-term consequences for minorities, including increased school dropout levels and contact with the juvenile justice system (Bradshaw et al., 2008; Fabelo et al., 2011).

School administrators typically justify exclusionary discipline practices as a safety measure to improve the school climate (Leung-Gagne et al., 2022). According to the National School Climate Council (2015), *school climate* is "the quality and character of school life and reflects norms, goals, values, interpersonal relationships, teaching, learning, leadership practices, and organizational structures." School climate is a multifaceted concept that describes school conditions that influence student learning, including the academic, disciplinary, and physical environments. Research indicates a positive school climate reduces absenteeism, aggressive behavior, dropouts, drug use, suspensions, and truancy (Benbenishty et al., 2016; Berkowitz et al., 2017; Thapa et al., 2013; Wang & Degol, 2016). Despite administrators' goal of improving the school climate through exclusionary disciplinary practices, schools with higher suspension rates are correlated with worse school climate and safety even after controlling for student and community characteristics (Johnson et al., 2011; Leung-Gagne et al., 2022).

Elementary and secondary school efforts to reduce exclusionary disciplinary practices and punishments have focused on identifying root causes, data analysis, establishing support

Table 10.5 CASEL's Core SEL Competencies

Core competencies	Definitions
Self-awareness	The abilities to understand one's own emotions, thoughts, and values and how they influence behavior across contexts.
Self-management	The abilities to manage one's emotions, thoughts, and behaviors effectively in different situations and to achieve goals and aspirations.
Social awareness	The abilities to understand the perspectives of and empathize with others, including those from diverse backgrounds, cultures, and contexts.
Relationship skills	The abilities to establish and maintain healthy and supportive relationships and to effectively navigate settings with diverse individuals and groups.
Responsible decision making	The abilities to make caring and constructive choices about personal behavior and social interactions across diverse situations.

systems, and implementing evidence-based practices. Social-emotional learning (SEL) is gaining widespread practice in K–12 schools. SEL refers to the knowledge and skills students require to communicate, interact with peers, resolve conflicts, and manage their emotional responses, particularly in stressful environments (Becker et al., 2022). The Collaborative for Academic, Social, and Emotional Learning (CASEL) defines SEL as:

> The process through which youth and adults acquire and apply the knowledge, skills, and attitudes to develop health identities, manage emotions, and achieve personal and collective goals, feel, and show empathy for others, establish, and maintain support relationships, and make responsible and caring decisions.
>
> (CASEL, 2024)

SEL includes a broad range of psychological and human development support services. Table 10.5 identifies CASEL's five core SEL competencies and associated capacities: self-awareness, self-management, social awareness, relationship skills, and responsible decision making (Becker et al., 2022).

Key Terms

achievement gap
administrator quality
administrators
charter schools
curriculum
dropout factories
dropouts
early education
magnet schools
mental health
neighborhood schools
opportunity gaps
pre-kindergarten
school choice
school discipline

school safety
school-to-prison pipeline
standards
standards and accountability systems
teacher quality
teacher retention
teacher shortages

Discussion Questions

1. How do high-quality early education programs improve student outcomes? What access do families and children have to high-quality early education programs?
2. What is school choice? What are school choice options? How does school choice impact student outcomes?
3. What are achievement gaps? What characteristics are associated with achievement gaps? What policies have been proven to reduce achievement gaps?
4. What are dropout factories? What factors are associated with school dropouts?
5. What are standards and accountability systems? How did standards and accountability systems develop? How can we improve state accountability systems?
6. What factors lead to teacher shortages? How can we improve teacher quality and distribution and reduce teacher shortages?
7. What factors lead to administrator shortages? How do school leaders improve student outcomes? What policy changes can be made to improve administrator quality and distribution and lower administrator shortages?
8. What factors have led to the rise of student mental health challenges? What can schools do to improve student mental health services?
9. What policy changes increased the prevalence of out-of-school discipline? What policy changes can be made to keep schools safe, while lowering the prevalence of out-of-school discipline?

Activities and Assignments

1. Choose one of the policies from this chapter and explain the scope of the problem.
2. Explain how you would revise the funding mechanism to mitigate your policy problem.

References

Annie E. Casey Foundation. (2021). *KIDS COUNT Data Book*. 2021 State Trends in Child Well-Being.

Balfanz, R., & Legters, N. (2004). *Locating the dropout crisis: Which high schools produce the nation's dropouts? Where are they located? Who attends them?* Center for Research on the Education of Students Placed at Risk.

Bartanen, B., & Grissom, J. A. (2019). *School principal race and the hiring and retention of racially diverse teachers (EdWorkingPaper 19-59)*. Annenberg Institute at Brown University. www.edworkingpapers.com/ai19-59

Becker, B., Beeson, E., Driscoll, C., Gillespie, C., Lowe, M., Nuland, L., & Wagner, A. (2022). *The state of social-emotional learning in K–12 public schools*. Hanover Research.

Bell, C. (2021). *Suspend: Punishment, violence, and the failure of school safety*. John Hopkins University Press.

Benbenishty, R., Astor, R. A., Roziner, I., & Wrabel, S. L. (2016). Testing the causal links between school climate, school violence, and school academic performance. *Educational Researcher, 45*(3), 197–206. https://doi.org/10.3102/0013189x16644603

Berkowitz, R., Moore, H., Astor, R. A., & Benbenishty, R. (2017). A research synthesis of the associations between socioeconomic background, inequality, school climate, and academic achievement. *Review of Educational Research, 87*(2), 425–469. https://doi.org/10.3102/0034654316669821

Bifulco, R., & Ladd, H. F. (2007). School choice, racial segregation, and test-score gaps: Evidence from North Carolina's charter school program. *Journal of Policy Analysis and Management, 26*(1), 31–56. https://doi.org/10.1002/pam.20226

Björklund, A., & Salvanes, K. G. (2011). Education and family background mechanisms and policies. In E. A. Hanushek, S. Machin, & L. Woessmann (Eds.), *Handbook of the economics of education* (Vol. 3, pp. 201–247). Elsevier. https://doi.org/10.1016/b978-0-444-53429-3.00003-x

Bleiberg, J. F., & Kraft, M. A. (2022). *What happened to the K–12 education labor market during COVID? The acute need for better data systems (EdWorkingPaper 22-544)*. Annenberg Institute at Brown University. https://doi.org/10.26300/2xw0-v642

Bradshaw, C. P., O'Brennan, L. M., & McNeely, C. A. (2008). Core competencies and the prevention of school failure and early school leaving. *New Directions for Child and Adolescent Development, 122*, 19–32. https://doi.org/10.1002/cd.226; PMID: 19021248

Bridgeland, J. M., Dilulio, J. J., Jr., & Morison, K. B. (2006). *The silent epidemic: Perspectives of high school dropouts*. Bill & Melinda Gates Foundation. https://docs.gatesfoundation.org/Documents/thesilentepidemic3-06final.pdf

Canady, M., James, B., & Nease, J. (2012). *To protect and educate: The school resource officer and the prevention of violence in schools*. National Association of School Resource Officers. www.nasro.org/clientuploads/resources/NASRO-Protect-and-Educate.pdf

Carver-Thomas, D., & Darling-Hammond, L. (2017). *Teacher turnover: Why it matters and what we can do about it*. Learning Policy Institute. https://learningpolicyinstitute.org/sites/default/files/product-files/Teacher_Turnover_REPORT.pdf

Casella, R. (2003). Zero tolerance policy in schools: Rationale, consequences, and alternatives. *Teachers College Record, 105*(5), 872–892. https://doi.org/10.1111/1467-9620.00271

Centers for Disease Control and Prevention. (2022). *Youth risk behavior survey: Data summary and trends report*. www.cdc.gov/healthyyouth/data/yrbs/pdf/YRBS_Data-Summary-Trends_Report2023_508.pdf

Collaborative for Academic, Social, and Emotional Learning. (2024). *Fundamentals of SEL*. https://casel.org/fundamentals-of-sel/

Currie, J. (2009). Healthy, wealthy, and wise: Socioeconomic status, poor health in childhood, and human capital development. *Journal of Economic Literature, 47*(1), 87–122. https://doi.org/10.1257/jel.47.1.87

Darling-Hammond, L., Bae, S., Cook-Harvey, C. M., Lam, L., Mercer, C., Podolsky, A., & Stosich, E. L. (2016). *Pathways to new accountability through the every student succeeds act*. Learning Policy Institute. https://learningpolicyinstitute.org/media/176/download?inline&file=Pathways_New-Accountability_Through_Every_Student_Succeeds_Act_04202016.pdf

Darling-Hammond, L., Sutcher, L., & Carver-Thomas, D. (2017, November 13). *Why addressing teacher turnover matters*. Learning Policy Institute. https://learningpolicyinstitute.org/blog/why-addressing-teacher-turnover-matters

Dietrichson, J., Bøg, M., Filges, T., & Jørgensen, A.-M. K. (2017). Academic interventions for elementary and middle school students with low socioeconomic status: A systematic review and meta-analysis. *Review of Educational Research, 87*(2), 243–282. https://doi.org/10.3102/0034654316687036

Dilberti, M. K., & Schwartz, H. (2023). *Educator turnover has markedly increased, but districts have to take actions to boost teacher ranks: Selected findings from the sixth American school district panel survey*. Rand Corporation.

Donald, E. (2001). *Give yourself the gift of a degree*. Employment Policy Foundation.

Egalite, A. J., & Wolf, P. J. (2016). A review of the empirical research on private school choice. *Peabody Journal of Education, 91*(4), 441–454. https://doi.org/10.1080/0161956x.2016.1207436

Fabelo, T., Thompson, M., Plotkin, M., Carmichael, D., Marchbanks, M. P. III, & Booth, E. (2011). *Breaking schools' rules: A statewide study of how school discipline relates to students' success and juvenile justice involvement*. Council of State Governments Justice Center and the United States Public Policy Research Institute.

Freeman, J., & Simonsen, B. (2015). Examining the impact of policy and practice interventions on high school dropout and school completion rates. *Review of Educational Research, 85*(2), 205–248. https://doi.org/10.3102/0034654314554431

Friedman-Krauss, A. H., Barnett, W. S., Hodges, K. S., Garver, K. A., Jost, T. M., Weisenfeld, G. G., & Duer, J. K. (2024). *The state of preschool 2023*. The National Institute for Early Education Research. https://nieer.org/sites/default/files/2024-05/2023_nieer_yearbook_4.24.24-compressed.pdf

Gershenson, S. (2013). Do summer time-use gaps vary by socioeconomic status? *American Educational Research Journal, 50*(6), 1219–1248. https://doi.org/10.3102/0002831213502516

Gottfredson, D. C., Crosse, S., Tang, Z., Bauer, E. L., Harmon, M. A., Hagen, C. A., & Greene, A. D. (2020). Effects of school resource officers on school crime and responses to school crime. *Criminology & Public Policy, 19*(3), 905–940. https://doi.org/10.1111/1745-9133.12512

Grissom, J. A., & Bartanen, B. (2018). Principal effectiveness and principal turnover. *Education Finance and Policy*. https://doi.org/10.1162/edfp_a_00256

Grissom, J. A., Bartanen, B., & Mitani, H. (2019). Principal sorting and the distribution of principal quality. *AERA Open, 5*(2). https://doi.org/10.1177/2332858419850094

Grissom, J. A., Egalite, A. J., & Lindsay, C. A. (2021). *How principals affect students and schools: A systematic synthesis of two decades of research*. The Wallace Foundation. www.wallacefoundation.org/knowledge-center/Documents/How-Principals-Affect-Students-and-Schools.pdf

Hart, B., & Risley, B. (2003). The early catastrophe: The 30 million word gap by age 3. *American Educator, 27*(1), 4–9.

Harvard University Center on the Developing Child. (2007). *InBrief: The science of early childhood development*. http://developingchild.harvard.edu/resources/inbrief-science-of-ecd/

Heckman, J. J. (2006). Skill formation and the economics of investing in disadvantaged children. *Science, 312*(5782), 1900–1902. https://doi.org/10.1126/science.1128898

Henig, J. R. (1994). *Rethinking school choice: Limits of the market metaphor*. Princeton University Press.

Irby, D. J. (2013). Net-deepening of school discipline. *The Urban Review, 45*(2), 197–219. https://doi.org/10.1007/s11256-012-0217-2

Irby, D. J., & Coney, K. (2021). The 1994 gun-free schools act: Its effects 25 years later and how to undo them. *Peabody Journal of Education, 96*(5), 494–507. https://doi.org/10.1080/0161956x.2021.1991690

Irwin, V., Wang, K., Cui, J., & Thompson, A. (2022). *Report on indicators of school crime and safety: 2021*. U.S. Department of Education, Institute for Education Sciences; U.S. Department of Justice Programs.

James, N., & McCallion, G. (2013). *School resource officers: Law enforcement officers in schools*. Congressional Research Service.

Jeynes, W. H. (2015). A meta-analysis on the factors that best reduce the achievement gap. *Education and Urban Society, 47*(5), 523–554. https://doi.org/10.1177/0013124514529155

Johnson, D. W., Steinberg, M. P., & Allens, E. (2011). *Student and teacher safety in Chicago public schools: The roles of community context and school social organization*. Consortium on Chicago School Research at the University of Chicago Urban Education Institute. https://consortium.uchicago.edu/publications/student-and-teacher-safety-chicago-public-schools-roles-community-context-and-school

Justice Policy Institute. (2020). *The presence of school resource officers (SROs) in America's schools*. https://justicepolicy.org/research/policy-brief-2020-the-presence-of-school-resource-officers-sros-in-americas-schools/

Karoly, L. A., & Bigelow, J. H. (2005). *The economics of investing in universal preschool education in California*. Rand Corporation. www.rand.org/content/dam/rand/pubs/monographs/2005/RAND_MG349.pdf

Kim, J. S., & Quinn, D. M. (2013). The effects of summer reading on low-income children's literacy achievement from kindergarten to grade 8. *Review of Educational Research, 83*(3), 386–431. https://doi.org/10.3102/0034654313483906

Kostyo, S., & Cardichon, J. (2018). *Making ESSA's equity promise real: State strategies to close the opportunity gap*. Learning Policy Institute. https://learningpolicyinstitute.org/media/297/download?inline&file=ESSA_Equity_Promise_REPORT.pdf

Kotok, S., Frankenberg, E., Schafft, K. A., Mann, B. A., & Fuller, E. J. (2017). School choice, racial segregation, and poverty concentration: Evidence from Pennsylvania charter school transfers. *Educational Policy, 31*(4), 415–447. https://doi.org/10.1177/0895904815604112

Kraft, M. A., & Lyon, M. A. (2022). *The rise and fall of the teaching profession: Prestige, interest, preparation, and satisfaction over the last half century (EdWorkingPaper 22-679)*. Annenberg Institute at Brown University. https://doi.org/10.26300/7b1a-vk92

Lehmann, P. S., Azimi, A. M., Fortney, K., & Alaniz, K. (2022). Racial and ethnic disparities in school discipline: The interactive effects of gender and parental educational attainment. *Crime & Delinquency, 68*(10), 1631–1669. https://doi.org/10.1177/00111287211029879

Leung-Gagne, M., McCombs, J., Scott, C., & Losen, D. J. (2022). *Pushed out: Trends and disparities in out-of-school suspension.* Learning Policy Institute. https://learningpolicyinstitute.org/sites/default/files/2022-09/CRDC_School_Suspension_REPORT.pdf

Losen, D. J., & Skiba, R. J. (2010). *Suspended education: Urban middle schools in crisis.* Southern Poverty Law Center.

Martin, C., Sargrad, S., & Batel, S. (2016). *Making the grade: A 50-state analysis of school accountability systems.* Center for American Progress. https://cdn.americanprogress.org/wp-content/uploads/2016/05/17094420/AccountabilityLandscape-report2.pdf

Musu-Gillette, L., Zhang, A., Wang, K., Zhang, K., Kemp, J., Diliberti, M., & Oudekerk, B. A. (2018). *Indicators of school crime and safety: 2017 (NCES 2018-036/NCJ 251413).* National Center for Education Statistics; Bureau of Justice Statistics. www.bjs.gov/content/pub/pdf/iscs17.pdf?ed2f26df2d9c416fbddddd2330a778c6=cbobieglen-cbbigine http://hdl.handle.net/11212/3786

Na, C., & Gottfredson, D. C. (2013). Police officers in schools: Effects on school crime and the processing of offending behaviors. *Justice Quarterly, 30*(4), 619–650. https://doi.org/10.1080/07418825.2011.615754

National Center for Education Statistics. (2023a). *Characteristics of public school teachers: Condition of education.* https://nces.ed.gov/programs/coe/indicator/clr

National Center for Education Statistics. (2023b). *Recovery from the coronavirus pandemic in K–12 education: Condition of education.* https://nces.ed.gov/programs/coe/indicator/toa/k-12-covid-recovery

National School Climate Council. (2015). *School climate and prosocial educational improvement: Essential goals and processes that support student success for all.* Teachers College Record.

Newburger, J. C., & Beckhusen, J. (2022). *Average teachers' earnings declining, lower than similarly educated workers.* United States Census Bureau. www.census.gov/library/stories/2022/07/teachers-among-most-educated-yet-pay-lags.html

Nguyen, T. D., Pham, L. D., Crouch, M., & Springer, M. G. (2020). The correlates of teacher turnover: An updated and expanded meta-analysis of the literature. *Educational Research Review, 31,* 100355. https://doi.org/10.1016/j.edurev.2020.100355

Nguyen, T. D., Pham, L. D., Springer, M., & Crouch, M. (2019). *The factors of teacher attrition and retention: An updated and expanded meta-analysis of the literature. (EdWorkingPaper: 19-149).* Annenberg Institute at Brown University. https://edworkingpapers.com/ai19-149

Olneck, M. (2005). Economic consequences of the academic achievement gap for African Americans. *Marquette Law Review, 89,* 95–104.

Perera, R. M., & Diliberti, M. K. (2023). *Survey: Understanding how U.S. public schools approach school discipline.* Brookings Institution. www.brookings.edu/articles/survey-understanding-how-us-public-schools-approach-school-discipline/

Slates, S. L., Alexander, K. L., Entwisle, D. R., & Olson, L. S. (2012). Counteracting summer slide: Social capital resources within socioeconomically disadvantaged families. *Journal of Education for Students Placed at Risk (JESPAR), 17*(3), 165–185. https://doi.org/10.1080/10824669.2012.688171

Thapa, A., Cohen, J., Guffey, S., & Higgins-D'Alessandro, A. (2013). A review of school climate research. *Review of Educational Research, 83*(3), 357–385. https://doi.org/10.3102/0034654313483907

United States Department of Health and Human Services. (2022). *Head start program facts: Fiscal year 2022.* https://eclkc.ohs.acf.hhs.gov/sites/default/files/pdf/hs-program-fact-sheet-2022.pdf

U.S. Department of Education, Institute of Education Sciences, National Center for Education Statistics. (2024). *School pulse panel 2023–24.* https://nces.ed.gov/surveys/spp/

Wang, M.-T., & Degol, J. L. (2016). School climate: A review of the construct, measurement, and impact on student outcomes. *Educational Psychology Review, 28*(2), 315–352. https://doi.org/10.1007/s10648-015-9319-1

White, K. R. (1982). The relation between socioeconomic status and academic achievement. *Psychological Bulletin, 91*(3), 461–481. https://doi.org/10.1037/0033-2909.91.3.461

York, A., Welner, K., & Kelley, L. M. (Eds.). (2023). *Schools of opportunity: 10 research-based models of equity in action.* Teachers College Press.

11 Higher Education Policy

Postsecondary education faces numerous challenges, including college affordability and student debt, equitable access, remediation, low graduation rates, and for-profit institutions. This chapter examines some of the problems facing American postsecondary education and possible ways to solve them. This chapter answers the question: How can policymakers and educational leaders improve postsecondary access, affordability, and equity?

For the past two centuries, the United States has led the world in educational access, expanding secondary access in the 19th century and postsecondary access in the 20th (Goldin & Katz, 2008; Page & Scott-Clayton, 2016). The U.S. led the world in the expansion of postsecondary education access in the second half of the 20th century. Between 1947 and 2010, U.S. postsecondary enrollment increased from 2.3 million to more than 21 million, an annual increase of nearly 13%. Postsecondary educational attainment has numerous benefits including improved lifetime earnings, employment rates, health outcomes, and relationships (Carnevale et al., 2021; Oreopoulos & Salvanes, 2011).

Despite these historical gains, U.S. higher education has witnessed some troubling trends in the 21st century. After 2010, U.S. postsecondary enrollment leveled off and then declined to 18.6 million in 2021. During the 2010s, undergraduate enrollment declined by 15%, 2.6 million fewer students, due to declines in the youth population, low unemployment rates, and increasing educational alternatives to traditional postsecondary programs. Among Organisation for Economic Cooperation and Development (OECD) countries, the United States has fallen to 14th in postsecondary education (OECD, 2023).

According to the National Center for Education Statistics (NCES, 1985), undergraduate enrollment increased by an average of 2.2% annually from 1985 to 2010, rising to a high of 18.1 million students. In 2008, the global financial crisis led to the Great Recession, prompting unemployed and underemployed workers to return to postsecondary education. Between 2007 and 2010, college and university enrollment increased from 18.3 to 21 million students (Ortagus & Hughes, 2021). During the past 14 years, enrollment has decreased at an average annual rate of 1.5%. Public 2-year institutions witnessed more dramatic enrollment declines of 38% between 2010 and 2021. Postsecondary enrollment declines are the product of several factors including declining birth rates, decreased immigration, rising tuition costs, and the COVID-19 pandemic. Nationally, 38% of 18- to 24-year-olds are enrolled in postsecondary education. Only two states, Rhode Island (57%) and Massachusetts (53%), and the District of Columbia (56%) have postsecondary enrollment rates above 50%.

More concerning than the overall decline in postsecondary enrollment rates is the growing gap in postsecondary enrollment by family socioeconomic status and race. Eighty-nine percent of students from families in the top socioeconomic quintile enroll in college, compared to 51% of students from families in the bottom quintile (Reber & Smith, 2023). Racial

DOI: 10.4324/9781003231561-15

Table 11.1 College Enrollment and Academic Performance by Race, 2010–2021

Race/ethnicity	2010	2021
Total	41	38
American Indian/Alaska Native	41	28
Asian	64	60
Black	38	37
Hispanic	32	33
Pacific Islander	36	45
White	43	38
Two or more races	38	35

disparities also pervasive, with **72%** of White students, **63%** of Hispanic students, and **62%** of Black students enrolling in college within a year and a half of high school graduation (Reber & Smith, 2023). According to NCES, only **32%** of students in the lowest socioeconomic quintile enroll in postsecondary education, compared to **79%** of students in the highest income quintile. Table 11.1 illustrates the racial disparities in college enrollment rates.

Despite these challenges, the demand for higher education is high, with more than **90%** of respondents saying a postsecondary credential is valuable (Gallup Lumina Foundation, 2024). College graduates are half as likely to be unemployed as their peers with a high school diploma. High school graduates earn an average of $1.3 million in lifetime earnings, compared to $2.8 million for college graduates, a $1.2 million difference (Carnevale et al., 2011, 2021).

College Affordability, Access, and Student Debt

During the past 20 years, college costs have skyrocketed. Between 2004 and 2024, average private school tuition increased from $20,150 to $46,652. Public school tuition increased from an average of $4,633 to $11,790 for in-state tuition and from $12,404 to $28,217 for out of state. The rising cost of postsecondary education is driven by slow productivity growth, a highly educated labor force, high standards of care, lower state appropriations and private fundraising, and more tuition discounts (Archibald & Feldman, 2018). Postsecondary education has seen limited productivity growth: student–teacher ratios remain stable because increasing them would lower educational quality. Postsecondary education relies on highly educated employees who have received real wage growth even as the wages of workers with high school degrees have stagnated. Postsecondary institutions seek to provide a minimum standard of care even if such changes raise costs. Decreasing state appropriations increase reliance on tuition.

The United States relies on a high-tuition, high-aid model. Discount rates, the total institutional grant aid awarded to students by colleges and universities as a percentage of total tuition and fees, are at an all-time high. Discounting means lower income students pay less than higher income families. The net price paid is the difference between the tuition and fees and the grants, scholarships, and other financial aid students and families receive. According to the National Association of College and University Business Officers (2023), the average tuition discount rate for private colleges in 2023–2024 was **51.9%**, meaning students and families pay approximately half the tuition sticker price.

In 2023, according to the Federal Reserve, U.S. student loan debt reached an all-time high of $1.77 trillion spread across 44 million borrowers, an increase of **66%** over the past decade. Between 1982 and 2012, average federal student loan debt increased from

$2,000 to $28,000 per student. In the 2021–2022 academic year alone, students and families borrowed $94.7 billion in student loans. Federal unsubsidized loans constitute 46% of this, and federal subsidized loans another 16%. Student loan debt can impact student career choices and quality of life and delay achieving other financial goals. The U.S. financial aid system perpetuates inequities in the distribution of financial burdens in postsecondary education. The U.S. has no national or state mechanism to restrict higher education tuition and fees (Dill, 2022).

The student loan debt burden disproportionately impacts lower income and historically underserved populations. Black student loan borrowers have the highest average debt, $34,089 (Rodriguez & Szabo-Kubitz, 2024). College costs, even after accounting for discount rates, have continued to consume a higher percentage of family budgets. Students from families in the lowest income quintile spend half their annual income on college expenses even after accounting for financial aid. Between 1975 and 2024, federal Pell grant program maximum awards declined from covering 75% to 29% of the cost of attending a 4-year public college (Rodriguez & Szabo-Kubitz, 2024). Despite increased discount rates, rising higher education costs have made it difficult for lower income families to afford college tuition and increased the debt burden on students and families.

How can college be made more affordable, particularly for underserved populations? The federal government can expand need-based financial aid through the expansion of the Pell grant program and other federal grant and loan programs. The federal government can also promote transparency in college and university costs, discounts, and value by collecting and sharing data with families and students. State policy efforts to improve college affordability have ranged from free community college to freezes on public tuition increases. Tuition and fee caps have had mixed results because tuition caps lead to fee increases and vice versa. Thirty-two states offer tuition-free community college programs. Improving college access and affordability requires policy solutions that combine federal, state, and institutional resources and planning.

Equitable Access – Affirmative Action

As discussed at length in Chapter 2, the U.S. postsecondary system historically excluded women, racial minorities, and members of religious groups, including Catholics and Jews (Dill, 2022). In the 1960s, affirmative action policies developed in response to this history of discrimination in educational opportunities. Civil rights protests on college campuses, disproportionately in the North, and their moral and ethical implications for university leaders were the main impetus for institutional change in admissions criteria (Anderson, 2005; Bowen & Bok, 1998; Douglass, 2007; Duffy & Goldberg, 1998; Skrentny, 1996; Stulberg & Chen, 2013). There is no federal mandate for colleges and universities to engage in affirmative action in admissions decisions. Each institution determines whether and how it employs such actions (Arcidiacono & Lovenheim, 2016). College and university admissions departments began voluntarily considering race as a factor in admissions decisions to improve the diversity of the student population and redress the history of educational exclusion.

College and university affirmative action policies elicited "reverse discrimination" claims as White applicants pushed back. The U.S. courts slowly restricted permissible affirmative action policies. In 1978, Allan Bakke, after being denied admission to the University of California at Davis's medical school, sued the university contending he was excluded from admission exclusively based on race. The school reserved 16 of 100 seats in each entering class for "qualified minorities" to address historical minority exclusion from the medical profession. The U.S. Supreme Court in *Regents of the University of California v. Bakke* ruled that using racial quotas violated the equal protection clause of the Fourteenth Amendment.

At that time, the justices also ruled that using racial identity as a criterion in admissions decisions was constitutional. In 2003, in *Gratz v. Bollinger*, the U.S. Supreme Court struck down the University of Michigan's undergraduate admissions system, ruling the Fourteenth Amendment prohibits a system that awards points for demographic characteristics and fails to treat applicants as individuals. However, it also ruled that the University of Michigan Law School's narrowly tailored use of race in admissions decisions did not violate the equal protection clause of the Fourteenth Amendment or Title VI of the Civil Rights Act of 1964. Justice Sandra Day O'Connor, writing the majority opinion, reasoned that each applicant receiving a highly individualized review during the admissions decision did not unduly harm nonminority candidates. The decision also held that fostering diversity in higher education is a compelling government interest.

On June 29, 2023, the Supreme Court ruled Harvard University's and the University of North Carolina's consideration of race in colleges admissions violated the equal protection clause of the Fourteenth Amendment (Arrojas, 2023). In *Students for Fair Admissions (SFFA) v. Harvard University* and *SFFA v. University of North Carolina (UNC)*, SSFA alleged that as a federally funded program, Harvard race-conscious admissions policy violated Title VI of the Civil Rights Act of 1964, which provided that no person could be excluded from participation in any program receiving federal financial assistance on the grounds of race, color, or national origin. SSFA alleged that UNC's race-conscious admissions policy violated the Fourteenth Amendment. The Supreme Court clarified that universities may consider race within the context of a student's college admissions essays if it is related to quality of character or the ability of that applicant to contribute to the institution. Chief Justice John Roberts argued in the majority opinion that race-conscious admissions policies are not measurable enough to permit judicial review as required by the Fourteenth Amendment.

Justice Sonya Sotomayor argued in the dissenting opinion that the Fourteenth Amendment allows policies that increase equality. Minority students are disadvantaged in the college admissions process because they are more likely to attend underfunded elementary and secondary schools. Race-conscious admissions decisions reduce those inequities. In her dissent, Sotomayor stated:

> For 45 years, the Court extended Brown's transformative legacy to the context of higher education, allowing colleges and universities to consider race in a limited way and for the limited purpose of promoting the important benefits of racial diversity. Today, this Court . . . subverts the constitutional guarantee of equal protection by further entrenching racial inequality in education, the very foundation of our democratic government and pluralistic society.
>
> (Sotomayor, 2023)

The liberal justices argued Congress enacted Title VI of the 1964 Civil Rights Act and the equal protection clause to counter racist policies towards African Americans rather than to prevent any type of race-conscious policies.

As the relationship between educational level and earnings has increased in recent decades, so has opposition to affirmative action in higher education admissions (Dill, 2022). According to the Pew Research Center (2023), 50% of Americans disapprove of colleges considering race and ethnicity in admissions decisions and 33% approve. Racial disparities in affirmative action exist, with 47% of Black respondents approving race- and ethnic-conscious admissions decisions, compared to 29% of White respondents. The failure of the courts to ban affirmative action policies in U.S. higher education motivated opponents to turn to state ballot initiatives and gubernatorial executive orders. Between 1996 and 2020, nine states – Arizona, California, Florida, Michigan, Nebraska, New Hampshire, Oklahoma, Texas, and Washington – banned affirmative action in U.S. higher education admissions decisions. These bans are shown in Table 11.2.

College Remediation and Graduation Rates

College and career readiness refers to the knowledge, skills, cognitive strategies, and disposition required to be successful in postsecondary education or a professional career. The focus on college and career readiness stems from high remediation and low completion rates (Camara, 2013). Many students enter postsecondary institutions without the academic skills to be prepared for college. Postsecondary institutions offer remedial coursework to prepare students to complete standard degree requirements. College remediation refers to supplementary education courses to help students achieve the required academic skills to complete the college curriculum. According to NCES, 68% of students at public 2-year institutions and 40% of students at public 4-year institutions enrolled in a remedial course (Chen, 2016). More alarming, only 59% of public 4-year college students and 49% of public 2-year college students pass all their remedial courses. Many college entrants lack the skills to succeed in college coursework (Bailey et al., 2010). Remedial courses do not count toward degree completion, so they place an additional financial burden on students academically unprepared for postsecondary education. Remedial education is estimated to cost over $9 billion annually, with much of that cost falling on college students and their families (Jimen et al., 2016; Scott-Clayton et al., 2013).

Remediation stems from several sources including inequalities in elementary and secondary college preparation. Remediation rates are higher for minority students, delayed entrants, older returning students, and students at open-access institutions (Kurlaender & Howell, 2012; Merisotis & Phipps, 2000; Sanabria et al., 2020). The costs of college remediation fall disproportionately on lower income, minority students from low-performing secondary school systems. Despite the cost, remediation is necessary for many students. Students who complete college remediation courses achieve positive outcomes including remedial placement, enrollment persistence, and degree attainment (Attewell et al., 2006; Bahr, 2008; Bettinger & Long, 2009; Chen, 2016; Hodara & Xu, 2016). Remedial education can also harm students, particularly students in 2-year colleges and those who fail remedial courses

Table 11.2 U.S. State Affirmative Action Bans

State	Year	Method
California	1996	State ballot initiative – constitutional amendment
Washington	1998	State ballot initiative
Florida	1999	Gubernatorial executive order
Michigan	2006	State ballot initiative – constitutional amendment
Nebraska	2008	State ballot initiative – constitutional amendment
Arizona	2010	State ballot initiative – constitutional amendment
New Hampshire	2011	Legislative statute
Oklahoma	2012	Legislatively
Idaho	2020	Gubernatorial executive order

Note: Pew Research Center (2023).

(Clotfelter et al., 2014; Crisp & Delgado, 2014). Remedial placement lowers the likelihood of earning an associate degree or transferring to a 4-year college by diverting remedial students away from earning college-level credits and expanding the time and expense of achieving a degree (Clotfelter et al., 2014; Scott-Clayton & Rodriguez, 2015).

Many state governments have developed systemwide remedial education assessment and placement policies in recent years to minimize its cost while continuing to meet the needs of students who lack college-ready academic knowledge and skills. Thirty-two states have adopted systemwide remediation assessments and placement policies. Table 11.3 highlights some of the remediation policy requirements. States have also approved state policies to prohibit institutions from requiring remediation for students who meet certain benchmarks on state exams, to limit remediation to one semester, to embed support for college-level courses, and to use multiple measures to assess remedial placement.

Only two thirds of students graduate from 4-year postsecondary institutions, as shown in Table 11.4. College students who do not graduate acquire significant debt without the benefit of a degree to increase their earnings potential. Research has identified three sets

Table 11.3 State-Level Remedial Education Assessment and Placement Policy

State	Policy	Requirements
Connecticut	Conn. Gen. Stat. Ann. § 10a-157a	State statute requires that if the Connecticut State University System or a community technical college determines a student is likely to succeed in college-level work with supplemental support, the institution must offer developmental education support that is embedded in the college-level course.
Illinois	110 Ill. Comp. Stat. Ann. 175/100–30	State statute requires each university and community college to submit to the Board of Higher Education or the Illinois Community College Board a plan to scale evidence-based reforms to maximize the probability a student will be placed in and successfully complete an introductory English or math course within two semesters.
Massachusetts	Board Policy No. AAC 19–23	The Massachusetts Board of Higher Education recommends institutions use multiple measures to make placement decisions, adopt multiple mathematics pathways, and implement corequisite support.
South Carolina	Commission Policies on Developmental Education in South Carolina	The South Carolina Commission on Higher Education requires that only 2-year institutions offer developmental education courses, and notes that the University of South Carolina decided all developmental students would enroll in enriched sections of entry-level courses.
Washington	Wash. Rev. Code Ann. § 28B.77.020 (7) (a)(ii)	State statute requires the Student Achievement Council to work with the State Board for Community and Technical Colleges, the Workforce Training and Education Coordinating Board, and 4-year institutions to encourage the use of multiple measures to determine course placement.

Note: Education Commission of the States (2021).

Table 11.4 Graduation Rates at 4-Year Institutions Within 6 Years by Control of Institution

Student demographic	Public	Private nonprofit	Private for-profit
Total	63	68	29
Female	67	71	28
Male	60	64	31
White	62	69	34
Black	40	43	18
Hispanic	54	62	30
Asian	72	79	48
Pacific Islander	52	55	25
American Indian or Alaska Native	36	49	20
Two or more races	56	68	32

of factors that influence graduation rates: institutional, student, and financial. Institutional factors include student support services like academic support, student life, and first-year experiences that can provide the academic, residential, and social support students require to persist in college. These services are particularly valuable for underserved populations and first-generation students. Support services can lead to a higher level of student engagement, a critical factor in student persistence and retention (Millea et al., 2018). Student characteristics also influence persistence and retention. Academic preparation, family characteristics, and parents' degree attainment prepare students for the academic rigors and social demands of college. First-generation students have less academic, social, and financial support than their peers. First-generation students do not benefit from previous generations guiding them through the application, enrollment, and college experience. Financial factors also influence student persistence and graduation rates. Institutional financial supports are typically based on merit rather than need, placing lower income populations, who disproportionately receive lower quality elementary and secondary education, at a disadvantage. Each factor perpetuates inequity by placing underserved populations at a disadvantage.

For-Profit Institutions

Private for-profit colleges offer programs from nondegree certificates and associate degrees to doctoral degrees. They differ from nonprofits because they seek to make a profit and thus cost more. For-profit college companies receive investor funding, and those investors expect a return. The Higher Education Act of 1965 Title IV expanded federal aid to college students through grants, subsidies, and loans (Tucker, 2021). In 1972, the Higher Education Amendments authorized the use of federal aid at for-profit colleges and universities. Amendments in 1979 and 1986 expanded the federal loan funds available to students in the for-profit sector, leading to its massive expansion (Watkins & Seidelman, 2017). Between 1970 and 2010, for-profit enrollment increased from 111,714 to 2,022,785, a 1,700% increase.

Public budget shortfalls in the early 21st century led to crowded and underresourced community colleges and the subsequent increase in for-profit enrollment (Deming et al., 2012). Between 2010 and 2018, for-profit enrollment decreased from 2,022,785 to 982,410, a 51% decrease. In 2008–2009, the University of Phoenix was the largest for-profit postsecondary institution in the U.S., with an enrollment of 532,000 students. In 2021–2022, enrollment had declined to approximately 85,000 students. Despite the decline in for-profit postsecondary enrollment, this sector still enrolls **38%** of higher education students. Today, **828,875** students are enrolled in for-profit 4-year institutions, which is approximately **9%** of total postsecondary student enrollment. The for-profit sector is top heavy, with the largest 15 institutions accounting for **60%** of enrollment. The for-profit sector offers primarily career-focused curriculum. This sector provides almost no general education or liberal arts programs that prepare students for additional postsecondary training (Deming et al., 2012).

Private for-profit colleges and universities disproportionately enroll African American, Hispanic, older, and low-income students (Deming et al., 2012). African Americans account for **13%** of all postsecondary students but **22%** of those at for-profit institutions. Student outcomes in for-profit colleges and universities have fallen behind those in other postsecondary education sectors. A Third Way report found that the 6-year graduation rate for Black students was **44.2%** at public and private nonprofit 4-year institutions but only **14.2%** at for-profit 4-year institutions (Ortagus & Hughes, 2021). Hispanic students' 6-year graduation rates were **56.1%** at public and private nonprofit 4-year institutions but only **28.1%**at for-profit 4-year institutions.

The Servicemen's Readjustment Act of 1944 provided funding for 7.8 million World War II veterans to receive education benefits, which led to an unprecedented expansion in higher education enrollment. The extraordinary federal investment also led to fraud, particularly in for-profit postsecondary institutions. According to a 1950 report by the Veterans Administration, 963 of the 1,237 educational institutions identified as utilizing fraudulent practices were for-profit institutions. More than 300 educational institutions lost their accreditation in the scandal; more than **90%** were for-profit schools (Whitman, 2017). In 1992, Congress enacted regulations to reduce fraud in postsecondary financial aid programs. Among these regulations was the 85/15 rule, limiting to **85%** the share of revenues that higher education institutions could receive from federal aid programs. The logic behind the rule was that high-quality educational institutions should attract investors beyond the federal government (Lee & Looney, 2019). Between 1990 and 1999, student loan default rates declined from a high of **37%** to **12%** (Looney & Yannelis, 2015).

The 1998 Higher Education Act reauthorization lowered the non-Title IV funds proprietary postsecondary institutions were required to earn from **15%** to **10%**. The 2008 Higher Education Reauthorization, also known as the Higher Education Opportunity Act, gave for-profits 2 years to meet the 90/10 rule as a condition of Title IV institutional eligibility (Hegji, 2021). The 90/10 rule only applies to for-profit institutions. Proponents argue all higher education sectors should be held to the same standard. Opponents argue the historical record singles out for-profit institutions as disproportionately dependent on federal aid yet producing poor student outcomes (Hegji, 2021). Research indicates almost all public and private nonprofit institutions would meet the 90/10 requirement (Lee & Looney, 2019). A report by the Brookings Institution recommended strengthening the 90/10 rule to improve higher education oversight and said that repealing the 90/10 rule would increase enrollment at low-quality institutions and increase default rates (Lee & Looney, 2019).

How can federal and state governments limit for-profit institutions that target underserved populations and provide less effective education at higher costs? The federal government could reinstate the gainful employment rule that reduces federal funding to institutions that do not meet debt-to-earnings ratios. Federal programs including the GI Bill should count toward the 90/10 limit to require for-profit institutions to attract more students willing to pay full price.

Key Terms

affirmative action
college access
college affordability
for-profit institutions
graduation rates
Gratz v. Bollinger
high-tuition, high-aid model
postsecondary enrollment
proprietary postsecondary institutions
remediation
student debt
Students for Fair Admissions (SFFA) v. Harvard University and *SFFA v. University of North Carolina (UNC)*

Discussion Questions

1. How has postsecondary enrollment changed in recent decades?
2. How has college affordability changed in recent decades? How has this influenced college access?
3. What has led to historic levels of student debt? What are policy changes that could mitigate student debt?
4. Why has the need for college remediation continued to increase?
5. What are the differences in college graduation rates by type of institution? Why do graduation rates vary by institutional type?
6. What are for-profit institutions? What policy changes can improve for-profit student outcomes?

Activities and Assignments

1. Choose one of the policies from this chapter and explain the scope of the problem.
2. Explain how you would revise the funding mechanism to mitigate your policy problem.

References

Anderson, T. H. (2005). *The pursuit of fairness: A history of affirmative action*. Oxford University Press.
Archibald, R. B., & Feldman, D. H. (2018). *Drivers of the rising price of a college education (ED588510)*. ERIC. https://files.eric.ed.gov/fulltext/ED588510.pdf
Arcidiacono, P., & Lovenheim, M. (2016). Affirmative action and the quality – fit trade-off. *Journal of Economic Literature*, *54*(1), 3–51. https://doi.org/10.1257/jel.54.1.3
Arrojas, M. (2023). *Supreme court strikes down affirmative action in college admissions*. BestColleges. www.bestcolleges.com/news/supreme-court-strikes-down-affirmative-action/
Attewell, P., Lavin, D., Domina, T., & Levey, T. (2006). New evidence on college remediation. *The Journal of Higher Education*, *77*(5), 886–924. https://doi.org/10.1080/00221546.2006.11778948
Bahr, P. R. (2008). Does mathematics remediation work? A comparative analysis of academic attainment among community college students. *Research in Higher Education*, *49*(5), 420–450. https://doi.org/10.1007/s11162-008-9089-4
Bailey, T., Jeong, D. W., & Cho, S. W. (2010). Referral, enrollment and completion in developmental education sequences in community colleges. *Economics of Education Review*, *29*, 255–270.

Bettinger, E. P., & Long, B. T. (2009). Addressing the needs of underprepared students in higher education: Does college remediation work? *Journal of Human Resources, 44*(3), 736–771. https://doi.org/10.1353/jhr.2009.0033

Bowen, W. G., & Bok, D. (1998). *The shape of the river*. Princeton University Press.

Camara, W. (2013). Defining and measuring college and career readiness: A validation framework. *Educational Measurement: Issues and Practice, 32*(4), 16–27. https://doi.org/10.1111/emip.12016

Carnevale, A. P., Cheah, B., & Wenzinger, E. (2021). *The college payoff: More education doesn't always mean more earnings*. Georgetown University Center on Education and the Workforce. https://cew.georgetown.edu/collegepayoff2021

Carnevale, A. P., Rose, S. J., & Cheah, B. (2011). *The college payoff: Education, occupations, lifetime earnings*. Georgetown University Center on Education and the Workforce. https://cew.georgetown.edu/wp-content/uploads/collegepayoff-completed.pdf

Chen, X. (2016). *Remedial coursetaking at U.S. public 2-and 4-year institutions: Scope, experiences, and outcomes (NCES 2016-405)*. National Center for Education Statistics.

Clotfelter, C. T., Ladd, H. F., Muschkin, C., & Vigdor, J. L. (2014). Developmental education in North Carolina community colleges. *Educational Evaluation and Policy Analysis, 37*(3), 354–375. https://doi.org/10.3102/0162373714547267

Crisp, G., & Delgado, C. (2014). The impact of developmental education on community college persistence and vertical transfer. *Community College Review, 42*(2), 99–117. https://doi.org/10.1177/0091552113516488

Deming, D. J., Goldin, C., & Katz, L. F. (2012). The for-profit postsecondary school sector: Nimble critters or agile predators? *Journal of Economic Perspectives, 26*(1), 139–164. https://doi.org/10.1257/jep.26.1.139

Dill, D. (2022). Access and inequality in U.S. higher education: Policy issues. In O. Tavares, C. Sin, C. Sa, & A. Amaral (Eds.), *Equity policies in global higher education: Reducing inequality and increasing participation and attainment* (pp. 47–70). Palgrave Macmillan.

Douglass, J. A. (2007). *The condition of admissions: Access, equity, and social contract of public universities*. Stanford University Press.

Duffy, E. A., & Goldberg, I. (1998). *Crafting a class: College admissions and financial aid, 1955–1994*. Princeton University Press.

Education Commission of the States. (2021). *50-state comparison*. https://reports.ecs.org/comparisons/developmental-education-policies-07

Gallup Lumina Foundation. (2024). *The state of higher education 2024*. http//www.luminafoundation.org/wp-content/uploads/2024/05/State-of-Higher-Education-2024.pdf

Goldin, C., & Katz, L. F. (2008). *The race between education and technology*. Harvard University Press.

Hegji, A. (2021). *The 90/10 rule under HEA title IV: Background and issues*. Congressional Research Service.

Hodara, M., & Xu, D. (2016). Does developmental education improve labor market outcomes? Evidence from two states. *American Educational Research Journal, 53*(3), 781–813. https://doi.org/10.3102/0002831216647790

Jimen, L., Moralez, J., Sargrad, S., & Thompson, M. (2016). *Remedial education: The cost of catching up*. Center for American Progress. www.americanprogress.org/article/remedial-education/

Kurlaender, M., & Howell, J. (2012). *Collegiate remediation: A review of the causes and consequences*. College Board Advocacy and Policy Center.

Lee, V., & Looney, A. (2019). *Understanding the 90/10 rule: How reliant are public, private, and for-profit institutions on federal aid?* The Brookings Institution. www.brookings.edu/wp-content/uploads/2019/01/es_20190116_looney-90-10.pdf

Looney, A., & Yannelis, C. (2015). A crisis in student loans? How changes in the characteristics of borrowers and in the institutions they attended contributed to rising loan defaults. *Brookings Papers on Economic Activity, 2015*(2), 1–89. https://doi.org/10.1353/eca.2015.0003

Merisotis, J., & Phipps, R. (2000). Remedial education in colleges and universities: What's really going on? *The Review of Higher Education, 24*(1), 67–85.

Millea, M., Wills, R., Elder, A., & Molina, D. (2018). What matters in college student success? Determinants of college retention and graduation rates. *Education, 138*(4), 309–322.

National Association of College and University Business Officers. (2023). *2023 NACUBO tuition discount study*. NACUBO. https://www.nacubo.org/Research/2023/NACUBO-Tuition-Discounting-Study

National Center for Education Statistics. (1985). *Higher education general information survey (HEGIS): Fall enrollment in colleges and universities surveys, 1970 through 1985.* https://nces.ed.gov/programs/digest/d22/tables/dt22_303.70.asp

Oreopoulos, P., & Salvanes, K. G. (2011). Priceless: The nonpecuniary benefits of schooling. *Journal of Economic Perspectives, 25*(1), 159–184. https://doi.org/10.1257/jep.25.1.159

Organisation for Economic Cooperation and Development. (2023). *Education at a glance 2023.* OECD Publishing. www.oecd-ilibrary.org/education/education-at-a-glance-2023_e13bef63-en

Ortagus, J., & Hughes, R. (2021). *Paying more for less? A new classification system to prioritize outcomes in higher education.* Third Way. www.thirdway.org/report/paying-more-for-less-a-new-classification-system-to-prioritize-outcomes-in-higher-education/

Page, L. C., & Scott-Clayton, J. (2016). Improving college access in the United States: Barriers and policy responses. *Economics of Education Review, 51,* 4–22. https://doi.org/10.1016/j.econedurev.2016.02.009

Pew Research Center. (2023). *More Americans disapprove than approve of colleges considering race, ethnicity in admissions decisions.* //efaidnbmnnnibpcajpcglclefindmkaj/https://d1y8sb8igg2f8e.cloudfront.net/PP_2023.06.08_college-admissions_REPORT.pdf

Reber, S., & Smith, E. (2023). *College enrollment disparities: Understanding the role of academic preparation.* Center on Children and Families, Brookings Institution. www.brookings.edu/wp-content/uploads/2023/02/20230123_CCF_CollegeEnrollment_FINAL2.pdf

Rodriguez, E., & Szabo-Kubitz, L. (2024). *Equitable college affordability policies and practices (ED644606).* ERIC. https://files.eric.ed.gov/fulltext/ED644606.pdf

Sanabria, T., Penner, A., & Domina, T. (2020). Failing at remediation? College remedial coursetaking, failure and long-term student outcomes. *Research in Higher Education, 61*(4), 459–484. https://doi.org/10.1007/s11162-020-09590-z

Scott-Clayton, J., Crosta, P. M., & Belfield, C. R. (2013). Improving the targeting of treatment. *Educational Evaluation and Policy Analysis, 36*(3), 371–393. https://doi.org/10.3102/0162373713517935

Scott-Clayton, J., & Rodriguez, O. (2015). Development, discouragement, or diversion? New evidence on the effects of college remediation policy. *Education Finance and Policy, 10*(1), 4–45. https://doi.org/10.1162/edfp_a_00150

Skrentny, J. D. (1996). *The ironies of affirmative action: Politics, culture, and justice in America.* The University of Chicago Press.

Sotomayor, J. (2023). Dissenting Opinion, Students for Fair Admissions, Inc. v. President and Fellows of Harvard College and the University of North Carolina, et al. Supreme Court of the United States.

Stulberg, L. M., & Chen, A. S. (2013). The origins of race-conscious affirmative action in undergraduate admissions: A comparative analysis of institutional change in higher education. *Sociology of Education, 87*(1), 36–52.

Tucker, F. (2021). For-profit colleges: Neither educationally nor economically equivalent. *Research in Higher Education Journal, 40.*

Watkins, J. P., & Seidelman, J. E. (2017). A Veblenian analysis of for-profit universities. *Journal of Economic Issues, 51*(2), 366–374. https://doi.org/10.1080/00213624.2017.1320910

Whitman, D. (2017). *Truman, Eisenhower, and the first GI bill scandal.* The Century Foundation.

Index

Note: Page numbers in *italics* indicate figures and page numbers in **bold** indicate tables.